Some H2O damage 5/17/23

W9-BTI-691

THE NEW WORLD OF ECONOMICS
Explorations into the human experience

The Irwin Publications in Economics
Advisory Editor **Martin S. Feldstein** *Harvard University*

Third edition 1981

THE NEW WORLD OF ECONOMICS

Explorations into the human experience

Richard B. McKenzie
Department of Economics
Clemson University

Gordon Tullock
College of Business
Virginia Polytechnic Institute
and State University

RICHARD D. IRWIN, INC. Homewood, Illinois 60430
Irwin-Dorsey Limited Georgetown, Ontario L7G 4B3

ISBN 0-256-02494-4
Library of Congress Catalog Card No. 80–84325

Printed in the United States of America

1 2 3 4 5 6 7 8 9 0 ML 8 7 6 5 4 3 2 1

To
Professor Duncan Black

Preface

Economics traditionally has been defined by both its method and its subject matter. That is to say, there are economic methods—models and statistical tests based on a set of assumptions about the way people interact. In addition, there is an area of human life, which is hard to describe in a brief phrase but is known to all economists, in which these methods are applied. We believe that the methods have a much wider scope than previously has been thought. Like the first two editions, this third edition attempts to introduce the student to the new work that has been done in applying economic methods to problems outside the traditional subject matter of economic study. This new field of research is, we think, more exciting, more interesting, and even more relevant than the more traditional applications to traditional economic problems.

Economics has developed over two centuries. During this 200 years, almost all of the places where a simple line of reasoning can be applied to an important and interesting problem have been explored. The remaining areas for economic research are, in general, those where the reasoning is difficult and the amount of progress made in each investigation is comparatively small. The result has been that more and more complex and sophisticated methods have been applied to smaller and smaller problems.

This book attempts to break out of the narrow confines of economic subject matter as traditionally defined and to seek out new and refreshing problems that can be dealt with in a simpler way. In this edition, we have added a chapter on the new, emerging field of sociobiology (which, as it so happens, has as much or more to do with economics as it does with either sociology or biology—see Chapter 12). We have also added several chapters on current public-policy issues like taxes (Chapter 23), supply-side economics (Chapter 14), and rent seeking (Chapter 15). Past users of the book will recognize that we have rearranged several chapters and condensed and combined others, making for what we believe is a much more usable book.

By using the tools of economic analysis as we have (admittedly in some cases, in an exploratory and venturesome manner), there is the ever-present possibility for misunderstanding. Economic method does not cover all phases of human life. Hence, when economics is applied to new areas (and in this book it is applied to many new areas), it does not give a complete picture. We study supply and demand without studying the consumer tastes which have so much to do with the demand schedule. This problem is left to the psychologists simply because we do not know enough to deal with it. Similarly, in many of the areas we discuss in this book, our approach is a partial, rather than a complete, modeling of the real world. In many subtle ways, especially in Chapter 1, we have in this new edition attempted to place greater stress on the limitations of economic analysis. Nevertheless, we think that these economic models are enlightening even if they do not give complete answers. The growth of human knowledge is a matter of step-by-step progress, and the fact that we are unable completely to explain crime by economic methods does not imply that these methods should be abandoned.

As the reader may deduce as he goes through the textbook, we have found it an interesting and exciting book to write, and we hope that both the professors and the students will also find it interesting and exciting. If it is merely used to teach elementary economics, we will have achieved only part of our goal. We hope that the readers of this book will learn enough so they can apply economic methods to various problems that occur, both in public life and in their own private lives, outside the traditional areas. We also hope that they will find the process more fun than more traditional economics.

A few of the chapters in this book are based upon articles which have appeared in the economic literature. Since we have not been deluged with critical comments on these articles, we assume that they contain no serious errors. We have made every effort to eliminate all errors, but it is possible that we have missed some. We hope that professors and, for that matter, students who detect such errors will share them with their classes but will also let us know about them. This will make it possible for us to improve the quality of the book in future editions.

As a last note, the authors must admit frankly that this book is rather controversial. Both of us have been involved in controversy of one sort or another during our entire professional lives, so we, in any event, do not find this at all unusual. We have attempted to present the truth as we see it. But we should not be surprised if some of these chapters lead to very vigorous discussion. We only request that students reading the book attempt fully to understand our arguments. Perhaps, even after having fully understood them, they will prefer some other approach. But at least they should give us that small benefit of doubt which involves reading carefully enough to understand before making a judgment.

In writing a book of this nature, the authors are, of necessity, indebted to others for ideas and criticisms which have improved the book. Accordingly, we would like to express our gratitude to James Buchanan, Stephen Buckles, Paul Combs, Lila Flory, Allan Freiden, Charles Haulk, Roger Leonard, Thomas Ireland, Michael McPherson, Alan Mandelstamm, Dennis O'Toole, Joseph Prinzinger, Lloyd Reynolds, Robert Staaf, and Gilroy Zuckerman for giving us their views on various portions of the first edition of the manuscript. In addition, we would like to recognize the expert editorial assistance of Gloria Cline, Eva McClain, Mary Ann McKenzie, and Jillana Williams and the gracious way they handled these responsibilities. Further, the first section in Chapter 2 was first published as a short article in *Common Sense Economics,* and we thank the editor for giving us permission to reprint the article here.

Finally, over the six-year period that the first two editions were available, we received a number of comments and suggestions for improvements in this volume from economists across the country. Their comments on the classroom usefulness of *The New World of Economics* have been encouraging, and their suggested changes have helped us a great deal in the revision process. We would especially like to thank J. Fred Bateman, Raymond Battalio, Ann Fisher, Jane Humphries, John Kagel, Maren Marie Kiilsgaard, Virgil L. Mitchell, Guy Schlick, Alain Sheer, and Eliott R. Sussels.

Richard B. McKenzie
Gordon Tullock

Contents

xiii

PART 5
THE PUBLIC'S FINANCES AND POLICIES

PART 6
COLLEGE AND UNIVERSITY EDUCATION

PART 7
ECONOMICS AND ITS SCIENTIFIC NEIGHBORS

PART 1

INTRODUCTION

The economists' stock-in-trade—their tools—lies in their ability and proclivity to think about all questions in terms of alternatives. The truth judgment of the moralist, which says that something is either wholly right or wholly wrong, is foreign to them. The win-lose, yes-no discussion of politics is not within purview. They do not recognize the either-or, the all-or-nothing, situation as their own. Theirs is not the world of the mutually exclusives. Instead, it is the world of adjustment, of coordinated conflict, of mutual gains.

From James M. Buchanan, "Economics and Its Scientific Neighbors," *The Structure of Economic Science: Essays on Methodology,*" ed. Sherman Roy Krupp (Englewood Cliffs, N.J.: Prentice-Hall, 1966), p. 168.

The economic approach
to the study
of human behavior

Economics is a constantly changing discipline. This can be said about most disciplines, but it is particularly applicable to economics. At one time students could think of economics as being neatly contained within the sphere of commercial life, and most courses and books on the subject have traditionally revolved around such topics as money, taxes and tariffs, stocks and bonds, and the operation of the market as it pertains to the production and sale of automobiles and toothpaste. In recent years, however, economists have greatly expanded their field of concern, and, as a result, the boundaries of economics as a discipline are rapidly expanding outward, encroaching on areas of inquiry that have historically been the exclusive domain of other social sciences. The change in direction and scope of the discipline has been so dramatic that the economists who have been involved in bringing about the change are no longer inclined to debate the issue of what is or is not economic in nature. They merely ask "What can economics contribute to our understanding of this or that problem?"

This book reflects this expanded vision. Accordingly, we will introduce you to topics and points of discussion you may never have imagined would be included in an economics book. We will talk about family life, child rearing, dying, sex, crime, politics, and many other topics.[1] We do this not because such topics add a certain flair to the book, but rather because we believe that these are extraordinarily important areas of inquiry and that economic analysis can add

---

[1] Actually, Adam Smith was concerned with several of these problem areas in *The Wealth of Nations*, which was published in 1776. He would not be surprised that economists are now giving such topics more attention.

much to our understanding of them. In addition, we are convinced that you will learn a good deal about economics through their consideration.

In dealing with such topics, we cannot avoid coming to grips with human behavior and making it the focus of our concern. The simple reason is that crimes cannot be committed, children cannot be reared, sex cannot be had, and governments cannot operate without people "behaving" in one respect or another. We argue that before we can ever hope to understand social phenomena, we must understand why people behave the way they do. To do this, we must have some perception, or model, of how behavior is motivated and organized from which the revealed actions of people can be interpreted. Economists have such a model, which has been developed and refined since the days of Adam Smith, and it is because we employ this model in our discussion, that we consider this to be an economic treatise. All we intend to do here is to extend the application of this model into unconventional areas.

This is not to say, however, that economics can give a complete understanding of these problem areas. Other social scientists have long considered many of the topics included in this book, and their contributions to our understanding of human behavior cannot be overlooked. By viewing these topics through the thinking process of economists, we must be ever mindful that what we are dealing with is one particular point of view, which can be complemented by many of the findings in other disciplines.

You may at times have reservations about accepting what we have to say, but this is not necessarily unwelcome to us. We could easily write a book with which the reader would readily agree; however, we imagine that such a book might deal only with trivial issues and very well be a monumental bore. We take the view that at any given time, there are many important issues that are to some degree unsettled; we believe that learning not only requires that an individual know the settled issues but also be able to explore those issues over which there may be some disagreement.

You do not need to have a large reservoir of economic knowledge in order to understand what we have to say. We will provide you with the necessary principles on which later discussion will be founded. Furthermore, we do not intend to waste your time with a lot of esoteric theory that will never be used. We understand that you want to make as efficient use of your time as possible, and we intend to cooperate with you. (Remember, this is a book on economics!) The principles that we do develop and the points that we make will at times be very subtle and a little tricky to handle—we cannot escape this. You may be pleasantly surprised, however, at how few in number these principles are and at how useful they will be in thinking about topics that are and are not included in this book. First we need to lay the foundation—to explain how economists look at their subject and at human behavior.

THE MEANING OF ECONOMICS

For nearly 200 years, economists have periodically struggled with the problem of defining economics, and it is still a live issue. At times the subject has been defined as "what economists do," as that part of human experience that involves money, or as a study of how men attempt to maximize their material well-being. Different people perceive a discipline in different ways; therefore, no one can ever claim to offer readers the definition of the subject. All we can hope to accomplish is to lay out our own perception of the subject and in that way suggest how we will proceed.

The approach taken in this book is to define economics as a *mental skill* that incorporates a special view of human behavior characteristic of economists.[2] It is, in short, a thought process, or the manner in which economists approach problems, rather than an easily distinguishable group of problems that sets an economist apart from others. Sociologists and political scientists have dealt with many of the problems considered in this book, but the reader may notice that our approach to these problems is substantially different from theirs. This mental skill or approach has several distinctive characteristics that can be discussed as follows.

ABSTRACTIONS

First and foremost, economists are prone to think, as are all other scientists, in terms of *abstractions,* not in the sense that the notions

---

[2] In fact, it is the thought process or the mental skill developed below that defines an economist. Indeed, in the context of the discussion that follows, there are no doubt many people who call themselves economists but who do not meet the description offered here, and there are many persons in other disciplines who can, according to our definition, accurately be classified as economists. However, given the differences in policy conclusions of economists and noneconomists, it is apparent that not everyone possesses the mental skills developed in this book. By the same token, economists are well advised to develop some of the skills possessed by other social scientists.

are vague or nebulous, but rather in the sense that their first impulses are to reduce reality to the relationships that are important and that bring the inquiry down to manageable proportions. The ideal approach to the study of human and social phenomena would be to treat the world as we confront it. However, the world is terribly complex; at any point in time it encompasses literally billions of bits of information and tens of thousands (if not millions) of relationships. On the other hand, the human mind has a limited capacity to handle such data; it can only consider so much at any one time. It is, therefore, literally impossible for a person to think about the world in its totality and deduce anything meaningful. As a consequence, scientists must restrict the information they do consider. They must *abstract* in the sense that they pull out from the total mass of information a limited number of relationships they think are important and can handle.

This means that the analysis that then follows will lack a certain degree of realism. The analysis is based on abstractions that represent only a small portion of what we might call the *real world*. The expectation is, however, that such an approach will increase our understanding of the real world and will increase our ability to predict events in it. Economists heed the principle concisely laid out by economist Kenneth Boulding: "It is a very fundamental principle indeed that knowledge is always gained by the orderly loss of information; that is, by condensing and abstracting and indexing the great buzzing confusion of information that comes from the world around us into a form which we can appreciate and comprehend."[3] (Take a moment and think about this.) If you have difficulty understanding the world we live in, we suggest that your problem is likely to be that you are attempting to consider too much information, *not too little*.

Since the theory or model that is handled is, by its very nature, "unreal," the test of its acceptability is not dependent solely on the degree of its "realism" but also on the extent to which the model is able to accomplish its purpose—that is, to explain events in the real world and to make correct predictions. At times, the reader is likely to think to himself that our analysis is, in one respect or another, unreal or that the model we employ does not represent the "fullness of the human experience." To such a comment we agree, but we must follow with the question, "Are our conclusions not

---

[3] Kenneth E. Boulding, *Economics As a Science* (New York: McGraw-Hill, 1970), p. 2.

borne out in the real world? Are our predictions not more accurate than can be obtained by other means?"

There is a story of an economics professor who was lecturing on a very esoteric topic before his graduate class. In the middle of the lecture, the professor was interrupted by a student who said, "Sir, I hate to break in, but in the real world. . . ." The professor snapped back, "Mr. Waldorf, you must remember that the real world is a special case, and, therefore, we need not consider it!" Before one gets the impression that we may be taking the same view as this professor, let us emphasize that everything we say, although it may be discussed in terms of models, is directed at our understanding of the real world, and we believe that economics has a very efficient way of doing that.

VALUES

The approach of the economist tends to be (but is not always) *amoral*. Economics is not so much concerned with what *should be* or how individuals should behave, as it is with understanding why people behave the way they do. Accordingly, our analysis is devoid (as much as possible) of our own personal values. We treat each topic as something that is to be analyzed and understood, and in order to do that, we must avoid the temptation to judge a given form of behavior as contemptuous, immoral, good, or bad. Therefore, in the context of our analysis, the services of a prostitute are treated no differently than the services of the butcher; they are neither good nor bad—they exist and are subject to analysis. Criminal activity is considered in a manner similar to that of legitimate enterprise, and religion is treated as a "good" (for some) that is sought after and procured.

Our reason for taking this tack is that in this book, we are not interested in telling people how they should behave or what is good or evil; we are interested in gaining understanding of the behavior of others *given their values*. Further, we are interested in evaluating the effects of institutional settings on human behavior and in suggesting how institutions may be rearranged to accomplish whatever objective is desired. Note that our intention is to suggest changes in institutions and not in behavior.

Like everyone else, we have our own value systems, and we could easily make recommendations regarding how people's behavior *should be* changed to accomplish what we, as humanists, think is right. We also recognize that you have your own values, and we in no way wish to suggest that you dispense with them. You may violently disagree with prostitution or with political corruption—we do not quarrel with this. All we ask is that you allow us the opportunity to address the question of why such phenomena occur. In the process, you may find a solution to the problem that is more consistent with your values than the solution you may now perceive.

THE INDIVIDUAL

The focal point of the study of economics is the *individual*. It is the individual who possesses values, makes choices, and, if given the freedom, takes actions. All group decisions and actions are thought of in terms of the collective decisions and actions of individuals. Social goals are considered only to the extent that they reflect the collective values or choices of individuals. All too often we hear such expressions as "society disapproves of this or that," "Congress is considering legislation," or "government has made a decision to enforce a given policy." If the expressions are meant to suggest that individuals are involved, we have no qualms; if, on the other hand, the expressions are intended to suggest that these bodies have a behavior of their own that is independent of the behavior of individuals, we must take issue. We ask, how can a group *act*? What is group behavior if it not the behavior of individuals? How can a society, as an independent organism, have a value? Where must the values come from?

Do not misinterpret us; we are interested in understanding group behavior. However, we argue that to do this, we must first understand the behavior of the individuals that make up the group. We take it as a given that only individuals can act.

RATIONAL BEHAVIOR

Economists begin their analysis of human behavior with the assertion that *human beings act* and do so with a purpose. That purpose is to improve their lots—to change the situation from something less desired to something better, or as economist von Mises put it:

> Acting man is eager to substitute a more satisfactory state of affairs for a less satisfactory. His mind imagines conditions which suit him better, and his actions aim at bringing about this desired state. The incentive that impels a man to act is always some uneasiness. A man perfectly content with the state of his affairs would

have no incentive to change things. He would have neither wishes nor desires; he would be perfectly happy. He would not act; he would simply live free from care.[4]

This is the ultimate foundation of economics as a discipline. Philosophers and social scientists in general still debate the issue of whether or not human beings have free will. We do not mean to detract from the importance of the debate. From our point of view, it is not necessary to discuss it. Whether people make free decisions or whether they are "programmed" to make the decisions is irrelevant from the economic standpoint. We only need note that they do make decisions. Such a position has several implications. First, in economics people are assumed to be rational in the sense that they are able to determine within limits what they want and will strive to fulfill as many of these wants as possible. People are able to offset environmental, social, and biological forces that would otherwise determine what they do. To what extent they are able to accomplish this depends on the resources at their commands and the intensity of desire to overcome these forces. Although taken for granted by many, these points need to be made because not all social scientists agree with this perspective. Many will argue, at least for purposes of their theories, that a factor such as the environment *determines*— not influences—human behavior. The economist, on the other hand, looks at such factors as constraints within which the individual's preference can operate.

This position implies that the individual will always choose more of what he or she wants rather than less. It also means that he or she will choose less of what he or she does *not* want than more. For example, if the individual desires beer and pretzels and is presented with two bundles of these goods, both with the same amount of pretzels and one with more beers, the rational individual (that is, college student) will take the bundle with the greater number of beers. If he or she does not like beer, then that is another matter. In a similar vein, if one bundle contains a greater variety of goods or goods with a higher quality than the other bundle, the individual will choose that bundle with the greater variety or higher quality.[5]

If there is some uncertainty surrounding the available bundles,

---

[4] Ludwig von Mises, *Human Action: A Treatise on Economics* (New Haven, Conn.: Yale University Press, 1949), p. 13.

[5] For all intents and purposes, goods of differing quality can be treated as distinctly different goods.

the individual will choose that bundle for which the *expected value* is greatest. People do make mistakes mainly because they have incomplete information, but this does not negate the assumption of rational behavior. We only assume that the individual's motivation is to do that which he or she expects will improve his or her station in life, not that he or she always accomplishes this. There are such things as losers.

Economists are often criticized for assuming that man is wholly materialistic—that man wants material things. The criticism is unjustified. All we have assumed from the start of this section is that an *individual has desires*. These desires may be embodied in material things, such as cocktails and clothes; however, we also fully recognize that human beings *want* things that are aesthetic, intellectual, and spiritual in nature. Some people do want to read Shakespeare and Keats and to contemplate the idea of beauty. Others want to attend church and worship as they choose. Even a few may want to read this book! We have no quarrel with this (particularly with those who are interested in this book). We accept these as values with which we must deal in our analysis. They are part of the data we handle. We emphasize, however, that what we have to say regarding material things is also largely applicable to those values that are not material. We may talk in terms of goods, but what we mean are those things people value.

COST

Another implication of our basic position is that as far as the individual is concerned, Nirvana will never be reached. The individual will never obtain a perfect world and, as a result, must accept second best, which is to maximize utility through behavior. This suggests that the individual will undertake to do that for which there is some expected net gain. He or she will in this sense pursue his or her own self-interest. This does not mean that the individual will necessarily lack concern for his or her fellow human beings. One of the things that he or she may want is to give to others. Such behavior can yield as much pleasure as anything else and, if so, will be done. Why do people give gifts, say, at Christmas time? There are many motives that can be separated out; however, we suggest that the overriding reason is that the person involved gets some pleasure (gain), in one form or another, from doing it. Even the Bible admonishes that "it is better to give than to receive," indicating that there are gains to be had for acts of charity. Can you think of anything you or anyone else have done for which you or they did not *expect* some gain? (Remember, you have, no doubt, made a mistake and lost, but this is not involved in the question.) Certainly there have been instances in which direct self-satisfaction was not the basis for your action. However, we wish only to make the point that *much,* but certainly not all, human action is founded upon the desire of people to gain from what they do. To the extent that they behave the way we assume they do, then our predictions about their behavior should be accurate.

If we are seeking to maximize our utility, then it follows that we must make choices among relevant alternatives. It also follows that in the act of choosing to do one thing, we *must* forgo doing or having something else. There is no escaping this. Although often measured in terms of dollars, *the cost of doing or having something is the value of one's best alternative forgone when a choice is made.* Therefore, for every act there is a cost, and it is this cost that will determine whether or not (or how much) something will be done. Cost is the constraint on action. In other words, is there anything such as a free lunch? Free TV? Free love or sex? How can these things be had if choices are involved? No money may have changed hands, but, again, *cost is not money.* Money (or more properly, dollars) is just one means of measuring cost. To have such things, we have to give up something in the way of time, psychic benefits, and/or resources that may be used for other purposes.

In an attempt to explain social phenomena we will, throughout this book, address the question of the costs and benefits of any given form of behavior. In understanding behavior, cost is a very powerful explanatory factor as we will see. Consider the following problems:

1. Why do the poor tend to ride buses and the rich tend to fly? It may be that there are differences in the educational and experience levels of the two groups, resulting in different behavior patterns. It may also be that being rich, the rich can afford such extravagances as airplane tickets. All these factors may explain *part* of the behavior; but we wish to stress that it may be cheaper for the poor to take a bus than to fly and for the rich to fly than take the bus. Both rich and poor pay the same price for their tickets, and, consequently, the difference in cost must lie partly in the difference in the value of the time of the rich and poor. If by rich person we mean someone whose wage rate is very high, it follows that the rich person's time is much more valuable (in terms of wages forgone) than the poor person's time. Since it generally takes longer to take a bus than to

fly, the cost of taking the bus, which includes the value of one's time, can be greater to the rich than the cost of flying. The poor person's time may be worth, in terms of what he could have earned, very little. Therefore, the total cost of a bus ride can be quite inexpensive. As a case in point, consider Johnny Carson who makes over $1 million per year and a poor man who is unemployed. Determine the *total* cost for each to take the bus and plane from Washington to Chicago. You may think that Johnny Carson has a lot of free time for sunbathing on the beach. Regardless of how you view the situation, it is still true that Carson can sell his time for a considerable sum to many willing buyers. Given your calculations, would you ever expect Carson to take the bus?

2. Why do the British use linen table napkins more often than Americans? In part, the answer may be that the differences in culture have had an effect on the willingness of people to use one form of napkins or another. However, one should also realize that the British have to import virtually all of their paper or pulpwood and that paper is relatively expensive there. Paper napkins are much less costly in the United States. Furthermore, linen napkins require washing and ironing, and since wages are generally higher in the United States, the cost of using linen napkins is much greater to Americans than to people of Britain. Again the differences in cost provides a partial explanation.

3. Why do some people resist cheating on their examinations? It may be that they fear being caught and suspended from school, which means they attribute a cost to cheating. Barring this, they may have a moral code that opposes cheating, at least in this form. If they cheat, they would have to bear the psychic cost of going against what they consider right. This does not mean that all those with a moral code or conscience will not cheat to some degree. (Why?)

4. Why do some men forgo asking women out on dates? They may be shy (or gay), but they may feel that the cost of the date in terms of the money and time expenditures is too great. They may also be reluctant to ask women out because in doing so they have to incur the *risk cost* of being turned down.

5. Why are people as courteous as they are on the highways? They may have a streak of kindness in their hearts, but they may also be fully aware of the very high cost they can incur if their rudeness ends in an accident.

When trying to sum up the economist's view of human behavior, we are reminded of a little ditty for which, unfortunately, we do not have the source:

Oh, little girl with your nose pressed up against
the windowpane of life,
There is no jelly doughnut.

MARGINAL COST

In determining how many units of a *given good* we will consume,
we must focus on the additional cost of each additional unit. Another name for this cost concept is *marginal cost.* In other words,
before we can proceed to the consumption of the next unit, we must,
at each step along the way, ask how much does that additional unit
cost?

If we are allowed time to make choices, there is substantial reason
to believe that, as a general rule, the marginal cost of successive
units we provide for ourselves or others will rise. At any point
where a choice must be made, we are likely to have a whole array
of opportunities we can choose to forgo to do this one thing. These
opportunities are likely to vary in their value to us. In making the
choice to consume the *first* unit of a good, which opportunity will
we give up? We will forgo that opportunity we value least, and we
will forgo that opportunity if the value of the unit produced is

FIGURE 1–1

greater than the value of the opportunity forgone. Since cost (or as in this case, marginal cost) is the value of that opportunity given us, this means that the cost of the first unit is as low as possible. If we then wish to produce or consume a second unit, we will have to give up that opportunity that is second to the bottom in value. This means that the marginal cost of the second is greater than the first. Given this choice behavior, we should expect the marginal cost of successive units to rise progressively. Therefore, if we were to describe the relationship between the unit of the good provided and the marginal cost, we would expect to have a curve that is upward sloping to the right as in Figure 1–1. In this graph, marginal cost is on the vertical axis, and the quantity of the good is on the horizontal axis. We economists refer to such a curve as the *supply curve*. Because of this relationship, we can argue that the higher the benefits (or price) received per unit, the more units of the good that we can justify providing.

There are cases in which the marginal cost of providing additional units is constant. More units of the good can be provided by forgoing alternatives that are equal in value. (Can you think of such cases?) In this event the supply curve will be horizontal. See Figure 1–2.

There is no reason to believe that the supply curve will remain sta-

FIGURE 1–2

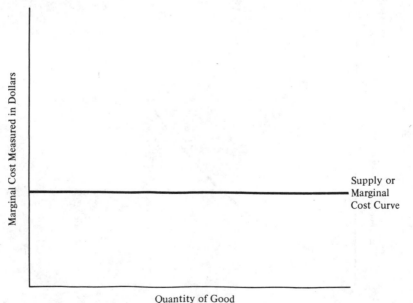

Supply or
Marginal
Cost Curve

Marginal Cost Measured in Dollars

Quantity of Good

tionary over time and under all conditions. Basically, the curve is set where it is because of a given cost structure of providing the good. It follows that anything that changes this cost structure will cause the curve to shift in one direction or the other. If the cost (which means the value of alternatives) of providing the good rises, then the curve will shift upward and to the left. If the cost goes down, the curve will move downward and to the right.[6] (Can you think of changes that would change the cost structure?)

DEMAND

The assumption that the rational individual maximizes his utility implies that he will fully allocate his income among those things he wants. When we say income, we mean *full income*, which includes not only what a person can earn on a conventional job and which may be *measured* in terms of dollars, but also what a person can earn by doing things for himself outside of his job, such as cooking meals. How can a person not fully allocate his income? Even when a person saves, the individual is allocating his income and generally doing it for a purpose. That purpose may be to acquire a certain degree of security for himself or his family or to buy something he wants in the future. By saving, we might rightfully argue that the person is buying something.

The assumption also implies that the individual will continue to consume a given good until the marginal cost (MC) of the last unit obtained is equal to the marginal utility (MU). (Like the concept of marginal cost, marginal utility [or benefit] is the additional utility on each additional unit of the good.) If this were not the case and the marginal cost of the next unit of the good were less than the marginal utility of it, the individual could increase his level of satisfaction by consuming additional units. He could get more additional satisfaction from the additional unit or units than he would forgo by not consuming something else. Note that the marginal cost is the value of that which is forgone. If the marginal cost exceeds the marginal utility, the individual can increase his satisfaction by consuming at least one unit less. (Can you explain why?)

---

[6] For a more detailed discussion on the concept of supply, see any standard textbook on principles of economics. For example, see Armen A. Alchian and William R. Allen, *University Economics: Elements of Inquiry,* 3d ed. (Belmont, Calif.: Wadsworth Publishing Company, 1972); or Richard B. McKenzie and Gordon Tullock, *Modern Political Economy: An Introduction to Economics* (New York: McGraw-Hill, 1978), chap. 4.

This rule is readily applicable to production and consumption decisions involving, say, carrots or candy, but we suggest that it has a much broader application than may be first realized. If you are a student, what rule do you follow in determining how much you study for a given course? We expect that you will follow the $MC = MU$ (or "equimarginal") rule developed above. You will continue to study until the marginal cost of an additional minute spent studying is equal to the marginal utility gained from studying that unit of time. If the marginal utility of an additional minute is greater than the marginal cost, is not this another way of saying that you would gain more by studying this particular course than doing whatever else you could do with the time? Would you, therefore, not study the additional minute?

In determining the length of her skirt, what rules does a woman follow? Again we argue that she will shorten the skirt until the marginal utility of taking it up one additional inch is equal to the additional cost. (What are the costs and benefits of shortening the skirt?) For different people in the same situation and for the same people in different situations, the costs and benefits of a skirt's length are different. Therefore, we would anticipate a variety of skirt lengths.

Consider a person—yourself, if you like—who is preparing to eat dinner. What rule does he use in determining how many beans he will dish onto this plate? By now, you should have it; he will add beans to his plate until the marginal cost of the additional bean is equal to the marginal utility.

No individual is really able to act in as precise a manner as the above discussion may imply. He may not have the capacity to do so, and the benefits to be gained from such precision may not be worthwhile. (Explain.) Actually, we are interested only in making the point that the rational individual will approximate this kind of behavior.

When considering more than one good, say, two goods such as beer and pretzels, the utility maximizing condition of $MC = MU$ translates into the following condition:

$$MU_b/P_b = MU_pP_p$$

where

MU_b = marginal utility of beer
MU_p = marginal utility of pretzels
P_b = price of beer
P_p = price of pretzels

If this is not the case and MU_b/P_b is greater than MU_p/P_b, then we can show that the person will not be maximizing his utility. No one really knows what a "util" of satisfaction is, but for purposes of illustration, let us assume that utils exist and that the additional saisfaction acquired from the last unit of beer (MU_b) is 30 utils, the additional satisfaction of the last unit of pretzels (MU_p) consumed is 10 utils, and that the price of both beer and pretzels is $1. It follows that

$$MU_b/P_b > MU_p/P_p \qquad (30/\$1 > 10/\$1)$$

The individual can change his consumption behavior, consume one less unit of pretzels, and use the $1 to consume one additional unit of beer. He would give up 10 utils of satisfaction in the consumption of pretzels, but he would gain 30 utils of satisfaction in beer. He would be better off, and he would continue to reorganize his purchases until the equality set forth above is met. (You may find this a little tricky. Do not hesitate re-reading what you have just finished. It is imperative that you understand what has been said above before going ahead to the next point.)

Now, let us suppose that the individual has fully maximized his satisfaction and that $MU_b/P_b = MU_p/P_p$. Further suppose that MU of beer and of pretzels is 20 utils and that the price of beer falls to, say, $.50 and the price of pretzels remains at $1. This means that $MU_b/P_b > MU_p/P_p$ (20/$0.50 > 20/$1) and that the individual can get two units of beer (40 utils) for the price of one unit of pretzels; he can gain utility by switching the beer. Notice what we have said: *if the price of beer goes down, the rational individual will buy more beer.* This all falls out of our general assumption that the individual is simply out to maximize his utility.

This inverse relationship between price and quantity is extremely important in economic theory and in the analysis of this book. It is so important that economists refer to it as the *law of demand.* It is important because it adds an element of prediction to economic analysis. We can say with a great deal of confidence that if the price of a good or service falls, *ceteris paribus,* people will buy more of it. It is, perhaps, the strongest predictive statement a social scientist can make with regard to human behavior.[7] The law of demand can

---

[7] The relationship is held with such complete confidence that one prominent economist has reportedly argued that if an empirical study ever reveals that people buy more when the price is increased, there must be something wrong with the empirical investigation. Other economists like ourselves, taking a more moderate view, may recognize possible exceptions to the rule but argue that they are extremely few.

be graphically depicted by a downward sloping curve as in Figure 1–3. As the price for the good falls from P_2 to P_1, the quantity purchased rises from Q_1 to Q_2.

Courses in economics generally deal with the law of demand in the context of conventional goods and services such as peanut butter, detergent, and meals at a restaurant. Although we agree with such application, we wish to stress that the law has a much broader application. In fact, we go as far as to assert that the law of demand applies to a wide range of things that people value and the procurement of which is revealed in human behavior. Consequently, we argue that the law of demand can be applicable to such "goods" as sex, honesty, dates, highway speeding, babies, and life itself! We predict that if the price of any one of these things goes up, the quantity demanded will diminish and vice versa.

We will spend much of our time in this book discussing how the law of demand applies to areas such as these. For purposes of illustration at this point, let us consider the demand for going to church. Many people do place a value on going to church, and as strange as it may seem, there is a price to church attendance. The church may not have a box office outside its doors selling tickets,

FIGURE 1–3

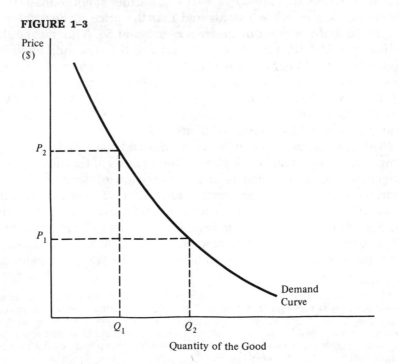

but people have to pay the price of their time, and they do understand that they are expected to contribute something to the operations of the church. (How many well-established people in the community would feel comfortable taking their families to church
week after week without contributing anything to the church?)
Through stewardship, sermons, and visitations the church does
apply pressure, as mild as it might be, to get people to contribute.
To that extent they extract a price. Suppose the minister and the
board of elders decide to raise significantly their demands on the
congregation. What do you think will happen to the church's membership, holding all other things constant? The membership may be
on the rise for a number of reasons. What we maintain is that because of the greater price, the membership will rise by less than
otherwise. In that sense, the "price" increase reduces the membership. This does not necessarily mean that people would be less
religious; it may only mean that some will react to the price change
and make use of other ways of expressing and reinforcing their
beliefs.

Suppose we return to the days when men were expected to be
the ones who asked women out on dates. (In recent years, this social
institution has broken down to a significant degree.) Given all the
attributes of a given group of women, men placed, as they do now,
some value on having dates with them. In other words, they had a
demand for dates. (In the event that you are concerned with the
approach we are taking, we could easily reverse the example and
talk about women's demand for dates. We only intend to use this
situation as an example. We do not wish to judge it as being good
or bad.)

Clearly, the utility-maximizing men will date women, if they can
get the dates, until the marginal utility of the last date during some
specified period of time is equal to the marginal cost of the date.
There is an implicit price to most dates. For the man, if they are
expected to bear the expense, it is equal to the money spent on
transportation, the entertainment, and refreshment, plus the value
of the individual's time. (There is also a price to the woman.) Suppose
that during this epoch when men were expected to pay for dates,
a group of women collude; they get together and decide that the
humdrum dates of yesterday are no longer up to their standards.
They decide to collectively require the men to spend more on them.
They in effect agree to raise the price of dates. If such a collusive
arrangement were to stick, what do you think would have happened
to the number of invitations issued to this group of women? No

doubt it would fall. It may fall because the men would then have an incentive to substitute other women for the women that were taking part in the cartel. Additionally, the increase in price of dates can induce several men to consume other goods such as watching Saturday night television or having a cold beer at a local tavern.

As the number of calls for dates begins to fall off, there would very likely be women who would begin to chisel on the collusive agreement by effectively lowering their demands (price). Thus, the agreement would tend to break down. Competition, as we will see on a number of occasions, will play a role in determining exactly what demands are made in areas of social interaction.

Many people value speeding in their cars. If caught speeding they may pay a fine of, say, $50. If they expect to be caught one out of every 100 times that they speed, the price they pay per time speeding averages out to $.50. Given this price, they will find a certain quantity of speeding desirable. Suppose, now, that the fine is raised to $10,000 per speeding conviction. The average price paid per time speeding would then rise to $100. Do you think that the people would speed less as the concept of demand predicts? (Suppose that the probability of being caught is increased. This can be accomplished by putting more patrolmen on the roads. What would be the effect?)

SUPPLY AND DEMAND

Measuring marginal costs and benefits in terms of dollars, we can draw both the demand and supply (marginal cost) curves on the same graph (see Figure 1–4). In taking this step we have constructed an *abstract* model of human behavior but one that can be quite revealing and useful in many contexts. We will repeatedly demonstrate this throughout the book. For now, we need only point out that the maximizing individual will choose to produce and consume Q_1 units of this particular good. It does not matter what the good is or where the curves are positioned; the individual will choose that consumption level at the intersection of the two curves. It is at this point that marginal cost is equal to marginal utility. If the individual chooses to restrict his consumption to Q_2, note that the marginal benefit, which is indicated by the demand curve and represented by MB_1, is greater than the marginal cost, which is indicated by the supply curve and is MC_1. This is true of every unit between Q_2 and Q_1. Therefore, the maximizing individual can raise his utility by consuming them. Beyond Q_1, the reverse is true; the mar-

FIGURE 1–4

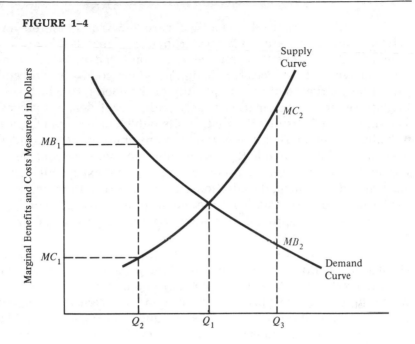

ginal cost is greater than the marginal benefit. For example, for the Q_{3d} unit, the marginal cost is MC_2 while the marginal benefit is less, MB_2.

Quite often, people find that it is less costly to trade with someone else than to produce the good themselves. To understand a social setting in which there are many producers and consumers trading for a particular good, we need to construct a model involving a *market* supply curve and *market* demand curve. We can derive a market supply curve by adding together what all producers are willing to offer on the market at each possible price. If each individual producer is willing to offer a larger quantity at higher prices, the market supply curve, like the individuals' supply curves, will be upward sloping.[8] To obtain the market demand curve, we can add the amounts demanded by all the consumers at each and every price. Since the individual's demand curves are downward sloping, the same will be true of the market demand curve. The market supply

---

[8] Strictly speaking, the market supply curve is not equal to the horizontal summation of the individuals' supply curves. Nothing is lost for our purposes, however, by leaving this refinement for more advanced treatments of the theory of supply.

and demand curves are depicted in Figure 1–5. The quantities involved in this graph are much greater than in Figure 1–4.

In a highly competitive market situation—one in which consumers have many sources for obtaining a given good—we will still expect the market to offer that quantity of the good (Q_1) which is at the intersection of the market supply and market demand curves. The simple reason is that if only Q_2 units (which is less than Q_1) are provided on the market, there will be many more units demanded (Q_3) than will be available (Q_2). Also note that there are consumers who are willing to offer the producers a price that exceeds the marginal cost of producing the additional units. As a result the suppliers can be induced to expand their production from Q_2 to Q_1. Beyond Q_1, the marginal cost of providing an additional unit is greater than what any consumer is willing to pay for it. If one producer refuses to expand production to Q_1, the consumers can, since we are talking about a competitive market, turn to other producers who may be in the market or may be enticed into it. In a monopoly market, one in which there is only one producer of the good, the consumers do not have the option of turning to another producer (i.e., competitor). To that extent, the monopolist has control over the market: he can restrict the number of units provided and thereby demand a higher

FIGURE 1–5

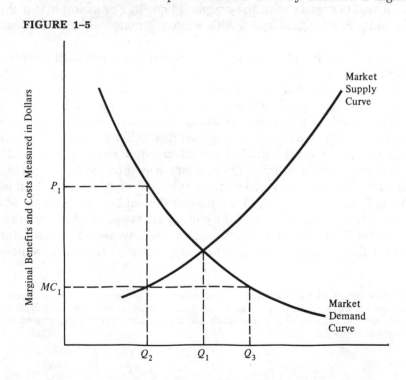

price from the consumer. By restricting output, the monopolist can reduce his total cost of production and can receive greater revenues. (Why?)

Similarly, suppose that the suppliers offer more than Q_1. The only way they can justify doing that is to charge a price higher than what consumers are willing to pay. Note that at Q_3 the marginal cost of the last unit is greater than the price the consumers are willing to pay for it. There will, as a result, be more units offered than will be purchased by consumers. Hence, the suppliers will be in a dilemma. They can either cut back on production and lower the price to the point that consumers will buy what is produced, or they can continue to produce more than can be sold at the price necessary to cover the cost of production. The suppliers can also produce the good and sell it at a price less than the cost incurred. Which option do you think the rational producers will choose? They will cut production back to Q_1, of course. To the extent that the competitive market produces where marginal cost equals marginal benefit, which is the optimizing condition of individual's as explained above, economists say that it is "efficient."

Now that we have outlined the basic framework of the economist's model, we can use it to consider changes in market conditions (meaning environmental, social, or whatever). We consider such changes in the discussion of most topics in this book.

THE LIMITS OF ECONOMIC ANALYSIS

Although we consider many diverse dimensions of the human experience in this book, we do not suggest that economic analysis can be used to explain all human behavior. The interaction of individuals in a social state, with each reacting to the actions of the others, is indeed very complex; some would say that it is so complex that precious little or nothing can be gained by the scientific study of it. We, of course, dispute such a claim. On the other hand, we must approach the complex task that we have before us with full recognition of our limited ability to understand social behavior, and we should be careful that we do not exaggerate the importance of the insights we gain from our study. Scientific insights about people's behavior achieve a degree of prominence not so much because they rank high on some absolute scale of useful knowledge but rather because they say a little something we may not otherwise have known. In short, these insights should always be kept in perspective; they are not, for the most part, monumental and unchanging truths but tentative statements of the way we perceive the world at this time, and they should be coveted as small nuggets because of their relative durability in the give-and-take of scientific debate.

You now know that economic analysis is founded upon an assumption that people know what they want or, what amounts to the same thing, that they have values. Given these values, people make choices, and we can, as we have, talk about the logic people follow in maximizing the attainment of what they want. An obvious limit to economic analysis is implied in what we have just said because much human experience is founded not so much on the attainment of what we want but in trying to figure out just what we want in the first place. Economist Frank Knight made the point with more flare several decades ago:

> Since economics deals with human beings, the problem of its scientific treatment involves fundamental problems of the relations between man and his world. From a rational or scientific point of view, all practically real problems are problems in economics. The problem of life is to utilize resources "economically," to make them go as far as possible in the production of desired results. The general theory of economics is therefore simply the rationale of life— in so far as it has any rationale! The first question in regard to scientific economics is this question of how far life is rational, how far its problems reduce to the form of using given means to achieve given ends. Now this, we shall contend, is not very far; the scientific view of life is a limited and partial view; life is at bottom an exploration in the field of values, an attempt to discover values, rather than on the basis of knowledge of them to produce and enjoy them to the greatest possible extent. We strive to "know ourselves," to find out our real wants, more than to get what we want. This fact sets a first and most sweeping limitation to the conception of economics as a science.[9]

Economics, unfortunately, has very little to say about what people value or why they value what they do. Values are the type of basic data that must be given or assumed as a part of the analysis. Once the values or goods are defined, then the individual can be assumed to maximize the attainment of those goods. However, note that this approach leaves little room for the individual, in the course of the maximizing process, to redefine what he wants; it leaves little room for spontaneous actions that spring from raw emotions. We do not mean to suggest that economic analysis is useless, only that, as might

---

[9] Frank H. Knight, "The Limitations of Scientific Method in Economics," *The Ethics of Competition and Other Essays* (New York: Harper and Brothers, 1935), p. 105.

be reasonably expected, it has its limitations. It can explain only a part of human experience, whether that experience involves crime, politics, sex, the family, or education. We must look to the other social sciences, philosophy, and the humanities for help in our quest for understanding of human behavior, and even with this help, we will probably always conclude that there is much about human behavior that is incomprehensible.[10]

CONCLUDING COMMENTS

How a person views the world and interprets the information he receives from it depends upon the preconceived model he or she has of it. The preceding has been an outline of how economists perceive the real world. For sure, this has been an incomplete description of the economists' way of thinking; there are many more refinements that can be made. (Because of space restrictions a book of this nature forces upon the authors, we have attempted to extend and refine the model until we thought the marginal benefits of an additional point was equal to the marginal cost of making the point.)

Because of this model—because of the concepts of supply and demand—the economists' first inclination is not to think in terms of absolutes, of whether or not something will be done or left undone, or whether or not a goal will be sought.[11] Most things have a price at which they may be obtained, and adjustments in behavior are made according to the price (benefit) that is charged (received). By concentrating on the general goal of utility maximization (and when talking about the firm, profit maximization) rather than on specific objectives, the economists are continuously seeking out new and nonobvious alternatives and thinking in terms of the substitutability, on the margin, of specific means of reaching the general goal. Years of life are, therefore, viewed as a possible substitute for cigarette smoking; low quality medical service in large quantities is one alternative to high quality service in more limited quantities; ice cream is a possible substitute for good dental care. Because economists view the individual as fundamentally seeking ways of gaining, whenever a person proposes a solution for any problem, economists instinctively ask: are there private interests

---

[10] For more on the limits of economic analysis, see Richard B. McKenzie, "On the Methodological Boundaries of Economic Analysis," *Journal of Economic Issues* (Fall 1977).

[11] See the quote by James Buchanan at the beginning of this section.

involved? Economists are trained to separate private interests from the fabric of proposals offered as solutions for social concerns, and they are trained to pull out value judgments from arguments that are put forth as matters of logic. The economists' proclivity to think in this way sets them and their discipline apart from others.

QUESTIONS TO PONDER

1. What role does utility maximization play in economic theory? Why does the economist not assume that the individual strives for something less than maximum utility?

2. What is the decision rule an individual will follow while driving in determining how far behind he will follow another car? What will be the impact of a reduction in the speed limit on the distance between cars? Explain.

3. Many university libraries across the country provide duplicating facilities and charge a nominal fee. Many lose money by doing this. Why do they charge low prices, knowing that they will go in the hole? What does this suggest about the demand for honesty?

4. If in the so-called economy size box of detergent, a consumer can actually get more detergent per penny, why do people buy smaller boxes? What are the costs and benefits of various box sizes?

5. The authors could provide the readers with a more highly complicated and sophisticated economic theory. What are the costs and benefits of doing so? Why do they not do it? How complicated should a theory be?

6. "If a theory can explain everything, then it can predict nothing." Do you agree? Explain.

7. Can economics explain all human behavior? Explain why or why not and cite examples.

RECOMMENDED READINGS

Kenneth Boulding. *Beyond Economics: Essays on Society, Religion, and Ethics.* Ann Arbor, Mich.: The University of Michigan Press, Ann Arbor Paperbacks, 1970.
——— *Economics as a Science.* New York: McGraw-Hill, 1970.
Israel M. Kirzner. *The Economic Point of View.* New York: Van Nostrand, 1960.
Ludwig von Mises. *Human Action: A Treatise on Economics.* New Haven, Connecticut: Yale University Press, 1949.
Mancur Olson, Jr. "Economics, Sociology, and the Best of All Possible Worlds," *The Public Interest* 12 (Summer 1968), pp. 96–118.

CHAPTER 2

Anything worth doing
is not necessarily
worth doing well

In the previous chapter, we stressed the role cost plays in guiding human behavior. In this chapter, we offer specific examples of the influence of cost.

ANYTHING WORTH DOING

From early childhood, most of us have been taught that "anything worth doing is worth doing well." If we were asked today if we still agree with the statement, many of us would say that we do.[1] It is only natural for a person to prefer a job that has been done well to one that has been done not so well; indeed, such a preference is fully consistent with the basic assumption in economics that more (quality) is preferred to less (quality). It is also easy to see why a person may not like to redo something that has already been done, particularly if the combined time involved is greater than the time that would have been required to do it right in the first place.

Obviously, people do not behave the way they profess they should. There is probably not a minister around who has not written what he considered at the time to be a poor sermon, and one of the authors recently built a bookcase that was more-or-less thrown together. Wives and husbands have cooked dinners they knew in their hearts were seriously deficient in one respect or another. Students regularly choose to work for a grade of C (or a grade point

---

[1] James Buchanan has suggested that an economist can be distinguished from a noneconomist by his reaction to the statement. "Economics and Its Scientific Neighbors," *The Structure of Economic Science: Essays on Methodology,* ed. Sherman Roy Krupp (Englewood Cliffs, N.J.: Prentice-Hall, 1966), p. 168.

average far less than 4.0) instead of going all out for an A. This is true even though the A is the preferred grade. How many, do you suppose, of the students who are reading this have written a paper that by their own standards fell far short of a well-done paper? In fact, can you say at this point that you have read the last few pages well?

Admittedly, people do some things well, but the point we wish to emphasize is that they frequently do things less than well, not because they do not want to do better, but because of the *additional* (or *marginal*) cost involved in improving the quality of whatever they are doing. Given the student's ability—which, as a matter of fact, is limited at any point in time—writing a good A paper generally requires more effort and time than writing a C paper. If the student spends additional time on the paper, he or she has less time for doing other things—less time to study the subject matter in other courses, in which case he or she may do less well or even fail. He or she cannot use the time for physical exercise, cannot spend the time in bed, or out on dates. To reiterate, there is usually an additional cost that must be borne for a higher quality paper, and it is because of this cost that he or she may rationally choose to turn in a paper that may just get by. (Even so, the student may still hope for an A. Can you explain why?)

If the cost is not greater for higher quality work, then one must wonder why the job may be done poorly. The student will be able to have a higher quality paper without giving up anything. The problem of the poorly done work may be one of perception; that is, the student may perceive the additional cost to be greater than what it actually is, in which case he or she should respond appropriately if provided with accurate information. He or she may, in addition, inaccurately assess the benefits of a better performance.

Quite often one person will admonish another to do a good job. For example, professors may be distressed at the quality of the papers they receive and may honestly feel that if their students are going to write a paper, they should write a good one. The professors may be even more upset if they find out that their students spent the last few days doing very little or having a good time.

The values the professors and students place on different activities obviously differ. Professors may view the paper as being of greater value than do the students; they may view the other activities as being of less value. Consequently, they believe it is in the students' best interests to do better papers. However, since students view the value of the other activities as being higher, they, in effect, view the cost of doing the better paper as being higher. Of course, it is clearly rational for professors to want the students to turn in better papers, but if they had to bear the costs, they might change their minds.

The same line of argument can be used to explain why the preacher's sermon is of low-quality even though he or she may have the ability to do better. By writing a better sermon, he or she may have to bear the cost of not seeing the parishioners at the hospital or of giving up something else that is considered valuable. In order to cook a better meal, the homemaker may have to forgo writing letters, discussions with neighbors, or hauling Little Leaguers to practice.

What should be the "quality level" toward which a person should strive? The utility-maximizing individual should raise the quality of whatever he does until the marginal benefit received from an additional unit of quality is equal to its marginal cost. Suppose that the marginal benefits for units of quality diminishes as the total quality of the work goes up. Assume also that the marginal cost of additional units increases as the quality level is raised. The diminishing marginal utility assumption is represented by the downward curve (which is equivalent to the demand curve) in Figure 2–1. The up-

FIGURE 2–1

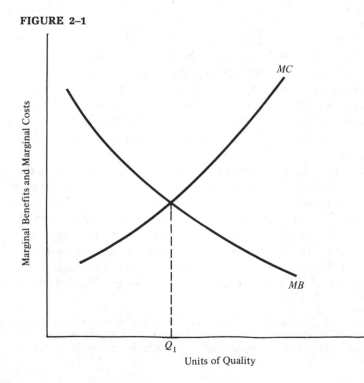

Units of Quality

ward sloping curve represents the increasing marginal cost. Notice that we have labeled the horizontal axis as *units of quality*. (The actual good or service involved can be anything.) The utility-maximizing quality level is Q_1. Before Q_1, the marginal utility of an additional unit of quality is greater than the marginal (or additional) cost.[2] By expanding the quality toward Q_1, the utility of the individual can rise. If the person extends the quality level beyond Q_1, notice that the marginal cost of doing so will be greater than the marginal utility. The result is that the person's total utility level will be less than it would be at Q_1. An outside observer (such as a teacher) may feel that the quality of the work done by the student, Q_1, may be quite low—and it may even be low by the standards of the individual student—but this does not make his behavior any less rational. In other words, anything worth doing is not necessarily worth doing well.

WHY THE YOUNG GO TO COLLEGE

College classes are predominantly made up of young adults between the ages of 18 to 22 years. A small percentage are in their middle or late 20s, but people who are over 50 constitute an extremely small minority. Why do the young go to college whereas older adults, as a general rule, do not? The list of answers conventionally cited may include (1) the young, having recently graduated from high school, are more accustomed to the routine and peculiar demands of the educational process, (2) the young do not have the family responsibilities that the older people have, (3) the young, as a rule, realize the value of education more than do their elders, and (4) the young are more intellectually alive than their parents.

All of these factors can have an influence in determining the composition of college classes, although our experience suggests the last two reasons are invalid. Although rarely cited, the difference in the cost of the two groups may be equally important in explaining the composition of college classes. The cost of a college education is more than the direct monetary expenditures made by the student at the start of each year or academic session. The total cost is the summation of all that the student must forgo. In addition to uni-

---

[2] Marginal cost can be viewed as the utility forgone in some alternative activity. Therefore, by consuming more quality, the individual can, when $MU > MC$, acquire more utility than he gives up in some other activity.

versity charges, this total may include the loss of income one may experience while in the classroom and studying, the transportation expense associated with going to and from the campus, the additional postal and telephone expenditures one must make to stay in contact with friends and family, the cost of books and materials, and the cost of fitting in culturally with the college community.

Although there may be differences, the essential one to the young and old is the opportunity cost of one's time. This, of course, will mean that the total costs will differ. Suppose, for example, that total university charges are $3,500 per year (approximately the average for all public universities in the country in 1980) and that all costs other than opportunity cost of time are $1,000 per year. (We realize that the older people *may* be inclined to spend less on such things as fitting in.) A younger person just out of high school can, over the course of the following four years, probably earn, at the best job he can get, about $32,000 for an average of $8,000 per year. On the other hand, the man who is 45 years old can conceivably earn about twice as much, $60,000 or even more. This means that the total cost to the young adult is about $50,000 for four years of college education; the cost to the older person is approximately $78,000 (see Table 2–1).

TABLE 2–1
Cost of college at present-day prices

Four years	Young adult	Middle-aged adult
University charges	$14,000	$14,000
Opportunity cost	32,000	60,000
Other costs	4,000	4,000
Total costs	$50,000	$78,000

Even if we assume that the two groups have the same values and are equal in every respect with regard to college education, we would expect a larger quantity of education to be demanded by the young than by the old. For example—and only as an example—assume that the demand for college by the young is exactly equal to the demand of the old, as depicted in Figure 2–2A and B. Since the price of a college education to the older person (P_b) is far greater than the price paid by the young (P_a), we would expect that the quantity of education demanded by the young would be greater. In the example of Figure 2–2, the quantity of education demanded by

FIGURE 2-2

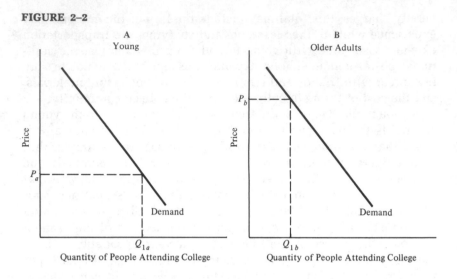

A
Young

B
Older Adults

Quantity of People Attending College

Quantity of People Attending College

the young would be Q_{1a}, which is greater than the quantity demanded by the old, Q_{1b}.

In addition, the young have a much longer period of time to reap the benefits of a college education. The 45-year-old man or woman has only 20 years left in his or her working life, whereas the 22-year-old college graduate has 43 years left until retirement. Therefore, the investment expenditure by the young is likely to be much more profitable. Finally, we should note that the total cost to the young can be much less than we calculated since their parents may foot the university bills. This is less likely to be the case of the much older persons.

WHY STUDENTS WALK ON THE GRASS

Walking on the grass may not appear to have anything to do with economics or to be sufficiently important to warrant discussion. We suggest, on the contrary, that the decision to walk on the grass, for example on the campus mall, is an aspect of human behavior and, therefore, economics. A study of the decision to walk on the grass can be revealing about the causes of pollution and human action in general.

Why do students walk on the grass? Why do people who may dislike to see paths form on campus or courthouse lawns walk in places where paths exist or are likely to exist? To answer these questions, one must begin by recognizing that there are benefits to walking on the grass. It can be a shortcut across campus and save time; the walk may also be personally gratifying, particularly in the spring and without shoes. The individual who strongly favors campus beautification must, in making the decision to walk on the grass, weigh the expected benefits against the expected costs. Before stepping onto the grass he must quickly reflect on the benefits and then calculate the costs involved. He may calculate that if he walks on the grass, he will be responsible for killing several blades of grass but it is very unlikely that anyone will be able to notice even if he regularly walked in the same places. Even if the student dislikes paths on lawns, he may reasonably expect the cost of the walk to approximate zero since each individual walk does not materially affect the environment under normal circumstances. Consequently, the calculated benefits exceed the costs, so he walks—and does it rationally![3]

The problem is that everyone independently making similar calculations may do the same thing. The result is that a path forms, an eyesore is created. This does not mean that it is rational for any one individual not to walk even after the path has formed. Since the person cannot control the walking of everyone else, the results of one's individual walks cannot be detected by anyone; therefore, the rational choice is to take the benefits of cutting across the lawn. If the path is there, one can reason that if one does not walk, no one will be able to tell that one did not—that is, the nature of the path will not be affected. So one walks, and everyone else walks, and the path remains and continues to deepen and possibly spread. This in miniature illustrates the evolution of a form of pollution.

Following this line of argument, one can deduce that if a *private* cost is incurred by the individual, then the logical thing to do may be to take the sidewalk or another route. If the lawn or path is prone to become a quagmire when it rains, then private costs *are* imposed for walking. The individual will have to clean his shoes, and since time is involved in doing that, there is a cost. The cost for some may still not be as great as the benefits, but, significantly, when such conditions exist, there is less walking on the lawns than on sunshiny days.

The connection between walking on the lawns and pollution of other forms should be clear. A person or firm may litter because he

---

[3] Before the reader becomes unduly disturbed by this statement, he should check the economic meaning of *rational action* in Chapter 1.

calculates that there are certain benefits to getting rid of a piece of paper. He may reason that one piece of paper by itself will not significantly affect the environment or materially affect anyone's sensibilities. Therefore, he discards the paper. The problem, again, is that if everyone follows suit, an environmental problem will develop. If the individual can control the behavior of all others, he may not pollute himself, but given his inability to control others, polluting may be rational. Also, cleaning up can be irrational; one may reason he cannot do enough to affect the general environment, particularly since others will be littering as he cleans up. (In fact, his attempts to clean up can reduce the cost of polluting to everyone else—the environment is less affected—and, therefore, one might anticipate, without an intervening change in people's values, more littering by some.) As a result he does not receive the full benefits of his actions and to that degree is less likely to clean up.

The analysis can be extended to conversations at a crowded cocktail party. If the reader has ever been at such a gathering, he probably remembers that often the sound level starts off at a low level and then increases, even though the number of people in the room has not changed. The reason for the crescendo in conversation volume is that at the start, people may be able to understand one another at a low volume. However, as everyone else begins to talk, the general volume begins to rise; this means that the volume that any one individual must use in order to be understood by the person standing next to him must be increased. Because he and everyone else increases his volume, talking louder can be rational. The result may be (as it has time and time again) that all persons in the room end up virtually shouting at one another. *If* each were to lower his own individual volume then all could have a more pleasant conversation. But the question is whether or not it is rational for any one individual to lower *his* volume. The answer is no; he could not be heard, because he cannot control the volume of the others in the room. In addition, he may not significantly affect the general volume level. Therefore, no one changes his volume.[4]

These problem areas point to the usefulness of some form of

---

[4] One qualification: as the volume goes up, several may decide to leave the room keeping the volume from going as high as it otherwise would. Additionally, the higher general volume can make the party more tiring and can cause it to end more quickly for some. The host could conceivably get up and ask that everyone quiet down; the immediate effect can be a sharp reduction in volume. This is, however, likely to be a short interlude before the sound increases.

collective action the purpose of which may be to impose private costs on the actions of individuals so that they may be expected to act in the general interest (which can also be in their own interest). In the case of walking on the grass, the government can plant hedges or thorny bushes along the edge of the sidewalks. If people want to walk on the grass, they will have to incur the cost of jumping the bushes or of runs in stockings. In the case of industrial pollution, taxes or fines for polluting can be imposed. Since people's demands for these activities slope downward, the quantity demanded will be reached.

THE DILEMMA OF ALTERNATE WAYS OF CONSERVING ENERGY

In the 1970s, most people were concerned about the developing shortage of energy. Many attempted to conserve energy by cutting down their thermostats a few degrees and perhaps driving a little slower. The effects of such voluntary actions were, however, not sufficient to eliminate the shortage. Drastic government action in the form of rules on speed limits, thermostats, and fuel consumption of automobiles was necessary to partially remedy the situation. Why did people who were concerned about the energy crisis leave their lights burning and continue to zip along the highways at high speeds? Was it solely because people did not care (as many did not)? Why were price increases on energy necessary to get people to cut back on their energy use at home and in the automobile?

Imagine, for the moment, John sitting in an overstuffed chair watching television. He knows that a light has been left on in an adjoining room, but he does not get up and turn it off.[5] Leaving the light on for an additional half hour until he happens to walk by the room will increase his electric bill, but we must also recognize that getting up requires effort and diminishes the entertainment value of the television program. In other terms, turning the light off is costly. Moreover, given relatively low rates on the use of electric power, John may calculate that the cost of turning the light off is greater than the increase in the electric bill. If John is concerned about the total community consumption of fuel through the generation of electric power, he may still reasonably assume that his decision to leave

---

[5] We recognize that there are times when a person will get up and turn the light off; our purpose here, however, is to explain why at times he may not.

the light on, or even leave every light in his house on, will not appreciably affect the total amount of fuel consumed by the power company. During the winter of 1977 and 1978, natural gas supplies were in critically short supply. Many workers were being laid off because of the gas shortage. All during this period, the gas street lights in a townhouse development in Blacksburg, Virginia were left on *day* and *night!* The townhouse residents met to consider turning them off; they decided to leave them on, however, because an "insignificant" quantity of gas was being used.

The problem, as in previous examples, is that many people, viewing the situation only in individual terms, may decide to leave their electric and gas lights on, in which case, *significantly* more fuel will be consumed by the generating facilities. The reader should understand that we do not necessarily condone this behavior; we are merely attempting to explore the logic of what can be considered a deplorable circumstance. If you question the legitimacy of this explanation, suppose then that John knew that leaving lights on for the duration of the program would cost him $50. Would you expect him to get up and turn it off? Suppose the price of natural gas were three or four times higher, what would the townhouse residents have decided to do?

When the shortage of gasoline began emerging in the spring and summer of 1973, Exxon and other petroleum companies advertised a saving in gas consumption if a driver were to drive at 50 miles per hour instead of 70. The Exxon commercial demonstrated that a car going 70 miles per hour will use a 20-gallon tank in 253 miles; if the car went 50, the 253 miles could be covered with four gallons of gas to spare. Should Exxon or anyone else have expected the ad to make a significant dent in total gasoline consumption? Not really, because it would take the driver approximately one and a half hours longer to travel the 253 miles at 50 than it would at 70. The value of the gasoline saving is, at $.60 per gallon, approximately $2.40. This means that the driver would have had to value his time at $1.60 per hour (or far less than the minimum wage) to justify (on purely economic grounds) slowing down. It he has the public interest at heart, he may slow down, but he will have done so without materially affecting the long-run fuel problem of the United States. It is also very difficult for anyone to slow down in the public interest while others, including public officials, are cruising along at higher speeds.

If the price of gasoline were to rise to $2.00 per gallon, several effects can be predicted. First, and as a generality, a greater private cost will be incurred for energy consumption. Second, the saving from going 50 miles per hour (instead of 70) would be $8.00 (four gallons times $2.00). This means that anyone who would then value his time at less than $5.32 per hour would find going slower economical; economists would expect more to do so. (Why?) Third, economists would also expect that, since the demand curve for travel is downward sloping, people will drive fewer miles, buy smaller cars, use more car pools, and make greater use of mass transportation. All this will further reduce the amount of energy consumed. Fourth, since people will be going slower and the highway fatality rate declines with lower speed, there should be fewer deaths on the highways. The dollar value of damage per wreck should also fall, causing a reduction in insurance rates. Not having made a detailed study of the possible effects, we cannot say *how great* the effects will be, but we can predict with confidence the favorable direction of the effects and that the "shortage" will be eliminated with some increase in price. (Why?) By 1980 the price of a gallon of gasoline rose in some areas to $1.50 and above, and all of the above consequences (predicted in the first edition of this book in 1975) have been observed.

No one likes to see the prices of things increase. The problem is that when the quantity demanded exceeds the quantity supplied, how is the shortage to be eliminated? How is the available quantity of gasoline, natural gas, and fuel oil going to be distributed among the potential buyers? The pricing system has drawbacks. The real income of many people is going to be reduced; most will be unable to buy as much. The question is not, however, whether or not the pricing system is perfect for allocating supplies but rather how its advantages and disadvantages stack up against alternative systems.

The pricing system may not be fair, but is a formal coupon-type rationing system fairer by your own definition? The question which emerges is how do we distribute the coupons? Do we distribute the coupons according to the number of cars that a person has? If we do, wealthy people (who tend to have more cars) will be getting disproportionate shares of the gasoline. Do we give the people who live two miles from work more than the people who live 20 miles away? Do we give the family with six children and one car less gasoline than the person with two children and two cars? Do sales representatives get more gasoline than college students who commute to and from school? Can we really say that being able to go to work for a middle-aged worker is more important, in some ultimate sense, than an afternoon ride for an elderly couple who may have no other principal form of entertainment? These questions have no easy answers, but if the pricing system is not employed, these questions and many, many others like them must be addressed. If we do adopt a nonmarket rationing system, then it follows that the price of the good will be kept lower than otherwise but that there will still be people who are willing to violate the rules and sell the gas on the black market at a higher price. Control of black markets is likely to be necessary.

If an economist ever suggests that the price should be raised to reduce the quantity demanded, he will normally be confronted by the argument that the rich will be able to continue to buy all the gas that they need, but the poor will not, and the poor need the gasoline to go to work. We are inclined to believe that both rich and poor will cut back on their gasoline consumption. In addition, it is not at all certain that the poor will, under a coupon system, end up with the gasoline.[6] If the price of gasoline goes to $2.00 per gallon and the poor are unwilling to buy at that price, will they not be willing to sell their coupons at that price? If they do, they will have more money, but they will not have the gasoline which, as suggested, they need.

RECKLESS DRIVING

There are many drivers on streets and highways who are, for all practical purposes, numskulls. They do not know how to drive, are drunk when they do, or generally do not think about what they are doing behind the wheel. Others take out all of their pent-up aggressions when driving their cars.

We can attribute a large percentage of the deaths that occur each year from automobile accidents to these types of drivers. There are, on the other hand, many conscientious people who are careful and continually think about the consequences of their driving behavior. They are the ones who purposefully stay on their side of the road, observe speed limits, do not tailgate, or, in general, do other things which may be deemed reckless because they calculate the costs of having an accident to themselves and the other people in the car. They are careful because the costs of being less careful are greater than the benefits that can be achieved.

---

[6] If the government is interested in setting up a coupon system to minimize people's disutility under a bad situation, then they should permit people to sell their coupons. By the fact that people freely choose to buy or sell coupons, we must conclude that they are better off by doing so. Otherwise we must wonder why they make the trade. If coupons are sold, it means that the price of gasoline will, in effect, rise.

Actually, the cost of driving recklessly is not *necessarily* equal to the cost incurred from any given accident but, rather, is equal to the cost of the accident discounted by the probability of having the accident. Granted, the probability of having an accident under such conditions is very close to one; however, under other conditions (for example, driving 85 miles an hour on a freeway), the probability of having an accident can be far removed from unity. The calculated costs of reckless driving is correspondingly lower. The reader should think in terms of the probability of having an accident as well as the cost of the accident if it occurs. When discussing reckless driving, too often people tend to think only in terms of the cost of the accident if it occurs; consequently, they tend to overestimate the cost and fail to understand why so many people drive recklessly.

Those people who weigh the costs and benefits of driving recklessly should respond in a predictable way to changes in the expected costs and benefits. If the benefits of going faster, making U-turns in the middle of the street, and driving on the wrong side of the road were to increase, then obviously driving of this nature from drivers as a group would increase. For example, if a child were to have a serious head injury requiring immediate medical attention, would you not expect the parents to break speed limits, ignore stop signs, and generally take more chances attempting to get the child to the emergency room than they otherwise would? This is a clear example of an increase in benefits from reckless driving; we suggest that similar responses will occur even if the change in the benefits were less dramatic. Take, for example, a person who may be late for an important meeting. How would he behave, relatively speaking, behind the wheel? At least, would you not expect drivers as a group to respond in the way an economist would predict?

In a similar manner, we would expect people to respond to changes in the expected costs of reckless driving. There should be less reckless driving when the expected cost of doing so goes up and more when the cost goes down. If these statements are reasonable, the reader should agree that one reason for the large volume of accidents on highways is that the expected cost to the drivers is relatively low.[7] This is simply another application of the law of demand.

---

[7] We recognize that in an absolute sense, the cost of an accident may be quite high. The cost that the driver will operate on, however, is the cost of the accident discounted by the probability of having the accident. Besides, we are merely suggesting in different words that if the costs were even higher, the quantity of reckless driving would be lower.

Admittedly, not everyone will respond to changes in cost—for example, those who do not think about what they are doing, and those who do not consider cost as a factor—but so long as there are people who do consider cost as a factor, the downward sloping demand curve should hold. The number of people who think or act randomly will determine the position of the demand curve and not the slope. To illustrate this basic point, would the reader not agree that students have more collisions in the hallways of their classroom buildings than they do on the streets when they are in their cars? It appears clear to us that, although students are involved in large numbers of automobile accidents, the number of hallway accidents is far greater. One explanation for the difference in the accident rate is possibly that bumping in the halls does not cost the individual very much, whereas automobile collisions can be considerably more costly. If the student knew that if he bumped into someone in the hall, he would be fined $50, would you expect the same amount or less bumping? Would your answer not apply to people's behavior in traffic?

Finally, there is an ironic implication of our argument. Safety devices such as seat belts, padded dashes, and air bags reduce considerably the probability of death and severity of injury in the event of an accident. The government, by making such equipment mandatory, is, in effect, reducing the expected total cost of an accident to those in the car, thereby reducing the cost of reckless driving. (The total cost of an accident is the damage done to the car plus the personal injury.)

Therefore, required seat belts and other similar internal safety devices should, contrary to the good intentions of those who supported the legislation, increase the amount of reckless driving. The effect may not be very great (just how great it is will depend upon the elasticity of demand), but it should still be positive. This means that there will be a tendency for people who have such devices to inflict a greater cost on the drivers around them. This was not, undoubtedly, what the Congress had in mind when it passed the legislation.[8]

---

[8] We have suggested that seat belts will reduce the private cost incurred from driving recklessly and increase the social cost—that is, the cost of one's own reckless driving borne by others. If the government is interested in reducing the social cost from automobile travel, then it should develop requirements for proper headlights and brakes and annual safety inspections. Internally, the car can be made less safe, thereby increasing the private cost of an accident to the driver. As an extreme example, suppose the driver had a dagger mounted on the steering column and pointed at his chest. Would he

QUESTIONS TO PONDER

1. Is life priceless? What evidence can you offer to support your contention?

2. In the fall and winter of 1973, gasoline production was falling behind consumption partially because of the Arab embargo of oil shipments to the U.S. State governments were beginning to order cutbacks in speed limits for cars to 55 miles per hour. CBS News reported (November 28, 1973) that the cutback in speed could result in approximately 14,000 fewer deaths on the highways. Given this benefit, why would the states not reduce the speed limits under more normal circumstances?

3. By the end of 1970, the federal government had spent more than $700 million on the development of the SST (supersonic transport). The reader may know that Congress, in December 1970, cut off funds for the project. However, at that point, should the Congress have considered the $700 million already spent in their decision on whether or not the project should have been completed?

4. In most democratic organizations, such as student governments and faculty senates, motions will pass and candidates will be elected if they secure a simple majority of all votes. Provide an economic explanation as to why such organizations would generally be opposed to the adoption of a rule that required unanimous consent.

5. Explain why there is congestion on highways.

---

not be inclined to drive more safely? We are not proposing that such devices be required; we are merely attempting to make general points concerning how people may respond as a result of automobiles being made less safe.

PART 2

INTERPERSONAL
RELATIONSHIPS

Sexual behavior

If you are at all typical of readers of this book, these are the first words that you have read. We understand why you chose to start at this chapter. However, you must realize that you have skipped over some important introductory material. In the first two chapters, we developed several economic concepts that will be used in this chapter, and you may not at times bo able to follow the discussion. More importantly, we emphasized in the first chapter that economics cannot explain all dimensions of the human experience. This is a particularly relevant point when we deal, as we do in this chapter, with sexual behavior. We demonstrate in this chapter that economic analysis can provide us with several important and interesting insights about people's sexual behavior. However, there is much about people's sexual behavior we simply cannot explain, and several of these areas arc, perhaps, the most meaningful. In our dealings with others, we can intuitively grasp the patterns and, therefore, the sense of other people's behavior. And although we may not be able to explain logically how or why we react, wc are indeed able to react—and other people are able to react to our reactions. People's sexual behavior represents very complex patterns of actions and reactions; it involves varying degrees of romance and love, which are patterns of behavior that largely defy explanations.

There is a possible pitfall in trying to explain any pattern of behavior like that of sexual behavior—it is that the writer or reader will assume that those parts of behavior we can explain are more important than those we cannot explain. Unfortunately, this is probably not the case with regard to people's sexual behavior. However, we should be able to take the analysis for what it is, nothing more or less. In our view, anyone who thinks that the sexual experience can be fully described and understood with economic analysis is a seriously deprived individual. Having said this let us proceed.

INTRODUCTION

To those who may be unfamiliar with developments within the field of economics over the past decade, sex—or human sexuality—may appear to be a peculiar topic for discussion among economists and for inclusion in an introductory book on economics. However, for those who view economics as a study of human behavior (as do the authors), concern with sex is not at all peculiar, bizarre, or sensational. Clearly, a major impetus for human action is the sexual drive, and concern with matters relating to sex, in one way or another, occupies a significant portion of most people's time. Indeed, given the dominance of sex in human experience, one must wonder how economists have been able to avoid the topic in their classes and books for so long.

If one thinks about what is normally considered to be within the traditional boundaries of economic science and considers the ramifications of sex as a part of the human experience, the discussion in this and the succeeding chapter may not appear to be at all out of place. To the layman, economics may be thought of as a discipline that (1) is founded on the study of goods and services that yield benefits or, in the jargon of the profession, utility to the buyers; (2) concentrates on the give-and-take, exchange, or trading relationships between and among people; (3) deals with scarce resources and, thereby, with goods and services that involve costs in their production and can command payments from persons who desire them; (4) is grounded in such concepts as opportunity cost and on such laws as the laws of supply and demand, diminishing marginal utility, and diminishing marginal returns; and (5) is concerned primarily with that domain of human behavior in which the individual is rational—that is, attempts to maximize his or her well-being.

Consequently, economics is normally associated with the development of a theory that is readily applicable to such goods and services as football games, peanut butter, ice cream, brickmaking machines, Rembrandt paintings, and, perhaps on occasion, with prostitution as an institutionalized profession. In the remaining portions of this chapter, an attempt will be made to show how the sexual behavior of people other than prostitutes or buyers of the services of prostitutes can be discussed and partially analyzed and understood within the context of economic concepts and theory. No claim is made to the effect that economic theory can explain all, or even a major part of, human sexual behavior.

CHARACTERISTICS OF SEX

Sex as a service

Sex is a classification of a whole range of services one person provides for himself or another which yield utility to the recipients. The list of services provided under the heading of sex may include such normal heterosexual experiences as holding hands, kissing, petting, and intercourse. A sexual experience (or service) may also include the stimulation one receives from watching the girls (or boys) go by, from reading *Playboy*, *Playgirl*, or *National Geographic*, and from the tales of those who write to "Dear Abby" or Dr. David Reuben. For junior high school boys and girls, a gratifying (and permissible) sexual experience may be nothing more than the frequent and purposeful bumping and shoving that goes on outside the class. The list of sexual services can be considerably lengthened.

Many people are quick to condemn one sexual practice or another as inhuman or immoral. Although the authors, and most everyone else, have their own sexual preferences, they submit that they are just that—their preferences. The issue of what is immoral will not be our concern, mainly because such a discussion is likely to be worthless to anyone who disagrees with the writers. Moreover, it would be an unnecessary diversion from the central purpose of this chapter, which is to explore the question of *how people do behave* and not how they should behave.

The utility that one receives from a satisfying sexual experience may in the psychic realm be similar, but certainly not identical, to the satisfaction a person receives from eating a good peanut butter sandwich, drinking a chocolate milkshake, or watching a performance of Sir Lawrence Olivier in a Shakespearean play. Indeed, for most people the distinctive, but not the only, difference between a sexual experience and other more "normal" goods and services consumed may be in the intensity of the pleasure received. For most persons, sexual intercourse and all the trappings that go with it probably give the recipient more satisfaction than a peanut butter sandwich; that is evidenced by the cost that a person is willing to incur for sex relative to the cost he or she is willing to incur to obtain the sandwich. For some people, however, the sandwich can deliver more utility than intercourse: everyone may not consider sex to be within his or her own choice domain just as everyone may not wish to purchase pickled pigs feet. Oddly enough, even the person who never engages in sexual activity can receive considerable utility from sex. He (or she) may refrain from engaging in sexual activities because of the extent of the cost. Because of this, it is extremely risky (if not impossible) to make interpersonal utility comparisons regarding the absolute psychic value of sex just as it is risky to suggest that the people who attend Shakespearean plays enjoy the plays more than those who never attend.

Given that sexual experiences can yield utility like other goods, it follows that for the fully rational person the quantity of sex demanded is an inverse function of the price—that is, the demand curve is downward sloping in as in Figure 3–1. If the price goes up, the quantity demanded does down; if the price goes down, the quantity goes up. This means, in effect, that given the price of sex, the "consumer" will want only so much sex supplied by another and will vary his consumption with the price that is charged. The reason for this relationship is simply that the rational individual will consume sex up to the point that the marginal benefits equal the marginal costs (or until $MU_s/P_s = MU_a/P_a = \ldots MU_n/P_n$, where Mu and P denote marginal utility and price, respectively, and where s rep-

FIGURE 3–1

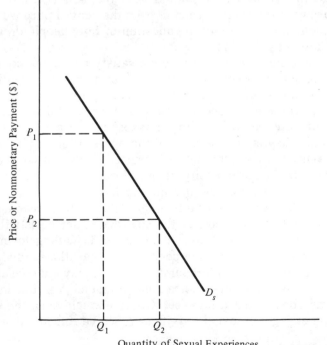

Quantity of Sexual Experiences

resents sex and a and n, other goods). If the price of sex rises relative to other goods, the consumer will rationally choose to consume more of other goods and less sex. (Ice cream, as well as many other goods, can substitute for sex if the relative prices require it.)

The law of demand, as stated above, is a fundamental principle of business operations the prostitute cannot ignore. By raising her (or his) price, the prostitute will not only sell fewer "tricks," but may find that if there are a number of other readily available competitors, the quantity demanded from her (or him) can fall to the point that total revenues will fall.[1] Revenues can rise if the demand she (or he) faces is inelastic. In other words, the prostitute (he or she) must remember that although the demand for sex in general may be inelastic because of the relative necessity of the service to those who want it, the demand for any particular sex service from any particular person can be highly elastic. (Can you explain why?)

The law of demand is also applicable to the more ordinary sexual relationships. A male may demand very few units of sex from the girl he is dating or from his wife, in part because of his sexual preferences. However, closer examination of the individual's circumstances may reveal that the price he would have to pay—although in nonmonetary terms—may be so great that he must rationally choose to be "gentlemanly" and ask for very little. The same may be said for women; in fact, the difference in the quantity of sex demanded by men and women may reflect in part the relative difference in the cost of sex to men and women. If the price of sex to women were lowered, one might anticipate a relatively larger quantity of sex demanded by them. The problem of men obtaining more sex from women, if viewed this way, becomes one of how to reduce the cost of sex to women (or, in addition, how to increase their preferences for it—that is, increase their demand).

The cost of sex

Sex is a service that is produced and procured. The sexual experience must be produced by one party for another. Like all other production processes, the production of any sexual experience entails costs. This is because not only may some materials, such as contraceptives, be required and a direct expenditure made (as in

---

[1] The reader should recognize that there are male prostitutes, although they may presently account for a relatively minor portion of the total membership in the profession.

the case of the prostitute), but also because the participants must generally forgo some opportunity that has value to them. That, by definition, is the cost. The actual experience requires at least a few minutes, and this, of course, implies that one cannot normally do anything else of consequence at the same time. (One can, perhaps, imagine eating an apple or reading a book while producing sex for someone else, but it may be difficult indeed to imagine playing a successful game of pool or efficiently carrying on one's normal business operations.)

The opportunity cost of the time spent in the sexual act in most instances may be a trivial part of the total cost involved in either the production or procurement of sex. The total cost may include such items as the cost of the "wining and dining," which, contrary to the general impression, may often be heavily born by females. Consider, for example, the number of times the girl may invite her male companion in for coffee and a snack after a date or over to dinner; or consider the possibility that she may be purposefully and skillfully arranging the situation in which the wining and dining may take place. Because the man may pick up the check, he is credited with the wining and dining. However, one must wonder who wined and dined whom. This is not meant to suggest that all such efforts by one party or the other are intended to procure and produce a sexual experience. The motive can simply be to have an enjoyable evening out. We are suggesting, however, that the wining and dining can, for some, be a part of the calculated cost of obtaining or producing a gratifying sexual experience.

The cost may also include the risk cost of pregnancy (which may be disproportionately borne by the female), the expenditure of effort (male orgasm alone requires approximately 200 calories), the psychic cost of violating one's own moral standards, and the damaged-reputation cost which may be incurred if one's family or friends find out about the sexual relationship. Lastly, there is the cost incurred in the time spent plotting and maneuvering into a position in which the type of sex desired can be had. Both female and male must assess the "market" to determine which persons and sexual experiences are within their choice domain and must develop a strategy tailored to the selected party(ies). The selected strategy may require a considerable expenditure on clothes, hairdos, makeup, and education. It may also require a time expenditure on being in the right places. The producer may also require the recipient to become involved emotionally as well as physically; coupling marriage with sex is, perhaps, the ultimate form of contracted involvements. The value of one's time, as approximated by his wage rate, will determine the cost of the sexual experience. The higher the opportunity wage, the higher the cost of the experience. Because of the different effects of higher income on sex consumption (and, perhaps, the associated education levels and lifetime experiences) and the different preferences between the high and low income groups, one cannot say theoretically which income group should be expected to have the higher rate of sexual activity. The economist can say, however, that the difference in the cost to the two groups, due to the fact that sex is labor-intensive, can partly explain the difference in the level of sexual activity that may exist.

Studies have generally revealed that the higher income groups consume as a group more sex than the lower groups. They tend to be more open-minded, are more educated, and have fewer psychological hangups regarding sex.

We can explain these facts by arguing that the demand for sex, because of the nonprice factors, is greater for the higher income groups. This situation is described in Figure 3–2A and B. The demand in 3–2A for the higher income groups is greater than the demand in 3–2B. Given the differences in cost—P_a for the higher income group and P_b for the other group—the difference in revealed sexual activity is $Q_{1a} - Q_{1b}$, where $Q_{1a} > Q_{1b}$. If the opportunity wage cost had been the same and equal to the wage of the lower income

FIGURE 3–2

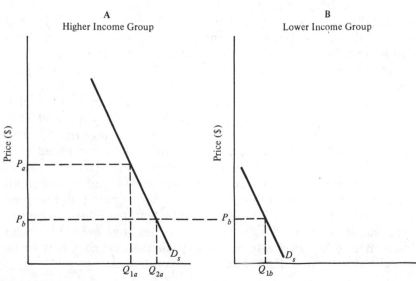

A
Higher Income Group

B
Lower Income Group

group, the difference would have been greater, $Q_{2a} - Q_{1b}$. The difference in the opportunity wage cost explains $Q_{2a} - Q_{1a}$ of the difference in sexual activity of the two groups.

In summary, a gratifying sexual experience can be quite costly. In economics there is an adage that is probably repeated in almost all principles courses: "there is no such thing as a free lunch." We suggest with equal conviction that there is no such thing as free love or free sex.

Sex as a cooperative experience

Sexual intercourse is a human experience that must be cooperatively produced and enjoyed. We have, perhaps, written nothing that is more obvious than that. However, stating the obvious can direct our attention to essential points. First, if one party shirks his or her responsibilities in the exercise, then both parties lose in terms of the satisfaction that could have been had. Another way of saying the same thing is that the productivity of one's efforts are integrally related to the efforts of the other person. Understandably, people seeking sexual experiences will try to find other persons who have interests similar to theirs. The search may be costly in terms of time and money expense, but it can be rewarded in terms of finding someone who will energetically apply himself or herself to the sexual experience, thereby increasing the productivity of the efforts of the person doing the searching.

Second, although it may be at times, sex is not always a give-and-take relationship like the relationship that exists between buyer and seller in the market place. In many or most instances, the relationship is fundamentally different from the relationship that exists between traders. Granted, both parties, in the course of the sexual experience, give to and take from the other. However, the sexual experience is much more: it is in large measure an exercise in which two (or more) people jointly pursue essentially the same goal. It is probably this dimension of the sexual experience that causes people to set it apart from other activities in which they are engaged on a daily basis. In so many activities, people work independently of one another—that is, they work competitively, each trying to undercut, undersell, or outdo the other. There is some competition involved in most any relationship, but because of the nature of the experience, sex is an activity that forces people to work together. This is, no doubt, one of the elements of the experience that causes it to be thought of as more human than other experiences.

Sex as an exchange relationship

As much as they may depend upon cooperation, sexual experiences can also involve exchanges—one person doing something for someone in return for something else. Generally, when exchanges are involved, the relationship is a barter one—no money is involved. One can provide sex to another in exchange for a similar but different sexual experience. However, the exchange need not always be in kind. One party can provide sex in exchange for security, clothing, candy, kindness, marriage, interesting company, conversation, being a part of the crowd, and entertainment. How many times has one person said or, perhaps, indicated in more subtle terms: (1) "I will give you sex if you will marry me or go out with no one else"; (2) "I will give you sex if you carry out the garbage or vacuum the house for me"; (3) "I will give you sex if you will stay home with me tonight." In the courting ritual, such implicit dealing is frequently, although not always, present. All such bargains imply nonmonetary payments. Since, as we believe, the supply of sex is upward sloping, the payments should result in a greater quantity of sexual experiences than will occur from strict cooperative efforts.

Why do exchanges occur in this dimension of interpersonal relationships? The answer must involve the fact that the sexual preferences of the two parties are not identical. Furthermore, the exchanges can increase the utility levels of both parties. Let us explain with references to Figure 3–3. Suppose both parties enjoy sexual intercourse, but they get different levels of satisfaction from different coital frequency rates. As can be seen in the top half of Figure 3–3, the utility level of the female is assumed to rise until her total utility peaks when intercourse is being experienced two times a week. From that point onward, her total utility falls as the coital frequency is raised. On the other hand, the male's total utility level rises, although less rapidly than the female's, until it peaks at a coital frequency of four times per week. (Remember, the shapes of the two curves in the figure can be anything; by drawing the curves as we have, we mean only to illustrate the fact that sexual partners can differ over coital frequency.) Given this information, how many times per week will the couple experience intercourse? That is not an easy question to answer precisely. We can say, however, that they will have intercourse at least two times a week. This is simply because between zero and two times per week, both of their utility levels rise, generated directly by the pleasure they receive from the sexual act and indirectly from seeing the other enjoy the experience.

FIGURE 3-3

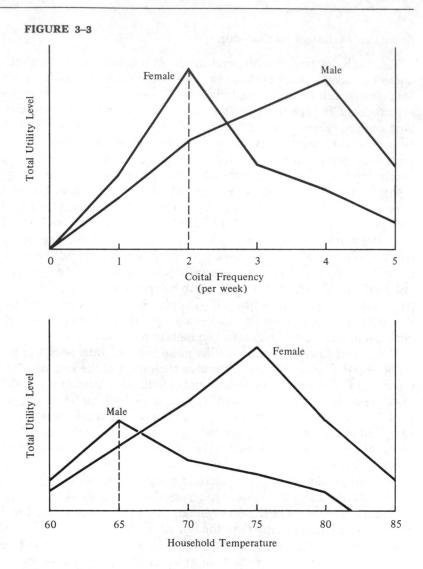

Beyond a coital frequency of two, the male's utility level continues to rise, but the female's falls. The female may engage in intercourse more frequently out of a sense of duty or sheer love; however, she may be induced to go even further by exchanges that may be made. Since both of their utility levels are falling beyond a coital frequency of four, we expect the couple to have intercourse between two and four times per week.

In the bottom half of the graph, we have illustrated another dimension of marital life—the temperature setting in the home. (This dimension can really be anything, like the frequency of cleaning the house, or cooking meals, or staying home at night.) In the lower graph, we have illustrated a situation in which the most preferred temperature setting for the female is much higher than the male's. The male would prefer a temperature of 65 degrees, whereas the female would prefer a temperature setting of 75 degrees. We know that they will cooperatively move to a setting of at least 65 degrees, because both are better off at that level than at any lower level. Again, the temperature may be raised even further for noneconomic reasons. However, the potential for exchange is indicated in the two halves of the graph. The female may agree to have intercourse more than two times a week if the male will agree to set the thermostat above 65 degrees. So long as the increase in the female's utility from setting the thermostat higher is greater than the loss in utility associated with a higher coital frequency, then she gains by the trade. The same holds for the male but, of course, in the opposite direction. The point of the discussion is that trade can increase the coital frequency over and above what it would otherwise have been, and, in the process, both parties can be better off. The actual trades, however, may not be viewed as such; the two sides of the deal(s) may be discussed in terms of compromises.

Because money is not normally a permissible part of the deal, people who desire heterosexual or homosexual experiences must have double coincidences of wants. One party must be able to provide what the other party wants and must want what the other party has to offer. This implies that the search cost of both parties can be considerable and can result in less sex being exchanged than otherwise. It is because of such search costs alone that people may be willing to make monetary payments to prostitutes.

Sex as a marketed product

Sex can be molded, packaged, advertised, and promoted like most other product groups. In the case of *Playboy* and *Penthouse*, the marketing process is direct and open; people know clearly what is being sold. In other instances, such as Dr. David Reuben's column, the intentions, which may include the simulation of a sexual experience, are not so obvious. Most watchers of television realize that sex is the medium through which other products are sold. Joe Namath's testimonial in the Brut cologne commercial, which ends with the statement: "If you aren't going to go all the way, man, why go at all?" is a less-than-subtle form of selling Brut by selling sex.

On a personal level, people use many of the same marketing techniques as do major manufacturers—they do package and advertise their sexual products. Short skirts, padded bras, no bras, tight slacks, deodorants, and body shirts are all forms of presenting one's sexual services in the best possible light and methods of attracting the attention of possible buyers. By using such devices and techniques, the individuals involved may be as guilty of fraudulent packaging and advertising as are producers of cosmetics, soaps, and toys. If one views much of the advertising of such products as wasteful, then it would be consistent to view much expenditure on makeup and clothing in the same light.

Why do people incur the costs associated with personal beautification? We must, at the start, admit that there is the prevalent "honorable" reason that people just want to look nice and/or feel good. Be that as it may, we wish to suggest that there are other reasons (which are no less honorable except in an individualistic sense). An individual may want to increase the number of buyers for what he or she has to offer in order to have a larger quantity of sex and a larger group from which to select the services that he or she desires. With an increased choice domain, the individual, in all probability, can select a higher quality service, *as he or she assesses quality.*

By looking attractive, a person can also possibly increase the nonmoney payment received for the sex services that he or she produces or can possibly lower the nonmoney payment that he or she will have to make for the sex services of others. All of these possible benefits make expenditures on personal beautification rational.[2]

In other words, people may attempt to look more attractive for the same reason that the professional prostitute does, although not necessarily in the same ways; how much expenditures are made depends upon the costs, the benefits, *and market conditions.* The girl (or boy) with no competitors may be expected to expend, *ceteris paribus,* less on improving the quality of her (his) sexual services.

---

[2] Personal beautification, once produced, becomes a public good because persons other than the one who is more beautiful receive benefits from the sense that their surroundings are more pleasant. This may mean that since the individual may consider only the private benefits from the personal beautification and not the total social benefits, there may be an underinvestment in such beautification.

There is one other economic explanation for looking attractive. The human mind has a limited capacity to absorb facts and information, such as who may be in our presence and their characteristics. On the other hand, an individual is bombarded by tens of thousands of bits of information. The mind is incapable of absorbing, analyzing, and registering all of the information. The individual must, by absolute necessity, make decision rules regarding the facts and information which will be permitted to register in the brain. As a result, he or she may decide to ignore some information as a general rule, meaning that he or she may not notice all people nearby. Before a person can have a meaningful relationship in any dimension with someone else, the fact that they exist as a distinct entity must register in the mind of the other person. Because of the construction of decision rules regarding which bits of information will actually be allowed to register, the person desiring the relationship must not only be present but must be able to somehow break through the decision rule in the event that it actually presents a barrier. This may mean that his or her actions have to be dramatic or flashy; a simple statement that "I'm present" can be ineffective. The extra nice clothes, the short skirts, the makeup, and the exceptionally nice manners may be means of breaking through the barrier of decision rules.[3] Once this has been accomplished—that is, his or her presence has registered—and the relationship has been established, the individual can drop back into his or her own manner of dressing and behavior.

A MODEL OF SEXUAL BEHAVIOR

The amount of sex that is produced and consumed is not in our view determined by the gods. Granted, men and women have biological drives, and there are bodily constraints on sexual behavior. Men and women, however, have some control over these drives (as a general rule) and do not engage in sex to the extent of their biological capabilities. The amount of sex produced and consumed is the result of the interaction of individuals within what we might call social space (or the market). For an explanation of how the amount of sex actually consumed and produced is determined, we must look to some of the forces these individuals bring to bear on this interaction process.

---

[3] For some, breaking through the decision rules of those with whom they wish to associate may mean that they dress down, dress hippy, or dress in such a way that they may be considered a part of the antiestablishment.

A restatement of principles that have been intrinsic in much of the discussion that has gone before would be helpful. These principles are the laws of demand and supply. We stress, however, that these principles cannot explain all sexual behavior—only a small portion of it. We assume that the demand curve for sex by either males or females is downward sloping and that, as a reasonable generality, the market supply curve of sex is upward sloping. Therefore, the quantity of sex supplied will increase with the price paid for it. As in Figure 3–4, which depicts the demand for sex by men and the supply of sex by women, the relative positions of these curves depend upon such factors as the relative preferences of the sexes and the relative costs of the sexual experience(s) borne by them.

If the supply and demand for sex were determined solely by biological drives and if these drives were equal for men and women (which may or may not be the case), the supply and demand curves could be so positioned on the graph that their interaction is on the horizontal axis; the price, or nonmoney payment, paid for the sex

FIGURE 3–4

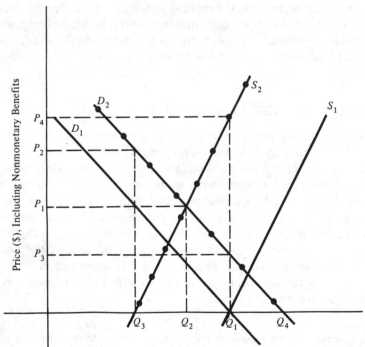

Quantity of Sexual Experiences

would be zero, as is the case with S_1 and D_1 in Figure 3–4. This does not mean that no costs are involved to the parties; there are, as discussed above. It only means that there will be no need for extra non-money payments or direct money payments made by one party to the other. The gratification one receives from the experience will compensate him (her) for the cost incurred in providing the sex.

Such a circumstance does not, however, realistically reflect the general state of the world. Women are restricted from fully revealing their biological drives. They bear a substantial portion of the risk cost associated with pregnancy (men, it must not be forgotten, bear a part of the cost). Although general standards are changing, many women still view sex as an activity in which they are not supposed to engage except under the umbrella of marriage. Many, because of their training from childhood, look upon sex as something dirty and not to be enjoyed. Virginity, in and of itself, can have positive value so that giving it up is an added cost of sex. Men, on the other hand, generally look upon sex as a service which is to be pursued for purposes other than the pleasure received directly from the experience. In tribal Africa, men may achieve status within the tribe from killing a lion barehanded. In more modern and less barbaric places, men can achieve the same stature among their peers by sexual conquests. The effect of these pressures is to raise the male's demand for sex and to decrease the female's supply of it (to say, S_2 and D_2 in Figure 3–4). At a zero price, there will then exist a shortage of sex to men since only Q_3 sex will be supplied by females and Q_4 will be demanded.

The upward sloping supply curve of female sex indicates that women are willing to offer a larger quantity of sex than Q_3 if the price (not necessarily in money form) is raised above zero. As indicated by the demand curve, D_2, men are willing to pay as much as P_2 for an additional sexual experience. We might anticipate, therefore, that nonmoney payments in any number of forms (security, dining out, and so forth) will be offered. The result will be that the quantity of sex will expand toward Q_2. Beyond Q_2 the side payment required by the women to bring forth an additional unit of sex is greater than what the men are willing to pay for the experience. (To see this clearly, the reader should ask themselves how much the men would be willing to pay for an additional unit of sex at Q_1 and how much the women would charge for the unit.)

The market for sex is changing along with individual values toward sex. The supply of sex by women is expanding. The availability of contraceptvies is reducing the potential pregnancy cost of intercourse to women. Virginity is no longer as important to many,[4] and more and more the message is getting out that women are capable of enjoying sex. Abortions are becoming more common, cheaper, and more acceptable. Assuming that these changes in cost and values have no effect on the demand side of the market, we can conclude that the quantity of sexual activity will increase and the price or nonmoney payment made to women can fall.[5] We are frankly uncertain as to what is happening to the demand for sex by men. If the demand rises, but by less than the supply increases, the same general predictions as the ones above would follow; the price, however, would not fall as much, but the quantity of sexual activity would rise by more than in the case above. (What may be the consequence of a drop in the men's demand for sex?)

We have been speaking in terms of generalities, and, of course, an oversupply of sex for some women does not hold for all women. For some women—for example, the not-so-pretty and the old—there can be a shortage of sex, and they may have to make the nonmoney payments to obtain the desired quantity of sex.[6] In fact, if we individualize the market, we can postulate that what the woman may view as her "standards" may really be a mirror image of her relative market position—that is, because a woman is beautiful she can maintain higher standards than the woman who is less endowed and who has no offsetting differences.

PROSTITUTION

Why does prostitution exist? Once the existence of the cost of sexual intercourse and of the positive equilibrium price in Figure 3–4 are recognized, the question is easily answered. The price

---

[4] Remaining a virgin for some women may now be considered a negative value. Some women may feel that it indicates they are not desirable or are in such limited demand that the price offered by men has not been high enough to seduce them into giving up their virginity.

[5] It is possible that the price will become negative. This would mean a reversal of roles: the women would be paying the men. For more on the emergence of male prostitution, see Thomas R. Ireland, "The Supply and Demand of Sex" (Paper presented at the Western Economics Association meeting, June 1974).

[6] From some points of view, such women may be viewed as deviates. However, such a designation may be inappropriate. These women can be behaving, in a sense, like everyone else; the only difference is the location of their equilibrium in the social market.

of the prostitute, even though it may be $50, can be much lower than the cost the man (woman) would have to bear in order to obtain the same pleasure from other, more legitimate sources.[7] The man can pay the $50, and by doing so he does not have to spend the time that may be required to seduce the nonprostitute. He does not have to send her flowers or other gifts and, more important, does not have to become involved emotionally or otherwise. He can satisfy his needs and leave anonymously.

Another reason why a man may seek the services of a prostitute is that the quality of the service can be higher. The prostitute is a professional; she may not only have had more experience than the conventional sex partner, but she can prorate the cost of "training" and improving the quality of her service over a larger number of sexual experiences. The investment cost per "trick" can be trivial if she operates in large quantities.

Legalizing prostitution can have several predictable effects. First, since the penalties of being caught soliciting buyers will be eliminated and the cost of searching for buyers (streetwalkers have to keep on the move) will be substantially reduced, the supply of prostitutes should increase. This should result in a larger quantity of output. The quality of the product should also rise, bringing about in part a reduction in the threat of venereal disease (VD). Houses of prostitution would be able to justify more expenditures on medical checkups for the prostitutes since the quantity of their business would reflect their reputation for cleanliness, just as in the case of Holiday Inns.

Furthermore, if we assume that the price or nonmoney payment charged for sex is competitively determined in the normal sex markets, the existence of clean, legalized prostitutes means a larger number of competitors for nonprostitutes, including wives. Legalization of prostitution should, where nonmoney payments are charged, reduce the nonmoney payments. Wives may be against legalized prostitution because of moral convictions; our analysis indicates, in addition, that they may (or should) be opposed to its legalization on the grounds that it can reduce their competitive position. In a similar vein, prostitutes probably do not look upon the changing values

---

[7] On the other hand, by adding in the cost of VD, we can understand why some men do not engage prostitutes. For some, $50 plus the cost of contracting VD can be a greater cost than the possible benefits (and lower than the benefits to others).

of women in general with much favor. To the degree that the price of nonprostitutes goes down, the price that the prostitute can charge must fall.

SEX AND LOVE

Our analysis has proceeded as if sex can be completely divorced from love. Obviously, it cannot always be, and this impression must be corrected. However, there is very little economics can say about love because love is an experience almost impossible to define or conceptualize. About all we can say is that love (whatever it is) and sex go together in many people's minds in much the same way as hotdogs and hotdog buns and razors and razor blades. Love and sex are viewed by many as complementary goods. This does not mean that the relationship between sex and love is exactly the same as the relationship of other complementary goods. We only mean to assert that a connection is drawn between the two, that the degree of love that exists will affect the demand for sex and, possibly, vice versa. Our assumptions concerning the normal slope of the supply and demand for sex can still hold; the demand can still be downward sloping and the supply can be upward sloping. The existence of the connection (although imperfect) between sex and love can determine the positions of the curves (and, possibly, their elasticities to a degree). A person's demand for sex can influence demand for a loving relationship, and the intensity of one's love for another can affect demand for sex. Generally speaking, the common requirement among women that sex be coupled with a feeling of love is a statement that their supply curve of sex is further back toward the vertical axis than it would be if the requirement did not exist. However, as a group, they can still be expected to respond positively to an increase in nonmoney payments as we have been using the term.

Admittedly, there are women (and men) who adopt the decision rule that they will not engage in sex unless they are married or have established a strong bond with someone else. They, in effect, rationally choose to ignore costs and benefits and changes in costs and benefits. Even though such people exist (and they may be quite large in number), the downward sloping demand curve and upward sloping supply curve hold so long as there are people who do weigh in their consumption decisions the costs and benefits of sexual experiences.

CONCLUDING COMMENTS

In this chapter we have tried to show how economic concepts and tools of analysis can be used to discuss people's sexual behavior. We have argued that men and women have downward sloping demand curves and upward sloping supply curves for various kinds of sexual experiences. This means that the quantity of sex supplied and demanded by men and women is affected by the explicit or implicit price that must be borne. In discussing sexual behavior in this way, we have been able to demonstrate a part of the logic—to the extent that it has any logic—people follow in pursuing sexual experiences. We have been able to draw several reasonable conclusions. However, the reader should be careful not to assume that we have said more than we have. We have said nothing about how sexual preferences are formed, and we submit that much sexual activity is actually more related to preference formation than it is to the process of making choices founded on preferences already known. This chapter reveals the limited usefulness of economic analysis, its strengths and weaknesses. Reflections on our own experiences suggest many instances in which the analysis is and is not applicable.

QUESTIONS TO PONDER

1. To what extent and in what ways is sex different from other "goods" people produce in the home or buy in the store. What makes sex different in many people's mind?
2. People often require that long-term commitments be made before they become involved in sexual activity. Why? What is the purpose of the commitment?
3. A new strain of venereal disease has been discovered that is not readily cured with the usual drug, penicillin. What effect will this discovery have on the sexual activity of the population?

CHAPTER 4

Exploitation of affection

The strength of most personal relationships is founded, to a significant degree, upon the affection one person has for another.[1] This is particularly true of the relationship between a man and a woman. The relationship works for two reasons. First, each person is concerned about the welfare of the other and is willing to do things for him or her. In this sense the relationship is largely charitable in nature; each person is both a donor of "gifts," broadly defined as any form of charitable expression, and a recipient of such expressions from the other.

Second, both persons understand that there is a need for implicitly defined limits to their own behavior and the behavior of the other person. These limits form the basis of the unwritten social contract between the two. Each person may then proceed in his or her own behavior, responding to the needs of the other, in the trust that the contract is being obeyed. This latter presumption makes possible behavior on the part of either person that is inconsistent with the agreed-on contract, implicit as it may be. It permits one party to, in a sense, exploit the other.

We intend to explain the logic behind this statement in the few pages that follow. We discuss the problem of exploitation after a chapter on sex because most of what is said has a direct application to man-woman relationships. We stress, however, that the argument is really very general in nature and can be applied to the personal relationship between parent and child and between close friends. The analysis provides an explanation of the breakdown in many personal relationships and, in general, why friends and

---

[1] As we intend to discuss in considerable detail throughout the book, such relationships can also be founded upon individual private interests that have nothing to do with affection. However, in this chapter, we want to focus on the affection aspect of the relationship.

loved ones can be "used." First, we briefly review the argument for what we call *charitable exploitation*.[2]

THE MODEL

The basic proposition underlying the charitable exploitation argument is that the donor of the gifts receives utility from giving to the recipient. This implies that he or she has a downward sloping demand curve for making gifts. Also, the rational donor will *freely choose* to extend gifts until the marginal benefits of doing so are equal to the marginal costs. We give *gifts* a very broad meaning here. A gift can, as is conventionally thought, be in the form of money or a material object. However, it can be the time one person spends doing something for someone else, and this can simply mean the time spent listening to another person. A gift can also be allowing the other person to listen to a record of his or her choice, scratching another's back, or providing him or her with a sexual experience of one form or another.

In Figure 4–1 we have placed marginal costs and benefits on the vertical axis and the quantity of the gift (which may be any single gift or a gift that represents a combination of gifts) on the horizontal axis. If we assume that the donor's demand curve (D_1) is downward sloping and, for simplification, that the marginal cost of units of the gift is constant at P_1 in Figure 4–1, then we can conclude that the donor will *choose* on his or her own to make gifts up to point Y, or a quantity of Q_1. At Y the marginal cost is equal to the marginal benefits.

Notice that it is only for the last unit—the Q_1^{th} unit—that the marginal costs and benefits are equal. Up to that point, the marginal benefits to the donor as indicated by the demand curve are greater than the marginal cost of each unit of the gift. As we have explained in Chapter 1, *the cost of something is the value of that which is forgone*. This means that the individual donor is getting more value in making each unit of the gift up to Q_1 than he or she could have gotten from the use of his or her resources in their best alternative. This excess value, referred to as *surplus value* by economists, can be described by the shaded area (P_1XY) in the graph. In simple language, when we do one thing we often say that we are better off

---

[2] This chapter is based on a short article by Wilson E. Schmidt, "Charitable Exploitation," *Public Choice* 10 (Spring 1969), pp. 103–4.

FIGURE 4–1

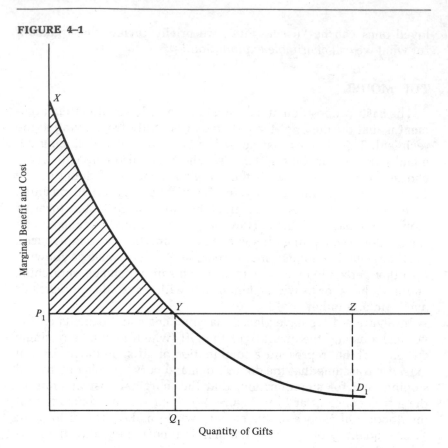

Quantity of Gifts

in some sense; in terms of our graph we would say that the donor is better off to the extent of the shaded area.[3]

Given the extent of the consumer surplus indicated by the shaded area P_1XY, the recipient, if he or she is the only recipient (or if all recipients act collusively), can force the donor to increase the gifts beyond Y by merely refusing to accept anything unless the donor abides by the recipient's wishes, which is for more units of the gift. Notice that we have not said that the recipient threatens overt harm to the donor but only threatens not to accept anything unless

---

[3] In more detailed terms, the total value that the donor receives from making Q_1 gifts is equal to $OXYQ_1$. The total cost is equal to OP_1YQ_1. The difference between the total costs and total benefits is equal to P_1XY, or the shaded area, which we have called *consumer surplus.*

the donor gives more. The recipient in effect presents an all-or-nothing deal to the donor: "either you give me more or I'll accept nothing."

If the recipient is able to pose the deal subtly, without the donor actually detecting the scheme in mind, the donor is presented with a choice problem. If he or she refuses to give more, then he or she must give nothing, which means that he or she must give up the surplus value that would have been received by giving Q_1 units of the gift. If he or she gives more, the marginal cost of each unit, P_1, will be greater than the marginal benefits of each additional unit. There is what we might call a *negative surplus value* attached to these additional units. As a result, the donor's total satisfaction level will be lowered by giving more. We can postulate that if the negative surplus value is greater than the shaded area in the graph, the donor will be better off by not giving anything at all. If the negative surplus value is less, the donor will be better off by extending his or her gifts.

This means that the recipient's ability to extract additional units of the gift, and in that sense exploit the donor, is not limitless. If at point Z in the graph the negative surplus value (area YZD_1) is just equal to the surplus value (P_1XY), then the smart recipient will ask for an amount of gifts equal to something *just short* of point Z. In this way, the recipient will insure that the negative surplus value is less than the surplus value and that the donor will give more. If the recipient asks for more than Z, the negative surplus value is greater than the surplus value, and the donor will be better off by not giving anything. If the recipient asks for Z, the donor will be *indifferent* to continuing the gift-giving and may, on some whim, stop giving. Therefore, the closer the recipient tries to come to Z, the more risk he or she must assume that he or she has misjudged the charitable feelings of the donor and may end up getting nothing. Remember it is not likely that the recipient will be able to make the calculations that are implied here with a great deal of precision and certainty.

Two points need to be stressed. The first is that the ability of the recipient to extract a larger quantity of gifts depends on the number of alternative recipients of the gift—that is, the number of what we might call competitors for the gift. If the recipient is one of many possible equal recipients and attempts to impose the all-or-nothing deal considered here, the donor can turn to someone else and in the end receive the full (or almost full) extent of the consumer surplus. The donor need not go beyond Y in Figure 4–1. The demand curve in Figure 4–1 is, in this case, the demand for giving in general and is not the demand for giving to any one individual.[4] If, on the other hand, the recipient is the only possible recipient *in the mind of the donor*, the recipient is, in essence, a monopolist; the donor must, in this circumstance, either accept the deal or turn to buying goods which yield less satisfaction.

Second, exploitation of the donor will occur only to the extent that the recipient is unconcerned about the welfare of the donor. If the recipient cares about the donor, then the recipient will be worse off to the extent that donor is worse off. By exploiting the donor, the recipient reduces the donor's welfare and, consequently, his or her own welfare.

ROMANTIC RELATIONSHIPS

Wilson Schmidt, who formulated the foregoing argument, suggested that the argument can be useful in understanding the behavior of welfare recipients under the conditions prevailing during the late 1960s. At the time, many welfare recipients were demonstrating against the welfare offices around the country, demanding larger checks. One might reason that the recipients were in effect threatening the government with the disruption of the welfare system. In such event, the government would have been unable to make the "charitable" payments. The protesting welfare recipients could have understood our argument to this point in an intuitive sense, recognizing that there may have been some consumer surplus that could be drawn out of the government bureaucrats and those who are in favor of giving to the poor.

We believe that the argument on charitable exploitation has a much broader application than originally conceived and is, perhaps, even more readily applicable to personal relationships. To show this, we turn to romantic relationships between men and women. A romantic relationship is, almost by definition, a charitable one in the sense that the man's utility is related to the utility level of the woman and vice versa. The relationship is built on the presumption that this is, to some degree, the case, and as a result, a certain amount of trust develops concerning the intentions of the other party.

---

[4] The donor's demand for making gifts to any one of the possible recipients under highly competitive conditions (that is, a large number of alternative recipients) will essentially be horizontal.

In a romantic relationship, the woman or man has a demand for giving in any number of dimensions. However, she or he will choose to freely give only so much, and that will be Y in our example, Figure 4–1. In the case of the woman, she may be willing to give Y because she feels confident in the man's feelings toward her. However, if she has been deceived, she can be exploited because of the existence of the surplus value. The man can drain the surplus value out of the woman in any number of ways. He can, to a limited degree, generally abuse her. He can make her go places and do things that she would not freely choose to do, and he can make her put up with quirks in his own behavior that he may find costly to change. In this sense, he can make her go further in giving in to him than she would otherwise choose to go. If, however, he pushes too hard—that is, asks her to go beyond Z—he will be dropped. The irony of this may be that the woman may still love the man, but she drops him because he has asked for too much. All of this can also be placed in the context of the woman exploiting the man, which occurs perhaps as frequently as the case of the man exploiting the woman. It is interesting to note that women's liberation has attempted to eliminate many economic and social barriers that interfere with women getting out of the home. The liberation movement has, in effect, been trying to increase the alternatives women have to the conventional marriage situation. Our analysis suggests that to the extent that women's liberation is successful, husbands will be less able to exploit their wives. To the extent that husbands have exploited their wives in the past and do not change their behavior, we would expect the divorce rate to rise because of women's liberation. (Can you explain why in terms of Figure 4–1?)

SEXUAL EXPLOITATION

The reader may sense that all of what we have said here can be readily applied to the physical-sexual relationship between a woman and a man. There may be activities in which a woman may freely choose to engage because they may give her direct pleasure or, more importantly for our purposes, may contribute to the pleasure of the man she is dating. Because of the woman's value system, however, and because there may be psychic costs associated with many forms of sexual activities, there are limits to the number of times in which she may *freely* engage in sexual activity (that is, make the gift). Because of the surplus value, the man, *if he wishes and if he is her only boyfriend,* can make the woman go further than she freely chooses to go. He can extract the surplus either in terms of an increased rate of specific, more readily acceptable activities (such as petting), or he can draw the surplus out in the form of an activity in which the woman may not *freely choose* to engage (such as intercourse). This does not necessarily mean that the man can "force" the woman to have sexual intercourse, because the size of the consumer surplus may not be great enough to push her to that point. But it does suggest that regardless of the level or kind of activity the woman chooses, the man *can,* in a sense and under the condition that he is a monopolist with respect to the woman's affection, exploit the woman to some degree. If the man is only one of many possible dates for the woman—that is, the relationship has not been permanently established—the all-or-nothing deal cannot work as effectively. In the event the man tries to make the woman go further than she desires, she can merely turn to one of her other possible dates and retain the full consumer surplus from giving to the opposite sex. She, in this event, has bargaining power.

The typical male may intuitively sense the essence of the foregoing discussion and realize that he can obtain more of what he wants if he is the only one as far as the woman is concerned. This line of analysis may explain why the man may refrain from trying anything on the first few dates. On the first few dates, he may intuitively understand that he is one of a number of candidates for the (charitable) affections of the woman. If he attempts anything physical, she can turn to someone else from whom she may at that point receive equal pleasure (in the sense we have been using the term); thus, she can ultimately receive the full extent of the consumer surplus from giving. By waiting and putting on his best manners, he effectively may be able to eliminate the competition in the *mind of the woman* and, by the delay, more accurately assess the size of the woman's consumer surplus. He may also be investing the time for the purpose of increasing the woman's charitable demand for him (in which case she will of her own accord go further), and he may be attempting to determine what would be the most appropriate way of presenting the all-or-nothing deal.

The reader must remember that if the deal is not carefully posed —verbally, by facial expression, or otherwise—the woman's preferences for giving to the man can be damaged, implying a reduction in her demand for him. In other words, a deal clumsily made can reduce the woman's demand to the point that her demand curve intersects the vertical axis at P_1. In such case she will decide to give nothing.

Many women do trade sex for other goods, such as security, and the object was covered in some detail in the preceding chapter. This, however, is not what is meant by *sexual exploitation* here; by the term we mean one party *forcing* the other party to go further sexually than he or she would freely choose to go. Many readers may believe—by thinking in terms of the over-sexed, male stereotype— that if women do in fact find it necessary to make men go further sexually than they would freely choose to go, it is only of interest as a peculiarity of the relationships between nymphomaniacs and highly religious men.

The possibility of the female sexually exploiting the male becomes much more plausible if the male stereotype is set aside and if specific circumstances are considered. First, it should be realized that men can bear a cost by engaging in intercourse; they may be liable for child support and/or may be forced, because of personal values, into marrying someone who, under other circumstances, they would not choose. The existence of such costs and the fact that once the woman is aroused, she may not want to stop short of intercourse may partially explain why the woman may have to say, or subtly indicate, that "if you don't go all the way, then you may do nothing at all." Because of the male's surplus value from engaging in petting or from stimulating the woman, he may go all the way because by doing so he will be better off than he would be if he were not allowed to touch. (He could be even better off if he could touch without assuming the risk of pregnancy.)

Second, a married man may want to establish a rather impermanent, now-and-then relationship with some women other than his wife. He gets pleasure out of doing things for her, but he still does not want the relationship to seriously encroach on his family life. The woman may require that he see her more often—engage in sexual relations more frequently—than he would freely choose. He may consent, again, because of the surplus value acquired from the first few "units" of the relationship consumed.

Lastly, one party may need to resort to sexual exploitation when his or her appetite for sex differs from the appetite of the other party. In any continuing relationship, it is quite possible that there will be times when the female appetite is greater than the appetite of the male. In such a circumstance, the female may find it necessary to exploit the male. Before closing, it should, perhaps, be noted that male foreplay may be one means by which the women have sexually exploited the men. They, in effect, say that "either you arouse me, or I will not be interested in anything you have in mind."

CONCLUDING COMMENTS

By suggesting that the woman (or man) can be exploited if she (he) has a "monopolist" for a boyfriend (girlfriend), we have been saying, in effect, that exploitation can more likely occur if the relationship is a well-established, permanent one—that is, if the woman and man are going steady or are engaged. We submit that the analysis supports many of the fears of parents in seeing their teenage son or daughter becoming tied down into a permanent relationship. In concluding, we emphasize that the analysis indicates what the man (woman) *can do,* not what he (or she) will do. What either does is, again, dependent upon their consideration of the other's welfare. If one person loves another or cares about his or her welfare, then exploitation affects the other's welfare and, therefore, his or her own welfare. It follows that exploitation is most likely to occur when feelings of love or caring are not fully reciprocal—that is, when the one party that wishes to do the exploiting does not care (to the same degree) about the other person. As we said at the beginning, the argument in this chapter is applicable to basic friendships.

QUESTIONS TO PONDER

1. Does the argument in the chapter suggest an explanation as to how children (and college students) can exploit their parents—that is, get more from their parents than their parents would freely choose to give?
2. Does the analysis suggest an explanation as to why an only child may more likely be spoiled than children who have several sisters and brothers?
3. Explain divorce in terms of Figure 4–1.

CHAPTER 5

Marriage, divorce, and the family

The family is generally considered to be the basic building block on which social order is founded. However, even with all the attention that social scientists and others have given it, the family remains perhaps one of the least understood institutions. The purpose of this chapter is to develop insights into the marriage and family processes. Our approach is somewhat unusual. Certainly we recognize the importance of love in marriage and the family. However, we also recognize that in considering the establishment of a family, individuals are driven by a variety of motives. Some of these are not fundamentally different from those that lead people to buy a car or new clothes.

In addition, we will treat the family in its function as a producing unit. It is a "firm" that takes resources, including labor from within the family and the goods that are purchased, and produces things desired by family members. We want to look inside the family unit and analyze its behavior in terms of the behavior of its members. In the process, we are able to make observations regarding the importance of the marriage contract, the difficulty of divorce, the economic implications of love, and organizational principles underlying the family structure.[1]

THE MARRIAGE CONTRACT AND DIVORCE

Marriage can be defined in many different ways,[2] but for our purposes, we view it as a contract between a man and woman (or

---

[1] Because of his pioneering efforts, we are indebted to Gary Becker for his work in the area. Gary S. Becker, "A Theory of Marriage: Part I," *Journal of Political Economy* 81 (July/August 1973), pp. 813–46; and "A Theory of Marriage: Part II," *Journal of Political Economy* 82, supplement (March/April 1974), pp. s11–s26.

[2] Webster's defines marriage as "the institution whereby men and women

between two parties of the same sex if homosexual marriages are ever legalized). Each party explicitly or implicitly makes certain commitments as to his or her responsibilities within the family. He and she agree to recognize certain rights and privileges of the other, and both agree, again explicitly or implicitly, to a set of rules by which household decisions and changes in the contract are to be made. This last provision is necessary because not all issues concerning the relationship are ever likely to be settled before the vows are said and because conditions do change.

Such provisions of the contract may only be vaguely understood and recognized as such, but nevertheless, they are generally present in one fashion or another. The couple may simply have an understanding that they will work things out together, tacitly realizing from their knowledge of the other's behavior what this means. The process of marriage may be compared with the development of a constitution and bylaws for any firm or organization. As in the case of any one organization, the rules of the game can be as restrictive or as flexible as the people involved desire. In fact, the central purpose of dating and engagement may be to give the couple a chance to work out such provisions and to develop the contract by which both agree to live. (All couples do not, however, avail themselves of this chance to the same degree.) The contract, for example, may incorporate a provision on whether or not (or how many) children will be included, who will do the housework and mow the lawn, and which decisions will be democratically determined by the whole family and which decisions will be administratively determined. Although we might like to think that everything regarding the marriage *should* hinge on love, the division of the responsibilities and rewards may be greatly influenced by the relative bargaining power of the two involved.

Without the opportunity to develop such provisions, or if they are left undetermined, considerable disagreement can arise in the future, resulting in divorce. Because people have different views on what a marriage should be, the marriage may never take place and very often does not. This is because the couple involved cannot agree on what the contract should be. In this sense, the dating process screens out some of those marriages that will otherwise fold. Resources are used in dating, but at the same time, the process

---

are joined in a special kind of social and legal dependence for the purpose of founding and maintaining a family." *Webster's New Collegiate Dictionary*, 7th ed., s.v. "marriage" (Springfield, Mass.: G&G Merriam Company, 1967).

saves resources from being tied-up (albeit temporary) in an un-satisfying marriage.

Divorce can often be the result of insufficient resources (time, energy, and emotional hassle) being invested by the couple in de-veloping the marriage contract. This may be because the two mis-judged how many resources are required; it may also be that either or both of the parties calculate that the expected gain from spending more time and energy on the contract will not be worth the cost.

Except in the case of divorce, most provisions of the marriage contract generally do not have the force of law. Occasionally there are cases in which a wife or husband takes her or his spouse to court (for example, for lack of support) but these are indeed rela-tively rare events. One reason is that the mutually agreed-upon contract is vague and rarely written down. Another is that the cost of one spouse taking the other to court can be considerable in terms of time and lawyer's fees and can be easily greater than any benefits that may be achieved. So many of the violations of the contract are of a trivial nature, such as one party's refusal to take out the garbage, to spend time with the children, or to refrain from flirting with other men or women. The potential benefits are just not that great, even if the court will consider the case. In addition, the court fight itself, which may generate a great deal of antagonism, can represent con-siderable cost.

If the provisions have any meaning, it is mainly because of the moral obligation such agreement engenders, the pressures that can be brought to bear on the parties involved by either party or by friends and others, and the threat of one party retaliating by shirk-ing his/her responsibilities. The main role of the court has generally been one of refereeing the division of the family assets (children included) between the husband and wife at the time of divorce. On occasion, the court does attempt to bring about reconciliation.

This role of the court in the divorce process is one that is not unimportant and without economic implications. The reason is that the court's intrusion insures that the husband and wife each has some property rights in the family assets, both tangible and intan-gible. To this extent, the husband and wife have a greater incentive to "invest" their time and other resources in the development of family assets and the building of a strong marital relationship. The family is an investment project in the sense that returns can be received over the span of years.

An analogy of an investment in a business is useful here. Suppose an entrepreneur is considering an investment in an office building.

Will he be willing to make the investment if he knows that after doing so he has no property rights in the building—that is, someone else can take it over without any objection from the courts? Although he may be willing to make some investment in the enterprise and to protect it, he will probably be more willing to do so and invest a larger amount if he has some rights that are protected by the state. The whole investment project will be less costly to him. The same can be applied to the willingness of the partners in a marriage to invest in the union. To the extent that the stability and durability of the marriage is favorably affected by such investments, the legal status of the marriage yields benefits to all parties in the family.

There is one problem here. By giving each partner property rights over the family assets and, to some extent, over the other and by making the dissolution of the marriage costly, the husband or wife *can,* if she or he desires, abuse the other. Since there is a cost involved in divorce, one may allow himself or herself to be exploited because he or she may be better off than if he/she incurs the cost. If the abuse is greater than the cost of going through with divorce, it goes without saying that the marriage will be dissolved. If the parties are single and living together, either party can walk away without legal constraints. This may force the other party to be more considerate.

THE COSTS AND BENEFITS OF MARRIAGE AND THE FAMILY

We have assumed that people's behavior with regard to marriage is to a degree rational. (Can you think of any reason we should assume differently?) This, of course, means that in choosing a spouse, both sexes are out to maximize their utility. It also means that in the process of becoming married, each individual must address two very fundamental questions: (1) what are the costs and benefits in general of being married as opposed to remaining single, and (2) given these benefits and costs, how long and hard should he or she search for an appropriate mate.

The costs of marriage

In assessing the pros and cons of marriage, the individual must reckon with several major cost considerations. One of the most important for some (but by no means all) persons is the loss (cost) of independence. Individuals are never completely free to do exactly what they please; they must consider the effects their actions have on others. However, in the close proximity of the family, the possible effects any one person's action can have on another in the family are more numerous and direct than for the person who lives alone. The result can be that everyone may willingly agree to restrict their own behavior to a much greater extent than would be necessary if they all lived alone. They may, and very likely will, also agree to make many decisions by democratic or collective action. In taking this step, the members of the household essentially agree to incur future decision costs, which include the time and trouble of reaching a decision. This is because it is generally more costly to make decisions with a larger number of people involved.

For example, it is more costly for one of the authors, McKenzie, who is married, to purchase a new car than Tullock, who is single. All Tullock has to do in buying a car is consider his own preferences. McKenzie, on the other hand, must not only consider his own preference, but also those of his wife and children. The result can be, and almost always is, that buying a car is a long drawn-out process for the McKenzies. Note that if McKenzie and his wife had identical preferences, which, to be sure, is never the case in marriages, their decision cost would be the same as Tullock's. In such event, McKenzie would not have to bring his wife in on the decision to buy the car or anything else, and she would not care that he did not. Because of identical preferences, they both could be assured that whatever he bought, each would like it as well as the other. We have used just one example of the numerous times in which decision costs are incurred in a family. (If the reader thinks that such costs are unimportant, he should try marriage for a convincing empirical study!)

It is because of such decision costs that husbands and wives often agree to have many decisions made administratively by one party or the other. Except under unusual circumstances, one party can be allowed, without consulting the other, to make decisions with respect to, say, the family meals. The other party can determine what clothes will be purchased for the children and what types of flowers to plant in the yard. Each party may make decisions not agreeable with the other; however, the savings in decision costs can yield benefits that more than offset the effects of wrong decisions.

Wives often have the responsibility of making decisions with respect to meals and the interior of the house in general, and husbands make decisons with respect to the yard and the exterior of the house. This fact has been attributed to inculturated values—that is, spouses are merely role playing. Although there may be some truth in the statements, we suggest that such argument does not explain why the responsibilities for decisions are divided in the first place. Our analysis indicates that the division of decision-making power within the home can be added efficiency to the operation of the household and that if roles are not assumed to begin with, they would tend to evolve. The division of powers may not end up in the same way that we now observe them, but given what they are, there may then be the criticism that inculturated roles are being assumed.

As suggested above, the family is involved to a considerable extent in the production of goods and services shared by all members of the family. These are basically of one type and available in one quantity and quality. Such a good—take for example the car considered above—may not be perfectly suitable for any one individual's tastes, but it is the good everyone agrees to buy. In this instance, and there are many of them, the individual must bear the cost of not getting the good in the amount and quality that is most suitable to his preferences.

This type of cost is not only incurred because of the goods consumed, purchased, or produced by the family—such as cars, television programs, recreation, and family life (which tends to defy definition)—but is also applicable to relationships with other people. Both spouses may agree to associate with certain people, not because either finds the people to be *best* suited to what they find desirable in friends, but because the selected friends represent compromises for both. This is not to say that each will not have several friends of his/her own, but only that they are likely to agree on mutual friends. To the extent that they associate with mutual friends, there is less time for them to be with their individual friends. We submit that this can be a legitimate cost calculation in marriage.

To the extent that household decisions are democratically determined, members of the household have a say on how the burden of the production of the household goods is to be distributed. In this way they can determine who pays, either in terms of contribution of money income or time and effort. The family can effectively "tax" family members in a way that is similar to any other collective, governmental unity. Any family member can, like any citizen, be forced to pay for collective goods and projects with which they may not be in perfect agreement. This can be considered a potential cost to a family member. This is evident from the complaints that one may hear in a home when the decision is made to go on a picnic and the burden of preparation is distributed or when one is asked to take out the garbage or mow the lawn.

Other costs associated with marriage and the family in general include the risk cost of developing strong emotional ties with one specific group of individuals and the forgoing of the opportunity to date and in other ways associate with other people. These factors may be of no consequence to some, and may in fact be an advantage to others. Further, the cost of marrying one particular person can be the loss of the opportunity to have married someone else who is not known at the time of marriage but who, if he/she were sought out, would be a more desirable spouse. The list of cost provided can, of course, be extended.

The benefits of marriage and family

The benefits of marriage and the family are derived mainly from the ability of the family to produce goods and services wanted. First, the spouses have the opportunity to produce things not readily duplicated in nonmarriage situations. Such a list may include children (at least ones that cannot legitimately be called bastards), prestige and status that can affect employment and the realm of friends, companionship that is solid and always there, a family-styled sex life that may be more desirable than sexual associations with which the individual may disapprove, and family life in general, which we indicated above defies definition. Granted, many of these goods can be had in certain quantities and qualities outside of the family; we are only suggesting that they take on special characteristics within the family and for that reason are valuable to people. (We recognize that to some these are costs.)

Second, the family operating as a single household—that is, more than one individual—can produce many goods and services more efficiently than can several single-person households. This is because there are economics of scale in household production. Take, for example, the problem of cleaning the household rug. Although there may be some selection in size and power of vacuum cleaners, generally speaking, the machines available are capable of handling the dirt of several people. However, one cleaner must be purchased. If more people are added to the house, the household need not increase the number, size, or power of the vacuum cleaner proportionally. The same can be said of many of the resources that go into the production of a garden, meals, and other household goods such as washing machines, rakes, mixers, brooms, electric toothbrushes, and so forth.

Indeed, many of the goods and services provided by individuals in the home are *public goods:* they benefit everyone involved and do not diminish in quantity or quality if additional people are added to the household. For example, many things done to beautify the house are this kind of good. If a picture that all like is hung on the wall, one person's enjoyment of it does not detract in any significant way from the enjoyment by others. Because they all live under the same roof, they each do not have to produce such goods for themselves individually, meaning that they can raise the quality of the goods that are had or they can divert resources to other purposes. Such goods may not be enjoyed or appreciated by a very large group of people, and because of the decision costs involved, as explained, there is some point at which the collective group would be too large. *Therefore, we would expect some unit in society to develop that would be small enough that people of similar tastes can be together to have them and large enough that they can be provided efficiently. The family, in our view, is that unit.* It is large enough to provide such goods as these efficiently yet small enough that the decision costs incurred are minimized. By having provision for numerous such family units, individuals are given considerable choice over the type, amount, and quality of these goods.

The efficiency of household production can also be greater because of the opportunities for the parties to specialize and effectively trade with one another. In this way the parties can take advantage of their comparative efficiency in production. Suppose that, for simplicity sake only, there are only two things for the household to do—clean a given size house and mow its lawn, which is of a given size. Suppose also that we are given the following information about the abilities of a husband and wife in doing these two things:

	Cleaning the house	Mowing the lawn
Wife	60 minutes	100 minutes
Husband	100 minutes	300 minutes

What this table shows is that the wife can clean the house in 60 minutes and can mow the lawn in 100 minutes. It takes the husband 100 minutes for the house and 300 minutes for the lawn. If they both live separately and have lawns to mow and houses to clean, it would take them a total of 560 minutes. If they lived together and each cleaned half of the house and mowed half of the lawn, it would take them a total of 280 minutes (80 minutes for the house cleaning and 200 minutes for the lawn). However, there is a possibility here for the two to specialize, one cleaning the house and one mowing the lawn. Since each will be doing something for the other, we can, in a sense, say they are trading.

To see this prospect, recognize that every time the wife cleans the house she gives up three fifths of the lawn being mowed. If she spends 60 minutes on the house, those are minutes she cannot be mowing the lawn. Since it takes her 100 minutes to mow the lawn, we can assume that she could have mowed three fifths of the lawn. On the other hand, each time the husband cleans the house, he gives up one third of the lawn being mowed. (Why?) We can thereby argue that it is more costly (in terms of the portion of the lawn not mowed) for the wife to clean the house.

If we want the cost of production to be minimized, we would then argue that the wife should mow the lawn, the husband clean the house. If they do this, the total time spent by both of them would be 200 minutes. If the wife cleans the house and the husband mows, the total time would be 360 minutes.

Notice what we have demonstrated here: by being under one common roof, the cost of the goods demanded by the members can be minimized by the husband and wife specializing and effectively trading. Notice also that we have made this demonstration even though one spouse, the wife, is actually more efficient in the production of both the mowed lawn and the cleaned house. By specializing, the wife and husband can also avoid many of the costs associated with developing the same skills. Each can concentrate his/her attention on a more limited number of household tasks, improving the efficiency with which they can be done.

This demonstration is important because it indicates that if husband and wife are interested in maximizing household production or minimizing the cost of household production, which amounts to the same thing, then they will specialize to some degree in the functions of the households. They will have what many derogatorily call *roles*. However, *these roles need not be what they presently are*. Further, it indicates that certain roles may be assumed by, say, the wife not because she is necessarily less efficient than the husband in the production of those things the husband does, but rather because her comparatively greater efficiency (called *comparative advantage*) lies in what she does.[3] The same is true for the husband. To acquire the efficiency benefits described here, the husband and wife need to have the appropriate preferences for the assigned tasks.

Furthermore, if the decision facing the family is the allocation of members' time between work internal to the home and work external to the home and if the family is interested in minimizing the cost of goods produced in the home, then it should use that labor with the lowest value outside of the home. The cost of cleaning the house is equal to the cost of the materials and supplies and the value of the individual's time outside the home who does the cleaning. Assume that it take two hours to clean the house, that the wage the wife can earn outside the home is $3 per hour, and that the wage of the husband is $5 per hour. (Here we are only attempting to use a realistic example; it is a fact, which is the subject of considerable complaint by women, that husbands do tend to earn more than their wives.) It follows that it would be cheaper for the wife to do the cleaning. If the man did the cleaning, it would cost an additional $4 since his wage is $2 per hour higher.[4]

Many sociologists and psychologists contend that roles, such as child care, are assumed within the house because of socially determined values. We are unwilling to argue that such forces have no effect on the organization of many households. All we wish to add is that much of what we observe in household relationships may very often be the result of a conscious, rational choice on the part of the couples. Clearly, women do tend to earn less than men in the market, a point made above, either because they are the victims of discrimination or because they are less productive. Given this, which is not something individual households can do much about, it is reasonable to expect households to delegate many responsibilities,

---

[3] If the wife takes as much as 180 minutes to mow the lawn and everything else about the example above is the same, it would still be most efficient for the wife to mow the lawn and the husband to clean the house.

[4] The same allocation of wife- and husband-time would result if the wife is substantially more efficient in the production of household goods. Consider the case of the wife being able to earn $5 per hour and the husband earning $3 per hour. Suppose that it takes the wife an hour to do some household task and it takes the husband two hours. If the husband stayed at home to do it, it would cost the family $6 (two hours at $3 per hour). However, it would only cost them $5 (one hour at $5 per hour) for the wife to do it. In such case, the family would choose to have the wife stay home if it were interested in minimizing production costs. Inculturated values would perhaps come into play as an explanatory factor if the couple did not obey these rules for time allocation.

such as child care, to wives. In this way, the cost of the child care is minimized, and the output of the family is maximized. If the household production is greater by the wife staying at home, then one can suggest that the output of the wife is actually greater than what is indicated by her work in the home; she should get some credit for the greater output of the household.

If the discrimination women face outside of the home is reduced and/or they are able to raise their productivity relative to men, we should expect their wages to rise relative to their husbands'. We should then expect to see more and more wives working outside the home and *relatively* more time being spent by husbands in housework. It is clear that the labor force participation rate of women has been on the rise over the decades. There are many reasons for this, including changes in attitudes of men and women toward women working in jobs. The greater wages of women can be another explanatory factor.

There are other possible benefits to marriage and the family, like the benefit of making communication less expensive. Communication is an important aspect of any production process. (Can you name other benefits?)

SPOUSE SELECTION

The rational individual, in search of a spouse, will attempt to maximize utility as in all other endeavors. He (by which we mean he or she) will not pretend to seek the "perfect mate" but only that one individual among those whom he knows and who are willing to marry him that *best* (not perfectly) suits his preferences. (Who do you know that has married the *perfect person?*) This means that he will seek to minimize the cost incurred through marriage and the family.[5] If he marries someone who agrees with him, the cost associated with arriving at the marriage contract is less than otherwise. There is not as great a need for (implicit) bargaining. If he marries someone who agrees with him as to what the family should do, what kinds of recreation they should have, and the number and way in which children should be reared, then the cost of having to give up friends and goods that suit his preferences better will be minimized. In other words, we would expect rational individuals to tend to

---

[5] In searching for a mate, he will extend his search until the marginal cost of extending the search is equal to the marginal benefits.

marry persons who have similar values and preferences and are in other ways like themselves. Interestingly enough, this is generally what researchers have found.[6]

Rational behavior has other implications with regard to search for a mate. It implies that the greater the benefits from marriage, the greater the costs a person will be willing to incur in searching for the spouse. This means that the greater the efficiency benefits that are to be achieved in family production or the greater the esteem people give those who marry, the more costs, in terms of time and effort, that a person will apply in looking. Greater costs may take the form of later marriages and a smaller fraction of the population married. Also, the longer the individual expects the marriage to last and the more stable it is expected to be, the more careful will be the search. This does not mean that mistakes will not be made; it only means that greater costs will be incurred in trying to avoid mistakes.

It also follows that the difficulty (cost) of divorce should affect the extent to which people search for a spouse.[7] It may affect the extent to which people marry, the extent of more informal arrangements, and the availability and economic well-being of prostitution as an institution. If a divorce is made impossible, a man (or woman) knows that if he (or she) chooses the right person, then there are more benefits to be had than if divorce were easier to come by. The impossibility of divorce will assure him that his spouse cannot freely marry someone else whom she may later prefer. If, on the other hand, he chooses the wrong person, the impossibility of divorce will mean that the decision would carry with it greater cost than if the marriage could be easily dissolved by divorce. Therefore, as Gary Becker has argued, we would expect the resources applied to search for a mate to be directly correlated with the difficulty of obtaining a divorce, and he writes that "Search may take the form of trial living together, consensual unions, or simply prolonged dating. Consequently, when divorce becomes easier, the fractions of the persons legally married may actually *increase* because of the effect on the age at marriage."[8] Alan Freiden has in part corroborated this hypothesis in a study of the effects of different state divorce laws. He

---

[6] See, for example, R. F. Winch, *Mate Selection* (New York: Harper and Row, 1958). This conclusion, of course, does not apply to the situation in which one party prefers a mate who will dominate him/her.

[7] Becker, "A Theory of Marriage: Part II," pp. s22–s23.

[8] Ibid., p. s22.

found that the more costly the divorce process, the smaller was the fraction of women married.[9]

If divorce is made easier, this line of analysis indicates that people will tend to incur fewer search costs, perhaps reflected in a younger age at which people marry. Aside from the experience of the last few years, the age at which men and women marry has generally been on the decline. One might reasonably assume that the durability of marriages in general is positively related to the extent to which people search the marriage market before they choose the one. If this can be accepted (and it might be a poor assumption), then making divorce easier can result in more divorces because they are less costly and also because people are expending fewer resources in search of a spouse and, therefore, making more wrong choices.

THE IMPLICATIONS OF LOVE

For our purposes we say that a person loves another if his or her level of satisfaction is in part dependent upon the satisfaction level of the other person.[10] In this sense, one person genuinely cares for the other person and cares what happens to him (or her). This is because he (or she) will have greater utility if it is known that the other person is in some sense better off. He will, therefore, be motivated to help improve the situation of the person who is loved. The more intense the love, the stronger is this motivation.

As we have explained, responsibilities are typically delegated to family members, and each member is dependent upon the others fulfilling their end of the bargain. In this way, the welfare of the family members will diminish if any one member shirks responsibilities.[11] Because shirking hurts others, the person who loves the others will be less inclined to shirk than the person who does not. It is for this reason that a person, if given the choice, would naturally want to marry someone who loves him and would also naturally want to marry someone whom he loves because what he does for

---

[9] Alan Freiden, "The United States Marriage Market," *Journal of Political Economy* 82, supplement (March/April 1974), pp. s34–s54.

[10] Here we are following Gary Becker in defining *love*. The central point we make is also his. See "A Theory of Marriage: Part II," pp. s12–s17.

[11] A person can shirk by failing to carry out any part of the contract or by making it more difficult (costly) for the other person to see that the contract is obeyed.

the family will also give him satisfaction to the extent that it makes everyone better off.

Where love does not exist, we will be more likely to find individuals shirking family responsibilities.[12] This in turn means that family resources will have to be diverted into the "policing" of family members. In this way love has an economic dimension. This does not mean that people will not marry someone they do not love or who do not love them. Because of the benefits of being in a family situation, people may prefer that to the single life. Many people do marry for money as well as other benefits.

All of this adds up to one interesting conclusion, and that is that the *efficient* marriage is one in which the two are in love and are alike in terms of values and preferences. Oddly enough, this is what most people would readily argue. The interesting thing about this conclusion is that it is derived from the perspective of economics and the family as a producing unit. The greater the love and the closer the preferences of the couple, the closer will the marriage approximate what may be considered the ideal. However, in the realistic world in which we live, it is clear that the maximizing individual does not always have the opportunity to choose a spouse who loves him (or her) and has similar preferences (at least to any great degree). He (or she) must often choose between a person who may love him very little but who may be in many ways like himself, and the person who loves him but who is very different. All the individual can do is maximize over the range of opportunities.

The discussion suggests that love adds to the efficiency of the household; we also argued earlier that differences in preferences can detract from the efficiency with which the household is operated. If this is the case and the individual is seeking to maximize the output from being in a family, then we must conclude that love is not all that is necessary for a successful family and marriage. Marriages have been known to break up in which the parties professed to love each other dearly. The problem was that they violently disagreed over what the marriage should be and do and the roles that each was to play. The gulf in preferences could have been so wide that the love, as intense as it was, could not bridge it. This seems to be fairly descriptive of the marriage and breakup of Cher and Sonny Bono, who, during the 1973–74 television season, had one of the top ten programs. They broke up telling reporters that they still loved each

---

[12] In the jargon of economics, love can be said to internalize the externalities generated from family living.

other but that they both had such markedly different interests that they had to go their own ways. In the same way, we might expect that many marriages are held together with little love; the partners' preferences are so much alike, they still find their relationship very beneficial, at least given their next-best opportunities.

CONCLUDING COMMENT

Marriage and the family are terribly complex subjects to discuss, and you probably detect there is a lot that has been left unsaid. We definitely agree. We believe that the field is wide open for future research. This has been only a sample of what economists are beginning to say about such basic social institutions, and we think that the economic approach shows great promise in contributing to our understanding of the subject.

QUESTIONS TO PONDER

1. Given the analysis in this chapter, would you expect married couples to "invest" more or less in their marriages (in the way of building up a permanent relationship) than people who are simply living together? Explain.

2. Consider the following true-life case: A movie star had been living with a woman for several years. He decided to break the relationship, but when he did, the woman sued him for the division of their common property and for a monetary settlement. The woman won her case. What affect will such a ruling have on the willingness of people to "live together?" On the willingness of people to marry? What effect will such a ruling have on the durability of the relationships that exist between people who are living together?

3. Given the following information, who will mow the lawn and who will clean the house:

	Cleaning the house (required time)	Mowing the lawn (required time)
Wife	75 minutes	150 minutes
Husband	200 minutes	200 minutes

(See the example in the chapter involving the division of household chores.)

Child production

Children may be little darlings in their parents' eyes, but they are also economic goods. They can provide considerable benefits to their parents and relatives, and they are the result of a continuously evolving production process. This process involves resource expenditures like everything else that is produced in the home.[1]

CHILDREN AS ECONOMIC GOODS

From children, parents obtain a good deal of companionship, resulting in benefits not unlike those received from other goods, such as a new car or a good martini. Children can be someone to talk to or go on a walk with, and they can be ready-made partners for a game of ping pong or checkers (if one can bear the hassle of getting them to do it). Their existence gives parents some hope that they will not be left alone later in life. Children also provide parents with the pleasure that comes from being respected and needed and, at least at some stages of a child's development, adored by someone else. There are very few parents who are not touched when their small children run to them when they return from work or a trip. Rightly or wrongly, children are used to fulfill parents' goals and to extend themselves beyond their own physical limitations. By having children, parents are able to negate the unspoken criticism of relatives and friends that they are incapable of having or, in some way, loving them. The motivation for having children may include a

---

[1] We are again indebted to Gary Becker for his work in the economics of fertility, which underpins the discussion in this chapter and the work of many other economists. Gary S. Becker, "An Economic Analysis of Fertility," *Demographic and Economic Change in Developed Countries* (Princeton, N.J.: Princeton University Press, 1960), pp. 209–40. For a critical evaluation of this literature, see Harvey Leibenstein, "An Interpretation of the Economic Theory of Fertility: Promising Path or Blind Alley?" *Journal of Economic Literature* 12 (June 1974), pp. 457–70.

means of fulfilling a sincerely felt need to make a contribution to society, to explore the unknown, or to test the hypothesis that they can do a better job in rearing children than others.

Children, at one time in our history (and this is still true in many undeveloped areas of the world), were a means by which parents could develop their own old-age pension plan. As the children grew up, parents paid into the plan by feeding and clothing their children; in later years, the children took care of the parents when they were unable to provide for themselves. This, incidentally, was at a time when security markets and insurance companies were not very well developed, particularly in newly opened territories. This kind of arrangement has not completely dissipated. However, for the most part, today people in the industrialized countries rely much more heavily on the impersonal, financially based retirement plans for old age income. The reason may be in part due to the fact that the market has provided alternative retirement schemes that are cheaper than those incorporated in children. As we will see, children can be extremely expensive. Further, the benefits in the financially based plans are contractual and to that degree are more certain or less risky. Another reason may be that the government has forced people to become a part of the social security system which may have contributed to reduced reliance on children for retirement maintenance.

Last but not least, children can be an important source of labor, particularly for families living on farms and places where child labor is less expensive than mechanization. The parents, in the beginning stages of the children's lives, "invest" resources in their growth and development in order that they can become workers. When the child is old enough to work, they reap the returns from their investment.

Granted, parents in general may not have children for the sole purpose of seeing them become good and loyal workers or for the purpose of gaining a sense of immortality. All of the benefits that can be listed are fused in the typical decision to have a child. But this is true in the decision to buy a new car or house; there are a multiplicity of reasons for buying or producing almost anything. All of the benefits of having children that can be enumerated add up to one total level of parental satisfaction and, to that degree, to the parents' demand for children. This demand for children—or, perhaps more properly, "child services"—can be reflected in the total *number* of children that are had or in the *quality* of the children born and reared. The one thing that can be said at this point is that the greater the benefits reaped from children, the greater the number and/or quality of children that will be had. This assumes, of course, that the cost of the children is held constant and that parents, or at least some of them, look upon the decision to have children in the same rational way as they do everything else. Because some readers will doubt the reasonableness of this latter assumption, we will return to it later.

The cost of rearing a child includes the family expenditures on giving birth, food, clothing, shelter, education, entertainment, medical expenses, insurance, transportation, and so on. Other major cost items, which are often overlooked, are the emotional drain and the value of the parents' time spent on rearing the child. Estimating the cost of children is a difficult problem at best. The actual cost of a child will depend on exactly how much the parents want to spend, and all costs will vary with the economic status and location of the parents. Given these problems, however, Ritchie Reed and Susan McIntosh have made estimates of a child reared on a "modest-cost" budget in an urban setting.[2] A summary of their estimates, by the educational level of the mother, is included in Table 6–1. (The estimates were originally developed for 1969. Those estimates have been adjusted upward in the table to account for inflation between 1969 and 1980.) The cost of giving birth, which includes prenatal and hospital care and the maternity wardrobe of the mother, is estimated at $3,314. The expenses associated with rearing the child until the age of 18 are estimated at $70,922. Reed and McIntosh made the simplifying assumptions that the parents' incomes and the prices of the things that go into determining these figures are held constant throughout the 18 years. The cost of four years of college education for the child is estimated at being $12,011 in a public institution. The total of these costs (referred to as total direct costs in the table) is $86,247, and they are held constant for all education levels of the mother. The reason for this is that Reed and McIntosh wanted to focus on the impact of the different educational levels of the mother.

The opportunity cost of the mother's time is dependent upon the wage she could have earned and the number of weeks she would have worked had she not had children. In the case of the mother who has an elementary school education, the estimated opportunity cost

[2] Ritchie H. Reed and Susan McIntosh, "Costs of Children," *Economic Aspects of Population Change: The Commission on Population Growth and the American Future*, ed. Elliot R. Morss and Ritchie H. Reed (Washington, D.C.: Government Printing Office, 1972), pp. 330–50. The authors, in their report, provide more detailed information than can be given here.

TABLE 6–1
Total cost of a child by educational level of mother, in February 1980 prices

Type of cost	All women	Elementary	High school	College, 4 years or less	College, 5 years or more
Undiscounted					
Cost of giving birth	$ 3,314	$ 3,314	$ 3,314	$ 3,314	$ 3,314
Cost of raising a child	70,922	73,922	70,922	70,922	70,922
Cost of a college education	12,011	12,011	12,011	12,011	12,011
Total direct costs*	86,247	83,247	86,247	86,247	86,247
Opportunity costs	126,240	95,314	127,249	178,152	222,559
Total costs of first child	212,488	181,561†	213,497	264,400	310,967
Marginal cost of each additional child spaced two years apart‡	105,407	100,447	105,566	113,726	120,844
Discounted					
Cost of giving birth	3,313	3,314	3,314	3,314	3,314
Cost of raising a child	37,969	37,969	37,969	37,969	37,969
Cost of a college education	2,687	2,687	2,687	2,687	2,687
Total direct costs*	43,970	43,970	43,970	43,970	43,970
Opportunity costs	84,841	60,046	85,510	119,721	149,062
Total costs of first child	128,811	108,016†	129,481	163,605	193,032
Marginal cost of each additional child spaced two years apart‡	62,484	57,681	62,637	70,537	77,427

* These costs may be somewhat overestimated because of possible duplication occurring when the cost of giving birth as calculated by perspective is added to the USDA figures on the cost of raising a child to age 16.

† For a woman with only an elementary school education, a low income figure for the cost of raising a child may be more appropriate. This would reduce the total discounted cost to $44,181 and the total undiscounted cost to $72,845.

‡ Differs from cost of first child in that the opportunity cost and the cost of giving birth are less. For additional children, the $500 cost of nursery supplies is subtracted from the cost of giving birth to the first child.

Source: Ritchie H. Reed and Susan McIntosh, "Costs of Children," Economic Aspects of Population Change: The Commission on Population Growth and the American Future, ed. Elliot R. Morss and Ritchie H. Reed (Washington, D.C.: Government Printing Office, 1972), p. 345. The cost of rearing a child was computed by Reed and McIntosh in 1969. Their calculations have been adjusted upward to take account of inflation between 1969 and February 1980. Because the consumer price index was used to make the adjustments, the costs should be considered rough estimates.

is $95,314. For the mother who had a four-year college education, the opportunity cost is estimated at $178,152.[3] This means that the total calculated cost for the first child is a whopping $181,561 for the mother with the elementary school education and $264,400 for the mother with four years of college.[4] The marginal cost for each additional child is $100,447 and $113,726 for the mothers with the elementary school education and college education, respectively. The reason the cost for the second and following child is lower than the cost for the first is mainly due to the fact that if the children are spaced closely together, the opportunity cost of the mother's time is not duplicated with additional children. Since 1969, prices have risen considerably, and if the same study were redone today, the figure would be inflated by more than 60 percent. Clearly, the cost of a child is, by most standards, substantial.

The costs given above are the result of the simple summation of the expenditures made and the earnings forgone during the rearing phase of the child's life. However, $1,000 spent today is worth more than $1,000 spent several years in the future. The reason is that the $1,000 spent today can earn interest during the course of years if it is deposited in a savings account or invested in interest-bearing securities. Therefore, to determine the *present value* of the expenditures made on the child and the earnings forgone in the future, Reed and McIntosh discounted the yearly costs by 8 percent, and the new cost figures are recorded in the lower half of Table 6–1. The result is that the *discounted* total cost is $108,016 for the mother who has an elementary school education and $163,605 for the mother with four years of college. The marginal cost of each additional child is reduced to $57,681 and $70,537, respectively. Certainly for most people, the first child is the biggest single "good" they are likely to buy during their life!

THE DEMAND AND SUPPLY OF CHILDREN

By pointing out the costs and benefits of children, the authors do not mean to imply that children are just like every other good a family purchases. There is substantially more emotion and risk and

---

[3] For a description of how these figures were determined see Reed and McIntosh, "Costs of Children," pp. 341–44.

[4] Note that we have not included an estimate for the opportunity cost of the father's time, the emotional drain, risk cost, or the cost that may be associated with the depreciation of the mother's market skills.

uncertainty in having a child than in buying a new house or almost anything else. Parents are not able to see the good (child) before they buy it; in fact, their task is to produce it from scratch. The child comes with a will of his own from birth. This adds an element of surprise that is not a feature of a new house. In the case of the house, the buyers can sell if they decide later that it is not what they want, perhaps recouping their investment and then some. In modern American society, to do the same with a child is frowned upon.

All of this means that the decision to have a child is more difficult than other decisions a family confronts and that there is more room for error in child production than in the production of other things. It does not follow that some parents will not attempt to approach the problem with the same rational *intentions* that they approach everything else.

Parents may conceive a child they did not plan to have because the momentary importance of sex was so great that they forgot to take the necessary precautions. This seems to be very likely if it is recognized that, based on a study in 1965, there are approximately 2 billion acts of sexual intercourse between married couples in the United States each year.[5] One could add a substantial number of acts between those who are unmarried. It is simply a matter of probability that some goofs will occur—no contraceptive is foolproof. To the degree that accidents occur, there will be children born and reared who are not the result of the conscious consideration of the expected costs and benefits. However, to the extent that there are parents who consider the costs and benefits in child-bearing decisions, the demand curve for children will be downward sloping. The cost of a child will influence the fertility level; more children will be had the lower the cost or price. Parents will, in addition, rationally balance off the number of children conceived with the quality.

In Figure 6–1 we have illustrated the total market demand for children (D). In our example Q_1 children will be born and reared because of impulsive or, in other ways, nonrational behavior on the part of parents. However, how many children will be had in total will depend also on the supply, which means cost, of children. If, for simplification, the supply of children is assumed to be horizontal

---

[5] Leslie Aldridge Westoff and Charles F. Westoff, *From Now to Zero: Fertility, Contraception, and Abortion in America* (Boston: Little, Brown & Co., 1971), p. 24. This estimate is based on a coital frequency of 6.7 times per month for all couples.

FIGURE 6–1

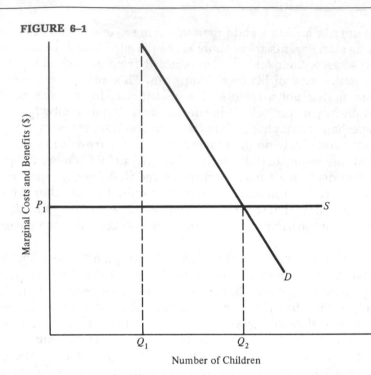

(S)—that is, the marginal cost is constant at P_1—the total number of children had will be Q_2. Of this total, Q_1 will be the result of "accidents" and $Q_2 - Q_1$ will be the result of cost-benefit calculations.[6] If you are inclined to doubt our assumption that many child-bearing decisions are conscious, rational acts, you should reflect on the number of times you have heard someone or yourself say, "Not me! I can't afford to have another child. There is just not enough time in the day to handle the two that I've got." This is just another way of saying that the cost of the additional child is too great for the expected benefits. We might expect the people who make such statements often go to great extents to avoid conceiving again.

If the demand for children falls, the economist would predict that the number of children had will fall. This situation is described in Figure 6–2 by a shift in the demand curve from D_1 to D_2. The number of children drops from Q_2 to Q_3. The number of accidentally con-

---

[6] It is quite likely that many of the births that are unplanned take the place of births that were planned for a later date. If this is the case, the demand curve will move in to the left to account for it. This does not affect the analysis.

FIGURE 6–2

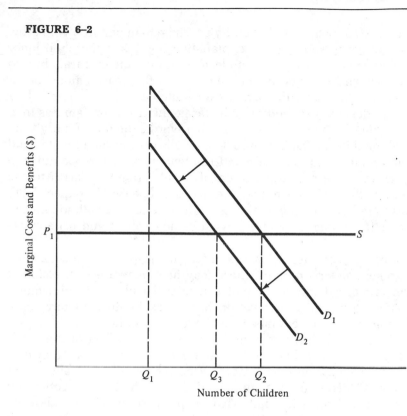

Marginal Costs and Benefits ($)

Number of Children

ceived children remains at Q_1; however, the number of rationally determined children falls, causing the drop in the total.[7]

This change in demand can result from an exogenous drop in people's "taste" for children. It can also result from a decrease in the relative prices of other goods produced and consumed in the home. If the latter happened, rational couples would tend to reallocate their resources toward the cheaper goods and away from children. It may be that one explanation for the declining birth rate has been the growing relative cheapness of goods, such as cars and all forms of entertainment, which may be substitutes for children.

In general, the location of the demand curve is dependent upon the *relative* benefits attributable to children and upon the family resources. Children who grow up on farms have many more oppor-

---

[7] The change causing the drop in the demand may make unwanted children more undesirable and may induce parents to take greater precautions in their coital relations.

tunities to contribute to the family's income than children who grow up in an urban setting. One explanation for this is the child labor laws, which do not restrict children from working on farms but do restrict them from working in industry. For this reason alone, economists would expect the benefits attributable to children and their parents' demand for children to be far greater for farm families than for families living in the cities. In other words, the farm family's demand for children (D_1 in Figure 6–2) will be greater than the demand of urban families (D_2). The result is a tendency for farm families to be larger. If there is a migration of people from the farms to the cities, as there has been over the decades, one would expect birth rates to fall and the population growth rates to taper off somewhat. Interestingly, this is precisely what demographers and economists who have tested these hypotheses have found.[8]

Over time, if there is a reduction in the price of mechanized equipment, *ceteris paribus*, there may be a decrease in the size of farm families if the equipment can take the place of child labor. Cheaper farm equipment would encourage families to buy more equipment and use less labor, i.e., have fewer children.

The leftward shift in demand can also be the effect of the availability of cheaper and better contraceptives. Because they are cheaper we may anticipate more extensive use of them and fewer accidental births; the summation of the accidental plus rationally determined births would fall. Also, people's preferences for children may turn away from *numbers* to *quality*, causing the demand curve based on the number of children to shift in.

The reader should understand that for parents there is the ever-present decision between using their resources for the purpose of having more children and using them for the purpose of giving the number they have more attention. This can be reflected in what the parents consider a quality improvement.

We have concentrated in this section on a drop in demand for children because that appears to us to be the current trend. The reader may want to extend the discussion himself by considering possible causes for an increase in demand and the consequences of such developments.

Given our model, anything that reduces the cost of children,

8 John D. Kasarda, "Economic Structure and Fertility: A Comparative Analysis." *Demography* 8 (August 1971), pp. 307–17; Stanley Kupinsky, "Non-Familial Activity and Socio-Economic Differentials in Fertility," *Demography* 8 (August 1971), pp. 353–67.

ceteris paribus, will shift the supply curve downward and increase the number of children had. In the case of Figure 6–3, the supply goes from S_1 to S_2, and the number of children demanded goes from Q_2 to Q_3. The reason for the expansion is that prior to the cost reduction, the cost of the additional children, Q_3–Q_2, exceeds the benefits indicated by the demand curve between Q_2 and Q_3. Once the supply curve shifts down, the benefits of the additional children become greater than the cost. It is therefore rational for the couple to divert more resources into child production.

Such a change may have been the consequence of an increase in efficiency of rearing children, making the whole process less costly. It may have also been attributable to a decrease in the prices of those resources purchased from the market that are peculiar to the production of children, or it may be attributable to changes in such exogenous forces as government policy.

As an example of a proposed change in government policy that can affect fertility rates, take the proposal of President Ford, who

FIGURE 6–3

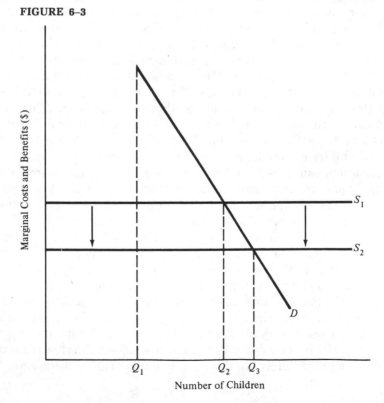

at the end of his term in 1976 recommended an increase in the personal exemption for federal income tax purposes. President Ford argued that the allowable personal exemption of $750 is too low to accommodate the high cost of rearing a child today and that it should be raised to $1,000. (The exemption was actually raised to $1,000 by 1980.) Clearly, such a policy effectively lowers the cost of having children. If a person were in a tax-rate bracket of 30 percent, Ford's proposal reduces a person's tax liability by $75 ($250 × 30 percent) per year. In this way, the proposal reduces the cost of having a child by $1,350 (undiscounted) over the first 18 years of the child's life. This may not seem like much of a saving since the undiscounted cost of an additional child can be upwards of $100,000.

Even though such a change in the tax structure is not likely to have an effect on everyone's decision to have a child, it can affect those marginal couples whose estimated costs and benefits of having an additional child are very close or who are more or less indifferent to the idea of having a child but are inclined to hold off. For illustration, suppose a couple figures that with the $750 exemption per child the undiscounted marginal cost of the additional child is $100,000 and the marginal benefits are $99,500. Since the marginal cost is greater than the marginal benefit, the couple would not have the child. However, if the Ford proposal is adopted, the marginal cost will be lowered to $98,650, an amount less than the marginal benefits of $99,500. The passage of the higher exemption will give the green light to this couple and to others in a similar position. Such a change in the tax laws will tend to make slightly more difficult the problem of population control. Welfare payments tied to the number of children, including payments to unborn fetuses, and public provision of education and day-care centers can, in a similar manner, encourage population growth. In a similar way, high rates of inflation like those experienced in the United States in recent years reduce the *real* value of exemptions, thus increasing the total real costs of having children. (The above analysis actually applies to increases in the real value of personal exemptions.)

As seen in Table 6–1, the major cost in the rearing of a child is the opportunity cost of the parents' time. The higher the potential wage of the parents' time outside the home, the higher is this component of the cost. The effect of greater cost can be to reduce the number of children had. This is illustrated in Figure 6–4 by the upward shift in the supply curve and the accompanying reduction in the desired children. On the other hand, the higher wage gives the

FIGURE 6-4

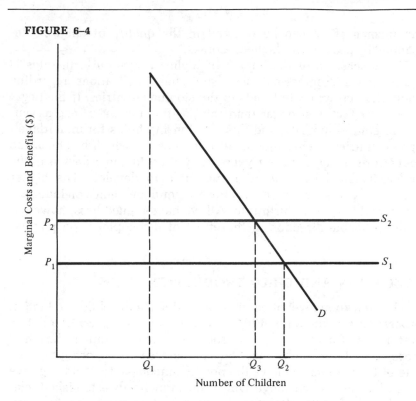

Number of Children

couple added income to allocate to family purchases, including children. This "income effect" can have a positive influence on the production of children.[9] If this is the case, the net effect of the higher wage depends upon the relative strengths of the negative cost effect and the possible positive income effect. The empirical studies that have been done on the subject tend to find a negative correlation between family income and number of children.[10] This suggests, but does not confirm, that the negative cost effect is stronger. As opposed to being reflected in the number of children,

---

[9] We recognize the possibility that children can be "inferior goods," meaning the income effect can be negative.

[10] Bruce Gardner, "Economics of the Size of North Carolina Rural Families," *Journal of Political Economy* 81, supplement (March/April 1973), pp. s99–s122; Dennis N. DeTray, "Child Quality and the Demand for Children," *Journal of Political Economy* 81, supplement (March/April 1973), pp. s70–s95.

the income effect can be realized in the *quality* of children demanded by people with higher incomes.[11]

The discussion of the impact of higher wages on birth rates is interesting and important because it has implications regarding population growth-rate trends in developing countries. If the negative cost effect is stronger than the positive income effect, as empirical studies indicate, and this relationship holds for underdeveloped countries, then the population explosion, which has been the concern of many in recent years, may fade *to some degree if the underdeveloped countries are ever able to develop.* The higher opportunity wage, coupled with the greater dependence on industry, could lead to a lower birth rate. All we have argued here, however, is the probable direction of the effect of development on population growth and not how strong the effect is.

EDUCATION AND CHILD PRODUCTION

The education level of parents can influence the child production process in several ways. First, it can change the parents' relative preferences for children by introducing them to things they find more valuable. Second, education can increase the opportunity wage rate of the parents and have the positive income effect and negative cost effect mentioned above. One of the more firmly established relationships in fertility literature is the negative correlation between the amount of education of the wife and the number of children she has—that is, as the wife's education level rises, the number of children tends to fall.[12] There is some evidence that shows that the relationship between the husband's education level and the number of children is positive.[13] One possible explanation for these findings is that, as many studies have found, the wife's time is relatively more important in child production than is the time of the husband, and

---

[11] Testing the relationship between income and child quality is a difficult task because of the problems associated with defining and obtaining data on *quality.* Nevertheless, Dennis N. DeTray made an effort by defining child quality as the extent of the child's education. He finds that the education of the mother, which can be mirrored in her opportunity wage, does have an effect on the "efficiency with which child quality is produced" (p. s93). Because of the data that was used, he considers his conclusions to be weak and tentative. ("Child Quality," pp. s70–s95.)

[12] Gardner, "Economics of the Size of North Carolina Rural Families."

[13] Masanori Hashimoto, "Economics of Postwar Fertility in Japan: Differentials and Trends," *Journal of Political Economy* 82, supplement (March/April 1974), pp. s170–s94.

the cost of her time will accordingly be more influential in the child-production decisions. In the case of the husband, whose responsibilities have traditionally included earning the money income, his education has had little cost effect (since the amount of his time involved may not be very great) but has had a positive income effect.

Third, education can increase the efficiency with which the "quality" of children can be raised. At least one empirical study tends to support this.[14] Even with a higher opportunity wage rate, greater efficiency can make a unit of "child quality," however defined by the parent, cheaper to the more educated person. For example, suppose it takes the parent with an elementary education two hours to teach his child a certain task which contributes to the child's quality. The parent's market wage rate is $2 per hour. The total cost is $4. On the other hand, if it takes the more educated parent, who earns $5 per hour, one-half hour to accomplish the same thing with his child, the cost is only $2.50. Everything else being equal, we would expect the more educated person to demand more units of child quality.

Fourth, the effects of education can show up in the parent's knowledge and use of contraceptives and in the number of unwanted children. A number of studies have found a direct relationship between parents' education and knowledge and use of contraceptives.[15] More educated parents tend to use the more effective contraceptive methods and use them to a much greater extent. Robert Michael gives three possible explanations for this: (1) Education makes the technical literature on contraception more easily understood and to that extent lowers contraception costs; (2) it raises the value of the couples' time and thereby makes more effective methods, which may be more expensive but less time consuming, more economical (the time expenditure for a couple does vary somewhat from the pill to the use of diaphragms and foam tablets); and (3) education raises the cost of children by raising the cost of parents' time and, thereby, increases the cost of an unwanted child. This makes knowledge and use of contraceptives more valuable.[16] In the process of developing his argument, Michael makes an interesting point regarding the

---

[14] Ibid.

[15] Robert T. Michael, "Education and the Derived Demand for Children," *Journal of Political Economy* 81, supplement (March/April 1973), pp. s128–s64. The author of this article refers to a number of studies connected with this point on page s140.

[16] Ibid., p. s159.

efficiency of contraceptive devices. He writes, "If a couple used a contraceptive technique that was 'only' 90 percent effective, in a 15-year period their expected fertility outcome would be 2.7 births. . . . Or, of a couple used a contraceptive technique that was 'only' 99 percent effective, the chance of a conception in a five-year interval exceeds 10 percent. 'Good' (but not perfect) contraception does not provide the long-run protection one might think."[17] He also estimated that if a fertile couple does not use any method of contraception for five years, the probability of conception is 100 percent.

CHILD PRODUCTION AND OVERPOPULATION

Economists are in general agreement that the optimum quantity produced of anything is that quantity at which the marginal cost of the last unit is equal to the marginal benefits of it. This will be the case if all costs and benefits are actually considered by the individual making the decision on the output, and this rule of thumb holds for the production of children. However, if the person making the decision does not consider all costs in the production of children (that is, someone else bears a portion of the cost), the perceived marginal cost will be lower than it really is. Using Figure 6–4, because not all costs are considered by the person making the child production decision, the couple will perceive that the cost of children is represented by supply curve S_1, whereas in fact the true supply curve, considering all costs, is at S_2. Couples will rationally choose to produce Q_2 children. Note that the true marginal cost (P_2), when all costs are included between Q_2 and Q_3, is actually greater than the demand curve. This indicates that the marginal cost of the children is greater than the marginal benefits, and as a result, too many children are produced.

In our present society, there are two basic ways in which couples deciding to bear children can underestimate the cost of their children. They may not consider the added congestion their children can create. This may mean that there are simply more people taking up the same limited area, reducing the freedom all persons have to move about without affecting others, or it may mean that more people are competing for resources, other than space, causing another form of congestion. This cost of an additional child is incurred in general by people not involved in the decision to have the child.

---

[17] Ibid., p. s141.

The other basic way by which the private decisions of parents can impose costs on others is through the tax system. Presently there are many public facilities, such as schools, that are provided with tax money. If the facilities are not free to the user, they are most often subsidized. To this extent, a portion of the total cost of a child is borne by the general taxpayer. The private decision of one couple to have a child can, therefore, increase the tax bill for the rest of the community. Because these costs may not, and to a substantial degree are not, considered by the child-bearing couple, the costs they consider will be understated, resulting in overproduction of children. (It is indeed an interesting thought that the tax burden of the general public is partly dependent upon the coital frequency of couples!) One way to turn this around is to have the child-bearing couples pay the cost by imposing a tax on them for each birth. To put it mildly, this is not likely to be a popular proposal with those who want children. They no doubt would prefer that the rest of us continue to pay the bill for their fortune or misfortune, as the case may be.

CHILD PRODUCTION AND THE FUTURE

Thomas Ireland in a paper on "The Political Economy of Child Production" suggested some interesting, but to some, we are sure, disturbing prospects for the future course of child rearing.[18] If it were not for the rather dramatic change over the past 15 years in the public's acceptance of abortions, we would indeed consider his ideas to be futuristic. But, as it is, Ireland's paper may indicate what is just around the corner.

His paper is based on two main propositions: first, scientists now have the capability to transplant an animal fetus from its mother to a "host mother" with the birth following in due course. There is every reason to believe that if medical science is not able to do it now, the know-how will be developed in the future to accomplish the same thing in humans. Second, the problems associated with pregnancies cause some women pain and inconvenience and make many unable to work in the market for several months.

The prospects of fetus transplant provides a potential solution to the dwindling number of adoptable babies and the moral problems surrounding abortions. Because adoptable babies are becoming very

---

[18] Thomas R. Ireland, "The Political Economy of Child Production" (Paper presented at the Public Choice Society meeting, University of Maryland, March 1973).

expensive, the mother who would like to bear a child but who cannot because of the sterility of the husband, would have some incentive to pay to have an aborted fetus transplanted into herself.[19] This may not sound so crazy if it is remembered that women now pay handsomely for artificial insemination and for the rights to adopt a child.[20] In fact, a public-interest group interested in the rights of the fetus' life may be willing to pay another mother to accept the transplant and carry the child to term. Such a solution may be disgusting to some readers who are concerned about the life of the fetus. Granted, this may be a less-than-ideal solution, but it may be a better solution than one of standing around discussing the question of when life begins while many fetuses are being destroyed.

In addition, there are possibilities for payment arrangements whereby the true mother and host mother gain by a fetus transplant. Suppose that there is a mother who earns $20,000 per year, who wants to have a child of her own, but who is not willing to endure the pain and loss of income associated with pregnancy. If there is another woman who earns $8,000 per year, then the mother can possibly agree through some institution, which is not yet established, to pay a host mother to carry the baby to term at which time the baby would be transferred back to the original mother. If the disability associated with the pregnancy is three months, the real mother could be willing to pay (ignoring taxes) as much or more than $5000 to the host mother. By making the payment, it will be the host mother who will lose time at work, which will cost her $2,000. She can receive from the real mother, say, $4,000 and her income will rise to $10,000. Furthermore, the total output of the economy can be $3,000 greater than what it would have been if the real mother had lost the time from work.[21] All of this may sound a little cold-hearted, but we really do not mean for it to be taken that way. These are, however, solutions which may be more than just attention getters in the relatively near future.

---

[19] Adoptable babies of minority groups are still relatively easy to obtain, but with the legalization of abortions, this supply is dwindling.

[20] In 1980 the phrase *surrogate mother* became popular. Surrogate mothers are women who agree to be inseminated with the sperm of a husband whose wife is sterile. In 1980, the surrogate mothers were agreeing to be impregnated and to carry to term a child who would then be given back to the natural father. The fee for surrogate mothers in 1980 was as high as $10,000.

[21] It may be found that transferring a fetus to a host mother will affect the quality of the child.

CONCLUDING COMMENTS

In recent years, it has been the fad to project the future course of the population trend and accompanying problems. Most of these projections are merely statistical extrapolations of the trends of the recent past. They do not assume that there will be adjustments made in the economy that will alter the course of the trend. We do not wish to understate the importance of getting the world's population growth under control. However, we suspect that the doomsday prophets will be mistaken in their projections because of certain anticipated changes in the child-production process. First, we expect that as the population grows larger, putting pressure on resources, the cost of producing children will become relatively greater, reflecting back on the private household decisions. Second, we suspect that as congestion becomes greater, there will be growing pressure on government to change the tax structure and to make abortion and contraceptive devices more readily and inexpensively available to the public. Third, we expect that with the growing cost of children, there will be a renewed incentive to find new technology for preventing pregnancies. In fact, we view the recent public concern over population growth to be a part of the self-correcting changes we see. Those that are projecting the population are alerting the voting public to the problem and setting the stage for changes in policy. Regardless, we have tried to demonstrate in this chapter how economics can be used to explain child-bearing decisions. The reader should once again, however, realize that economics cannot yield a complete explanation for these very complex social decisions.

QUESTIONS TO PONDER

1. Suppose that the prices of all goods and services rise faster than the cost of rearing children. What will happen to the population growth rate? Explain.
2. What effect have liberalized attitudes among the young toward hard drugs done to the number of accidental births and planned births?
3. What effect do new technological inventions in child-care services and other goods and services have on the birth rate?
4. What effect has women's liberation had on the population growth rate? Explain the several ways in which the movement has had an effect.

PART **3**

CRIME
AND
DISHONESTY

CHAPTER 7

The economic basis
of law

Primitive human beings probably had few formal laws; in fact, they may have had no formal laws at all. Today, however, wherever you go you find laws, and these laws have many things in common. In the United States, Russia, Chile, and China, murder, burglary, and theft are all illegal. In all four of these countries, when the laws are broken, a police system and a court apparatus deal with the crimes.

Needless to say, legal codes differ. In the United States, you are more-or-less free to say anything you wish, but this is emphatically not true in the other three countries listed above. Buying something with the intent of reselling it at an increased price is illegal in both China and Russia (the fact that it is illegal does not mean that there is not a great deal of it), while the same act is perfectly legal in the United States and Chile. The obscure doctrinal heresy of *revisionism* is a deadly crime in China and another heresy, *dogmatism-obscurantism,* is an equally deadly crime in Russia.[1]

CRIMES WITH VICTIMS

The fact that laws differ from country to country is not particularly surprising; but the fact that the laws of many countries are similar in a number of basic characteristics is striking. Why do we find burglary illegal practically everywhere?[2] One answer of course,

---

[1] These two terms, which might be translated, respectively, as favoring Russia and favoring China in the split between the two Communist powers, may well have become legal or perhaps reversed their position between the two countries by the time the reader sees this chapter. One of the characteristics of Communist politics is that it is subject to sudden change.

[2] In the Soviet Union and China, burglary is divided into two crimes—ordinary burglary and theft of state property. Theft of state property is much more severely punished.

is that it is immoral. We do not quarrel with this particular answer, but we would like to point out that there are good, practical reasons for making burglary, theft, and murder illegal. Since this is a book on economics, we are going to deal with these practical reasons not the moral issues; although if the reader keeps moral principles in mind, it will not detract from our discussion.

Illegal burglary

Let us consider burglary. The first thing to be said about burglary is that one person—the burglar—gains and one person—the victim—loses. The victim obviously objects to the burglary. Furthermore, as a practical matter, the injury to the victim (in terms of the market value of the stolen property) is likely to be greater than the gain to the burglar. This is because the victim characteristically has acquired the property that is stolen for his or her own use, while the burglar normally steals it in order to sell it. The use value of the object to the rightful owner is apt to be greater than the sale value to the burglar.

Although this is normally true, it is not inevitable. In exceptional cases, the burglar may put a higher value on what is stolen than the original owner. Still the transaction would appear to be a pure transfer with one person benefiting and the other losing, and not everyone is opposed to all such transfers. During the strong New Left movement in the late 1960s and early 1970s, the view that "ripping off" the system was a positively virtuous act was held (or at least proclaimed) by a fairly large number of people. However, the members of the New Left spoke only of theft from "the system," not theft from their own pockets.

Legal burglary

It may be argued that if burglary were perfectly legal, everyone would engage in it and no one would suffer any great loss. What A stole from us, we would steal from C, who in turn would steal it from A. This is not true. Consider the situation that would occur if burglary were legalized, and suppose that you have some property. In order to retain it, you have to either guard it yourself—and this may not be sufficient if the burglars come in groups[3]—or to

---

[3] Strictly speaking, if they came in groups to use force or overawe you, it would be robbery not burglary, but this technical distinction is of no great interest to nonlawyers.

strengthen your house so that people cannot break in. Clearly, strengthening your house can be a difficult and expensive business, but if burglary were legal, people would have far more protection against burglary than they do now. They would have better locks, stronger doors, grills on the windows, and so forth. They would also, no doubt, spend a fair amount of time guarding their property, and this would cut into their time applied to productive activity. Their total living standard would go down as they expanded resources in protecting all that they have earned. Further, the return on their productive work would be lower because what they have earned might be stolen from them.

On the other hand, those individuals in society who consider burglary a suitable profession would devote their time and attention to stealing their neighbors' property. First, this means that a segment of the labor force is involved in acquiring good burglar tools. The stronger our neighbors build their house, the more complicated the devices we need to get into it. On the other hand, the more complicated the devices we have to get in, the stronger our neighbors will build their houses. Once again, resources are diverted from productive activity and labor switched from production activity to uses which cancel each other out.

When we buy a new lock for our doors, we injure the burglar by making it harder to get into our houses. Similarly, when the burglar buys some new burglar tools, the gain made from them is accompanied by a loss to us. They make it easier for the burglar to get our property, and that, of course, is an injury to us. Thus, with no laws, everyone's plundering and protective behavior inflicts severe externalities on everyone else, and total production will fall. This would be true even if we as individuals not only attempted to protect our own property but also if we engaged in burglary whenever we saw the opportunity. Certain individuals may not do too badly by such a modus operandi, but clearly, society as a whole loses.

Private police

Situations in which individuals can make private gain by activities that lower total social product are generally undesirable. We would like to have society designed in such a way that this is impossible. As a matter of fact, we cannot totally avoid such situations, but we can certainly make them less common than they would be if burglary were legal.

Making burglary illegal means, in essence, changing from the technique of trying to prevent burglary by locks and bars to trying to deter burglary by the threat of detection and punishment. Note that the threat of detection and punishment can be offered privately. Most of our readers have seen window stickers saying that this or that establishment is protected by such-and-such private detective agency. These private detective agencies will, in fact, make an effort to capture and deliver to the regular court system anyone who commits crimes against the protected establishments. The fact that people hire them would seem to indicate that they do a better job or, at least, do a job which provides protection in addition to that provided by the regular police. There are, indeed, some so-called right-wing anarchists who believe that we should depend on this technique entirely for the prevention of crime.[4]

The last proposal, although it usually surprises people, is not quite as radical as it first appears. As a matter of historical fact, legal systems began with a court but no police force. It was up to the people who were the victims of the crime to seize the criminal and bring him to the court, and the court would simply inflict punishment. The gradual development of a government-operated police force is probably an improvement, but it is conceivable that the other system can work as well. Certainly, in ancient times, this system was employed, although we do not know how efficiently it worked since there are no statistics available.

Deterrence

Today, however, we normally depend upon the government police force to prevent crime. It commonly does this not by physically stopping burglars from entering the house but by attempting to catch them after they have stolen and imposing a punishment upon them. As we will show later, punishment does deter crime, and, indeed, this seems to be a fairly efficient way to deal with it. If we know that burglarizing our neighbor's house will bring us $100 but that we will be running a 1-in-50 chance of getting a year in prison, we are likely to decide that it is not a good bargain. Under the circumstances, we will not commit the crime.

This analysis assumes that the police are available at reasonable rates, which seems to be a reasonably accurate statement about the world. Although local governments frequently complain about the cost of running their police forces, these costs are usually a very

---

[4] Some of them even favor private courts. See David Friedman, *The Machinery of Freedom: Guide to a Radical Capitalism* (New York: Harper Colophon Books, 1973).

small fraction of total government expenditures. This does not mean that they are optimally efficient; most government activities have very large built-in inefficiencies.

Suppose, then, that by making crime illegal and appointing a police force to protect us against burglary, we can get rid of a great many of our locks and bars and reduce the amount of time we spend guarding our property. Suppose, further, that this police force is not unbearably expensive. Under these circumstances, almost everyone in society will favor introducing a police force. This would not be because everyone in society wanted to avoid burglary themselves. There might well be some persons in society who would prefer a law which gave them the right to commit burglary and prevented everyone else from commiting burglary to a law which prevented burglary for everyone. However, they would realize that this was impossible.[5]

Consider professional burglars in a state in which burglary is illegal, and then contemplate a change in the law which will make burglary perfectly legal. First, the burglars will realize that the result of making burglary legal will be that they will no longer have to worry about the police arresting them. Second, they will now have to spend a great deal of time guarding their ill-gotten gains and in buying elaborate locks, window bars, and so on to protect themselves. Surely their living standards in net would go down.

Thus, even without any reference to moral principles, we can demonstrate that we should have laws and that these laws are similar, even in different societies. They would also have certain differences. For example, it is easy to see why dictatorships pass laws that make it dangerous to criticize the dictator or to conspire against him or her. It is also easy to see why Communist countries enforce their ideology by making disagreement or even lack of apparent enthusiasm a criminal offense. Democratic countries, however, normally stick to those laws that seek to prevent things such as burglary and murder and have little in the way of laws against "political crime."

Private versus public protection

As we have discussed, you can, to some extent, protect yourself against crime by improved locks, bars on your windows, and so

---

[5] There have been times in human history in which something like this did exist. Individuals or groups might have the right to prey on others without any reciprocal injury to themselves.

forth. In countries that do have laws against burglary and murder, we see people depending in part on this kind of private protection as well as on the public protection of the police. No doubt, that is the pattern in your family. Why don't we depend entirely on the police and courts rather than partially on the police and courts and partially on locks and alarm systems? Clearly, if a person leaves the door unlocked, it will increase the likelihood that the house will be robbed. However, this assumes that we cannot change the size and effectiveness of the police force. Suppose that we take all of the money that we now use in putting locks on our doors and on our cars and bank vaults and use this money to hire additional police officers. Will this be more efficient than our present technique?

The answer is probably "no," although we do not know enough about the exact parameters to be sure. The point is that as we increase resources for police, we encounter declining marginal returns in crime prevention, just as we do in anything else. The same is true with private locks and bars. As we increase the number of them that we have, each additional dollar makes less difference in reducing the probable crime rate.

To say that private provision of locks and bars is subject to declining marginal returns is the same thing as saying that as you reduce the amount you spend on them, you get increasing returns. The fact that police resources as they are expended face reduced marginal returns, combined with the fact that private protection as it is reduced faces increased marginal returns, means that there is probably some equilibrium value in which at least some private production of protection by way of locks and barred windows is sensible.[6] Whether our present balance is that particular optimal amount, we do not know, but we do know that no society would be well advised to depend entirely on public protection against crime.

In sum, there is a good argument for provision of a legal structure which, by threats of punishment, lowers the crime rate. However, this argument does not indicate that we should depend entirely on this technique. Further, it does not suggest that we should spend infinite resources on protection against crime by either public or private means. Crime is like other bads in that we do not want it but we are not willing to spend infinite resources in reducing it to

---

[6] Note that this works the other way, too. Reducing police expenditures increases the marginal return, and increasing private protection reduces marginal return.

absolute zero; the objective should be to reduce it to the point where the present discounted value of the reduction of the crime by a certain amount is the same as the present discounted value of the cost of so reducing it.

"VICTIMLESS" CRIMES

A category of crime in which no one is injured directly is the so-called victimless crime. In recent years, a number of people have taken the view that these victimless crimes should not be illegal. They argue that these crimes involve consenting adults dealing with each other in a way that harms no one else and that the government should not attempt to "legislate morality." There is clearly something to be said for this view, but the issue is by no means as simple as the normal newspaper discussion indicates. Experience with advocates of abolition of laws against victimless crimes normally suggests that they want to abolish the laws against only some of such crimes. For example, if you ask a person who is strongly in favor of abolishing the laws against homosexuality whether he or she thinks a consenting adult should be permitted to sell another consenting adult a new car without a seat belt, he or she may very well say no. On the other hand, many people who would favor making it legal to sell cars without safety equipment are in favor of banning homosexuality. The simple slogan victimless crime does not encompass or explain all the possible individual reactions to it, nor does it necessarily follow that this type of behavior is inconsistent.

Before turning to a more careful examination of the problem, let us produce a list of crimes that do not, in any direct sense, have victims. These will be crimes that have been against the law in various places at various times, but concerning which most of the people who are affected by them have given consent and therefore cannot be regarded as victims. As we shall see below, it is not necessarily true that all those people affected will have given consent.

First, let us consider crimes in which only one person (a single consenting adult rather than a group) is involved:

1. Carrying a concealed pistol.
2. In many states, carrying a pistol at all, concealed or otherwise (note that in New York this applies also to such disabling but nonfatal weapons as Mace).
3. Riding a motorcycle without a safety helmet.

4.   Carrying a wirecutter in saddle bags (illegal only in Texas, but it is regarded as important enough in Texas so that it is part of the constitution).

These crimes involve the direct action of only one person, although, as we shall discuss later, it may be argued that such crimes can indirectly affect others.

Let us now turn to crimes which involve more than one person:

1.   Sex acts between consenting adults, whether homosexual, heterosexual, sodomy, and so forth.
2.   Sale of an unregistered gun.
3.   Sale of drugs, which may be (a) heroin, (b) marijuana, (c) alcohol, (d) others (LSD, barbiturates, and so on).
4.   Constructing and selling new cars without safety belts to knowing purchasers.
5.   Gambling. (Note that this is perfectly legal in many places, if a heavy tax is paid or if a state bureaucracy is acting as bookie; it is illegal, however, in many places regardless of these considerations.)
6.   Selling cimetidine to ulcer sufferers. This particular drug is the drug of choice in most of the world, but its use is illegal in the United States essentially because the Food and Drug Administration takes a very long time to make up its mind about new drugs.
7.   Sale of pornography.
8.   Hiring an individual to work in a factory that does not meet the safety standards required by the federal government. (Note that the individual hired is assumed to *know* the safety standards are not met.)
9.   Prostitution.
10. The sale of meat that has not been slaughtered under approved conditions. (Note, once again, we must assume for purposes of this example that the customer knows this.)

This list has been produced with some care. It is our opinion that almost everyone looking over it will find some activities between the consenting adults he feels should be illegal and some activities which he thinks should be legal. We also think, however, that different people will select different items from our list to ban by law and to permit.

Presenting this list to people with different political views and asking them to indicate which ones should be banned and which ones should not is an interesting experiment. We presented the list to a conservative lawyer and a moderately liberal criminologist who had just debated the subject of victimless crimes in a legal journal. The conservative lawyer had argued that victimless crimes should be banned if they were immoral. The liberal criminologist, equally obviously, had argued that if only consenting adults were involved, there should be no legal prohibition. The reader will not be surprised to hear that the conservative lawyer simply checked (from the more-than-one-person crime list) 1, 3a, 3b, 5, 7, and 9. The response of the liberal criminologist was almost equally predictable. He could not bring himself either to argue that selling a car without safety belts should be legal or that there was a victim in this case. In consequence, in a rather involved and complicated letter, he copped out.

The desirability or undesirability of banning these acts is not entirely determinable from an economic standpoint. The economist can offer some advice as to which if any, of the above items should be illegal, but there are clearly noneconomic considerations here. Since, again, this is a book about economics, however, we are primarily going to deal with the economic considerations and only briefly discuss two noneconomic criteria.

Morality

First, many people make their decisions about what should be legal and illegal almost entirely in terms of morality. As economists, we have very little to say about this issue. Each of us has his own moral code, but we cannot argue on economic grounds with people whose consciences tell them something different than our consciences tell us. What we are going to say, then, has little to do with morality, and the reader who wishes to give precedence to moral principles is perfectly free to do so. We see no reason, however, why he should object to at least considering arguments which center on the issue of efficiency.

Paternalism

Leaving aside morality any law banning or requiring certain types of activities may be justified on what are essentially paternalistic grounds. In other words the state may decide whether or not an activity should be made legal or illegal because the individual is not capable of making decisions on his own. For example, it may be said that an individual who is offered a car without a safety belt at $50 less than one with a safety belt may choose the less expensive car because he does not properly appreciate the safety advantage of the safety belt. Since most people who have cars with safety belts do not use them, people who make this argument frequently suggest that wearing the safety belt should be compulsory—and indeed it is in Australia.

This argument seems to be much more suitable for dictatorial governments than for democracies. If we are pledged to permit the individual to make decisions by voting on such matters as who should be president, whether we shall be in the Vietnam War and how hard we shall fight if we are, or whether the local school board is to be permitted to float a bond issue in order to build a new school, then there is some difficulty in arguing that the same citizen should not be permitted to choose whether or not he should wear a safety belt. Note that there is no logical inconsistency in the paternalistic argument. But the argument has an ironic twist because the individual is assumed to be capable of voting on the political leaders who will appoint the civil servants who will restrict his decision-making power but he is assumed not capable of making the decision on the car directly. This is odd but not a logical inconsistency.

Inadequate information

Sometimes people who favor this kind of restriction on individual choice will argue that people are not well informed enough to make the decision. Once again, feeling that people are well informed enough to make decisions on the city schools, traffic laws, and our relations with Chile but not well informed enough to make decisions about safety belts seems a bit odd; but if the problem is one of inadequate information, providing the information is certainly possible. Indeed, there is a great deal of legislation requiring that information be provided—cans have to be labeled with a list of contents, and so on.[7]

---

[7] There are also many laws restricting information. This is particularly true with respect to price information. In many places, advertising the price of prescription drugs or even informing people concerning the internal rules of the Internal Revenue Service with respect to auditing tax returns are all examples of the government's making a strong effort to prevent people from obtaining information. Perhaps the strongest single example of this is the complete and total censorship of all reports of the discussions of appellate court judges before decisions are rendered. Juries are also supposed to deliberate in complete secrecy, and no one is ever supposed to know how they reached their decisions. In this case, the secrecy is not complete. Nevertheless, it probably would be illegal for anyone wanting to better understand our judicial system to set up a project in which ex-jury members are asked to fill out a questionnaire about their decision procedures.

It can be argued, of course, that even if information is provided, people will not bother to read it or that, if it is provided, complications can arise. Late in 1976, a swine flu inoculation campaign was announced. In some states, the physicians giving the free inoculations were required to give fairly careful explanations to the potential recipients about the relatively untried nature of the vaccine. As it turned out, after having these explanations, many people refused to have the inoculations. It is not obvious whether the citizens of the states where no explanation was given and therefore where there was a much larger inoculation level were better off or worse off than the citizens of those states where this additional information was provided, with a resulting lower level of inoculation. Persons who refused the inoculation did not only affect themselves. By remaining susceptible to the disease, they made an epidemic just a little more likely.

One of the new fields of economics is the economics of information. In general, providing and absorbing information is a costly activity—it consumes resources. If we compel every cannery to list the complete contents of its product on the outside of every can of beans, the additional cost will be slight. On the other hand, if we compel housewives to read and understand this list before they buy the can of beans, the total cost distributed over the country will be very considerable indeed. This is particularly so since there are a number of minor chemicals with long, complicated names put into canned goods.

In the case of informing people about seat belts or the "customers" of our judicial system about how the system actually works, the cost of absorbing the information may be more than it is worth. Those who feel that all victimless crimes (or for that matter, some of them) should be perfectly legal but that steps should be taken to see to it that people are well informed about the consequences should realize that it is at least possible that the information can be more costly than it is worth.

In this connection, one possible course of action is simply to see to it that relevant information is available but not demand that people actually "consume" it. This course of action is apt to appeal to the better educated or more highly motivated part of the population, of which we suspect our readers are a part. However, one should realize that, in a way, such a proposal benefits one segment of society more than another. Suppose we require the makers of some household remedy—for example, cold tablets—to include in their package a little pamphlet that carefully explains all of the scientific evidence on the dangers of their remedy. Let us suppose, also, that this raises the cost of the medicine by $0.02. Everyone who buys the medicine must pay the $0.02, but not all people will benefit. Basically, those who will benefit most are the better educated and/or conscientious people who are capable of reading and understanding the pamphlet. People who are unmotivated to read such instructions or have a low level of literacy are not apt to read the pamphlet. Further, they may be poor, so the $0.02 means more to them.

If they *do* read it, they may think the dangers discussed are greater than they really are, with the result that they fail to take pills which would help them. Thus, providing fairly detailed information and making its consumption or nonconsumption voluntary is, in general, an act that probably benefits better-educated people more and may injure the less well-educated. This is not proof that making consumer information available is undesirable, but it is something that should perhaps be taken into account in the decision-making process.

Additional reasons for making victimless crimes illegal

Some of the other victimless crimes are victimless in themselves, but the avoidance of the crime would not be any significant inconvenience for an honest person and might be quite inconvenient indeed for a criminal. For example, the honest person who has need for either a wirecutter or a pistol is not inconvenienced particularly by being compelled to carry them openly. The horse thief who hopes to cut the wire quietly and get away with some animals or the person who is in the business of armed robbery and does not want the police to know is very seriously inconvenienced indeed. Thus, these laws can be thought of as efforts to make the work of the police a little easier without imposing any great inconvenience on any honest person.

The argument for restriction on the type of drugs that can be sold is, in a way, similar. The argument is often made that in order to prevent people from making money by selling drugs that are useless or perhaps even harmful, it is necessary to license the sale of all drugs. Of course, once one begins licensing the sale of drugs, the approval of new drugs is delayed because they must go through a governmental procedure. The delay is set off against the benefit that comes from preventing bad drugs from being sold. As it happens, in the United States the average delay, which is now over seven years, probably inflicts a good deal more injury on the citizen than he would suffer from having a certain number of bad drugs made available.[8] However, this seems to be the result of bad administration rather than of the law being undesirable per se.

The sale of hard drugs is not a victimless crime in the sense that people who are under the influence of these drugs are likely to cause injury to others. At the moment, the most dangerous drug from this standpoint is alcohol. It seems likely that the reason that alcohol predominates is that, being legal, it is readily available; hence, a great deal more of it is consumed. If heroin and marijuana were readily available, they might cause as many automobile accidents and quarrels that end in fighting as does alcohol.

Needless to say, we are not arguing that laws against heroin, marijuana, and alcohol are desirable or, for that matter, undesirable. We are simply pointing out that it is possible to make an argument for such laws on the grounds that there are, perhaps somewhat indirectly, victims. If someone could design a legal system that permitted people to consume these drugs freely but kept them off the roads while they were under the influence, it would presumably sharply lower the automobile accident death rate. In fact, this has been attempted in various foreign countries and for a time, in any event, was successful in England.[9] The arguments for the remainder of these activities being made illegal mainly turn on the theory that they do lead to injury of people other than the persons who have given their consent by indirect means. For example, if the government does have a policy providing medical attention to victims of accidents, assaults, and so on, then the cyclist who rides a motorcycle without a safety helmet may be imposing tax costs on other people. Of course, this can be avoided by making the cyclist buy personal insurance. Similarly, prostitution (and, indeed, sexual promiscuity in general) is a more-or-less necessary condition for the continued viability of the social diseases. A strictly puritanical sexual morality would lead to the extinction of these diseases fairly quickly.

---

[8] See S. Peltzman, "An Evaluation of Consumer Protection Legislation: The 1962 Drug Amendments," *Journal of Political Economy* 81 (September–October 1973), pp. 1049–91; and W. Wardell, "Therapeutic Implications of the Drug Lag," *Clinical Pharmacology and Therapeutics* 15 (January 1974), pp. 73–96.

[9] See H. Laurence Ross, "Law, Science, and Accidents: The British Road Safety Act of 1967," *Journal of Legal Studies* 2 (January 1973), pp. 1–78. With respect to Sweden, Denmark, and Norway, Ross finds that the Swedish and Norwegian laws actually have had no effect, apparently because of poor enforcement.

The reader may feel that the arguments we have given for making these victimless crimes illegal are very weak. Our point, however, is that such arguments are not nonexistent, and it is possible to make at least some case for banning almost all of the activities we listed at the beginning of this section as being victimless. The situation is not that these crimes are truly victimless but that they have what we might call weak and indirect effects on people who can be called victims. Since many perfectly legal activities have at least as serious indirect, injurious effects on people, it does not follow from this that these acts should be illegal, but it also cannot be said with absolute certainty that the laws against them should be repealed.

CONCLUDING COMMENTS

As we said earlier, most of the readers probably find that they would like to have some of these acts made illegal and others legal. Different people will favor different lists. The issue is controversial in the true sense—that is, there does not seem to be any definite way of reaching a conclusion. Reasonable men can simply disagree. The authors, as a matter of fact, split on the issue. Tullock would like all of them except the concealed-gun rule repealed. McKenzie is less radical. We should be very much surprised if, in the average classroom, there is general agreement as to which of these laws should be repealed and which retained.

QUESTIONS TO PONDER

1. Which of the list of victimless crimes do you think should be made illegal? Why?
2. The arguments with respect to burglary and robbery in the first part of the chapter in a direct sense apply only to efforts to obtain another's property. Can you apply them to crimes against the person, such as rape, murder, and assault? (Hint: if you have difficulty with this, Gordon Tullock, The Logic of the Law (New York: Basic Books, Inc., 1971), will explain how it is done.
3. Why do China and Russia punish theft of state property more seriously than theft of private property? Would it be efficient to run a system in which the government is the principal economic producer without this distinction?

CHAPTER 8

The economic aspects
of crime

In the preceding chapter, we were concerned mainly with the nature of victim and victimless crime. In this chapter, we develop more thoroughly the economic model of criminal behavior. As we will see, this model leads to conclusions about how criminals should be treated in order to solve those social problems considered to be criminal.

THE COSTS OF CRIME

Costs to the criminal

Crime is an economic as well as a sociological and psychological problem. There are definite benefits (at least to the criminal) and costs associated with criminal activity. Criminals can possibly increase their lifetime income even though at times they may be imprisoned. They can reduce the number of hours worked per week and, perhaps, improve their working conditions.[1] In addition, criminals can, within some socioeconomic groups, raise their status among their peers by commiting crimes and even by serving time.

To obtain these benefits, criminals must incur the costs of developing the right skills (unless they want to run the risks of bungling the job), acquiring the necessary tools such as guns and explosives, and making the contacts that may be necessary to pull off the job.[2] In the narcotics business, criminals must invest in raw

---

[1] Remember that even though you may consider the working conditions of the criminals to be bad, they may still be better than the alternative available to him or her.

[2] As may have been suggested in Chapter 2, there is some optimum amount of risk the criminal may rationally decide to assume. How much education or, for that matter, any other resource input the criminal is willing to buy depends upon the probabilities of being caught, the extent of the punishment, and the degree to which the criminal is risk-averse.

materials, storage facilities, and processing and transportation equipment. Criminals may, like other business people, have to meet a payroll, which may include sales and administrative personnel. In the business of shylocking, the accumulation of financial assets is important. Prostitutes may have to incur the costs of physical abuse and medical treatment.

If criminals are specialists in armed robbery or burglary, they must spend the time required (which implies opportunity cost) to case the site of the crime, to wait for the opportune moment, to pull off the crime itself, to fence the stolen goods, and to stay undercover until things have cooled. If caught, they have the additional costs of legal help (unless a court-appointed lawyer is secured). If convicted, they must forgo the income they could have earned while incarcerated; and because of their records, they can suffer a reduction in earning ability after being released. There may also be, for some, the psychic cost of having done something wrong and the loss of respect within the family and community structure. (Consider the cases of former President Richard Nixon and former Vice President Spiro Agnew.)

The cost to the individual of committing his or her own crimes can be viewed as rising as the general level of criminal activity rises. As the crime rate rises, the public can be reasonably expected (beyond some threshold) to respond by applying more resources to crime prevention making it more difficult (more costly) for the criminal to commit crimes. In addition, one might expect all criminals to commit those crimes first that will yield the largest amount of booty per resource expenditure, meaning the lower cost crimes. This implies that to extend the level of criminal activities, criminals will have to seek out lower cost alternatives or more lucrative opportunities. Like all other production processes, one might also expect criminal activity to be subject to the law of diminishing returns. (Why?)

Costs to the victim

The victim of a robbery or burglary will suffer the loss of the stolen property and, possibly, bodily and mental injury, implying medical bills and loss of income. In the case of rape, the victim may not only be subjected to an extreme amount of violence but also to community gossip; and even though she may be innocent of any wrong-doing, her reputation can be damaged. This may be particularly true if the victim takes the rapist to court. The defense attorney, in an effort to make the strongest possible case for his client, may parade the victim's past (questionable) relationships before the press and community, distorting them wherever possible. The cost of legal fees and time spent in lawyers' offices and the court can be, for her and other victims of other crimes, a substantial portion of the total cost borne by victims. It is because of such cost, no doubt, that many crimes go unreported. In the case of murder, the victims may be, in addition to the one murdered, the family and friends who lose income and friendship.

Costs to society

The total cost of crimes extends far beyond those directly involved in the crime itself. Nonvictims must, in an attempt to avoid being victims, incur the costs of locks, burglary alarm systems, outside lights, and the many other devices used to make crime more costly to prospective criminals. The nonvictim may also have to incur the cost required to avoid high crime areas. In early January 1974, the *Charlotte Observer* took a survey of approximately 300 persons who had moved from Charlotte, North Carolina to surrounding suburbs, and they found that a primary reason for over half of the respondents moving out of the city was to get away from the high incidence of crime.[3] Many of the people who had moved then had to commute longer distances to work.

Crime will also impose higher taxes on victims and nonvictims alike since police protection and judicial, penal, and (to a limited extent) rehabilitation systems are not likely to be avoided. Society may also experience a loss of social interaction. Because of fear of being sexually molested, children are taught not to speak to strangers and, above all, not to get in their cars. Women may avoid speaking to or walking on the same side of a street with men they do not know. Since police officers are given a considerable amount of discretionary power over whom to stop, search, and arrest, crime can impose on the general population a "liberty tax." Finally, people shopping in stores often go out of their way to insure that they do not give the impression that they are shoplifting.

---

[3] *Charlotte Observer,* January 6, 1974, p. 1. Charlotte, deservedly or not, has acquired the reputation among many as being the murder capital of the South.

RATIONALITY AND CRIME

The rational criminal

To the degree that crime involves benefits and costs, crime can be a rational act, and the amount of crime actually committed can be determined in the same manner as is the amount of any other activity. The only difference may be that crime involves behavior that is against the law. The criminal can weigh-off the benefits and costs and can choose that combination that maximizes his own utility, and he will maximize his utility if he commits those crimes for which the additional benefits exceed the additional costs.

Because of the cost of crime, the amount of crimes committed can fall far short of the amount that can, technically speaking, be committed. This would be true even if we ignore or dismiss the costs of being caught and punished. For example, suppose that the benefits of committing a particular crime, such as robbery, for a prospective criminal are illustrated by the downward sloping demand curve in Figure 8–1. (Why is the demand downward sloping?) (In this graph the quantity of crimes is on the horizontal axis and the marginal costs and benefits are on the vertical axis.) Suppose,

FIGURE 8–1

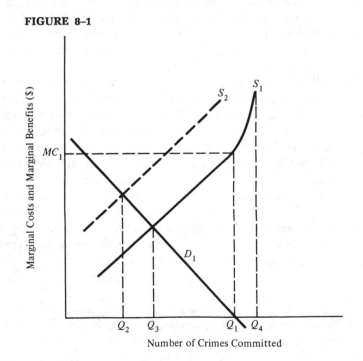

Number of Crimes Committed

also, that we consider only nonpunishment costs such as raw materials, labor, and equipment. Further, assume that the supply curve (or marginal cost curve, S_1) in Figure 8–1 is upward sloping. As indicated by the graph, there are benefits to committing additional crimes until Q_1 have been committed; beyond Q_1, the additional benefits to further criminal activity become negative. However, at Q_1 the cost of committing the Q_1th crime (MC_1) is far greater than the additional benefits, which, at that level of activity, are zero. The criminal, if he is operating at Q_1, can increase his personal satisfaction by reducing the number of crimes committed. If he reduces the number of crimes all the way back to Q_2, the marginal benefits from the Q_2th crime would then exceed the cost, in which event it follows that he could improve his utility by increasing the number of crimes. Needless to say by now, the rational criminal can maximize his utility by committing up to Q_3 crimes, at which point the additional benefits are equal to the additional costs. The analysis can be extended to include the total "market" for crime by adding horizontally the individuals' demands and supplies. The total community crime level would then be established at the intersection of the market demand and market supply curves.

There are three important points that should be given particular attention. The first one is that the number of crimes committed by the rational criminal will not be equal to the maximum, which for our purposes can be defined as Q_1, where the demand curve intersects the horizontal axis, or Q_4, where the supply curve becomes essentially vertical. The second point that needs to be emphasized is that, given the demand for crime, the amount of crimes perpetrated is dependent upon the cost. If punishment is introduced into the analysis and the type of punishment employed represents an increase in cost to the criminal, the supply curve will decrease (that is, move upward and to the left) to, say, S_2. As a result, the number of crimes the criminal will choose to commit will be lowered. One can also suggest that anything that reduces the cost of crime, such as reduction in the cost of handguns or an increase in the leniency of the courts, can increase the supply of crime and, thereby, the number of crimes actually committed. This would also be the case if society became more tolerant of or sympathetic toward criminals. (Why?)

The third point is that although one can observe that a large number of crimes are committed, such as Q_2 in Figure 8–1, one cannot conclude that the severity of punishment has no effect on criminal activity. If the difference between S_1 and S_2 represents the cost imposed on the criminal by the penal system, then one can deduce that the penal system has deterred Q_3-Q_2 crimes. In other words, the effectiveness of a penal system can be judged by how many crimes are committed. However, a more appropriate indication of the effectiveness of punishment, or any other policy that increases the cost of crime to the criminal, is how many crimes are never committed because of that punishment. This, we believe, is a point policemen readily see but one which other concerned individuals often overlook.

If the booty from committing crimes increases while the cost remains constant, one could also predict from our model that the demand for crime would rise to the upper right as in Figure 8–2. The number of crimes committed, we predict, would go up.

FIGURE 8–2

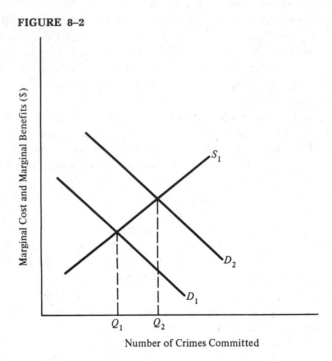

Number of Crimes Committed

The irrational criminal

There is a common notion among lay and professional criminologists and sociologists that certain criminals who commit certain types of crime do not behave rationally. They do not weigh-off the benefits and costs of their actions, and we will treat this controversial issue in greater detail in the next chapter. However, at this point, we want to insure the reader that we concede the point that there are "sick" criminals just as we would concede the issue if anyone ever suggested that there are sick plumbers, businessmen, and professors.[4]

To the extent that they do not measure the consequences of their actions, the demand curves for sick criminals are vertical. However, this does not mean that the demand for the crime in general is not downward. The market demand curve will still be downward sloping so long as there are rational criminals in the market. The existence of the irrational criminal just moves the market demand curve for crime out to the right and does not change the slope. The supply of crimes will also increase since there are more criminals. For example, suppose that there are rational and irrational criminals in the market and the market demand for crime by rational criminals is equal to D_1 in Figure 8–3. If, for purposes of illustration, there are

FIGURE 8–3

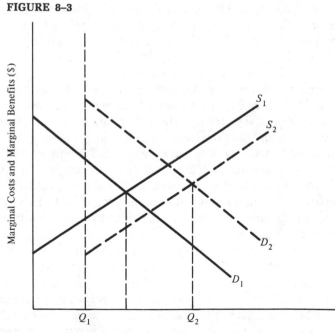

Number of Crimes Committed

[4] We are also willing to concede the point that "sick" criminals may specialize in certain bizarre types of crimes rational criminals do not. As we argue in the next chapters, there is presently little evidence that suggests, however, what these areas may be.

Q_1 crimes committed by irrational criminals, then the total market demand and supply curves would be at D_2 and S_2. The total number of crimes committed would then be Q_2, Q_1 by irrational criminals and Q_2–Q_1 committed by rational criminals.

The reader should recognize that so long as the market demand for crime is downward sloping, the changes in the cost of crime as discussed above should lead to changes in the number of crimes committed *by the rational criminals*. Since the irrational criminals, by definition, do not consider costs in their behavioral decision, one should not expect their level of crime to be affected; therefore, the total market response should be in the same direction as predicted for rational criminals. (The percentage change in the amount of crime would not be as great.)

THE ECONOMICS OF BEING A NONVICTIM

Victims of crimes suffer, and in that sense, people can benefit by actively avoiding crimes. For certain types of crimes, such as aggravated assault, the benefits of crime avoidance can be considerable; for other types, such as having a potted petunia plant stolen from one's backyard, the benefits can be very slight mainly because the value of the stolen property can be very low. In any event, people have a demand for crime avoidance which implies a demand for locks and other devices and means of thwarting crimes. Furthermore, if nonvictims are rational, their demand for crime avoidance is downward sloping as is the case for everything else they value.

As illustrated in Figure 8–4, this means that a person will avoid more crimes the cheaper it is to do so. If the price (which must be imputed from the cost of equipment and time) of avoiding a particular crime is P_1, the number of crimes avoided will be Q_1. More pointedly, people will do only so much to reduce the risk of crimes being committed against them.[5]

This means, of course, that they will "permit" in a sense some crimes to be committed. Granted, if there were no cost involved in crime avoidance, everyone would prefer never being a victim to at times being one. However, if people did everything necessary to avoid ever being a victim, the cost (including time cost) of avoiding certain types or crimes, such as petty larceny or even burglary, can, over the long run, be greater than what they would have lost had

---

[5] Operationally speaking, reducing the risk of being a victim is the same as increasing the number of crimes he avoids.

FIGURE 8–4

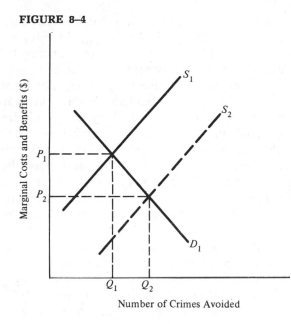

Number of Crimes Avoided

they been less cautious and at times been a victim. To put the problem in a little different perspective, would you expect someone to spend $100,000 to avoid being robbed of $75,000? This is an extreme example, but do people not address similar questions when they consider taking measures to avoid crimes?

Clearly, people do limit the number and quality of locks on their doors; college professors (the authors included) generally have locks on their doors they know can be picked by any reasonably good thief. In fact, one of the authors is inclined to leave his door wide open when he is out on errands or in class. One reason is that any prospective thief will have to pass by a secretary and can be observed by others who may be close by. Another reason is simply that he calculates that there really is not all that much in his office to steal and that, quite honestly, he generally figures the value of his time spent locking, searching for his keys, and unlocking the door can, over the long run, far exceed the value of the property likely to be stolen. You can be assured, however, that when he has an expensive calculator in his office, he closes and locks his door upon leaving. (Is his behavior inconsistent?)

People do not put bars on their windows; the major cost here is likely to be the deterioration of the outward appearance of their homes. People are also willing to walk in some areas at some times well aware that the probability of being mugged is above zero. Admittedly when the probability is quite high, such as may be the case in New York's Central Park at midnight, they may be willing to forgo their walks. However, just because people may not be willing to walk in Central Park, one cannot conclude that they are unwilling to assume any risk or take any chance of becoming a victim. If individuals tried to avoid ever being a victim of crime, we are convinced that they would lead a very dull life! In other words, rational behavior can make the criminal's work a little easier than otherwise.

Given the above discussion and Figure 8–4, it follows that if the cost of avoiding crime falls, the supply of crime avoidance will expand downward and to the right, resulting in an increased number of crimes avoided—that is, a person will buy more locks and/or take more time to avoid being caught in a threatening situation. Again, it should be stressed that given the cost reduction, the rational person will do only so much to avoid crimes.

It also follows that if the benefits from crime avoidance increase, the individual will expend more effort and money in an attempt to avoid crimes. This increase in demand, as illustrated in Figure 8–5, can be the result of an increase in the value of that which could be stolen or perhaps an increase in a person's assessment of the worth of his own physical condition and/or life. A person who may

FIGURE 8–5

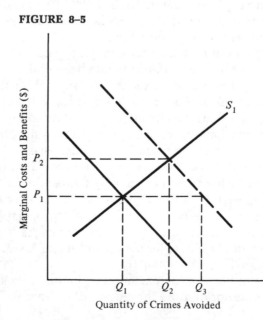

Quantity of Crimes Avoided

be depressed and care very little about living can hardly be expected to divert many resources to avoid being killed. In addition, the increase in demand can result from an increase in the probability of being a victim; in such a circumstance it is reasonable to expect a person to be willing to pay a higher price for crime avoidance. Notice that in all of these cases, the increase in the cost of avoiding crimes curtails the number of crimes that the individual will attempt to avoid. In our graph, if the price of crime avoidance had remained at P_1, the quantity of crimes avoided would have been Q_3; however, because the price of crime avoidance rises to P_2, the number of crimes avoided is Q_2. This quantity is higher than the original number Q_1, but still is not as great as it would have been had the price remained at P_1.

POLICE PROTECTION

The individual citizen, not the police, is society's first line of defense against crime. The citizen may be an amateur, undisciplined and untrained in modern police techniques, but he does have one thing going for him and that is his own private interest in protecting those things that to him are valuable. If it were not for such motivation, we can be assured that the work of the criminal would be greatly eased. Police can contribute to crime control, but one should understand that, in urban areas today, there are only about two police officers for every 1,000 residents.

From this perspective, police protection and law enforcement should be viewed as a supplement to the basic protection people provide for themselves. Generally speaking (but not always), the services of police are provided by local government, and this is done for two basic reasons. First, it may be more efficient to provide the additional protection through some collective organization. As opposed to having every store owner check to insure that his doors are locked after closing hours, the duty can be assigned to a police officer on that beat. A great deal of traveling time can be saved. Such services need not be provided publicly and often are not. Shopping centers, for example, do provide their own security guards; in a sense they are selling police protection along with the floor space.

Second, police protection is not always the type of service that can be bought and sold in the market on a customer-by-customer basis. There are activities for which the police could *conceivably* charge in much the same way as Coca Cola does for its drinks. This might be where the service is specifically intended to benefit one particular individual (or group) and the service can be withheld unless the individual pays the prescribed fee. An example might be a police officer's retrieval of stolen property for a particular individual; if the individual does not pay for the service, the service can be withheld.[6]

On the other hand, the benefits of police activity can be spread quite generally across the community. The presence of the police can provide an additional threat to all criminals operating in the community, and the police can contribute to the removal of criminals from the community by making crime less profitable or putting them behind bars. In such cases, all members of the community benefit (albeit in varying degrees) since the risk of becoming a victim is lowered. In addition, the community can, because of the police presence, reduce their own private actions intended to thwart crime.

If such generalized benefits are provided, then all members of the community must share in those benefits. The police can deny some benefits to some people by denying them some services, as discussed above, but they cannot deny to anyone those benefits that pervade the entire community. Consequently, it may be extremely difficult (if not impossible) for the police to charge for the generalized benefits. If a resident benefits regardless of whether or not he pays, then it is understandable why he may refuse to pay on a voluntary basis. For one thing, he can figure that he can get the protection free if it is provided. Secondly, he may reason that the amount he would be willing to contribute to the "police fund" may be so small in relation to what is needed that any contribution he makes will neither determine whether or not the police protection is provided or significantly influence the amount of protection he receives. Therefore, police protection must be financed by some extra-market means—that is, by taxation.

The members of the community may gladly consent to some additional taxation because they know there are benefits to be reaped from police services; and without the intervention of government, meaning taxation, police protection may not be provided. This can be particularly true in the larger communities where social pressure is impotent. By voting for the additional taxes, not only may the

---

[6] We are merely suggesting here that the police could charge for certain types of services. The reader should not interpret our remarks as advocating such a system. Besides, the administration of such a system might be so expensive that other means of collecting may be more desirable.

individual acquire the very slight benefits from the taxes he himself pays, but he can also benefit from the taxes paid by others.

There are limits, however, to amount of police protection acceptable to a voting public, mainly because, as we have seen elsewhere in this chapter, there are costs involved. As the level of protection is increased, taxes must be raised and people will have to give up other things, such as ice cream and clothes, which they value.[7] As tax rates are raised, we can reasonably assume that there will be more and more people who will find that the benefits received from the additional protection will be less than the additional costs they must incur in the form of taxes. At some point, there will be a sufficient number of votes to defeat any proposal to expand police activities further. The reader should recognize that by restricting the size of the police departments, the voting public is limiting the number of crimes that will be prevented. *They are also allowing, in a sense, some crimes to be committed.* The voting public may not like to have crime in their midst, but at the same time they may not want to see their taxes increased either. We personally see very little chance of the public ever voting to wipe out all crime, even if it were possible.

Having only limited resources with which to prevent and investigate more crimes than they can handle, the police themselves must make certain economic decisions. They must decide whether or not their resources should be applied in residential or business areas or whether they should attempt to prevent or investigate burglaries, murders, or rapes. If they apply their resources in preventing burglaries, then they must allow other crimes, such as speeding violations and murders, to occur or go unsolved. In recent times, the police have been required to enforce price controls that have been mandated by the federal government. Having used their resources in this way, they cannot use them to solve other crimes. This is one aspect of wage-price or other control systems that is not readily appreciated by the public who may favor controls.

TWO HYPOTHESES ON CRIME: THE ECONOMIC VERSUS THE SOCIOLOGICAL VIEWS

The editors of the *Washington Post* are against private ownership of guns and devote part of its editorial content to denouncing it. As

---

[7] You may feel that police protection is much more important than, say, ice cream. However, remember that is your preference; others may not agree with you at all levels of police protection.

part of this campaign, they found a professional robber in Washington and interviewed him quite extensively.[8] Under guarantee of anonymity, he was—as far as we can tell—very frank and explained fairly accurately his motives and *modus operandi*. His special field was armed robbery, and he was apparently making a very good income from it. He was vaguely unhappy about his occupation because he realized it was risky, but as he said, "I want to go to barber school, but I know there's not that kind of money in barbering." In general, he calculated the risks with care: "Now I know if I's gonna rob somethin' it ought to be big, because I'm gonna get the same time. I stay in the District where the police is too busy. . . . It's too risky in Prince Georges." He read the paper daily "for crime. . . . I want to know how much people out there are gittin' and who's gettin' what kind of time."

Thus, this young criminal explains his own behavior largely in terms of calculations of profits and risk of cost. It is notable that the *Washington Post* reporter seemed to pay little attention to this aspect of the matter, although he reported verbatim lengthy statements made by the criminal. The crimes in the article are blamed on the environment. The article begins by pointing out that the criminal came from a poor family background, but it devotes far more attention to the simple fact that guns are readily available in Washington, D.C. than to any other aspect of the environment. Further, there seems to be no evidence that the reporter thought of the ready availability of guns in Washington as merely a reduction in the cost of criminal activity. He regards these environmental factors as direct causes of crime rather than as changes in technological conditions that may conceivably lead profit-seeking individuals to choose a life of crime. We get the impression reading the article— albeit we must read between the lines for this—that the reporter feels that the statements the criminal makes about the risks and profits are evidence of the fact that he has had a bad environment, rather than statements about the cost-benefit calculations that lead him to continue his life of crime.

It is possible we are misrepresenting the reporter's attitude by imputing to him values and positions we find in the *Washington Post* and, indeed, in a very large part of all modern discussions of crime. The conventional wisdom in this field holds that criminals are either sick persons who require treatment or are the result of environmental deprivation (which seems to amount to much the same thing

---

[8] "Dodge City on the Potomac," *Washington Post*, May 11, 1969, p. D-1.

operationally), and that the possibility of punishment—which plays such a large part in this criminal's calculation—actually is unimportant in determining whether a person does or does not commit any crime. It is argued that people commit crimes not because they see an opportunity for profit but because they are somehow socially deformed. Further, it is thought that the way to deal with this problem is to change the basic environment so that no person is deformed by the environment or to rehabilitate the criminal once captured. This is one of two dominant hypotheses in the criminal activity. The other hypothesis, the one that immediately occurs to any economist, is that criminals are simply people who take opportunities for profit by violating the law. Under this hypothesis, changing the costs of crime—that is, increasing the likelihood of being put in prison, lengthening the period of imprisonment, or making prisons less pleasant—would tend to reduce the amount of crime. As discussed in the preceding chapter, the reasoning is simply that the criminals' demand for crime, like their demands for other more normal goods and activities, is downward sloping; the greater the cost or price, the lower the quantity demanded. Rehabilitation for such criminals would be relatively pointless, since the individual is not "sick."[9] He is simply behaving rationally.

People with economic training are apt to take the latter of these two hypotheses as true and those with sociological training, the former. Until recently, in any event, sociologists were inclined to dismiss the economic view of crime:

> This misplaced faith in punishment may rest upon the unrealistic assumption that people consciously decide whether to be criminal —that they consider a criminal career, rationally balance its dangers against its rewards, and arrive at a decision based upon such pleasure-pain calculations. It supposedly follows that if the pain element is increased by severe punishment, people will turn from crime to righteousness. A little reflection reveals the absurdity of this notion.[10]

The problem, however, is basically one for empirical research. Before turning to a discussion of what empirical research has been

---

[9] Our prisons, in point of fact, devote practically no effort to rehabilitation. This is probably wise since those experiments in rehabilitation that have been undertaken seem to show that we do not know how to do it. See Robert Martinson, "What Works?—Questions and Answers About Prison Reform," *The Public Interest* 35 (Spring 1974), pp. 22–54.

[10] P. B. Horton and G. R. Leslie, *The Sociology of Social Problems* (New York: Appleton-Century-Crofts, 1960), p. 155.

done in the field, we should like to clarify the two hypotheses a little bit to explain the difficulties of testing the difference between them. The economic hypothesis holds that crime would tend to occur whenever the cost fell below the receipts. The costs, in a very straightforward and simple way, would be the energy and equipment put into the actual crime—which is usually quite small—plus the expected value of punishment, which in our society is apt to be imprisonment. From the sociological standpoint, these two variables would appear to be largely irrelevant. Indeed, we have never been able to understand how people who believe in the conventional wisdom favor imprisonment at all.[11]

The costs and benefits, however, are to some extent affected by environmental variables in which the sociologists are interested. First, a poor person is probably less injured by being put in jail than the wealthy person. Thus, one would anticipate that the poor would count the cost of imprisonment as being lower than would the wealthy; hence—other things being equal—opportunities for crime that would attract the poor person would appear to be unprofitable from the standpoint of the wealthy person. Second, the size of the booty would be of interest. Large concentrations of wealth would attract potential criminals who would not be interested in small quantities.

These two factors, taken together, would indicate that wide disparity in income might increase crime. A wide disparity of income means that there are some people in the community for whom imprisonment has a low cost and some targets for crime that would pay off very well. Both poverty and disparity of income might increase the crime rate under *either* the sociological or the economic explanation. Lastly, life in the larger city may reduce the cost of crime as opposed to life in a smaller city. The reasons may be that crime targets are located more closely together and that there is a lower degree of social interaction (implying lower social costs). Ethnic groups may be more willing to protect their own, and, in general, it is harder for police to catch criminals in large cities.

It will be observed that we have listed a number of variables—which the sociologist might consider as causes of crime—as factors that affect the cost and benefit and hence, somewhat indirectly, the cause of crime. This might appear to make the test of the two hy-

---

[11] Indeed, some of them have drawn the logical conclusion from their reasoning and *are* opposed to imprisonment. This opinion, however, is more apt to turn up in private conversation than in print. For one example in print, see *The Nation*, September 27, 1971, pp. 258–59.

potheses difficult, and indeed it would, were it not for the fact that there are some remaining variables. If we believe that criminals are sick and are not deterred by threat of punishment, then we would predict that changes in the rate of punishment would have no effect on the crime rate. From the economic viewpoint, we would predict that such changes *would* have an effect on the crime rate. Both the sociologist and the economist would expect the same outcome if statistical tests were made of the first several factors; but when it came to the effect of imprisonment upon the crime rate, there would be a clear difference in the expected result.

It should be noted that, although the significance or nonsignificance of the effect of punishment distinguishes between these two hypotheses, it cannot, strictly speaking, prove the economic hypothesis. A much weaker hypothesis that people respond to costs whether sick or well would lead to the same result as what we have referred to as the economic hypothesis. Indeed, Gary Becker (an economist) and his students have always used this simpler hypothesis quite explicitly. Most of the research we shall discuss below, then, goes to the question of whether or not punishment deters crime but does not directly relate to the rationality or sickness of the criminal. This is, however, enough. If punishment deters crime, then the sociological approach falls to the ground, and much of the advice given to governments by sociologists over the past 50 years is clearly wrong. Indeed, such advice might well be one of the major reasons for the rising crime rate.

Before going on to the question of whether punishment deters crime, it is necessary to make a brief digression on the type of punishment to be used. At the moment, there are only two forms of punishment in general use in the United States, fines and imprisonment. Of these two, fines are clearly superior because of the immense dead-weight loss involved in imprisonment. Not only is output largely lost because very little useful work is performed by prisoners, but the cost of imprisonment, which must be borne by society, is very substantial. Unfortunately, a large percentage of all criminals cannot pay fines large enough so that we would be able to regard them as having the same deterrent effect of, let us say, ten years in prison. Under the circumstances, we are driven back on imprisonment; but we should be more than willing to explore other possible alternatives.

Prevention of crime by such things as better locks, more careful police patrols, and so forth is one way of reducing the crime rate. To some degree, in any event, it is cheaper than the imprisonment threat. Rehabilitation of criminals would be desirable if we only knew how to do it.[12] Going back a little bit in time, there is, of course, the death penalty which will be discussed below; and going back several hundred years, the use of torture and other physical punishments. The latter, of course, are constitutionally prohibited in the United States. Various African and Arab countries, however, are returning to public floggings as a basic deterrent mechanism.

DOES PUNISHMENT DETER CRIME?

Until recently, almost all of the empirical work on whether punishment deters crime was done by sociologists.[13] In practice, however, this work was both scanty and technically rather poor. Further, the small number of tests that had been undertaken mainly dealt with the death penalty. It is not necessarily true that if the death penalty did not deter murder, then imprisoment would not deter burglary.

Testing the deterrent effect of the death penalty on murder is rather difficult because, in the United States where most of the research has been done, death sentences have always been quite rare. Even in the 1930s, murderers had only about one chance in 60 of being executed, whereas their chance of going to prison for a long period of time was 20 to 30 times as great. Under the circumstances, changes in the frequency of the death penalty would tend to be less significant by a wide margin than other variants in punishment policy. There are modern statistical techniques that permit taking a number of factors into account at the same time. The most common is multiple regression. These early studies of the death penalty, however, used simpler and less effective methods of statistical analysis. In part, this is no criticism of the sociologists because many of these studies were performed before large computers were available. It is notable, however, that the studies were not repeated with more modern methods by the sociologists until the economists entered the debate.

---

[12] A very thorough study of published rehabilitation research is summarized in Martinson, "What Works?" It includes a few that seem to show some possible promise for the future. None, however, showed a statistically valid ability to rehabilitate the criminal. During the three years between publication of his article and preparation of this second edition, the situation has remained as Martinson depicted it. Indeed, some of the techniques he thought promising have falsified their promise during that time.

[13] For a survey of the early sociological research, see Hugo Adam Bedau, The Death Penalty in America, rev. ed. (Garden City, N.Y.: Doubleday, 1967).

Even with the most modern methods, however, the results are poor with respect to the death penalty. The problem is simply that the death penalty has always been too rare to provide an adequate number of observations. The first economic study on the subject by Ehrlich showed that each execution prevented somewhere around eight murders.[14] More recently, critics have run a number of additional studies partly using additional data and partly questioning Ehrlich's methods. At the moment, we think an honest statement would be that the matter is in doubt. As economists, we tend to think that the death penalty would indeed reduce the frequency of murder, but that is a theoretical rather than an empirical statement.

However, the problem is an extremely theoretical one. Data in crime are almost incredibly bad, even for murder. Still, we can see little evidence that the sociologists have tried to apply really suitable methods to the problem. These inadequate tests of the deterrent effect of the death penalty were, however, until recently the *only* empirical investigations that had been undertaken on the deterrent effect of punishment. In spite of the fact that this evidence was extremely weak, sociologists and criminologists continued to say that it had been demonstrated that punishment had no deterrent effect.

The widely popular view that criminals are sick is based not on a few poor empirical studies but on zero empirical studies. Some criminals are indeed mentally ill, and they are customarily segregated from the other criminals during the trial process. Thus, most states maintain facilities for the criminally insane as well as for ordinary criminals. There seems to be, however, absolutely no evidence that criminals who are in the ordinary prisons are more likely to be insane than people outside or that what neuroses they do have, have much to do with their crimes.[15] In addition, if investigations deal exclusively with criminals who are in prisons and who are by definition failures at their jobs, one can easily get a distorted picture of the criminal population. We would obtain the same type of distorted picture if we attempted to judge the intelligence and sanity of the business community as a whole by primarily observing those businessmen who go bankrupt.

What, then, have the criminologist and sociologist investigated?

---

[14] Isaac Ehrlich, "The Deterrent Effect of Capital Punishment: A Question of Life and Death," *American Economic Review* 65 (June 1975), pp. 397–417.

[15] One of our ways to investigate this subject has been to ask people if they can refer us to such empirical research. We repeat the question here.

The answer is the environmental background of the criminal. As we have pointed out, people from poor backgrounds are apt to have a lower cost of crime; hence, even under the economic explanation, we would anticipate that they would commit more crimes. Studies of this sort, then, do not differentiate between the two basic hypotheses, and such studies have dominated the work on the determinants of crime by sociologists and criminologists. Indeed, until very recently, those economists who turned their attention to crime simply accepted the dominant opinion of sociology and criminology and repeated the sociologists' studies, albeit with somewhat different methodology.[16] Thus, until really very recently, most "experts" on crime believed that punishment did not deter crime. This belief indicated that we were wrong to put people in prison, although this conclusion was seldom drawn. Further, it was based on an extraordinarily small quantity of very inferior work, which in turn was mostly addressed to one very special case.

Once economists began working on crime, however, it was inevitable that they would begin to investigate the possibility that crimes—like everything else—are affected by price. The deterrence theory of punishment is, after all, simply a special version of the general economic principle that raising the price of something will reduce the amount purchased.[17] The first serious empirical research by an economist to test this proposition was undertaken by Arleen Smigel Leibowitz under the direction of Gary Becker.[18] Presumably the basic research design was his, and it set the standard and style for the bulk of empirical research that we shall discuss.

For certain types of crime, Arleen Leibowitz ran a multiple regression routine in which the crime rate by state was a dependent variable and the punishment was the independent variable(s). She

---

[16] See, for example, Belton M. Fleisher, *The Economics of Delinquency* (Chicago: Quadrangle Books, 1966).

[17] For earlier and more rigorous discussions of the economic approach to crime, see Gary S. Becker, "Crime and Punishment: An Economic Approach," *Journal of Political Economy* 76 (March–April 1968), pp. 169–217; and Gordon Tullock, "The Welfare Costs of Tariffs, Monopolies, and Theft," *Western Economic Journal* 5 (June 1967), pp. 224–32. The latter refers to the deterrent effects of punishment only in passing.

[18] Arleen Smigel Leibowitz, "Does Crime Pay: An Economic Analysis" (A.M. thesis, Columbia University, 1965). In not being published, it is typical of the research in this area. Many of the papers have not been formally published, presumably because journals regard their conclusion as beyond the pale. We have obtained copies of these, mainly in mimeographed form, through the "invisible college." It seems likely that we do not have all of them. We would appreciate being informed of further examples.

found a pronounced deterrent effect. The technical excellence of this study, together with the conflict between it and the conventional wisdom, set off an immense flood of further research. This started slowly, but as time goes by, it has become a true torrent.

Some of this work was done by sociologists, mainly students of Jack Gibbs,[19] but the bulk was done by economists. Further, a number of the individual studies were undertaken by people who felt confident that there must be something wrong with the hypothesis that deterrence prevented crime; hence, they had a very critical attitude. The fact that they ended up with the same results is fairly good evidence that bias does not determine the result in any case.

In the first edition of *The New World of Economics,* we had a fairly lengthy discussion of this empirical research, together with a bibliography.[20] We decided to leave this out here simply because the volume of evidence is now so overwhelming that merely listing it would take up too much space. Further, the rate at which new work of this sort with improved data is being produced would mean anything we published would tend to be obsolete by the time it reached the reader. As a good start, however, the reader may turn to the earlier edition of this book or to the Tullock article cited above.

Basically, the Leibowitz design has now been repeated with many, many different bodies of data and with many, many different specifications of the details of the equation. All of these studies of which we are aware have indicated that punishment does deter crime. The studies have been carried on in the United States, in Canada, in England, and in Germany. International comparison, although a little dubious, seems to show the same results. Students in search of new data have turned to local rather than national figures and have compared counties in various states rather than the states as a whole. On the whole, the data have become overwhelmingly favorable for the deterrence hypothesis. Indeed, the more recent studies normally accepted the deterrence hypothesis and investigated something else, with deterrence appearing in their equations not as the primary hypothesis but as a variable included to reduce what otherwise

---

[19] Jack P. Gibbs, "Crime, Punishment, and Deterrence," *Southwestern Social Science Quarterly* 48 (March 1968), pp. 515–30.

[20] McKenzie and Tullock, *The New Work of Economics,* 1st ed., pp. 153–55. For an earlier, and therefore somewhat shorter, discussion of the empirical evidence, see Gordon Tullock, "Does Punishment Deter Crime?" *The Public Interest* 36 (Summer 1974), pp. 103–11.

might be noise. This continues to test deterrence, even though that is not the major objective of the researcher.

CONCLUDING COMMENTS

Ideas influence the real world. The fact that most specialists in the study of crime have believed, written, and taught that punishment does not deter crime has had an effect upon public policy. Legislatures have been more reluctant to appropriate money for prisons than they otherwise would have been; judges have tended to feel that imprisonment had little effect on crime and, hence, at the intellectual level in any event, were less willing to put people in jail for long periods of time. Further, the shortage of prisons so induced has made it impossible to keep people in jail for long periods of time for serious crimes. As a result, halfway houses (which are very inexpensive), parole, and probation have been resorted to on a very large scale, and this has sharply reduced the cost of crime. This in turn leads to a rise in the crime rate that leads to further clogging of facilities and, hence, further reduction in the cost of crime. The rising crime rate in the United States to a very considerable extent can be blamed upon our intellectual community.

QUESTIONS TO PONDER

1. Jeremy Bentham referred to the English common law as "dog law." He pointed out that dog trainers sometimes simply punish a dog every time it does something they want it to refrain from doing. With time, the dog learns not to do the act that brings the punishment. Do you think this is a fair description of our law? Do you think it is true of other legal codes also? Do you think it is a good or bad thing?

2. Many of the people who allege that punishment does not deter crime seem to make exceptions for violations of the antitrust law and tax evasion. Is this consistent?

3. Good performance in school is usually rewarded with good grades and poor performance penalized with bad grades. Even sociologists, who argue that punishment does not control people's behavior, use this method of grading their students. Is this consistent with their basic position?

CHAPTER 9

Cheating and lying

CHEATING

Cheating is a continual problem in all educational institutions. Exactly how much cheating is likely to go on across a university campus is unclear at this point, but we do have several very interesting studies. Charles Tittle and Alan Rowe, both sociologists, designed a study to determine the influence that moral appeal and threat of sanction had on the amount of cheating that went on in their classes.[1] To do this, they gave weekly quizzes to their students; the instructors took the quizzes, graded them without marking the papers, and then, at the next class meeting, returned them to the students for them to grade. Without any appeal being made to the students that they were on their honor to grade them correctly, the students in one test group took 31 percent of all opportunities to cheat; the other test group took 41 percent of all opportunities. Next the instructors made an appeal to the students' sense of morality in grading the papers, and the instructors concluded that "emphasizing the moral principle involved in grading the quizzes was also ineffectual. A moral appeal had no effect whatsoever in reducing the incidence of cheating."[2] In fact, in one of the test groups, the amount of cheating went up substantially after the appeal was made. Finally the instructors threatened to spot check the quizzes for cheating, and the amount of cheating fell sharply from the 41-percent range to 13 percent in one class and from 43 percent to 32 percent in the other. They also concluded from the study that the instructor who had a reputation of being "lovable and understanding" had the greater amount of cheating in his class, and they found that ". . . Those who were most in need of points were willing to take

---

[1] Charles R. Tittle and Alan R. Rowe, "Fear and the Student Cheater," *Change* (April 1974), pp. 47–48.

[2] Ibid., p. 47.

greater risks (that is, cheated more). This is consistent with the theory that the greater the utility of an act, the greater the potential punishment required to deter it. And perhaps it shows the futility of a moral appeal in a social context where all individuals are not successful."[3]

One of the authors of this book replicated the above study in a somewhat different form and, in this case, for a slightly different purpose. He wanted to see how many students would cheat on a test which the students were told would not be considered in their grades. He gave his classes in Principles of Economics a test on the first day of the term; he had their answer sheets photocopied and the copies graded by a graduate student. During the next class session, his secretary gave back the original answer sheets and called out the correct answers. Later, by comparing the copy and the original answer sheet, it was found that 15 percent of the students cheated, and *this was on something that had no bearing on their grades.* As a point of interest, one student was rather ingenious in the way in which he cheated. In taking the test, he had left the last eight answers blank; when he was given a chance to correct his own, he filled in the answers. Because he apparently did not want it to appear too obvious what he had done, he intentionally missed three of them and marked them wrong like all the others that he had missed! This is no new development. Several decades ago, Hartshorne and May undertook a study of several thousand children in the fourth through eighth grades.[4] Their study, which has not been seriously disputed, is considered a classic within the psychology profession. One of their tests was to give the students a set of examinations in which the students could cheat with ease but the instructor would always know that they had cheated. Approximately 97 percent of the students cheated at least once. The Hartshorne and May conclusion is striking: "No one is honest or dishonest by 'nature.' "[5]

Less dramatically, Nicolaus Tideman invented a statistical method of determining how many times a particular type of cheating occurs. This type of cheating, copying the paper from the person sitting next to you on a multiple choice examination, can be detected by a complicated computer analysis of the examination papers. Tideman's

[3] Ibid., p. 48.
[4] Hugh Hartshorne and Mark May, *Studies in the Nature of Character: Studies in Deceit* (New York: Macmillan Co., 1930).
[5] Ibid., p. 412.

studies showed the number of cheaters in various classes as low as zero or as high as 20 percent. The problem, then, is a common one; but economically we have to ask two other questions. What is the gain and loss from cheating, and who, if anyone, gets hurt?

Consider Pete, a student who is worried about his grade in a given course and thinks it would be possible to cheat. The gain if he does cheat is, of course, the improvement in grade he can expect from cheating times the probability that he will get away with it. This is true regardless of how much he learns in the course. How well he has studied is, of course, relevant to how much his grade will improve. If he will get an A anyway, why cheat?

The cost of cheating is, first, the fact that the cheater's conscience may bother him. If Pete has been ethically indoctrinated with the view that cheating is a bad thing (and it must be remembered that this is not true of everyone), then there is some positive cost to him for violating that ethical rule. For some people, this cost is so high that they would never violate the rule against cheating, no matter what the benefits they could expect. For other people it is so low that they would violate it any time they saw a chance. President Carter's principal press spokesman, Jody Powell, was expelled from the Air Force Academy for cheating. In this case, the expulsion was permanent. Senator Edward Kennedy, it may be remembered, was expelled from Harvard for cheating on a Spanish test and being caught. Presumably at the time he hired a classmate to take the exam for him, he thought the chances of being caught were low; but surely he realized there was some chance and took it into account. (Incidentally, Harvard's decision to readmit him was in no way unusual.)

It is not only people toward the lower socioeconomic classes who cheat. A student contemplating cheating, then, will compare the benefit with the cost. The moral issue is real but not the only one. A very immoral student may decide that the risk is too great, and a student of more than average morality may be tempted by a very good chance under circumstances where the benefit was very great (suppose that a fellowship turns on the grade in that course) and the chance of being caught is very low.

Who is injured by cheating? Most students tend to think of it as a game with the teacher, but the teacher is, in fact, not hurt particularly by a student cheating. It is true that most teachers rather dislike it and tend to feel that they have been made a fool when the students succeed, but it does not really injure them. The people who are injured are the other students. In saying this, however, it should be kept in mind that the injury caused by any one student cheating is spread over a number of other students, so that the injury to any one from a single student cheating is so small as to be almost invisible. Only if a considerable number of students cheat is the injury to any individual student serious.

Suppose a teacher in a class of 100 normally grades on a curve—that is, he gives the top 20 an A, the next 40 a B, the next 30 a C, and the bottom 10 are flunked. One of the students who normally flunks is successful in cheating and therefore gets an A. This means that one of the noncheating students who otherwise would have received an A gets a B, one who otherwise would have gotten a B gets a C, and one of the ones who otherwise would have gotten a C flunks. In this case, the injury is concentrated in three specific people, but it is hard to tell in advance which three they will be. Thus, at the time the student contemplated cheating, the potential injury was spread out because no one knew who would be the lowest A, the lowest B, or C, and so on.

Curve grading of this sort is not, of course, the only way of grading, and many professors use absolute standards. Suppose, for example, that there were 50 questions on the test and the professor intended to give an A to those who got 45 or more correct, B to those who got 37 or more correct, and C to those who got 30 or more correct. The cheater moves himself from 20 correct and a flunking grade to 47 correct and an A. This does not make any other single person flunk, but it does mean that there are more As and fewer Fs than there would be otherwise; hence, in a way this depreciates the value of the As and Bs and makes the pain of flunking somewhat greater than it would be otherwise.

It is an intriguing, indeed paradoxical, characteristic of this reasoning that the cheater injures other people who cheat just as much as those who do not. Let us return to our original example where the teacher is grading on a curve, and suppose that Pete has succeeded in raising his grade by cheating so that he is the 20th student in the series and has an A. Another student now cheats and gets a higher grade, with the result that Pete is moved down to a B. Of course, the students who have not cheated are injured by both of these students cheating, so they are doubly injured; but it is still true that any student who cheats is to some extent injured by other students who cheat.

The discussion of cheating has assumed that students are injured by receiving low grades and benefit by receiving high grades. This is not absolutely certain, and there are people who maintain that the entire grading system is unimportant. Surely the individual who does not care what grade he receives is not injured by having his grade lowered because other people have cheated. However, the student who hopes that his grades will help him get a fellowship for graduate study or a good job is injured by cheating. Note that he is also injured if the cheating simply increases the number of As rather than moving anybody down in grade, because this means that As are regarded as less valuable by future employers or future graduate schools.

Looked at from the standpoint of society as a whole, cheating reduces the information content of grades. If there is a good deal of cheating, then the grading system does not give very much information as to the quality of students; hence, it is harder to make decisions as to whom to hire, to whom to give graduate fellowships, and so forth. The size of this cost depends on how good the grades are as a predictor of later success, and, unfortunately, we do not have very much data on that issue. Nevertheless, there must be at least some cost.

Rather ironically, we have come to the conclusion that the students should be strongly in favor of rules against cheating, at least insofar as these rules are enforced against other people, and teachers should feel less concern. An unscrupulous student should favor a rule that prevents other people from cheating while permitting him to do so. Unfortunately, rules of this sort are not in the cards. In general, we have to choose between institutions that make cheating difficult for everyone or institutions that make cheating easy for everyone. For most students, the former set of institutions will have a net payoff because the gains they may make from cheating, even ignoring the possible conscience problems of cheating, will be less than the loss they will suffer from other people cheating. From the standpoint of teachers, there is little cost either way. It is the students who should be opposed to cheating.

LYING

Let us leave cheating, which is after all a special form of dishonesty, and turn to the more general problem of lying and, a little later, to the law of frauds. Beginning with simple lying, an individual who is thinking of telling a lie once again has the problem of conscience. One of the costs he must face if he is to tell a lie is the moral cost. As we have said before, for some people this is a very large cost and for some people it is a very small cost. In addition to that cost, there is the possibility that he will be caught telling a lie, and this must be multiplied by whatever injury he will suffer from being caught. Since we are talking about simple lying and not about fraud at the moment, this injury will be a loss to his reputation. If you are once caught telling a lie, people are likely to think you will tell lies in the future; hence, you may have difficulty getting them to accept your word, even when you are telling the truth.

For example, a sales representative who sells gadgets door-to-door has little need to be concerned with this type of cost. It is unlikely that he or she will return to the same home again. If the buyers find out that the gadget is not what it was said to be, there will be little cost inflicted on the sales representative. On the other hand, someone who sells to the same people again and again, particularly if it is valuable enough so that they will give careful thought to transactions, can lose immensely from lying. For example, take the vice president of a large steel company who has the duty of acting as principal sales representative to General Motors, Ford, and Chrysler. The cost to him of losing the confidence of his customers is so great that he would be a fool to lie to them.

This is particularly so since they will be experts and likely to catch him if he does lie. In any event, they will have an opportunity to make a very thorough test of his product if they buy it. In the real world, arrangements of this sort are so honest that the sales representative will rarely make an effort to sell a product if a competitor has one that is clearly more suitable to the purchasers' needs. Store clerks are trained to suggest a more expensive brand. Our vice president may frequently suggest a cheaper grade of steel where it would be adequate. Certainly he is very unlikely to make a misstatement on this subject.

Most cases of purchase and sale are intermediate between these two. The manufacturer of canned goods had better have a satisfactory product if he wants to stay in business; but exact truth on the label is not all that important because the purchaser probably does not read it.

These are the nonlegal costs of telling a lie. We have ignored the costs of possible legal penalties because we want to put off the question of punishment for fraud until after we have dealt with the problem of simple lying. The benefits from lying are a little more complicated. Presumably the reasons for telling a lie are that you want to influence someone to do something they would not do if you told them the truth. The door-to-door sales representative, for example, if he or she accurately described the product, might sell very few of them. On the other hand, by a suitably colorful sales pitch, he or she may make quite a nice living. The benefit from the lie, then, is the profit (whatever it is) from influencing the victim's behavior. For example, suppose that if the sales representative correctly describes the object, he or she has a one in ten chance of selling it. Assume a suitable lie increases the chances to 50–50. Assume further that the commission on the sale is $5. If the sales representative lies, he or she moves from a one in ten chance of making $5, which is worth $0.50, to a 50–50 chance, worth $2.50, and the payoff on the lie is then $2.

But this is the gross benefit. Obviously you have to subtract from it the possible cost of the lie. Ignoring possible legal penalties, this cost, as we said above, is the reduction in credibility. For the door-to-door sales representative, this may have substantially zero value; hence he or she can say that a $2 profit was made by telling a lie. For our vice president in charge of sales for a major steel company, on the other hand, the payoff to him from completing a sale by telling a lie might be $100,000 or so, but the cost to him of being detected in a lie might be $2 or $3 million in reduction of lifetime earnings.

The fact that people may tell lies, of course, has an effect on the behavior not only of potential liars but of the people who will hear the lie. Most housewives are properly skeptical of door-to-door salesmen selling complicated devices. On the other hand, most purchasing agents who deal in large sums of money are so convinced of the honesty of the sales vice presidents with whom they talk that they may actually use them as sources of technical information.

All of this, of course, depends on the fact that the people to whom a potential liar might make a dishonest statement try to estimate his truthfulness. The individual who hears a statement by someone else will put resources into determining whether or not it is true. In some cases, he may have great respect for the person making the statement or he may realize that the person making the statement has no particular motive to tell a lie. Hence, he would put high credence on the statement and not do a great deal of individual investigation. This is, of course, the reason that having a reputation for truth as opposed to a reputation for lying is valuable to people in business or, indeed, in any walk of life.

Consider, then, the situation that confronts Mike, a salesman, dealing with a potential customer. If Mike is known to be honest, the customer will invest fewer resources in checking his statements. In consequence, the cost of the sale will be lower. This honesty on Mike's part generates a net and perfectly genuine social gain for the joint society of the two of them: part of this value goes to Mike and part to the customer. Thus, social institutions that improve the reliability of information can have a positive payoff. Note that this argument has nothing to do with morals, although it is in accord with the received moral code. There are simply economies to be gained if all statements made are truthful. These economies partly have the effect of reduction in resources invested in checking the accuracy of statements and partly in the reduction of errors made because false statements are believed. No matter how many resources we invest in checking the truth or falsity of someone else's statements, we will be fooled occasionally if he or she tells enough lies. There is a further saving in the reduction in the sales effort of the salesman.

One way of investing resources in preventing lying is simply refusing to believe the word of someone whom you have caught lying in the past. This superficially appears to be costless but it is not because it means that you disregard many statements that are true. Hence, there is the cost of obtaining the same information from someone else or remaining ignorant. The problem is almost a game. The more skeptical we are of things you say, the more resources you will have to invest to convince us and the more resources we will invest in checking what you have to say. Further, the chance exists that we will disbelieve you when you are telling the truth. Under the circumstances, there is a net social loss from our belief that you may be lying.

There is, of course, an optimal amount of resources for us to invest in checking your statements, given that we have some idea of how likely it is that you are lying. Knowing the resources we will invest in checking your statements, there is an appropriate amount of resources you should invest in "improving" your lie. For example, you may generate false data, misinterpret true data, improve the attractiveness of your statements by various means, and generally respond to our skepticism by resource investment. This resource investment, of course, should lead to more resource investment by us in detecting possible lies. It is not sensible, however, for the potential victim of the lie to invest an infinite amount of resources into reducing the likelihood that he will believe an untrue statement. In this case, the cost of further information should be offset against the benefit from the reduction in the likelihood that we will be fooled. Similarly, the potential liar should not invest an infinite amount of resources in making his lie believable because, here again, the potential resources do cost something and should only be put in if the potential gain is greater than the cost.

FRAUD

Under these circumstances, with a net social gain by reducing the number of lies or, put differently, by increasing the reliability of the statements, we should search for social institutions that will make lying less common. There is one such social institution that is very widely used: laws against fraud. Although there are laws against fraud, in most cases not all untruthful statements are covered. Let us consider briefly an optimal law against fraud and why we might permit people to tell lies under some circumstances (in the sense that we may be unwilling to do anything about it).

The problem, of course, is that there are costs to enforcing any law. The first and obvious cost is the necessity of providing police, courts, and prisons. These have been discussed earlier in the discussion of crime and tax evasion. These costs in the laws against fraud do not differ particularly from those in other laws, but there is a special cost in the case of fraud. The probability that the court will go wrong is exceptionally high in cases of fraud. Suppose that we have bought something from you, and, for various reasons, it is unsatisfactory. If we simply say that you lied to us when selling it and bring a fraud accusation against you, the possibility exists (and the probability is not close to zero) that the court will go wrong—it must, after all, determine which of two people is telling the lie, and human beings are not terribly good at doing that. Thus, the prospect of many erroneous decisions in fraud cases is a very significant cost. Most court systems thus attempt to restrict the number of fraud cases that can be brought. In general, they try to get evidence other than the oral statements of the two parties for fraud prosecutions, and they restrict them to cases where something of substance is at issue. It is not obvious that real-world institutions in this regard are ideal, but they are at least sensible.

A very important situation in which lying occurs in most governments—democracies or dictatorships—is politics. The average man has a very low opinion of the honesty of politicians, and this opinion is completely justified. The basic problem is that the voter has very little motive to check up on the statements of the politician; hence, politicians can get away with a good deal of dishonesty. The reason why the voter has little to gain by checking up on the honesty of a politician comes essentially from the fact that the individual voter has very little effect on the outcome of an election. If we devote a good deal of resources to determining that one of the two candidates is lying and vote against him, in the presidential elections this has less than a 1-in-10-millionth chance of having any effect on the outcome. Under the circumstances, we are not even likely to remember very accurately what the politician has promised.

There are complicating factors which make lying in politics even more likely. Most democracies, and the United States government in particular, have governmental structures that disperse power. The arguments for seeing to it that no individual has too much power are very strong, but it does have the characteristic that it is very hard to tell whether a politician has broken his promise. A man running for Congress who promises to do his best to get Blacksburg, Virginia (which is in the Appalachian Mountains) converted into a deepwater port by a massive and expensive government dredging program may in fact do his best, but Blacksburg may never become a port because he is only one congressman. Thus, we cannot tell whether he kept his promise or did not. Further, it is certain that conditions will change between the time the man is elected to office and the time he has an opportunity to act on one of his promises. Whether the change is such that the voters would agree that he should not carry out his promise is, once again, a matter for dispute.

There is one area in which politicians are well advised to keep their promises, but unfortunately this is no great benefit for the functioning of our democratic system. If members of Congress make a promise concerning some matter of great moment to a few constituents, then it is likely that the constituents will be very well informed on whether or not their representatives make a real effort. Since the matter is of great interest to them, they will try to be informed on what the representatives did for them in Washington. In general, they are apt to punish or reward them in the future in terms of whether or not they carry out their promises. Thus, this is the kind of promise politicians try to keep. Unfortunately, this type of special-interest activity does not make the political system function well, and, indeed, politicians may be simultaneously making public statements against some program and privately telling a small group of people that they will back it. In many cases, this is the optimal course of action for a suitably unscrupulous person. (Do we not observe this kind of special-interest legislation?)

Under the circumstances, it is unlikely that people attracted into politics are those who have very strong moral objections to lying. In many cases, of course, they do not consciously think of themselves as lying; they just are not very careful in examining their own motives. It is very easy to convince oneself that whatever is good for oneself is good for the country. Politicians probably do this a great deal and, hence, do not consciously feel that they have done anything immoral.

Political lies are one area in which we have great difficulty making use of the government to control lying. The government, by definition, is in control of politicians, and the politicians are more likely to make use of the political process to injure their opponents than to seek absolute truth. In consequence, most democratic societies have very little in the way of controls on lying by politicians. Politicians, of course, take advantage of this. Granted the possibilities for the government in power to use any legal process that punishes telling political lies as a means of punishing political opponents, we can see why laws against political lying are rare. Unfortunately, this means that the politicians are even freer in telling lies than they would be if we changed the institutions.

In the United States at the moment, this is rather compensated for by the fact that it is fairly safe to tell lies about politicians too. The laws of libel and slander have been adjusted by the Supreme Court recently so that it is almost impossible for politicians to sue a person who has maligned them. There are special circumstances in which such a suit is possible, but they are extremely narrow, and most statements anyone might choose to make, either in print, on TV, or simply in conversation, are perfectly safe no matter how untrue they are. Unfortunately, although this may even things up with respect to the politicians, it does not mean that public communication on political matters is particularly honest.

This chapter was originally written right in the middle of the Watergate scandal. It was clear that the newspapers had uncovered a good deal of dishonesty on the part of a whole pile of politicians. But a careful reading of the *Washington Post*, the newspaper with which we have the most contact, indicated that it was not entirely honest itself. To take an example for which the *Washington Post* later half-heartedly apologized, they ran a column on Patrick Buchanan, the president's aide (complete with a picture of him), in which a large number of documents were cited as evidence of his personal unscrupulousness. As a matter of fact, he had had nothing to do with any of them. But this is only an extreme example, and, indeed, the *Washington Post* is to be commended for permitting him to publish a letter attacking their handling of this matter and for making a sort of weak apology for the matter. This is, on the whole, above the normal standards with which newspapers handle politics.

CONCLUDING COMMENT

In sum, then, lying and cheating, like most other human behavior, have positive payoffs, and they have costs. They also have moral implications, and for many people, these moral implications are more important than the economic calculation. Unfortunately, there are also many people for whom the economic calculation is the controlling one. Any set of social institutions for controlling lying or cheating should be based upon firm recognition of that fact.

QUESTIONS TO PONDER

1. Would you expect small children to cheat more or less than college students? Why?
2. Generally speaking, colleges can be divided into two categories, one using the honor system and another in which there is supervision to make cheating at least hard. In some cases, the honor system fails, and there is a great deal of cheating; but in other cases, it has been successful. How would you account for this?
3. How do you account for the fact that students usually object to procedures that will make cheating harder?

PART 4

POLITICS, BUREAUCRACY, AND GROUPS

Presidential elections

In recent years economists have used their tools to investigate political problems. Political scientists, in fact, have begun learning economic tools to apply them in their own discipline. As a result of this movement, there is now a large and very complicated literature in which economics is applied to political problems. As a sort of sampling of this literature, in this chapter we will develop a very simple economic model of a presidential election and then use this model to analyze the elections of 1960 to 1980. The model is very simplified and presents only a partial picture of elections. Still, it does cast a little light on the 1976 election and a good deal on earlier elections. We think it will both give you an idea of the new type of political reasoning and improve your understanding of the elections, even if it is not a complete picture.

A SIMPLE MODEL

Our simple model, Figure 10–1A, shows all possible political positions on some issue or some group of issues. Although it will get more complicated later, for the moment you can think of it as being a rather typical liberal–conservative continuum. Any individual voter has some point on this spectrum that corresponds to his or her own personal preferences. Suppose, for example, it is point B. In moving away from point B, the voter feels less and less satisfied. For example, point C is preferred to point D. The bell-shaped distribution line shows the arrangement of voters between conservative and liberal positions. There are more in the middle than at the ends. For our reasoning, the bell-shaped distribution is not necessary, although in our opinion it is realistic. To make this clear, in Figure 10–1B we have drawn in another distribution of voters with some skew and then labeled it in the same way as Figure 10–1A. The student can follow our line of reasoning on either of these two figures or draw in another.

FIGURE 10–1A

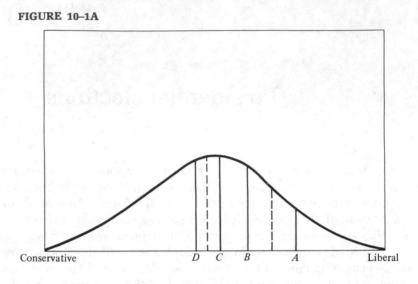

Conservative   D   C   B   A   Liberal

For a contest between two parties, a simple diagram of this sort is frequently sufficient. For the 1968 election where there were three parties, we will have to use something else, and as a matter of fact, we will find it desirable to use a more complicated diagram for the 1964 election also. Nevertheless, this very simple diagram is suitable for an astonishing number of political problems in a two-party system.

FIGURE 10–1B

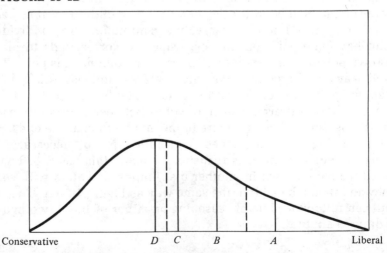

Conservative   D   C   B   A   Liberal

If one of the candidates for president chooses position A and the other chooses position B, then all of the voters to the right of A will prefer point A and all those to the left of B will prefer point B. The voters between will divide roughly in accordance with the dotted line, and B will win very easily.

In a two-party system, the intelligent politician attempts to find the middle of the distribution. If he or she chooses the exact middle, then the other party leader has the choice of choosing exactly the same location (which is not a very good policy) or choosing one a little away from the middle and, hence, will be thought to be inferior by slightly more than half of the voters—that is, he or she is certain to be beaten.

In practice it is rather hard to choose the *exact* middle of the distribution because politicians do not have perfect information, and in a way, electoral contests in a two-party system as contests to get as close to the middle as possible. Of course, there are other matters and issues involved in elections—personality, incumbency (which seems to be a big advantage in most elections, but probably not in 1976), past record, and so forth; but the positions the party takes should be close to the middle. Assume, then, that the first politician takes position C, which turns out not to be quite in the middle. The other politician obtains a little more information on popular preferences from the reaction to the position of the first candidate. This second politician realizes which direction from the middle the first position is and takes a position at D, a little to the left of C (in this particular case because C was a little to the right of the middle), which is just far enough away so that the voters can tell the two candidates apart. Under the circumstances, if the two candidates have done their jobs with a high degree of skill, they will divide the vote evenly among them. In practice, of course, they are never quite that accurate; hence, one party or the other will have an advantage.

THE 1960 ELECTION

The 1960 election is an example. It is indeed so much of an example that it is not all obvious who actually got the most votes. Not only is there the question of whether or not the Illinois and Texas voters actually cast the majority of their votes for John F. Kennedy,[1]

---

[1] In both cases, there was a rather dishonest Democratic machine that might well have generated enough false votes to provide for the margin in the official figures.

but the situation in Alabama was so confused that it is not clear who some 250,000 voters voted for. If they voted for Kennedy, then he had a majority of the popular vote. If it is assumed that they or, let us say, half of them voted instead for Senator Harry Byrd (who received six electoral votes from Alabama), then Richard Nixon had a majority of the popular vote. In any event, it was a very close election, much closer than normal.

In this simple model we see an explanation of one of the outstanding characteristics of two-party democracy as we are familiar with it in the United States. The two parties tend to be very close together and near the middle of the political spectrum. It is often said that this does not give the voters a real choice. To take an early and probably not now popular example, one of the first books urging Sen. Barry Goldwater's candicacy called for "a choice, not an echo." More recently, George Wallace in 1968 said, "there isn't a dime's worth of difference" between Nixon and Humphrey. The 1976 election also presented the voters with two candidates whose positions were very nearly indistinguishable. This is the normal rule, and the 1964 and 1972 elections, which will be dealt with later, must be regarded as most unusual in a two-party system. Historically, two parties with very nearly indistinguishable programs, located very near the "middle of the road," are the norm.

It is not clear, however, that this is something we should criticize. The voters have no choice because both parties are trying vigorously to please them. A position in the middle of the distribution, as these two are, minimizes the total loss individual voters receive from not getting their first preference. This, of course, involves comparison of different people's preferences, which economists are not supposed to do, but the numbers are very large and there is no strong reason to believe that intensities are more severe on one side of the middle than on the other. Hence, a simple mechanical process of computing the loss an individual suffers from not having his ideal political position win by taking the distance between his position and the position that does win seems not unreasonable. With this calculation, the total loss is minimized by central position.[2]

Politicians are not always perfect in their decisions; they may

---

[2] Another way of putting it would be that the total gain is maximized. There is an unfortunate tradition, that one of the authors of this book had much to do with starting, under which political activities are largely talked of as ways of reducing losses rather than obtaining gains. This is merely a matter of semantics, but it does give a sort of negative sound to all economic discussions of political matters.

take a position far from the center, either through mistake or because they are driven by an ideological commitment to some other position. For example, suppose that one of the candidates takes position A. This, by definition, almost guarantees defeat unless the opponent makes an equally large error by taking a position just as far or farther from the center in the other direction. Under these circumstances, however, it is probably not wise for A's opponent to get as close to A as possible. If one candidate has chosen a highly eccentric position, then it is sensible for the opponent to try to emphasize the difference between the two, which means that he or she must take a position farther from the opponent's position than he or she would have had the first politician taken position C. Thus, one would anticipate that if one of the candidates takes a position well away from the center, like A, the other party will take a position on the same side of the center as position A but nevertheless well away from it as is shown by line B in our diagram.

In essence, this is what happened in the 1972 election, although full discussion of that election will be deferred until later. Sen. George McGovern took a position very far from the middle of American politics, and Nixon, insofar as he took any position at all (he did no campaigning), adopted a position clearly distinctive from McGovern's but nevertheless rather in the McGovern direction. Nixon had already stolen much of the political Left's clothing by introducing price control, visiting Peking, and encouraging détente with Russia. These moves had, of course, been made before McGovern was nominated, but they were parts of the Left's political program.

The need to distinguish one's position from that of the other candidate (which means that it may not be very close to the other candidate's if an eccentric position has been taken) can also occur in one other situation. George Wallace in 1968 was attempting to start a completely new party. Under the circumstances, he could not depend upon any of the existing political capital upon which the two major party candidates could draw. He quite wisely chose a position that was markedly different from that of the main candidates to attract voters by a differentiated product. Once again, full discussion of this must be postponed until later.

A MORE COMPLICATED MODEL

To discuss the 1964 and 1968 campaigns (and, indeed, to demonstrate why the 1972 campaign was different), it is necessary to complicate our model a bit. Politics is not actually fought along a single dimension but in a many-dimensional issue space. There are many different matters that are considered by politicians and by voters, and for each of these we should really have a separate dimension. This would involve the use of many-dimensional Cartesian algebra and would produce great complications. Fortunately, the single one-dimensional continuum we have been using is suitable for most problems involving two-party politics. When there are three parties, as in 1968, it is necessary to use two dimensions, and, for some rather complicated problems in connection with two-party systems, two dimensions are also necessary.

Figure 10–2 shows a two-dimensional model in which parties may differ not on one general issue but two. We have labeled these simply issue 1 and issue 2 because we want to use the same diagram to discuss a number of elections, the earliest of which occurred in 1896 and the last of which occurred in 1972. During this period, the issues under discussion changed radically. However, in all of these cases, we can analyze the situation with the use of two dimensions even though what is meant by the dimension differs from election to election.

Each voter is assumed to have some point in this issue space that

FIGURE 10–2

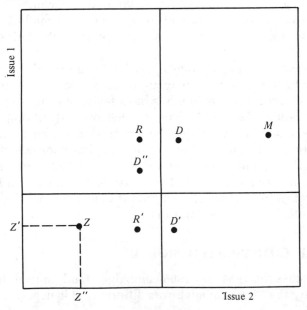

is his or her optimum. This means simply that he or she has some ideal policy on issue 1 and some ideal policy on issue 2. Suppose, for example, it is point Z in the diagram. This means that Z' is optimum on issue 1 and Z'' is optimum on issue 2. He or she then becomes less and less satisfied as the political outcome moves away from the optimum, and, for simplicity, we assume that this lack of satisfaction is equal in all directions—that is, moving an inch away in any direction makes him or her just as unhappy as in any other direction.

Once again, the voter's optima would be distributed across the issue space in some general form, probably a normal distribution. For simplicity, we are going to assume that there is a normal distribution with its peak near the middle. This assumption is not, of course, necessary. It is possible to duplicate the same line of reasoning using different distributions, but this is rather complicated. Therefore, we will not provide a second diagram for your enlightenment but merely suggest that if you are curious about this problem, you may turn to Chapter 4 of *Toward a Mathematics of Politics*.[3]

In this kind of issue space, there is a very simple rule for determining the division of the voters among the parties. A line halfway between the position of any two parties and vertical to a line connecting the two positions will divide the voters between them. If there are three or more parties, these lines will meet as on Figure 10–3, and the space is thus divided into more than two areas.

If there are only two parties, we normally expect them to be near the middle. Point R and point D, for example, will divide the voters between them according to the vertical line: all lines to the left of the vertical line are closer to R, and all points to the right are closer to D. They divide the voters approximately between them, and neither can gain by moving away from the center to some point such as M. Indeed, if the party now located at D moved to M, one could predict electoral disaster.

Two parties are once again likely to be found near the middle of this two-dimensional issue space for much the same reasons as they were likely to end up near the middle of the one-dimensional issue space in Figures 10–1A and 10–1B. But with more than one dimension, and of course in the real world there usually is more than one dimension, it is possible for the two parties jointly to make a mistake. Over a series of elections, they can drift off the center down the line dividing them. Thus, if the parties gradually slip from posi-

[3] Gordon Tullock, *Toward a Mathematics of Politics* (Ann Arbor: University of Michigan Press, 1967).

FIGURE 10–3

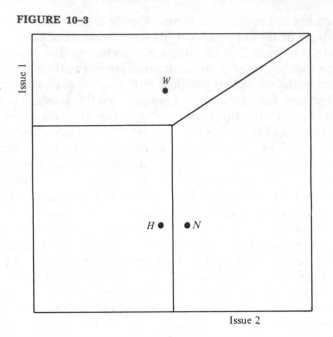

tions R and D to positions R' and D', they will continue dividing the voters about evenly between them, and the managers of the two parties might not realize that they are away from the center. This provides an opening for a political entrepreneur to enter and reorganize politics. There have been two such cases in recent history, William Jennings Bryan and Barry Goldwater. In each case, they came at a point in time where their party had been maneuvered into a position where it actually had somewhat less than a majority of the vote and its long-run prospects were not very good unless something drastic could have been done.

THE 1896 AND 1964 ELECTIONS

Assume that we are considering William Jennings Bryan. The two parties are now (1896) at R' and D' in Figure 10–2, and he restructured politics by moving to D''. This involved deliberately abandoning a number of traditional Democratic voters. Although Bryan himself failed to win, there is no doubt that he set the general outlines of American politics for the next 50 years. The reasons he failed to win the election are probably the extreme inertia built into the system plus the fact that it would appear that he had miscalculated. Although the Republican and Democratic parties had drifted away from the center in the last few years prior to the 1896 election, they had not drifted far enough so that this maneuver gave the Democrats a clear advantage. Indeed, from Bryan's time until the election of Franklin D. Roosevelt, only one Democratic president (Woodrow Wilson) was elected, and that was the result of a split in the Republican party.

Barry Goldwater is a more recent example. He and his backers felt that there was a good possibility of removing the "solid South" permanently from the Democratic side by a similar restructuring. The fact that John Kennedy was assassinated with the result that they found themselves running against a southerner scuppered any possibility of the tactic winning in 1964; like Bryan's attack, it probably would not have won anyway. Nevertheless, the experience in the 1968 and 1972 elections indicates that the two parties had drifted far enough away from the center that Goldwater had a better chance than Bryan. The bloc of voters was huge, of course. The southern whites, whom Goldwater proposed to move from the Democratic to the Republican column, make up 20 percent of the total population of the United States. Today a majority of them are voting Republican, although almost all voted Democratic from the Civil War until very recently.

The combination of Watergate and the Carter candidacy may once again shift the southern vote permanently into the Democrats' column. Carter, a Southerner who attracted a great many of the traditional "red-neck" votes—party because he was a Democrat and "grandpappy had voted Democratic" and partly because of his accent—was able to retain the black votes which are generally solidly Democrat. The combination permitted him to sweep the South, albeit his majority there was much smaller than the Democratic majorities in the "solid South" before 1960. He shows every sign of wishing to keep this unlikely alliance of the southern red-neck and black alive, and he may be able to do so. The Republicans, of course, who already have a majority of white votes in the South, are making efforts to increase that majority to the point where they dominate elections.

In the case of both Bryan and Goldwater, it was necessary for the candidate seeking to restructure politics to move fairly far away from his opponent. This was necessary simply because the information problem was difficult. In 1896 there was little or nothing in the way of traditional attachment to the Democratic party in the upper left-hand square shown in Figure 10–2. The only way of attracting people from that area into the party was to take a very firmly differentiated policy from the Republican policy. Bryan, of course, did so, but it turned out that he was not able to succeed. The same is true with Goldwater; indeed, the Goldwater defeat was much more severe than Bryan's.

THE 1972 ELECTION

This type of thing must be clearly distinguished from Sen. George McGovern's campaign. The McGovern campaign took the form of abandoning a number of traditional Democratic voters but not appealing to any significant bloc of traditional Republican voters. In essence, it was a move away from the center, which made no serious effort to restructure the nature of politics, although the managers of the campaign referred a good deal to the new politics. They moved to M in Figure 10–2.

The explanation for this phenomenon can be seen in a statement made by McGovern early in his campaign. He said that getting nominated was much harder for him than getting elected. We believe this was indeed true. If he had taken a more central position, he would have been unable to attract the support within the Democratic party (in particular, within the left half of the Democratic party) which put him over the top in Miami. He may have thought that the policy he backed was highly desirable for ideological reasons or, indeed, that in fact it would appeal to the majority of the population; but it seems more likely that he intended after being nominated to play the campaign by ear. He could, after all, hope that the Republicans would make a series of ghastly errors. Indeed, it should not be forgotten that the newspapers gave more attention to Watergate than any other single issue during that campaign.

McGovern's ability to take advantage of this, of course, was reduced by his own vice-presidential problems. But in fact, his loss of the election was largely predetermined by the method he chose to get the nomination. It does not follow from this that he was politically inept. Granting that he was correct, that getting the nomination was harder than winning the election, then the course of action he followed was the only one open to him. If he had taken a more central position in the nominating campaign, he would have had the traditional snowball's chance in hell of being nominated. Once nominated, he surely would have had a better chance of becoming president than he would have had he been eliminated in the first round of voting in Miami.

THE 1968 ELECTION

We now turn to the 1968 election, which is both the most complicated and, in many ways, the most interesting because there were three candidates. Two of the candidates, Nixon and Humphrey, were almost pluperfect examples of the *genus Politician*. As we would expect, they took political positions that were very hard to tell apart. The third candidate, however, was a most extraordinary politician. Before a formal analysis of the election, it is sensible to make a few remarks about Gov. George Wallace. There is no effort here to indicate his complete character or political position, but certain statements about him are necessary to apply the model we have developed so far from the 1968 election.

First, Wallace was clearly one of the best political tacticians who has ever lived. In addition, interestingly enough, he was also one of the worst political strategists who has ever lived. His short-range decisions were politically brilliant. His long-range decisions were usually terrible. Indeed, he frequently made decisions that had major long-run effects in terms of very minor short-run considerations, with the result that he had long-run difficulties. He also seemed to be unable to organize anything on the order of an efficient central campaign organization. On occasion, his campaigning was carried on brilliantly but mainly by a series of local decisions.

No doubt his major single achievement was getting on the ballot in substantially the entire United States in 1968. No other third party had ever succeeded in doing this in such a short period of time, and it should be noted that his own party by 1972 was unable to stay on the ballot in more than about two thirds of the states. The two major political parties, Republicans and Democrats, have formed what amounts to an implicit cartel to reduce competition from third parties, and on the whole, it is very effective. Nevertheless, Wallace carried out the almost impossible achievement of beating the electoral restrictions in 1968.

Wallace was a poor political strategist and was generally rather badly organized. His approach to politics has been a series of short-run improvisations. The fact that he was as successful as he was turned partly on his brilliance in the short run and his appeal as a speaker to a significant part of the American population and partly to the fact that the two major American parties had gradually drifted into a position where there was a significant minority—a minority to which Wallace appealed—who were quite dissatisfied with the political system.

This minority, the Wallace group, probably amounts to between 20 and 30 percent of the population. These numbers come from the public opinion polls in the early part of the 1968 campaign and Wallace's astonishing performance in the 1972 Democratic primaries. It would appear, however, that his backing, though substantial, was pretty much limited to that group. In other words, he was a candidate who could have had a great effect on who won the presidency, but he was very unlikely to make it himself. Even if he had gotten the Democratic nomination in 1968, 1972, or 1976, it seems very dubious that he could have come even as close to winning as McGovern or Goldwater did.

Another aspect of Wallace's support is that it was almost entirely drawn from traditional Democratic voters. It consisted essentially of Southern whites and blue-collar workers. Both are groups who have formed in the past part of the Democratic coalition. Indeed, it may well be that his backers were an actual majority of the people who normally vote Democratic, although we would estimate that this is not so. In any event, in 1968 a majority of his backers had the Democratic candidate as their second choice rather than the Republican candidate, probably not so much because their position was closer to Humphrey than Nixon on the issues (indeed, Wallace's statement that there was not a dime's worth of difference between the two was only a modest exaggeration), but because they were accustomed to voting Democratic and had a good deal of emotional involvement with the Democratic party together with antagonism to the Republican party.

Of course, during the latter part of the 1972 campaign and all of the 1976 campaign, the terrible injuries that had been inflicted upon him in the assassination attempt made his success even more unlikely. In almost constant pain, weak, and about as thoroughly crippled as it is possible to be and still stay alive, it is astonishing that he was able to do anything in the way of effective campaigning, and it is not surprising that he was not completely effective. It also seems likely that the particular portion of the population to which he appealed was those for whom his injuries would appear particularly undesirable in a president.

Under the circumstances, Wallace's effort to start a third party was doomed from the start; but judging it simply as political theater, it was a brilliant effort. He began by taking a position markedly different from the center of the political spectrum. We have graphed it on Figure 10–3 as being a little closer to Humphrey than to Nixon simply because, as a matter of fact, in 1968 the Wallace voters normally listed Humphrey as their second choice. Indeed, during the campaign, a good many people who had originally listed Wallace as their first choice decided to vote for Humphrey, apparently on the grounds that Wallace could not win and they preferred Humphrey to Nixon. This was practically the only shift among voters that occurred during the course of the campaign, but it was large enough to convert Humphrey from an almost hopeless candidate to a man who came within an ace of beating Nixon.

We have not labeled the two issue dimensions because, in a way, the distinction between Wallace on the one hand and Humphrey and Nixon on the o er was more sociological than an issue; but there were certain issues. The most obvious of these, of course, was attitude toward race, which was seldom mentioned during the campaign. There were, however, other issues, such as law and order, and during the campaign, there was some tendency on the part of Humphrey and Nixon to move toward the Wallace position. Indeed, one comedian summed up the campaign as follows: "Nixon says 'law and order is the issue'; Humphrey says 'law and order is the issue'; Wallace says 'plagiarism is the issue.' "

THE 1976 AND 1980 ELECTIONS

The 1976 election was, in many ways, a unique event. The capture of the Democratic party by a rank outsider[4] and the aftermath of Watergate made it radically different than any previous campaign. The actual developments of the campaign were, in many ways, unique also. Both the candidate of a party which had a large majority in the House and Senate (Carter) and the sitting president (Ford) campaigned strenuously against the establishment in Washington. The fact that they both thought this a good campaign platform probably indicates that it was near the center of the opinion spectrum, but the voters can hardly have thought that either of these men would, in fact, carry on an anti-establishment policy, and, of course, the winner, Jimmy Carter, did not.

---

[4] "Jimmy who?" as his early detractors referred to Jimmy Carter.

It seems likely that both Ford and Carter were traditional politicians in the sense that they tended to try and hold positions rather near the middle of what they perceived as the voting constituency they faced. Of course, the voting constituency in Carter's Georgia and the congressional district in Michigan which Ford had represented for so many years were different; hence, the midpoints were not identical, but both could be depended on when it came to a national election to try and be fairly close to the center.

In both the Republican and Democratic primary, more extreme candidates were eliminated. The situation in the Republican primary was particularly interesting because in the contest between Reagan and Ford, it wasn't absolutely clear which was the most extreme candidate. Traditionally, one would have thought that a presidential candidate who appealed primarily to the conservatives such as Reagan would be farther away from the center than someone like Ford and, hence, less likely to win the election. In the particular circumstances of the 1976 election, however, this is open to some doubt. It used to be that the South automatically voted Democratic, but this is no longer true. The Democratic candidate can depend on getting the votes of the Northeast, but the South is now up for grabs. Thus, there was another dimension in addition to the usual Right-Left dimensions which one might list as an appeal to the South. Though Democrats nominated Carter, a man with impeccable southern credentials, it is possible that Reagan's greater appeal to the South would have permitted him to take some southern states even away from Carter. He would probably have taken the same midwestern and western states that Ford took if he were able to swallow his distaste for agricultural parity. The fact that he would have lost more popular votes in the northeastern states, which were taken by the Democrats anyway, would have made little difference in the outcome in the electoral college.

Reagan's attitude on parity, which did a good deal to lose him the Republican nomination and which might well have lost him the election, was a case of a politician who was unwilling to abandon his convictions in order to win an election. Ford and Carter, of course, had no such scruples. It should be said, however, that Carter has since infuriated the farmers badly enough so that Reagan, still unwilling to endorse parity but concealing his opposition to it by saying he doesn't understand it, may have a good chance in the farm states in 1980.

There is, however, another possibility raised by the 1964 and the 1976 elections. Since the Civil War, the South has been almost automatically Democratic, but no southerner was elected as a Democratic president[5] until 1964.

It may be that with the alliance of the South and the Northern elements of the Democratic party breaking down, the South will become a wavering part of the Democratic party. Granted that there are very few political issues upon which the South and the Northeast, the other foundation of Democratic power, agree, a policy program which is essentially tipped towards the Northeast and a presidential candidate with a strong southern accent may be the ideal strategy.

But the above is merely a suggestion. This section is being written not only before the 1980 election but before the nominating conventions. Still, the general principles of this chapter apply. Reagan, for example, moved distinctly towards the center from his 1976 position and has, of course, done better in the primaries. It should be kept in mind, even in the 1976 nomination contest, Reagan selected a liberal member of the Republican party as his vice president in an effort to shift his image towards the center. That he has been compelled to move leftward in 1980 is not surprising. It can be predicted that once he is safely nominated, he will move still closer to the center.

In the Democratic camp, Kennedy has appealed basically to the left wing of the Democratic party but has been, at least at the date of this writing, unable to corral enough votes to throw out the sitting president. One could predict that if he did throw out Carter, he would immediately move towards the center.

An even more interesting candidate is John B. Anderson.[6] Anderson is a man of very considerable character, and he is deeply religious. Nevertheless, the strong forces which lead politicians to seek out vote-maximizing strategies have affected him too. He moved from being a member of the extreme right wing of the Republican delegation in the House of Representatives to being a moderate when his constituency changed, and in his presidential candidacy, he has moved even farther to the Left. Indeed, at the time of writing this chapter, he is perceived by the intellectual Left as the best candidate of the three. Even a man of character with strong convictions finds himself ruled by the blind forces of politics.

---

[5] Woodrow Wilson spent part of his childhood in the South, but his actual connections were largely northern.

[6] John B. Anderson and Gordon Tullock were on the Rockford High School debate team together long, long ago.

The reader of this chapter will know much more about the 1980 election than either of the authors for the simple reason that he will read it afterwards and we are writing it before. Nevertheless, we think the principles contained in the chapter will apply to 1980, 1984, and 1988 as well as the elections where we have historical data to analyze.

QUESTIONS TO PONDER

1. In England there are now a number of local parties. Two of them, respectively Scotch and Welsh, call for the independence of those regions and another, from Northern Ireland, in essence wants more British support and less British control in Northern Ireland. How would you graph parties like this on the diagrams in this chapter?

2. Historically, the United States has had long periods of one-party dominance—the Democrats from about 1820 to 1856, the Republicans from 1860 to 1932. Since 1932, and in particular since 1948, things have been more evenly divided. How do you account for the earlier periods?

3. Elaborate the simple one-dimensional model of Figure 10–1 to show both primaries in the two parties and the ultimate election.

CHAPTER 11

Bureaucratic
entrepreneurs

*Presidents come and presidents go, reaping the
calumny, but the bureaucrats endure. These
soldiers of the swivel chair remain nameless
and unnoticed. But now and then, we pause to
shine the spotlight briefly upon them in their
backrooms.*

Jack Anderson[1]

Although elected officials are surely important in our government,
they are massively outnumbered by their bureaucratic employees.
Further, it is not clear who is actually the employee. Bureaucrats
now make up such a large share of the total voting public that it
is almost possible to say that the politicians are the employees of
the bureaucrats. This is particularly so since bureaucrats are more
likely to vote than the citizens who are not. Bureaucrats, then, constitute a larger share of the voting public than of the actual population.[2] Clearly, this is the kind of voting bloc no politician can
afford to ignore.

However, for purposes of simplicity, let us assume that the politicians hire the bureaucrats, rather than the other way around, and
proceed on that basis. There is now a small but scientifically re-
spectable amount of literature in which economic concepts are
applied to bureaucracy. Once again in this chapter, instead of attempting to cover the entire scope of this rather difficult literature,
we will deal with only one aspect of it and use a rather simple
model. We hope that this model will be useful in and of itself and

---

[1] Jack Anderson, "Washington Merry-Go-Round," *Raleigh News and Observer*, July 15, 1974.

[2] Thomas E. Borcherding, ed., *Budgets and Bureaucrats: Organization of
Government Growth* (Durham, N.C.: Duke University Press, 1977).

provide an introduction to a much larger amount of literature for those who are interested.

THE BUREAUCRATS

Bureaucrats are not markedly different from other people. Most citizens of the United States are to some extent interested in helping their fellow men and in doing things in the public interest. Most citizens of the United States, on the other hand, tend to devote most of their time and attention to their own personal interests. The same is true of bureaucrats.

In one way, the single most important contribution of economics was to make it clear that the market economy converts private desires into public benefits. We can drive our cars not because the automobile workers, the stockholders, and the sales force want us to have good cars but because the car is generated as a sort of by-product of the achievement of their own goals, which in this case are income goals. During much of history, economics was taught by people who were under the impression that merchants, farmers, and so forth were attempting to do what was morally right. Since Adam Smith, we take a different view. Naturally, this is no implication that people in these occupations are particularly immoral; but it is also true that they do not produce their products primarily because they want to benefit their customers but because they want to benefit themselves.

The same is true of politicians and of bureaucrats. They are basically in the business to make a living, although, of course, on occasion they sacrifice their own interests to those of others or to charity just like anyone else. However, most of the time they generate what public good or public benefit they do generate as a by-product of attempting to maximize their own interests.

The market, *if there are no monopolies or externalities present,* is so organized that the individuals attempting to benefit themselves end up benefiting others. We should attempt to organize the government in the same way. The government that organizes itself so that self-interested and dishonest politicians or bureaucrats can benefit themselves greatly by injuring the public is subverting its service capabilities. Bureaucrats are like anyone else. They will rarely commit crimes or be consciously dishonest, but most of the time they act in their own interests and only occasionally sacrifice for others or for the public interest. What we want is a government so designed that people like this will generate benefits for others as they do in the nonmonopolistic part of the market. Such a government design is by no means impossible.

The question to which we now turn is how should we organize a bureaucracy in order to achieve this goal. We cannot cover this entire problem in the short space of one chapter and are only going to discuss one particular aspect of it. It is characteristic of most modern governments, although not always true, that each bureau has a monopoly on supplying to the government some particular service. This monopoly is so common that most people think it is a necessary characteristic of government. Indeed, periodically commissions look into government efficiency. Almost uniformly, these commissions object to "duplication," which, in essence, is having competition between two bureaus.

Although the view that you cannot have competition between government bureaus is very widely held, this is usually an unexamined presupposition. It is, of course, true that having two different government agencies doing literally the same thing might cause inconvenience. Their employees would tend to bump into each other all of the time. But we can have competition without that kind of congestion. A more significant possible objection to competition in government would be the existence of significant economies of scale. Such economies may be important with respect to local governments, but there seems to be little evidence that economies of scale would require bureaus of the size we now have in our federal government. Indeed, as far as we can see, these government agencies are far beyond the optimal size from the standpoint of production efficiency.

As an example of competition, most American highways are made by private contractors. They submit bids for constructing certain segments of the highway. Once the bid has been allocated to one of these contractors, naturally the other contractors are not permitted to move their bulldozers, graders, etc., onto the right-of-way and get in his way. On the other hand, most American road repairing is done by a government agency that has a monopoly. Occasionally road repairing is also done by competitive bids and private contractors.

It is not necessary, of course, that the competing units be private companies rather than segments of government. The Department of Defense (DOD) is basically divided into Army, Navy, and Air Force. Many of the missions of the DOD can be accomplished by more than one of these agencies. In areas where this is so, the secretary of defense can (and frequently does) solicit programs and plans from two or, in fortunate cases, three services. Then the secretary can choose what seems the most efficient solution from among two or more competing programs. This method does not work perfectly, heaven knows, but certainly it works better than the DOD does in those areas where the mission is allocated to only one of the services; hence, there is no competition.

As mentioned previously, most people studying government efficiency in recent years have taken the opposite view and have objected vigorously to duplication. Think of the consequences of such a policy in the private market, where General Motors, Ford, Chrysler, and American Motors not only duplicate each other's services but are also duplicated by a lot of odd foreigners like Toyota, Volkswagen, Fiat, Renault, Mercedes, and so forth. Clearly, if efficiency means elimination of duplication, we should consider abolishing everything except General Motors and make General Motors stop producing both Chevrolets and Pontiacs.

MONOPOLY AND BUREAUCRATIC BEHAVIOR

Let us turn to a little formal analysis in which we will assume that the government has given one particular bureau a monopoly over performing some particular service. For simplicity, we shall assume that the government is the federal government, the agency is the FBI, and the service it performs is the collection of national police activities. It should be emphasized that there is no implication that the FBI is one whit less efficient or more bureaucratic than any other government agency. In fact, it is the view of the authors of this book that the FBI is among the more efficient bureaus of the federal government. We do not regard this, however, as very high praise. The choice of the FBI, then, is simply to give a concrete example, not because the FBI is in any way different from other bureaus.

In Figure 11–1 we have shown the usual demand and cost curves with which you are no doubt familiar. The cost and benefit measured in dollars are, as usual, shown on the vertical axis and the quantity, in this case of police activities, is shown on the horizontal axis. We assume that policing is measured in dollar units, therefore the cost line is the horizontal line P, C. The downward sloping curve (D) is Congress's demand for such police services from the FBI.

If we could somehow assume that this is a completely competitive market, then Congress would buy from the suppliers that amount Q_1 of police services at price P_1. This is, of course, the optimal quantity (as far as Congress is concerned) in the sense that marginal costs equal marginal benefits. On the other hand, if the FBI were an ordi-

FIGURE 11–1

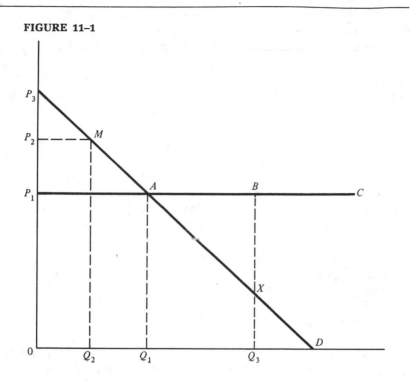

nary monopoly facing a myriad of small purchasers, then they would charge the price P_2 and would sell the quantity Q_2 to the purchasers. This would give them a monopoly profit equivalent to the square whose upper left-hand corner is marked P_2 and lower left-hand corner is at point P_1 on the vertical axis.

If we had a perfectly discriminating monopolist, he or she would sell the police services in small pieces at different prices to different people to obtain the full triangle above and to the left of A as monopoly profit and would produce the amount Q_1 at a cost P_1. In practice, it is rarely possible for a monopoly in the private market to perform in this way. It is possible that the government bureaucrat may be able to do so, however.

If the individual bureau has a monopoly on providing a given service, it also faces a monopolistic buyer called a *monopsonist* (one buyer) for that service. Congress has a monopsony status when dealing with the FBI because the FBI can sell its services to no one else. The problem of a monopolist facing a monopsonist is an extremely difficult one, and most economists say that in the general case you cannot tell very much about what the outcome will be. It is possible that the monopolist will be able to get the full gain of the monopoly or that the monopsonist will be able to get the full gain of the monopsony (which in our particular diagram simply means that Congress buys Q_1 units of police services from the FBI at price P_1). The solution can also be anything in between. Normally, it is said that the actual outcome depends on bargaining tactics and cannot be predicted.

In our particular case, however, it is possible to make a pretty good prediction as to the outcome. We have drawn the cost line in as a horizontal line because it is the easy way of measuring it. Congress, however, will not have any clear idea of the cost of providing services by a given bureau. Indeed, the bureau will do its best to guarantee that Congress does not have a clear idea of the minimum cost of providing various services. There are innumerable techniques available to the bureau to make it hard for congressmen to know what the bureau is doing in detail. Further, the bureau does not face a competitor producing the same commodity, so that Congress cannot simply compare its price with that of other people. In most of the negotiations between bureaus and Congress (which take the form primarily of committee hearings), it is clear that Congress never really gets an idea of the minimum cost at which a bureau can perform a given service. Indeed, the representatives in Congress who have many other demands on their time normally do not make any very strong effort.

The bureau, on the other hand, is rather well informed as to the shape of Congress's demand for its services. The reason it is well informed is that Congress's demand for the service of any given bureau is largely a reflection of the views of the voters on the value of that particular service. The bureau has a great many facilities for finding out what the voters think about the need for police services, or agricultural subsidies, or new parks, and so forth. It also can take careful note of any speeches that individual congressmen make on those subjects, which gives it further information. Last but by no means least, the bureaus are characteristically very well informed on any lobbying activities that may be going on in Washington with respect to the activities of that particular bureau. Indeed, in many cases, the bureaus themselves in essence organize the private lobbies, which push for more of their activities.

Edward Banfield, author of *The Unheavenly City*, in the earlier part of his life was a public relations man for one of the innumerable segments of the Department of Interior. As he is fond of recounting, on one occasion in the pursuance of his duties, he wrote a letter to the Secretary of Interior to be formally signed by the president of a citizens group that the Department of Interior had organized to press for further activities in his particular branch. The letter was sent to the secretary of interior, and in due course, it was referred to Banfield to draft a reply for the secretary's signature. Thus, he found himself carrying on the entire correspondence on both sides.

Under these circumstances, with the Congress having little idea of the minimum cost the bureau must put out to achieve its service and with the bureau having a very clear idea of Congress's demand for those services, the bargaining between the monopolist (FBI) and the monopsonist (Congress) almost certainly will go in favor of the monopolist. Thus, in this case we can predict the outcome with a fair degree of security, although in the general case it is a very difficult problem.

As the reader will have noticed, we referred to the bureau as being able to keep its minimum cost a secret to a considerable extent; we did not say that it could keep profit a secret. Indeed, those bureaus (and there are some continuously popping up) in which the head has worked out some way of getting a personal profit normally are detected after a period of time, and someone who has pocketed the profit is either fired or, occasionally, jailed. Thus, the bureaucratic monopolist is in a somewhat different position than a private monopolist. He or she cannot go live on the Riviera on ill-gotten gains. Indeed, if the comptroller-general and the various other agencies of the government that are directed at making certain that money is not diverted from its appropriate channels into private expenditures do their job, there is no direct way in which bureaucrats can benefit from their monopoly position. Unfortunately, there is an indirect way; and this indirect way probably causes considerably more social harm than would the simple waste of the profit we would anticipate if they could convert it into money to spend on riotous living.

Putting the matter bluntly, the bureaucrat can waste the funds. This waste, of course, is not pure waste in the sense that no one gets any benefit from it, but it is waste in the sense that there are very small benefits and those accrue to the bureaucrats. The obvious case that is always used in talking about this kind of thing (and it can occur in private businesses as well as in government) is the pretty woman secretary who is a poor typist. Since the busy man who has a pretty secretary who cannot type probably also has significant correspondence, two secretaries are necessary.

There are innumerable other ways in which the same kind of

thing can be done: elaborate offices, a lot of trips to important conferences that are held in places like Nice and Las Vegas, or the special dining rooms that are found so much in Washington. Recently the newspapers have talked a good deal about the presidential mess.[3] But this is merely froth, if one considers the whole thing. Surely the most expensive set of subsidized restaurants in the world are the restaurants in the capital building for members of Congress.[4] In addition, however, all over Washington there are small dining rooms for cabinet secretaries,[5] and below these establishments are special restaurants for senior officers (called flag officers in the Pentagon).[6]

Regarding the elaborate offices of bureaucrats, Jack Anderson was able to collect the following information on how tax dollars are spent:

> It is . . . a matter of solemn protocol that no bureaucrat with any status can move into a predecessor's lair without refurbishing it. Offices must be done over to fit the personality of the new personage.
>
> To determine whether this sacred rule is still in effect, we checked on several bigwigs who have been appointed recently. There is Alexander Butterfield, for instance, who was put in command of the Federal Aviation Administration after departing the White House. He was the man, it will be remembered, who broke the electrifying news that President Nixon was bugging himself.
>
> Sure enough, Butterfield has redone his chambers. New drapes and furniture were installed at a cost to the taxpayers of $5,400. . . .

---

[3] One of the authors was honored by an invitation to have lunch in the presidential mess on one occasion. It was by no means the best restaurant in Washington. On the other hand, this visit was in what we might call the "second division." There is a special, very small president's mess that serves lunch for eight high officials and then the main president's mess, which serves lunch for about 100 officials at the next rank. The second group of officials is divided into a first division—which has a late lunch—and a second division which has an early lunch. A late lunch is a status symbol among the staff of the White House.

[4] Once again, one of the authors has eaten in these *august purlieus* and can testify that the food was better than in the president's mess. It was also a good deal cheaper, which implies that the subsidy was larger.

[5] The only one in which either of the authors has eaten is the attorney general's dining room, and the food there is highly varying.

[6] The flag officers' mess, in which again one of the authors has eaten, is clearly subsidized, granted the prices they charge, but it is not really a very good restaurant. On the other hand, the Pentagon is a long way from any other restaurant. By rumor, the Supreme Court dining room outdoes all of the others in grandeur, cuisine, and, of course, subsidy.

We also checked with the Secret Service to see if the new director, H. Stuart Knight, had been able to manage with the luxurious suite the previous chief left behind. . . . Knight has somehow managed to spend $11,200 to do over his digs. Some $3,500 went for a new paint job alone.

At the Bureau of Standards, Director Richard Roberts splurged over $55,000 to remodel his office layout. He magnificiently extended the job to redo his secretary's office and adjoining conference room.

Social and Rehabilitation Administrator James S. Dwight, a stern critic of welfare cheats, didn't mind lavishing $120,000 upon his own welfare. The money was expended for plush carpets, tinted glass, sliding doors, a floor-to-ceiling bookcase, and other fancy fixtures in his domain. . . .

In recent years, the bureaucrats have become smitten with campaigns to trim the waistline bulges, which are an occupational hazard of too much time in the swivel chair. As a result, almost every large government agency has constructed recreational facilities where barrel-bellied bureaucrats can shed their flab—usually on government time, of course.

The State Department possesses a fitness room and gym, paid for by an employees' recreation association. A departmental volleyball team takes over the floor for over two hours at a time, much to the consternation of those on the sideline who want exercise when they are supposed to be working. . . .

Under the direction of former Transportation Secretary John Volpe, his department constructed a gym facility complete with the latest in physical fitness equipment, a soothing suana, and a Tartan track atop the headquarter building. Cost to the taxpayers: $34,195.[7]

The problem with all of these ways of spending possible monopoly profits is that they are conspicuous and Congress is apt to notice them. Thus, something can be done but not a great deal. There is another very large area in which money can be spent, which is something we think is best described as "bureaucratic aesthetics." A person who has devoted his or her life to, let us say, the FBI is apt to develop very strong ideas as to what is a good FBI operation. Thus, he or she might, for example, develop the idea that it is desirable to have an FBI office within 100 miles of any place in the United States, regardless of the density of the population. Congress would never be able to detect this kind of waste. It is omnipresent

---

[7] Jack Anderson, "Washington Merry-Go-Round."

in government. Congress may notice the elaborate special honor guard unit maintained by the Pentagon, but it is unlikely to realize that carriers are a few knots faster than they really have to be. For the devoted naval officer, those additional knots of speed have a real personal benefit. He or she thinks the fast carrier is better than a slower carrier, even though the combat capacity is probably not much affected.

There is an immense scope for this kind of waste in government, as indeed there is in private industry; but in private industry, the pressures to get what profit you can get in cash are so strong that this effect is probably rather minor. The federal triangle in Washington is a monument to President Hoover's feelings for this kind of aesthetics. That appalling monstrosity, the former War, Navy, and State Building, is a 19th century edition of the same thing. Anyone familiar with any given segment of the federal government can always find many, many further examples.

THE SIZE AND EXPANSION OF BUREAUCRACY

The most important form of waste is simply making the bureau larger than it needs to be. There are many reasons why a bureaucrat may want the bureau to expand and object to its contraction. First, the prestige of the person at the head of the bureau (and also civil service rank and pay) is very significantly affected by the absolute size of the bureau. Further, such things as the size of the office, whether there is a conference table, the type of chair in which the person is permitted to sit, and the type of water cooler near the desk depend on the size of the job. If this person can expand the bureau, he or she can anticipate over time that he or she will move up in these areas, and these areas are important to the bureaucrat who is conscious of their effect on status in Washington. An important consideration from the standpoint of almost everybody in a given bureau is that an expansion will mean that there are more possible promotions.

This list by no means ends the advantages of increasing the size of the bureau to a chief bureaucrat, however. Power obviously goes up as the bureau increases in size, and ability to control the bureau itself improves if he or she can hire new people. The reason is that under civil service rules, it is, to all intents and purposes, impossible to fire anybody. Under the circumstances, the only way in which he or she can get control over subordinates is to offer them the reward of promotions or improvements in the size of their staffs. Thus, he or she has more control over subordinates if the bureau is known to be expanding. He or she can dangle before the eyes of a number of junior officers the prospect of promotion to head of a new subsection.

Also, the relationship between the bureaucrat and Congress is advantageously affected by the expansion of the bureau. If the bureaucrat is going to be expending new funds, he or she usually has a good deal of freedom in deciding how they will be spent. Putting a new building in some particular representative's district may be a possibility, and this can pay off representatives for various favors they may do. Note that this also gives the representative a motive for expanding the bureau.

There is, on the other hand, substantially no motivation for reducing the size of the bureau. Insofar as government agencies are examined for efficiency (and, as a matter of practical fact, in spite of all the noise, there is not very much of this done), this concern for efficiency is concern for how well they do what they are doing. There is little or no attempt to discover whether or not they are doing things that are not worth doing. It is not generally true that government bureaus spend a great deal of energy doing things that are positively harmful to their constituents. *They may, however, do things that are worth a great deal less than their costs.*

In some cases, they actually work harm on society as a whole in order to benefit their constituents. The agricultural support program, which has been in existence now for some 30 years, used tax money for the purpose of making bread and other agricultural commodities more expensive. We could easily find innumerable examples of the same kind. However, these are all cases in which there is a distinct and direct benefit for the constituents of the bureau (i.e., the people who support it) and the cost falls on others. For example, farmers are much richer than they would be without this program, and the rest of us are poorer.

How can a bureau expand to too large a size? To return to Figure 11–1, we can see the explanation very easily. For simplicity, assume that the bureau is a monopoly and is able to get the entire monopoly profit of a differentiating monopoly from Congress because Congress does not know its production function. Under those circumstances, it can increase production to point Q_3 on the horizontal axis. Note that all the units of police service provided by the FBI between Q_1 and Q_3 have a positive value, but the value is less than their cost. Congress, on the other hand, is offered an implicit bargain under which the bureau proposes to produce the amount Q_3 of police services in return for a payment, which is the rectangle P_1-B-Q_3-O. The area of this rectangle is the same as the area under the demand curve and to the left of Q_3; i.e., it is the same as the area $O-O_3-X-P_3$. This is because the triangle P_1-P_3-A and the triangle $A-B-X$ have the same area. The monopoly has exploited its full monopoly profit out of Congress and then has used this monopoly profit to subsidize additional production which, from the standpoint of Congress, is actually not worth its cost. This is the solution that maximizes the size of the bureau and, hence, maximizes the various advantages of a large bureau, which we have enumerated above.

Probably few bureaus have actually achieved the goal equivalent to producing at Q_3 in our figure. For one thing, bureaucrats are like the rest of us in that they like leisure, therefore they do not work as hard as they might, even in generating excess capacity. Further, there are, as we have mentioned above, various other things that the bureaucrat can use his power to obtain. Last but not least, perfect adjustment, which would mean expansion to production Q_3, would be unlikely because if the bureaucrat reached this perfect adjustment, Congress would become indifferent between having the bureau continue to exist or not having it at all. Total benefit minus total cost would equal zero.

Nevertheless, it is likely that most bureaus have moved fairly far toward the size that is designated by Q_3 in Figure 11–1. In any event, it is fairly clear that if bureaucratic managers are as interested in their own well being as you and we are in ours, they will generate a bureau that is too large from the standpoint of the desires of the voters or at least those voters who are not employed in a bureaucracy.

Empirical tests of the hypothesis that bureaucracies are large—indeed, roughly twice as large as they should be—are hard to perform. The studies that have been done, however, do seem to indicate that the prediction is borne out. As an example of one study of this nature, there are a certain number of governmental services that are occasionally carried out by private companies on contract under fairly competitive situations. An examination of the costs private companies charge and those of a government bureaucracy seem to indicate that the private companies can generate the same level of service at much less than the cost of generating it by a bureaucracy.[8] Although this might seem to have nothing to do with

---

[8] Robert M. Spann, "Public vs. Private Provision of Government Services," in *Budgets and Bureaucrats*.

the absolute size of the bureaucracy, in general the greater efficiency is accomplished by simply using less equipment and personnel.

To take an example, fire protection is normally provided by municipal bureaucracies called fire departments. There are a few companies, primarily in Arizona, that provide fire service on a contract basis. In most cases, these companies have a contract with some city to provide fire protection in the city; but a good many of them also have private contracts with various individuals to provide fire protection in areas where there is no city government.[9]

These fire companies have developed a new way of dealing with a fire. They have, in essence, invented a new but simple technique. This technique consists of asking the person who telephones in what kind of fire it is and then sending equipment suitable for that fire, instead of sending two or three large engines to all fires. The usual equipment is a simple pickup truck with two men and a foam unit, which is adequate for most fires. In those cases where it is not, they, of course, send more equipment. Using this very inexpensive technique, they have been able to provide fire service that, judging by fire insurance rates, is just as good as that provided by conventional fire departments with far more equipment and manpower.

However, this is merely one example. To repeat what we said earlier, empirical work in this field is not easy, and the theoretical proposition that government bureaus will tend to be much larger—perhaps twice as large—as they need to be cannot be said to have been fully validated by empirical work as yet. It is true, however, that so far no empirical study attempted to test the proposition has indicated that the bureaus are less than oversized.

PROPOSED CHANGES IN BUREAUCRACY

What, then, can we do about this matter? The first thing that occurs to most people is simply to hire some experts to go to work to improve efficiency. We have now had a good deal of experience with this particular approach, and it does not seem to do very much good. The problem is that the efficiency experts have no way of measuring the demand for the government service, and although they can improve the efficiency with which the service is delivered,

---

[9] The individual contracts are of two types. The customer can pay them a flat amount per year, and they will then put out any fire that occurs on his property; or the customer can pay a much, much higher fee by calling them after the fire has broken out.

they cannot prevent the bureaucracy from being much larger than it should be and producing service that is not worth its cost. Further, in many cases, these efficiency studies seem to be positively perverse.

Almost all efforts to improve efficiency have led to attacks on duplication of services. As most economists have noticed, governments frequently organize cartels for private industry. For example, the Interstate Commerce Commission (ICC) was organized to reduce, and in fact has reduced, the degree of competition in transportation. The Civil Aeronautics Board (CAB) has changed the airways from a highly competitive industry to one of almost complete cartelization. We could go on with this list for quite sometime. It would appear that one of the functions of government efficiency studies is to promote cartelization within the government. Instead of suggesting that there be competition in the government, characteristically intragovernmental competition is strongly opposed. As we have said before, they attack duplication, which is another way of referring to competition.

If we did have competition for the provision of government services, we would move back toward Q_1 in Figure 11–1. This is, of course, the reason that the market, where there is competitive provision, can operate in such an efficient way. There is no obvious reason why the same thing will not occur if we can somehow introduce competition into government.

Under competition, if one bureau was offering quantity Q_3 of service at a price that included the welfare triangle, another bureau could expand its own total size by offering to add to its present duties quantity Q_1 at a price that reflected its price and give Congress the welfare triangle above and to the left. Thus, we would anticipate that under competition between bureaus, just as under competition in the private market, there would be a tendency to move toward the optimal quantity and price for the service provided.

The idea of competition between bureaus seems almost a contradiction in terms to many people, probably because of the long continued propaganda against duplication. In practice, bureaus do make a good many efforts to compete with each other to expand by taking someone else's business away from them. For a particularly striking example, the Department of Transportation does not sound like a very belligerent organization, but it played a major combat role in the war in Vietnam.

In this case, the Navy took the view that there was a minimum size below which combat vessels could not go. Presumably, this was a bargaining technique intended to get more money out of Congress. The Department of Transportation, however, has the Coast Guard as one of its subordinate agencies, and the Coast Guard expressed its willingness to provide small combat vessels in Vietnam. The contract went to the Coast Guard, and as a result, a large number of small speedboats equipped with machine guns were run up and down the rivers of Vietnam operated by Coast Guard personnel on temporary detail from their normal duties of preventing smuggling and rescuing people whose sailboats had overturned.

One can predict that if we have another war of this sort, the Navy will not again try to game Congress into giving them larger vessels than necessary because they will anticipate the loss of part of their budget to the Coast Guard. On the other hand, the Coast Guard, having won on this one, may try to compete with the Navy for some other type of combat mission in any future hostilities. If the Coast Guard continues outmaneuvering the Navy in this way, eventually it will be larger than the Navy.

Any rather careful reading of the appropriation hearings will indicate that this type of thing happens fairly commonly. Various bureaus propose to do things that are very close to or, indeed, exactly the same as things other bureaus are already doing or are thinking of doing. Usually these proposals are made with a good sales package claiming lower cost, better service, etc. The bureau whose ground is being trod upon then comes back by (a) cutting the price at which it is making its offer, (b) promising to improve the service, and (c) arguing that permitting the intruder to enter will lead to duplication. Over time, however, a good deal of this kind of duplication always develops.

Unfortunately, at this stage in the normal development of American government, a commission is appointed, usually by the president, to look over the government and improve efficiency. It goes through the entire civil service and military with the objective of eliminating duplication. In other words, it eliminates competition and reintroduces cartels. It has no more likelihood of creating actual efficiency in government than the Interstate Commerce Commission has of generating efficiency in transportation. The simplest remedy to all of this, of course, is to stop having presidential commissions look into efficiency. Since in the historic record they have always attempted to eliminate competition, we can at least stop them from existing.

But why not take a more positive approach? In the private market we do have something called the Sherman Act, which prohibits cartels and monopolies. Perhaps it is not well enforced, but at least it exists. Could we not have a somewhat similar approach to our government bureaus? There is no reason why Congress and the president should not encourage individual bureaus to propose the takeover of part or all of the duties of other bureaus at a better price and with better service. The more of this that happens, the more the individual bureau faces a demand curve that is not Congress's demand for, let us say, police services but Congress's demand for the FBI provision of those police services, as opposed to an expansion of the Secret Service, the postal inspectors, various police forces now run by the Pentagon for military purposes, or indeed simply expanding the Washington metropolitan police. Scotland Yard, which does most of the serious detective work all over England, is, after all, the police force of the city of London.

At the very least, this means that Congressional committees should be willing to listen to substantially any bureaucratic proposal for doing anything. If the Postal Service appears with the astonishing proposition that, although it cannot deliver the mail, it could run aircraft carriers more cheaply than the Navy, it should at least be listened to. It might not be sensible to transfer the carriers from the Navy to the Postal Service, but one could predict that the Navy would be impelled by such an offer to think long and hard about how they can make economies in the operation of their carriers.

Another way of introducing competition takes advantage of the fact that the United States is a rather large country. Various regions of the United States are much larger in geography, population, and in total income than many nations. Thus, a good many federal government agencies could be broken down into regional agencies responsible for areas larger than France or West Germany. Since there does not seem to be any evidence that our agencies function more efficiently than their French and West German counterparts, there is probably little in the way of economies of scale above that size for most government services. These regional bureaus could then apply to Congress for their budgets. At the end of each year, Congress could compare the service they had received and the cost and perhaps transfer a state or two from the region that did worst to another that did better. Thus, the regional bureaus would be put in a kind of marginal competition with each other and would be motivated to attempt to be efficient.

As the last and most radical proposal, many government activities do not have to be performed by the bureaucracy at all. There is no reason they cannot be contracted out to private people with, of course, precautions to make certain that the market remains competitive. A good deal of government activity is already done this way. Roads, dams, and government buildings are actually built by private contractors. Most military equipment is also produced in this way, although the military service does produce some of its own. We could go a good deal further. The Navy, for example, in addition to maintaining combat vessels, has a large collection of auxiliary and transport vessels. There seems no reason why these could not be contracted out to competitive private operation. The Weather Bureau, to take another case, does not seem to have any particular characteristics that make it necessary to have it operated by a bureaucracy rather than by a series of private companies, each of which gathers weather data and makes predictions in various parts of the country.[10] A good many park services are already contracted out in this way, and perhaps more could be. In general, we should take an experimental attitude about this kind of approach toward reducing the power of the bureaucracy; there certainly seems to be no reason to rule out contracting in many areas of government.

But this is only one of a number of possible approaches. Making it easier to fire bureaucrats would be a distinct improvement, and perhaps some kind of bonus system under which bureau heads are permitted to keep part of any saving they make without reducing the quality of service would be a good idea. In any event, we now have a bureaucracy that has "jus' growed"; it is not the result of careful planning or thought. Surely we can do better if we try.

QUESTIONS TO PONDER

1. Readers of mystery novels know that Scotland Yard investigates most murders in England. Actually, these novels exaggerate the role that Scotland Yard plays, but it does investigate a great many murders outside of London. Each of these murders is investigated by Scotland Yard on what amounts to an individual contract; that is, the local police force will call in Scotland Yard and pay its fee rather than investigating the matter themselves. Does this sound like an efficient arrangement? Explain.

2. In the area around Los Angeles, there are a number of cities that contract out substantially all of their government services, principally to other government agencies. A small city may, for example, have its taxes collected by the City of Los Angeles, purchase its

---

[10] The predictions could hardly be worse.

police services from the sheriff of Los Angeles County, and get its water and sewage services, street repairing, and so forth from other government agencies. In many cases, the city government (for a city of 100,000 or so) consists of the city council, one professional employee—who is usually either an engineer or lawyer and who negotiates these various contracts—and a secretary. Does this sound like an efficient arrangement? Why or why not?

3. Readers of Western novels know that there used to be a profession in the United States called *bounty hunter*. When a crime had been committed and the police of some area thought they knew who had committed it but were unable to find him, they would advertise a reward just as there are now reward posters for criminals in almost every post office. A professional bounty hunter would then attempt to find the person. The bounty hunter would make his living from the rewards. Even today there is something rather like this for people who skip out on bail from professional bail bondsmen. Would it be sensible to expand this institution and reduce the amount of money now spent on the regular police?

CHAPTER 12

Riots and panic

Riots, demonstrations, and, indeed, behavior of people in large masses have been studied primarily by sociologists or political scientists and little by economists. The purpose of this chapter is to demonstrate that economists have something to contribute too. In fact we suspect that an economic approach is far more fruitful than the approaches that have been traditionally used.[1] Most discussion of riots, demonstrations, and so forth turns on either one of two hypotheses. The first of these is that these riots or demonstrations are set off by generally bad conditions. For example, the blacks rioted all over the United States in the summer of 1967 because they had come to realize how bad their situation was and were taking action to change it. Since their situation was surely better than it had been in previous years, this theory has to turn on a sort of gradual realization on their part that they were not as well off as they could be, with this realization occurring faster than the actual improvement in their conditions. On the other hand, they have done very little rioting since then, and although their conditions have improved, they have not yet achieved full equality; so why they have not continued to riot is hard to determine from this hypothesis.

The second basic hypothesis (actually somewhat older) for the behavior of demonstrators, rioters, and so forth has to do with something called *mob psychology*. It is alleged that people in large groups somehow are different from when they are alone. Since we have never really understood this hypothesis, we are rather at a loss to

---

[1] A good deal of this chapter is based on the work of J. Patrick Gunning; although he has published only one article on the subject, he has actually done more work in the area. See J. Patrick Gunning, Jr., "An Economic Approach to Riot Analysis," *Public Choice* 13 (Fall 1972), pp. 31–46. Since he was a graduate student of one of the authors at the time, this is clear-cut proof that there is some educational activity carried on in universities. The students may learn nothing from the teachers, but the teachers occasionally learn something from the students.

explain it; but it will be found in the older literature on mob action.

The economist is apt to feel that the easiest way of explaining any change in human action is a change in the cost. Thus, if we observe people who never break windows when they are alone or in small groups but do break windows when they are part of a mob, we are apt to explain this in terms of such things as the fact that the cost of breaking windows is lower (that is, it is much safer) when you are in a mob than when you are alone and more likely to be caught.

Obviously, the difference between these different types of explanations should be subject to empirical investigation. Unfortunately, it is very hard to carry on empirical investigations during a riot. The only study of any sophistication of which we are aware was carried on by Nicos Devletoglou and certain of his friends during some riots in London. These riots or demonstrations were carried out by the English who were, for one reason or another, distressed by political conditions in Greece.[2] Devletoglou's experiment was solely devoted to finding out whether the people engaged in the demonstration/riot were well-informed about Greece and Greek politics. For this purpose he quickly designed a small questionnaire, and he and his assistants went out on the streets and presented the questionnaire to the participants.

Needless to say, this was a difficult task and required a great deal of tact on the part of the pollsters. In spite of the difficulties, they were able to get at least some answers and their results are reported in *Public Opinion Quarterly*.[3] As I suppose no one would be much surprised to learn, it turned out that the demonstrators knew something about Greece but not much. As a sample and politically neutral question, they were able to locate the city of Athens on a map of Greece but not the second largest city in Greece, Salonica. Their knowledge of the political issues about which they were demonstrating was, in Devletoglou's view, equally incomplete, but this is somewhat harder to measure.

Empirical work in which riots are examined after the fact by asking questions of rioters and/or police officers have been done on quite a large scale, but unfortunately, most of these experiments have not been designed in such a way that one can use the informa-

---

[2] This was before the establishment of the military dictatorship. Indeed, these riots in a somewhat indirect way had much to do with the institution of the Papadopolous regime.

[3] See Nicos Devletoglou, "Responsibility and Demonstrations: A Case Study," *Public Opinion Quarterly* 30 (Summer 1966), pp. 285–89.

tion to distinguish between the economic approach to rioting and the sociological and political explanations given above. For example, during some of the 1967 riots referred to above, blacks entered shops and removed TV sets they then took home. An economist would tend to feel that probably the largest single motivating factor that led blacks to go into stores and steal TV sets during a riot, when they did not do it under normal circumstances, was simply that the cost of such theft was much lower. In Detroit, for example, the police were under orders not to interfere.

The questions asked after the riot were unfortunately not designed to discover whether this was true or not. For example, suppose that a black who, during the course of the riot, took a TV set and now has it in his home is asked about his motives by an earnest young assistant professor of sociology. It is unlikely, to put it mildly, that he will say that he just wanted the TV set and saw an opportunity to get it without paying. Indeed, the earnest young assistant professor is rather apt to have appeared with a structured question in which the "thief" is asked whether his removal of the TV set was a protest against the establishment, a protest against the white merchants, or simply the enactment of his personal frustration from living in such a corrupt society. This gives him a choice of fairly pleasant-sounding motives, and he cannot be blamed if he takes advantage of them. The bulk of the research on the causes of riots has taken this form.

Note that this research simply offers no significant information on whether the economic or the sociopolitical explanation for rioting and demonstrations is correct; it does not disprove the conventional sociological wisdom. We cannot tell from this literature which hypothesis is true of the real world. This is unfortunate, and we hope in the future, riots and demonstrations will be investigated by people who have the economic hypothesis in mind and therefore design their research in such a way as to whether it is true or false.

Meanwhile, however, in the absence of empirical research, we will outline in this chapter the theoretical explanation for mob behavior that seems sensible from the economic standpoint. It is quite probable that if we had adequate empirical evidence, we would find that some aspects of both the economic and sociopolitical explanations are true; but since this is an economics book, we will present only the economic explanation and leave it to others to present the sociopolitical explanation. We would hope that there are no more riots, and, hence, there is no way to find out which of these explanations is correct or whether some intermediate point is better than either; but we doubt this will turn out to be true. There have been riots throughout history, and we see no reason for them to stop. Thus, future riots may provide the opportunity to test the hypothesis we advance here.

Let us begin by turning to a very special and indeed very minor type of riot the readers may think should not really be called a riot but which does raise somewhat the same issues. This phenomenon is *panic*. It is uncommon nowadays for theaters to burn, but at one time they did so fairly frequently. When this occurred, very often more people were killed by being trampled to death in or around the exits than in the fire. Further, when people were killed by the fire, they were usually killed because the exits were blocked by dense masses of people who were attempting to get through doors that were too narrow.

This phenomenon occurs in other settings, of course. People on sinking ships may mob lifeboats with the result that they are overturned, an occurrence clearly not in the best interests of the passengers. It is, of course, the possibility of panic that leads to fire drills and lifeboat drills. As a general rule, this kind of behavior leads to an increased death rate because the effort to put more people through a door than its design will allow or more people in a lifeboat than its normal capacity means that the actual capacity is less than it would be if people behaved in an orderly manner. Thus, a theater that has plenty of doors through which to evacuate the entire audience before the roof collapses during a fire—if they approach the doors in an orderly manner—may in fact have the doors clogged by struggling masses of people. The result may be that a good number of people are not only trampled but are killed in the theater because they are unable to get out of the theater.

That this behavior is not inevitable can be seen by considering the sinking of the Titanic as an example. The Titanic was thought to be unsinkable; hence, there were not enough lifeboats. The crew and passengers behaved with admirable restraint, although unfortunately with less than complete efficiency. Women and children and just enough crew members to handle the lifeboats were loaded into the boats, and no lifeboat was overturned or damaged in the process. The lifeboats, however, were by no means *fully* loaded; hence, a great many people died who did not have to do so. The people who remained on the Titanic, either because of inadequate lifeboats or because of the inefficiency in loading the lifeboats, were (at least to some extent) consoled by the lack of disturbance on the ship and by the ship's orchestra, which was playing hymns when the Titanic sank.

Most discussions of the phenomenon of the panic that was so conspicuously absent on the Titanic have put it down to a sort of change of character on the part of the participants. It is alleged that in unexpected periods of great danger, people stop acting rationally and crowd around doors or mob lifeboats. There is, however, a perfectly rational explanation. Consider someone in a theater that is on fire and has only a certain number of doors. Every minute that he remains in the theater increases the probability that he will be caught when the roof collapses. On the other hand, if he succeeds in fighting his way to the door, he will delay the exit of other people but not himself. Economically we refer to this as a public-good situation. Looked at from the standpoint of the entire collection of people in the theater, they would be better off if they leave in an orderly way, row by row and without any effort by individuals to get out ahead of the others. This will minimize the chance that any of them will be in the auditorium when the roof collapses and if it does catch some of them, will minimize the number. Further, it reduces to zero the prospect that people will be trampled around the doors.

But this is considering what we might call group rationality—how to get out the group as a whole. Individuals interested in benefiting themselves would realize that if they push toward the door, they reduce the possibility of dying themselves, whereas if they remain in their place and thus prevent congestion around the door (or reduce congestion if there are already people trying to force their way out), they increase the likelihood that they will be killed. Pushing toward the door benefits you and injures others. Remaining where you are and letting other people go out injures you and benefits others. Clearly, the latter type behavior is the nobler, and everyone who has considered the sinking of the Titanic has remarked on the courage of those who stayed on the ship, but it is not necessarily the rational thing to do.

Is there any way of telling whether the economic explanation—that each individual is making an individually rational decision—or the sociological explanation, which implies a breakdown of rationality, is correct? Well, there was an experiment run in the early 1950s that, although it does not conclusively settle matters, does cast a great deal of light on it. A professor of sociology tied a knot on one end of a large number of pieces of string. He placed these knots, one by one, in a bottle in such a way that the end of the string stuck out. The neck of the bottle was such that it was easy to pull the strings out including the knot, if only one or two of them were passing through the neck at a time, but that if all of the strings were pulled, the knots would clog the neck of the bottle.

He then gave the other ends of the strings to his students and told them he was running an experiment and that all of the students who pulled their string completely out of the bottle (that is, pulled the knot out) within 30 seconds would receive a nickel. Clearly there was no cause for panic here—the individuals were not in any way in danger; but, on the other hand, the economic arguments above would apply. Those individuals who did not pull on the strings and let other people pull theirs out first had less chance of getting a nickel. On the other hand, if everyone pulled on the strings, none of them would get their strings out, and no one would get paid. As I suppose the reader has already guessed, all of the students pulled on their strings immediately.[4] The neck of the bottle resembled the door of a burning theater when panic had set in.

Obviously this experiment does not finally settle the matter, but it does offer some support for the economic point of view. Unfortunately, when we turn to the other kinds of demonstrations and riots, we do not have even this kind of experimental information. We must, therefore, consider them in a theoretical way. Was Edward Banfield correct when he titled one of his chapters in The Unheavenly City, "Rioting, Mainly for Fun and Profit"?[5]

First, it must be admitted that a great many people do get some enjoyment from participating in riots. This enjoyment is probably greater if they can tell themselves and other people that what they are doing is politically important than if they do not have this rationalization, but there is not doubt that it is fun anyway. Until very recently, almost all American children engaged in minor acts of vandalism on Halloween. Clearly, this was a permitted violation of the normal rules much as Saturnalia was in Rome. Once the rules were lifted, a certain amount of physical damage to other people's property was carried out by otherwise quite controlled young people for entertainment. They did not, as a matter of fact, do very much

---

[4] One of the authors has repeated the experiment with students in his class with essentially the same result.

[5] Edward C. Banfield, The Unheavenly City: The Nature and Future of Our Urban Crisis (Boston: Little, Brown & Co., 1970), chap. 9, pp. 185–209.

damage, but on the other hand, the rules were only relaxed for small amounts of damage.

A certain amount of the kind of activity that goes on in riots is surely entertaining and more so if it is a substitute for attending school or working than if it is a substitute for leisure activity. Thus, one of the reasons why there was a good deal of university rioting and demonstrations in the latter part of the 1960s was no doubt that the students may have had to go to class if they had not been in the demonstration.

Profits from riot activity tend to be very modest, but at least in the black riots that peaked in 1967, there was material profit available. Some things were stolen, records of debts were sometimes destroyed in the course of a riot (which benefited the debtors), and there was, at least initially, a fairly good prospect that as a result of the riot a good deal of government money would be spent in the riot area. In practice, the latter "profit" tended to turn out to be rather unimportant. Indeed, in many cases, the physical damage to the areas with the consequent difficulty in shopping, and so forth was of greater importance to the inhabitants as a cost than were the various government programs as a benefit.

But the fact that these benefits existed does not prove that they explain the riots. Indeed, it is not really the intent of this chapter to explain these riots or any others. The problem with which we are concerned is people's behavior during riots. It is an observed fact that during riots, regardless of the basic motive of the rioters (which may be either good or bad), individuals do engage in vandalism, do sometimes start fires, do on occasion attack the police, and very commonly threaten the police even if they do not attack them. Further, there is usually a fairly widespread violation of a large number of minor laws against such things as walking in the streets, littering, and committing noise nuisances. All of this kind of activity is rare outside of the environment of a riot, and what we are interested in in this chapter is the explanation for this activity, not the explanation for the riot itself.

To repeat what we have said before, we will not be able to prove clearly one theory or the other. This requires empirical work that has not yet been done. We will simply present the economic explanation and hope that with time the empirical work to determine whether the theory is true or not true will be done. Granting that most people have at least some desire sometimes to commit minor vandalism —acquire property without paying for it, violate the traffic laws, litter, walk on the grass, or commit noise nuisances—why do we observe that all of the violations are so much commoner during riots than normally? Can we explain this without assuming that the people have changed at all but only on the theory that the cost they face has changed?

It is clear that the cost of all of these activities declines sharply during a riot. In the first place, it may be rather hard for the police to tell who in a large collection of rioters is committing the crime or misdemeanor. If, for example, a large number of people are facing a line of policemen and shouting insults or even throwing rocks, the policemen will normally be unable to determine which of the individuals has shouted the insult or thrown the rock, and therefore, a direct arrest is difficult. Under the circumstances, what the police normally try to do is seize the ringleaders. Since it is not at all obvious the police are able to detect the ringleaders, there is no strong reason to believe they get the right people; but they may, perhaps, not be completely random in their arrest patterns. In any event, it is clear that this activity is safer under these conditions than it would normally be.

This is particularly true because not only does the mob give some kind of concealment to the person who is, shall we say, throwing rocks at the police, but it also provides him with protection. The police are normally very heavily outnumbered by the rioters and, hence, are not really in a position to push quickly through and arrest any person they want. Unless the individual is in the front ranks or, better yet, actually somewhat in front of the mob, the police will find it quite hard to arrest him because of the prospects of physical violence from the rest of the mob. Thus, there is further protection for the individual committing this kind of act. His costs are clearly much lower than they normally would be.

Thus, if we consider that there are at least some people in society who would like to throw rocks at policemen or shout insults at them, then for them the cost of this activity goes down sharply during a riot and one would anticipate that their consumption of these "goods" would rise.

This, of course, assumes the kind of mob or riot in which there is no great internal discipline. Mahatma Gandhi, in the early part of the 20th century, organized a number of very large demonstrations in which the demonstrators were subject to extraordinarily tight disciplinary control from the mob itself. The benefits for this discipline were fairly obvious. He was attempting to appeal to the conscience of the English and realized that it was important that his followers do nothing that might offend the English newspaper reader. It is likely that, in general, public order was much better kept in and around one of his demonstrations than elsewhere.

But this is simply a further illustration of the same point. The mobs and demonstrations organized by Gandhi were extremely well behaved because the individual who committed some minor crime while participating would find not only the police but all the people around him would impose costs on him. He would certainly be immediately turned over to the police, accompanied by a group of witnesses, and he would find himself permanently barred from membership in the demonstrating political organization. Under the circumstances, these demonstrations were extraordinarily orderly, and the proverbial virgin with a bag of gold could have walked through them with much greater safety than she can walk today through Central Park.

A mob, then, changes the environment in which individuals operate. This change can be, as it was in the case of the Gandhi-organized demonstrations, a great reinforcement of the normal police activities in society because the members of the mob will enforce a set of rules and they are far more numerous than are the police. On the other hand, if the mob happens to feel the other way, it can mean a great relaxation of these principles. The ceremonial public murder by torture of a considerable number of political figures when the Nuri Pasha regime was overthrown in Iraq was as valid an expression of the change in environment in which the rioters operated as were the Gandhian demonstrations—in general, their opposite.

Once again, however, we have not proved that the economic explanation is the correct one. It is certainly true that when a mob is in the streets, the environment is different. The cost and benefits of various acts are different from the norm. We would, therefore, anticipate changed behavior, and we do observe it. But this is merely one hypothesis. The alternative hypothesis that people somehow change in a riot cannot be ruled out on this evidence. What we need is a further empirical work.

QUESTIONS TO PONDER

1. Earlier in this chapter, we described an experiment conducted by a sociologist that involved a bottle with a narrow neck and pieces of string with knots on their ends. Reread the description of the experiment. Try the experiment in class or with a large group of friends.

2. Whenever a commercial plane takes off in the United States, a stewardess at the front of the cabin explains where the emergency exits are. No one (almost no one) listens. Nevertheless, in many accidents in which the plane cabin remains intact, the passengers get out with remarkable speed and without jamming at the doors. How do you account for this? (There are safety regulations providing for both facilities and evacuation activity; you might be interested in looking them up.)

3. Suntzu, the first Chinese military theorist, urged very strongly that an army never completely surround its enemy but always leave a passage by which his troops can escape. Do you think this is a wise policy? Why?

PART 5

THE PUBLIC'S
FINANCES
AND POLICIES

CHAPTER 13

The inevitability of
taxes—and their
consequences

Benjamin Franklin once wrote to a friend that "in this world nothing is certain but death and taxes." Modern experience teaches that one more thing is for sure: Franklin had the order all wrong. All (or almost all) of us face a multitude of taxes from birth, and the taxes we pay seem always and everywhere to be on an upward spiral, taking a perpetually larger share of our purchasing power. We pay taxes on the income we earn, the goods we buy, the money we save, the property we create, and many of the gifts we receive. Death brings with it one more cruel stroke from the Internal Revenue Service, a tax on the estate we leave. Government seems intent upon insuring the validity of an old adage, "You can't take it (or at least, all of it) with you."

To many taxpayers, Howard Jarvis, author of California's Proposition 13 restricting that state's taxing power, had good cause for proclaiming that he was "mad as hell" and that he did not intend to take it any longer. In 1980, government at all levels collected in taxes over $820 billion, meaning that nearly 36 percent of the average worker's paycheck went to government.

Describing the importance of taxes in our lives is difficult, because many taxes are hidden and we don't realize we are paying many of the taxes we do in terms of higher prices for goods and services. Each year economists at the Tax Foundation, Inc. calculate how long the average American worker has to labor in order to pay his (or her) taxes and dubs the date on which his tax burden is satisfied as "Tax Freedom Day." In 1980 Tax Freedom Day was May 11, three days past Tax Freedom Day of 1979. Figure 13–1 indicates that Tax Freedom Day has gradually moved from February 13 in 1930 to progressively later dates in the year, reaching a plateau of sorts during the first half of the 1970s but then shifting again in the

FIGURE 13–1

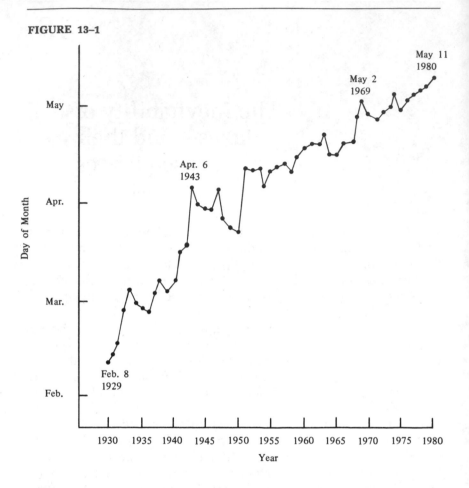

last few years of the decade. It should be noted that even during the early 1970s, government was growing and taking in more and more taxes; Tax Freedom Day remained fairly constant during the early 1970s simply because workers' income was rising faster than tax collections.

In a slightly different light, it now takes the average American worker 2 hours and 52 minutes each work day to pay his taxes. No other component of the typical family's budget takes a bigger share of the worker's time. It takes the average worker 1 hour and 1 minute of work to pay for his food and drink and 1 hour and 29 minutes to pay for his housing and utilities. Expenditures on clothing require 22 minutes of work; transportation, 41 minutes; medical care, 29 minutes; and recreation, 19 minutes.[1] In short, the frustration many people have felt toward government tax collections is real and, for many, well-founded.

Having said that, one would think that cutting taxes would be a simple matter in a democratic form of government. However, cuts in taxes spell cuts in government programs, and everyone has—or so it seems—their own little (or big) special interest to promote and protect. Hence, little or nothing tends to be done to control effectively the growth in taxes, much less reduce them. Many of the so-called cuts in taxes we read so much about in the newspapers invariably turn out to be cuts in the proposed growth of government taxing powers.

In this chapter we are concerned with the effects of government taxing powers. Much has been written elsewhere on what government does with its taxes—that is, what programs are supported with government dollars. Here we are interested in developing insights about the "allocative" effects of taxes themselves. We want to know how taxes, in addition to giving the government the wherewithal to conduct its business, influence people's consumption, savings, and investment decisions. We start with the very elementary example of how current tax codes affect the amount of reading your professors do. We then consider how poor people implicitly pay very high tax rates through the welfare (transfer) system. That discussion is followed by an analysis of the economic basis of what is termed the *subterranean economy*. Finally, we consider the effect that the windfall profit tax has on the current and future consumption of energy in this country.

THE PROFESSOR'S BOOKS

Go into almost any professor's office and you are very likely to be taken with the number of books he (or she) has. One can hardly resist wondering if the professor has really read them all. Why so many books? There are many more-or-less obvious answers to such a straight-forward question. First, the professor may need many of them for information relating directly to the research he has done in the past or is now undertaking. The books can also be useful in preparation of lectures. Second, academia tends to attract intellectual types, and heavy reading is the stock-in-trade of many intel-

---

[1] Tax Foundation, Inc.

lectuals. It's fair to say that professors as a group simply want or like to read more than other groups of people (although we all can also imagine groups of people, like ministers, who on average may read more than professors). In this regard, professors are effectively paid to pursue one of their favorite hobbies. (Nice job, you say? Many professors do like it and are willing to take a substantial cut in salary just to work behind the walls of ivy.) Third, professors tend to be paid more (and sometimes, a lot more) than other people, especially when income for summer teaching and outside consulting work is considered. In other words, the number of books the professor has on his office shelves can in part reflect his above-average purchasing power.

There are, however, other, not-so-obvious reasons for the number of books the professor has. Publishers are constantly attempting to sell books like this one to you, the student. They know you don't select your books, although you do have some hand in choosing the courses you take. They understand that the kingpin in the textbook-selection process is the professor. Accordingly, publishers must first sell your professors on their books before they can ever hope to sell them to you. And the best way to interest your professor in the book is to give him a copy for his perusal. Publishers figure a professor is not likely to adopt many books he or she has not seen (which is not always the case), and publishers are forced by competition for adoptions to give complimentary copies to faculty. A publisher can figure that if it does not give its books away and other publishers do, then it can not hope to secure adoptions. From this short analysis of the textbook market, you may understand why the publisher of this book distributed during its first year of publication somewhere between 4,000 and 8,000 complimentary copies of the book to professors. The publisher had to do it!

When told of these sales techniques, students are sometimes understandably disturbed. Some think the book market is one big rip-off of them; the books standing idle on the professor's shelves represent greater costs to the publishers and higher prices paid by students. To some extent, the concern is justified simply because the world we live and work in is slightly less than perfect. There are, without questions, some professors who, because they do not have to incur the cost of their actions, write every publisher in the country for all the freebies they can get and then sell them to a used-book seller at one-third to one-half their retail prices. You may imagine that these types of professors are an irritating concern to publishers; they represent many wasted books. The sales representatives of publishers are constantly attempting to spot these professors and to restrict their ability to get free books. However, with all of its imperfections, the giveaway program of publishers does not necessarily, in and of itself, result in higher prices to students. Why, you ask? The answer is very simple.

Publishers must sell their books in one way or another, and there will always be selling costs. (Of course, we could alleviate part of that problem by having state published and distributed books, but you can imagine there are difficulties with such a system also. What are they, by the way?) The question the private publisher faces is how to sell books in the most cost effective way. Giving books away is obviously one way that is cost effective. If it were not, then why do firms employ it? If increasing the size of the publisher's sales force were a more cost effective way, on the margin, then publishers would increase their sales force just to make an additional buck, if for no other reason. The moral of this short digression from the main topic of this section is clear: professors have as many books on their shelves as they do because of the cost of alternative ways of selling books, such as advertising. If, for example, the costs of advertising a book with glossy folders were to rise relative to the costs of printing books, then publishers would, on the margin, shift to giving more books away and using less advertising in their attempts to secure adoptions.

There is another, even less obvious explanation for the number of books a professor has and reads. Under the Internal Revenue Code, businesses are permitted to deduct their expenses of doing business in the process of computing their taxable income. The higher their deductible expenses, the lower their taxable income and the lower their obligation to government. That seems reasonable enough. However, you should also understand that a professor is, in a legal sense, engaged in the business of providing lectures for students and research for a university and outside funding agencies.

In the course of doing business, the professor must incur certain expenses, one of which is the purchase of books, journals, and related materials. All of these expenditures are deductible from the professor's taxable income. Hence, every time the professor buys a book he gets a tax break—that is, his taxes go down by a percentage of the purchase price of the book. For example, suppose a professor buys a book related to his work the price of which is $20. Because the book price is deductible, the professor's taxable income falls by that amount, $20. But the professor would have had to pay taxes on that $20 if it were not for the book purchase. If he or she were in a 35 percent marginal tax bracket, he (or she) would have had to pay $7 more in taxes. Hence, by buying the book, the professor saves, in a sense, $7 in taxes; and the book only costs, after allowing for the tax break, $13 ($20 − $7). In short, one perhaps important reason professors have so many books is the tax break they get from them. One reason professors buy, as a group, more books than other groups of people is that the relative prices of books to professors are lower (when the tax break is considered) than they are for other people.

In other words, if a given professor's demand for, say, books in economics were the same as a plumber's demand for books in economics (they both had the same income, tastes, and so forth), the professor would tend to buy more economics books than the plumber. The economics books are a deductible item for the professor, whereas they are not for the plumber. Because of the lower effective price paid, the professor is further down his demand curve for books than the plumber.

The tax break the professor gets on books is not the only professional advantage awarded people in academia. Any expense a professor incurs that is remotely related to his work can be deductible from taxable income as a business expense. Therefore, many professors not only deduct their expenditures on professional journals like the *Journal of Political Economy* and the *Journal of Economic Education* but also their annual subscription prices of magazines like *Newsweek* (professors must remain current) and newspapers like *The Wall Street Journal* and their local daily paper. Just what constitutes a business expense is, to a significant extent, left to the discretion of the individual professor. Although they might have a hard time explaining a deduction for *Playboy* and *Playgirl*, they could conceivably justify a deduction for *Life* magazine. Further, an economics professor may be able to justify the purchase of *All the President's Men* (a rather popular exposé of the Watergate episode by reporters Woodward and Bernstein) as a business expense on the ground that his (or her) professional interests extend to an understanding of political intrigue and its consequences on the economy.

If a professor has income from sources outside the university, then he can maintain an office in his home (which he might have maintained anyway without the extra income) and can deduct a part of the family's expenses on the house as costs of doing his outside business. The professor can even depreciate the furniture in his office, lowering the taxes paid. And he can claim purchases of hand calculators, home computers, and typewriters as business expenditures; take an investment tax credit (what is that?) on the purchases; and depreciate the equipment and deduct the depreciation from his (or her) business income. There is one case of a professor who set up an office in his home, paid $650 for a stereo to go in the office, and depreciated the stereo as office equipment on the grounds that the stereo was important to increasing office productivity. The deduction saved the professor about $240 in taxes, meaning the stereo on balance cost the professor $410. (Because of the anticipated tax savings, the professor bought a larger and better stereo than he otherwise would have purchased!) Worried about the fate of the professor? The deduction was approved by the IRS in an audit.

The point of this discussion is not to suggest that professors as a group act any more or less ethically than other groups. They are just people who, like all others, respond to the tax incentives afforded to them. And they respond in a fairly predictable manner: lower the after-tax price of any good professors buy, and they will buy more of it, a simple applicator of the law of demand. The central point of the discussion is that the tax system, by its very nature, gives people incentives to do a wide variety of things they would not otherwise have done. What people do in response to tax incentives may or may not be in the public interest (whatever that is) or even be intended; the important point is that an understanding of the incentives and disincentives of the tax system can be very helpful in our attempt to understand why people behave (on the margin) the way they do.

Consider the following examples of how tax incentives available to people other than professors affect behavior. In addition to salaries, churches give their ministers a housing allowance, which is not considered by the IRS to be taxable income. A minister who makes $20,000 in salaries and takes home a $5,000 housing allowance actually has more purchasing power than someone else who has a straight salary of $25,000. Further, everything else equal, we would expect the minister to buy more house than someone else with a $25,000 income; the minister's after-tax income is higher, and the relative price of housing (given the tax advantage) is lower to the minister than to the nonminister.

Generally speaking, a person's salary is taxable, but fringe benefits are not taxable. Therefore, a company can increase the effective income of its employees by switching compensation from salary to fringe benefits. And fringe benefits can be provided in a variety of forms: medical and dental insurance, life insurance, more attractive work environments, company parties, gymnasiums, company automobiles, conventions at vacation resorts, and fewer demands on the job. Sometimes the ingenuity of companies in developing dodges from the taxes borders on the bizarre. *The Wall Street Journal* reported in early 1980 that "Corporations are sending executives—and their wives—to have facelifts, and picking up the bills. 'Why not?' asked the plastic surgeon, 'It's unique, expensive, and tax deductible as a medical expense.' And in the tough world of business, every little advantage counts."[2]

As tax rates have risen over the decades, we have observed a growth in fringe benefits as a percentage of total worker compensation. Part (but not all) of this growth can be explained by the growth in the tax rates. We can expect that in the future many more people will take more and more of their income in fringes. Tax revenues will therefore not rise by as much, percentage wise, as tax rates.

THE WELFARE STATE AND THE HIGH TAX RATES ON THE POOR

Most, but not all, people have a heartfelt concern for the truly destitute people in their midst. Accordingly, many private charities have been organized for the relief of severe and not-so-severe poverty problems. Organizations like United Way and the Other Way, churches, and civic organizations spend literally hundreds of millions of dollars each year attempting to help people. The importance of these private relief efforts is oftentimes understated because the value of the time of the people who help others, without pay, is often left unrecorded. Newcasts also make us aware on a regular basis of the many unorganized private efforts to relieve the pains of poverty. We all know of instances in which people in a community take up a special collection to pay for, say, an infant's heart operation. In 1979 in a small South Carolina town, an impoverished man was caught just before Christmas rummaging through a garbage dump for toys he could give to his children for Christmas. He was charged with trespassing by the arresting officer. After the wire services picked up the story and told the country of the charges and the man's intent, the man and his family were deluged with gifts that Christmas. The family received more than $20,000 in cash gifts alone.

Still the voting public seems to believe that private charity is not

---

[2] *The Wall Street Journal*, March 29, 1980, p. 20.

enough, that under a completely voluntary charity system, many people are left without any aid at all or with less aid than is needed. Even conservative economist Milton Friedman makes a strong case for public charity: "... I am distressed by the sight of poverty; I am benefited by its alleviation; but I am benefited equally whether I or someone else pays for its alleviation; the benefits of other people's charity therefore partly accrue to me. To put it differently, we might all of us be willing to contribute to the relief of poverty, *provided* everyone else did. We might not be willing to contribute the same amount without such assurance."[3] An implication of Friedman's comments is that private charity is "sub-optimal," less than it "should" be or less than what people in the aggregate want it to be. The reason we do not have the optimal amount of private poverty relief is that aid is a kind of public good, meaning that people (who do not give) cannot be excluded from the benefits of charity relief given by others and that many people "free ride" on the private charitable contributions of others. According to Friedman and others who make this argument, poverty relief has many of the same characteristics of other public goods, like national defense and police protection, and must be provided publicly for many of the same reasons.[4]

Government efforts to help the poor frequently have, for several reasons, unexpected consequences. First, given the attention the welfare budgets of federal, state, and local governments receive in the press, it may appear to many that the poor are really "raking in the benefits." While it is true that the budget of the Departments of Education and Human Resources extends into the hundreds of billions of dollars (and was $283 billion for all social welfare programs in 1980), the amount of aid reaching the poor is actually a minor portion of the total expenditure (about 17 percent of all welfare expenditures in 1974, the latest year for which data is available). Further, welfare payments provided by the government usually lead to a reduction in private charity contributions. Indeed, public charity is many times designed to replace (and not just supplement) private charity.

---

[3] Milton Friedman, *Capitalism and Freedom* (Chicago: University of Chicago Press, 1962), p. 191.

[4] One of the authors has raised serious reservations about this argument. See Richard B. McKenzie, "The Construction of the Demand for a Public Good and the Theory of Income Redistribution," *Public Choice* (forthcoming). These reservations do not, however, affect the attainment of the limited objectives of this section.

Third, it is often believed that, because the poor earn little or no income, they pay no taxes. That is simply not the case. Even if their income is so low that they are not subject to an income tax, most poor people do pay social security taxes. Granted, the social security taxes are set up so that they are supposed to be shared equally by the employee and employer (each paying in 1981, 6.65 percent of worker's earned income up to $29,700), but in reality, the worker, even the very poor, pays both shares (for a total tax rate of 13.30 percent of income in 1980). (How does that happen? Why is that the case?) Poor people pay sales taxes on all store purchases, property taxes on their homes and cars, excise taxes on the beverages and gasoline they buy, and tariffs on the imported goods they purchase just to name a few taxes paid by all people. Further, when taxes are levied on the profits of corporations, costs of doing business (legally) rise, and the prices of the goods they sell follow the higher costs. The poor, along with everyone else, pay a part of these corporate income taxes through higher prices and reduced quantities of goods available to them. Indeed, because the poor tend to spend just about everything they earn and pay sales taxes on everything they buy, the effective tax rate (as a percent of income) from the sales tax alone generally means that the poor hand over a higher percentage of their income in taxes than do other, higher income groups.

Fourth, welfare benefits, whether in cash or in kind (like food, housing, and medical care), are generally provided in amounts that are inversely related to family or individual earned income—that is, the higher the earned income, the lower the benefits and vice versa. Scaling benefits downward as income rises eventually leads to some "break-even income level" above which the welfare recipient is on his or her own. Such a system is designed in part to provide the welfare recipients with an incentive to earn an income and get off welfare. If the benefits were not inversely related to earned income and if, for example, only people below a certain income level, like $7,000, were provided with benefits that would raise the recipients to $7,000, recipients with potential income in the vicinity of $7,000 would have little or no financial incentive to earn any income at all. Clearly, the welfare system would be a disincentive to work. Anything earned by an individual making less than $7,000 would effectively be taken away from the recipient by way of reduced government benefits; the recipient would be no better off, monetarily speaking, by his efforts. Reducing benefits as earned income increases insures the recipient is at least somewhat better off by working and earning part of his living.

Embedded in this type of graduated welfare system, however, is an *implicit* income tax paid by those on the welfare roles. Consider Table 13–1. It contains a hypothetical welfare program: as family earned income rises from $0 to $10,000 by increments of $1,000, welfare benefits (whether in the form of cash, food, and/or housing) fall gradually, leading to a rise in total usable income from $4,000 to $10,000. Every time the individual earns an additional $1,000, the government takes away $400 worth of welfare benefits. The recipient gains only $600 additional dollars from his or her efforts. This implies that the individual, through the design of the welfare system, confronts, on the margin, a 40 percent income-tax rate. That implicit tax rate should have much the same disincentive effect on a person's willingness to work as it would have on a much higher income person who actually pays taxes.

TABLE 13–1
Earned income and implicit taxes, example I

Earned income	Welfare benefits	Total usable income	Explicit tax on income	Tax rate as percentage of income
$ 0	$4,000	$ 1,000	$ 0	0
1,000	3,600	4,600	400	40
2,000	3,200	5,200	400	40
3,000	2,800	5,000	400	40
4,000	2,400	6,400	400	40
5,000	2,000	7,000	400	40
6,000	1,600	7,600	400	40
7,000	1,200	8,200	400	40
8,000	800	8,000	400	40
9,000	400	9,400	400	40
10,000	0	10,000	400	40

Granted, the government can reduce the disincentive effects of the implicit tax system. However, to accomplish that the government must (1) lower the benefits going to the lower income people, enabling the government to take less away as earned income rises (thereby reducing the implicit tax rate); and/or (2) keep the benefits the same for someone with no income but reduce the benefits by smaller amounts as earned income rises, decreasing again the implicit tax rate. The first alternative simply means that the welfare recipients will receive fewer benefits. A greater work incentive comes, in this case, with some sacrifice of the goal of helping the very poor in our midst.

The second alternative means that the break-even income (which is $10,000 in the table) is extended upward. As shown in Table 13–2, the marginal tax rate can be reduced to 20 percent by extending the break-even income level to $20,000. Obviously, in this case a lot of not-so-poor people are made beneficiaries of the welfare state, and the size of the welfare budget expands for two reasons: greater benefits going to the poor and benefits being extended to people who are not-at-all impoverished.

TABLE 13–2
Earned income and implicit taxes, example II

Earned income	Welfare benefits	Total usable income	Explicit tax on income	Tax rate as per-centage of income
$ 0	$4,000	$ 4,000	$200	20
1,000	3,000	4,800	200	20
2,000	3,600	5,600	200	20
19,000	200	19,200	200	20
20,000	0	20,000	200	20

Under our present welfare system, there are a number of programs the benefits of which are inversely related to earned income. The summation of the *implicit* marginal income tax rates associated with the welfare programs plus the *explicit* income tax rates the poor must confront when they earn and spend their incomes can spell a rather hefty tax-rate burden and disincentive for some or most of the poorest people in the country. Indeed, the combined implicit and explicit tax rate of the poor can (and does) exceed the marginal tax rates encountered by much higher income groups. Edgar Browning, on whose work this section is largely based, has provided us with an estimate (albeit venturesome) of the marginal tax rates paid by people with income below the official poverty level. The estimated marginal tax rate of the poor is 65 percent (and may, for many poor, be above 80 percent).[5] Admittedly, Browning's tax-rate estimates are based on several key assumptions that may be reasonably questioned by other researchers in public economics. However,

---

[5] Edgar K. Browning, "How Much More Equality Can We Afford?" *Public Interest* (Spring 1976), pp. 90–110; and *Redistribution and the Welfare System* (Washington, D.C.: American Enterprise Institute for Public Policy Research, 1975).

Browning's key finding that the poor pay very high marginal tax rates is rarely disputed by anyone. In short, if one is interested in explaining the relative willingness of different income groups to work for a living, they should look very closely at the welfare system and the implied tax-rate structure.

How much more should or can we expand the welfare state? That is an important question that Browning has also explored.[6] He suggests that there are greater restrictions on the ability of a society to help the poor than one might imagine on first thought. If more income is transferred to the poor, then we confront a very real dilemma, implying a real choice between greater help for the poor and greater disincentives for the poor to earn a living. If more income is transferred to the poor and if the break-even income level ($10,000 in Table 13–2) is not moved upwards, the greater initial benefits going to the poor must rise, and the benefits must fall faster in order for them to reach zero at the same break-even income level. The result: a higher implicit marginal tax rate faced by the poor and a greater disincentive for the poor to work and earn money. If, on the other hand, greater benefits are to be provided to the poor and the implicit marginal tax rate is not raised, the break-even income level must be moved up, meaning that many more people must be made beneficiaries of the welfare system and that fewer taxpayers will be available for meeting the welfare burden. Hence, to transfer an additional, say, 1 percent of the nation's income to the very poor, significantly more than 1 percent of the remaining taxpayers' income must be taken way.[7] Greater and greater aid going to the poor, with no change in the implicit marginal tax rate faced by the poor, spells progressively higher and higher explicit marginal tax rates applied to the income of the higher-income groups. The progressively higher marginal tax rates paid by the remaining taxpayers will be disincentives for them to earn the income that is transferred to the poor. In short, according to this line of analysis, if the transfer system is taken too far then the system can, as an old adage suggests, kill (or make very sick) the goose that makes the transfers possible. As suggested by Arthur Okun, former chairman of the Council of Eco-

---

[6] See especially, Browning, "How Much More Equality Can We Afford?"

[7] Morton Paglin has found that, as the welfare system expanded between 1959 and 1975 and the number of poor in the United States fell 17.6 million to 3.6 million (Paglin's "adjusted" estimates), the percent of the market value of in-kind transfers (food, housing, and medical care) actually going to the poor fell from 51.7 to 45.0. "Poverty in the United States," *Policy Review* (Spring 1980).

nomic Advisers, in any welfare system there are real and consequential trade-offs between equity and efficiency.[8]

TAXES AND THE SUBTERRANEAN ECONOMY

Mortimer Caplin, commissioner of the Internal Revenue Service under the Kennedy and Johnson administrations, is distressed with the development in the United States of what is called the "subterranean (or underground) economy." The subterranean economy includes those economic transactions that escape the watchful eye of the Internal Revenue Service and therefore result in unreported income and unpaid taxes. Caplin has written that according to the IRS study, the subterranean economy resulted in 1976 in at least $135 billion of unreported income and in at least $26 billion of unpaid taxes. Indeed, it is conceivable that the short-fall in reported income may have been in 1976 as much as four times the IRS estimate, or $540 billion, or more than a quarter of the year's gross national product.

Given inflation and the growth in income, it is very likely that much more income goes unreported today than it did back in 1976. Caplin concludes, "Participants in the underground economy place a heavy burden on the overwhelming majority of honest American taxpayers. National defense and other government expenditures must ultimately be met with taxes, and to the extent that some cheat, the rest of us foot the bill. Whether the annual tax gap is $26 billion or $100 billion, it contributes mightily to our unbalanced budget and by doing so, adds fuel to inflation."[9]

The IRS study of the underground economy found that failure to report income is widespread among taxpayers in the country.

Thirty-six to 40 percent of the incomes of self-employed people goes unreported. Indeed, wherever transactions are carried on mainly for cash, a high percentage of the earned income will very likely go unreported and untaxed.

Seventeen to 22 percent of all capital gains on the sale of properties escapes the capital gains tax by remaining unreported.

And 8 to 16 percent of all interest and dividend income is also unreported each year.

---

[8] Arthur Okun, *Equity and Efficiency: The Big Trade-Off* (Washington, D.C.: The Brookings Institution, 1975).

[9] Mortimer Caplin, "Uncovering the Underground Economy," *The Wall Street Journal*, March 31, 1980, p. 20.

Finding examples of how the subterranean economy works is not very difficult. All one has to do is ask a typical waitress or waiter how much of the tips collected is reported to the IRS. Very likely, only a minor fraction of the tips will be reported, meaning that the waitress or waiter's after-tax purchasing power is significantly greater than it would be if the income were reported. People who deliver wood for fireplaces generally insist that payment be made in cash. The purpose: to avoid traceable income and, therefore, taxes. In such a situation, the buyer may be pleased to pay in cash. He or she knows that the person who delivers the wood would probably charge a higher price if payment could not be received in cash. In short, both the buyer and the seller can share in the benefits of escaping taxes in the subterranean economy. And, of course, all illegal transactions in drugs, gambling, fenced merchandise, and prostitution result in income that is not taxed. It follows that a prostitute who collects, for example, $40,000 in fees actually makes the equivalent of about $67,000 in the above-ground economy.

The subterranean economy is not restricted to the United States. In fact, the subterranean economies of Britain, France, and Italy are believed by most to be far more extensive than the subterranean economy in this country. In Britain, vendors commonly offer buyers a 25-percent cash discount. The vendors figure they are better off giving the discount than they would be if the transactions were made by check and taxed at a rate much higher than 25 percent.

In his analysis of the subterranean economy, Caplin provides us with a list of three causes: "(1) the public's continued post-Watergate disrespect for government, (2) the financial pressures exerted by mounting inflation, and (3) the IRS's limited enforcement capabilities."[10] He points out that the IRS has only 19,000 agents and auditors to handle 140 million returns of all types and that "Today very few returns are ever subjected to real scrutiny. Over the last several years, IRS audit coverage—the percentage of tax returns reviewed by IRS examiners—has been below 3 percent and falling. In fact, audit coverage of the latest batch of individual income tax returns was only slightly over 2 percent—1.84 million examinations out of 87.3 million filings."[11] In other words, tax evasion is a good gamble for many.

As complete as Caplin's evaluation of the underground economy is, he overlooks what is perhaps the most important explanation for

---

[10] Ibid.
[11] Ibid.

its development and growth in recent decades: higher tax rates, especially higher marginal tax rates. Average tax rates (total tax collections divided by the adjusted net national product) rose from 25 percent in 1950 to 37 percent in 1977. When tax rates were very low, say, before the 1930s, people had very little financial incentive to escape the taxes by going underground in their economic dealings with others. The very limited taxes they would have had to pay were the price of *not* going underground. Now that tax rates and incomes are much higher, the price (in terms of tax liability) of not participating in the underground economy is much greater. Therefore, we would expect more underground activity today than decades ago, even if Watergate had never occurred and even if the chances of getting caught evading taxes today were the same as years ago. Inflation may be contributing to the expansion of the underground economy simply because inflation increases people's money incomes (although, not their real incomes) and pushes people into higher and higher tax-rate brackets. The higher tax rates then, in turn, induce more tax evasion.

Do tax cheaters impose a heavier tax burden on other honest taxpayers? The answer to that question is not as straightforward as Mr. Caplin suggests. If we assume that government is hell-bent on raising a given level of funds, then it follows that cheaters do impose a burden on other taxpayers. What is not collected from one must be collected from another. However, if we take a less gracious view of government and assume that government (i.e., the politicians and bureaucrats who run government) is out to maximize tax collections, then it may be that the tax evasion of cheaters is actually modulating the tax-rate demands on law-abiding taxpayers. A tax-maximizing government should be interested in achieving the greatest product from multiplying the tax rate times the reported taxable income. In an economy in which subterraneous activity is possible, it is reasonable to assume that when tax rates are raised, taxable income falls (part of the income goes underground). It is conceivable that tax rates can be raised to a point that taxable income falls to such an extent that the product of the tax rate times the taxable income actually falls. (The reader may recognize that we have here another application of the concept of the elasticity of demand.) In this event, the cheaters can actually be restraining the tax drive of government and reducing (from what it otherwise would have been) the tax burden of the noncheaters. Admittedly, which view of government and consequences of the subterranean economy is more correct is a question that can only be resolved by empirical work, which at this point has not, to our knowledge, been done. However, economic analysis of the sort presented here does provide one important benefit; it tells us what the empirical questions are.

THE WIND-FALL PROFITS TAX AND THE
OIL INDUSTRY

In 1974, the government began a program to strictly regulate the prices domestic oil companies could charge for each barrel of oil produced. Under the program, the then newly formed Department of Energy discriminated between "old" and "new oil," allowing a barrel of newly discovered oil (new oil) to sell for a higher price than a barrel of oil discovered prior to 1974 (old oil). The purpose of the price control program was, supposedly, twofold: first, to insure that oil companies were not able to reap wind-fall gains from the restrictions on world oil supplies brought about by the actions of the Organization of Petroleum Exporting Countries (OPEC); second, to insure that oil companies were still given some incentive (through higher prices on new oil) to search for new reserves.

Through succeeding years of actual operation of the program, it became clear to just about everyone that the Department of Energy was doing a poor job of controlling prices and that the price control program was restricting the search and discovery of new oil reserves. As a consequence, the demand for foreign oil was mounting, oil imports became a serious drain on the balance of payments, and the control program was enabling the Arab countries to charge higher prices than they otherwise would have been able to charge. (Explain how that could happen.) As a part of their program to achieve energy independence from foreign oil suppliers, President Ford and then President Carter proposed to deregulate the oil industry. A deregulation bill was not passed by Congress and signed into law until 1979. Under that bill, the oil industry would be freed from price controls in a step-by-step manner by 1985.

Once prices were decontrolled (and OPEC continued to restrict its production), the profits of the domestic oil industry soared, rising at triple-digit rates that caught the headlines of every newspaper in the country. In conjunction with his decontrol measure, President Carter proposed a wind-fall profits tax on the oil industry. After more than a year of political wrangling, such a tax finally passed in the spring of 1980.

The tax scheme that was actually passed is rather intricate; how-

222
CHAPTER THIRTEEN

ever, the principles are fairly straightforward. A percentage tax is applied to the difference between some base price per barrel, set by the Department of Energy, and the price per barrel on the oil market. If, for example, the base price was set at $13, the market price was $33, and the tax rate was 50 percent, the wind-fall profits tax would be $10 per barrel [.50 × ($33 − $13)].[12] From the so-called wind-fall profits tax, the government expects to collect $228 billion during the decade of the 1980s. In passing the legislation, Congress suggested that 60 percent of the collected taxes be used for reducing individual and business income taxes. The remaining portion of the taxes would be used to fund energy research programs (15 percent) and to aid low-income people in meeting their energy bills (25 percent.)[13]

Does the wind-fall profits tax contribute to economic efficiency? This is a question, as we will see, the answer to which depends upon one's perspective of how government does or should operate. The first impulse of many economists is to conclude that the wind-fall profits tax *reduces* economic efficiency. These economists point out that the wind-fall profits tax is not a tax on profits, per se. Rather, it is a tax that is related to the price of a barrel of oil and to the number of barrels that are produced. As the market price rises (and the base price remains constant), the tax per barrel rises. Further, the tax collections of the government rise with production and sales. Accordingly, the tax changes a firm's costs of doing business by increasing the marginal cost of production, decreasing industry supply, raising market price, and distorting consumer purchases away from oil products. In addition, the tax reduces the incentive firms would otherwise have to search for new reserves.

Granted, without a wind-fall profits tax, the oil industry would make greater profits. But, economists who object to the tax might argue that it is better for the industry to have the profits than for the government to have them, that the profits would provide the

---

[12] The actual base prices in 1980 ranged from $12.89 to $16.55 per barrel of different categories of oil. The tax rate was 30 percent on oil discovered after 1978 and on oil discovered with expensive "tertiary techniques." The tax rate on low-production stripper wells was 50 percent on the first 1,000 barrels per day, 60 percent on all additional barrels. The tax rate on all oil found before 1979 by major companies was set at 70 percent.

[13] Actually, the Congress in 1979 did not firmly commit itself to using the taxes for anything. The tax money was to be placed in an escrow account. Its use would be determined by legislation to follow.

industry with the necessary funds to expand their exploration efforts, and that the government should be more concerned with getting consumers the energy they want rather than with the equity of the income redistribution. Others might argue that it is the oil industry that found the oil, not the taxpayers, and that the oil industry is *entitled* to the oil that is discovered and delivered to the market.

From another, dramatically different perspective, the wind-fall profits tax might be viewed as efficient, contributing to total economic welfare. Economists with this point of view reason that in a *free* market system, the introduction of a profit tax on the oil industry can have all of the effects discussed above: it can lead to inefficiency because it reduces output from competitive levels. However, they point out that the current wind-fall profits tax was not superimposed on a free, unregulated market. Indeed, the oil market in 1979 was hamstrung with price controls and allocation directives from Washington. The controls themselves were contributing to economic inefficiency. The problem facing policy markets in 1978 and 1979 was one of devising a *politically acceptable means* of liberating the oil industry from the inefficient controls. A proposal to decontrol completely the oil industry, by itself, was doomed to failure. The Congress understood very well that decontrol of oil prices would mean higher gasoline prices for consumers in the short run, if not also in the long run, and would also mean constituency opposition to any politician who voted for the decontrol program.

How can a president achieve the necessary political support for a decontrol program? One way is to couple the decontrol of prices with a tax on the profits of the oil industry and an income-tax cut for consumers. If, indeed, decontrol is economically efficient, greater national income should result. Hence, it follows that the losers from the decontrol proposal (i.e., consumers of energy products) can be compensated with sufficient shifts of income from the oil industry to consumers. The energy industry may not be happy with the wind-fall profits tax. However, the viable political choices may not have been between, on the one hand, decontrol and no profits tax and, on the other hand, decontrol with a profits tax. The only viable options available to the Congress may have been: (1) the retention of the control program with no profits tax and (2) decontrol with a profits tax. So long as the industry profits go up by more than the profits tax (which they will under the wind-fall profits tax system actually passed), the industry is better off with decontrol and the profits tax than it would have been with control and without the tax.[14] In other words, the wind-fall profits tax may have been the price the industry had to pay in order to get out from under the price control system.

This view of the efficiency of the wind-fall profits tax can be illustrated with the aid of Figure 13–2. The graph includes the supply of domestic energy (S_1) and the demand for domestic energy (D_1). Assuming the industry is competitive (and there is no real reason to assume otherwise), a market completely free of government control will result in an output and consumption level of Q_3 and a

FIGURE 13–2

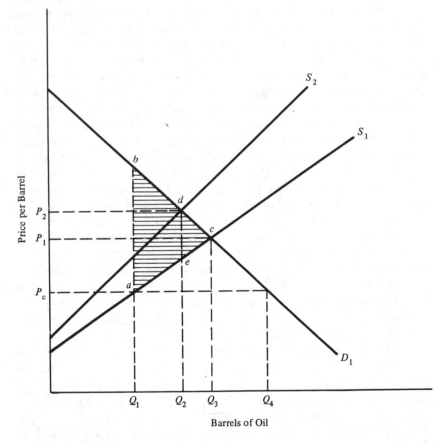

Barrels of Oil

price of P_1. However, the control program instituted in 1973 kept the price of oil below the market clearing level, say, at P_C. This control price graphically results in inefficiency equal to the triangular area abc, the difference between the area under the demand curve and the area under the supply curve between Q_1 and Q_3.[15] (The gap between the quantity demanded (Q_4) and the quantity supplied (Q_1) results in a higher demand for and price of imported oil.)

If the price is decontrolled and no tax is imposed, then the market will seek a price of P_1 and quantity of Q_3. However, if a windfall profits tax that rises with sales and price is imposed on the industry at the same time the price the industry can charge is freed from government control, then the supply curve will shift up and to the left to a position like S_2, reflecting what the industry perceives to be a higher cost structure of doing business. The combination of the two policy moves—decontrol and taxation—results in a higher than free-market price, P_2 instead of P_1, and lower than free-market quantity, Q_2 instead of Q_3. *However, output and oil consumption do rise, and economic efficiency does improve.* The inefficiency resulting from government policy falls from the triangular area abc to the smaller triangular area dce. Because the wind-fall profits tax makes possible (in a political sense) the decontrol of the industry, the wind-fall profits tax is viewed by some economists as an efficient and desirable policy course.

Which of the two perspectives developed is the correct one? That issue cannot be settled completely here. The view adopted depends partly on one's appraisal of the political options available to the president and Congress in the late 1970s. Because we doubt that a bill decontrolling the oil industry could have been passed in 1979 without the prospects of future passage of a wind-fall profits tax, we tend to side with those economists who believe the tax is efficient.[16] Such a position, however, does not mean we would oppose the elimination of the wind-fall profits tax if we could be assured that the prices of the oil industry would not once again be controlled.

---

[15] The area under the demand curve between Q_1 and Q_3 is the value consumers place on those additional units. The area under the supply (or industry marginal cost) curve is the cost of securing those additional units. When output is restricted to Q_1, consumers lose on balance the difference between the value and cost of Q_1 to Q_3 units. The triangular area abc is the net welfare loss—on inefficiency—of restricted output in the domestic oil industry.

[16] Backers of the wind-fall profits tax were, in early 1980, threatening to reimpose price controls on the oil industry if the wind-fall profits tax was not passed.

QUESTIONS TO PONDER

1. Make a list of tax advantages that are open to professionals like professors, doctors, and lawyers that are not available to assembly-line workers. If the tax code increases professors' purchases of books (as suggested in the chapter), what does it do to their purchases of goods not related to their work?

2. Consider the following welfare benefits that are available to various types of households:

Type of household	Welfare benefits
Family of four with two adults and two children	$7,000
Single individual	3,500
Family of three with one adult head and two children	5,000

    What incentive system does the welfare system set up for a family of four with income below the poverty line? What does the welfare system do to family stability? Can you think of a way of modifying the welfare benefits in order to neutralize the effects of the welfare system on family composition? What are the consequences of your proposed plan?

3. Make a list of activities that you have personally observed and that can be properly classified as a part of the subterranean economy. In what ways (if any) have you dealt in the subterranean economy? How do buyers benefit from sellers being able to escape taxes on their income? What economic factors other than taxes affect the extent of the subterranean economy in the United States?

4. What economic factors will affect the amount of federal tax collections from the wind-fall profits tax? How will the policy decisions of OPEC affect the wind-fall profits tax collections of the federal government? How will the wind-fall profits tax affect the pricing decisions of OPEC, domestic production, imports from abroad, the discovery of oil, and investment in alternative energy sources? Where possible, use supply and demand curves in your explanation.

CHAPTER 14

The Laffer (not laughter) curve

For several decades, the name of John Maynard Keynes was treated with considerable reverence in economic literature. He was the British economist who, back in the 1930s, literally revolutionized the way most economists and government policymakers thought about the function and importance of government fiscal (i.e., tax and expenditure) policy. Before Keynes, economists tended to argue that any unemployment or sluggishness in the economy will be eliminated by "natural" movements in market prices and wages. If there are more people seeking jobs than there are jobs available, then through competitive forces, wages will fall; the number of jobs will expand; the number of people looking for work will contract; and eventually the market will clear. Unemployment that persists for a long period of time can be attributed to "obstructions" in the market, such as minimum-wage laws and union contracts, that prevent the wage rate from falling.

After Keynes, economists—following the lead of Keynes—argued that unemployment can persist "naturally" in free, uncontrolled markets of consumers and investors. The cause of the persistent unemployment, insufficient (aggregate) demand. The so-called Keynesian economists reasoned that the demand of consumers for goods and services is determined by, among other things, the income level; the higher the income, the greater the consumption demand and vice versa. Investment, on the other hand, is determined by a number of factors, such as expected profits on plant and equipment and the interest rate on borrowed funds. Since savers and investors were different groups of people and since (or so it was believed) interest rates do not necessarily adjust downward when savings (at a given income level) exceed investments, the total demand of consumers and investors may at times not be sufficient to buy the total output of the economy. Hence, realizing that their inventories are

227

piling up (when goods that were produced are left unsold), businesses will cut back on production, incomes will fall, and unemployment will arise. In short, Keynesians argued that at the full-employment income level, the total demand in the economy may fall short of total production and unemployment can then emerge and can persist. Again, the cause of persistent unemployment, insufficient demand.

Before Keynes, most economists tended to believe that aside from removing obstrucions to downward wage movements, the government has no role to play in alleviating unemployment. After Keynes, most economists came to believe that government has a very important function in the macroeconomy: the stimulation of aggregate demand through its own purchases and through cuts in its tax collection. If unemployment is caused by insufficient aggregate demand, then it can be alleviated by greater government demand and/or by greater consumer demand that is induced by cuts in the taxes people pay.

Before Keynes, most economists equated deficits in government budgets with "irresponsible" government spending. After Keynes, budget deficits were seen and promoted as a means of increasing aggregate demand, thereby, as a means of stimulating an expansion in the national income level and reducing persistent unemployment. (A deficit in the government's budget means the government is spending more than it is collecting in taxes. Therefore, the government contributes more to total demand in terms of its own expenditures than it subtracts from total demand through the taxes it collects.)

During the 1950s, the federal government frequently ran budgetary deficits. However, the deficits were never (openly) advocated as a means of stimulating the domestic economy. The Eisenhower administration was always defensive about its deficits, blaming them on Congress. Congress, in turn, blamed the deficits on each other and the administration. President John Kennedy openly adopted Keynesian fiscal remedies for unemployment and retarded growth in national income. In the 1960s and through the early years of the 1970s, much of the professional attention of economists was directed at finding means of expanding, in the most effective way, total demand in the economy. In 1962 Kennedy proposed a tax reduction of about $10 billion (or 10 percent of total tax collections at that time) and suggested that the resulting budgetary deficit was "good" for the economy; it would get the "economy moving again" through its effect on demand.

Throughout the late 1960s there was a small band of economists at schools like the University of Chicago (called monetarists because of their emphasis on the need for a stable monetary policy) who contended that fiscal policy cannot possibly achieve the social benefits attributed to it by Keynes and his followers. However, most of the attention of professional economists during the 1960s was directed at finding effective means of expanding total demand in the economy. Little attention was given to the supply side of the macroeconomic equation and how taxes and government expenditures affected total supply and, therefore, employment and unemployment.

The 1970s were a period of "stagflation," a time during which the Nixon, Ford, and Carter administrations faced the twin problems of inflation and stagnation in national income and employment. It became apparent to a growing number of economists during the period that Keynesian economics did not provide ready-made solutions for all of the problems associated with stagflation. Indeed, many wondered if there were not stringent tradeoffs to be made between solving the problems of inflation and unemployment. The search began for new ways of looking at the problems facing the macroeconomy of the 1970s. This chapter deals with one of the new ways of thinking about policy. It deals with the development in the 1970s of what has come to be called the Laffer curve, named after its originator, economist Arthur Laffer at the University of Southern California. As we will see, this chapter is also concerned with the influence government tax policy has on individual incentives to work, save, and invest and, therefore, on the national income and employment levels. Briefly, the chapter deals with the supply, rather than the demand, in the macroeconomy.

TAXES AND INCENTIVES ONCE AGAIN

Keynesian economic theory implicitly assumes a direct relationship between the rates at which incomes are taxed (i.e., tax rates) and total tax collections of the federal government. As we have seen, this view of the relationship between tax rates and tax collection leads to the conclusion that economic activity can be stimulated by a reduction in tax rates: lower tax rates mean more purchasing power for consumers, more purchases and greater consumption demand, more production and national income, and less unemployment. Further, the view leads to the conclusion that inflation can be suppressed by an appropriate increase in the tax rates: higher tax rates spell more taxes for the government and less purchasing for the consumer, fewer purchases by consumers, lower consumption demand, and the elimination of any excess demand in the economy that is putting upward pressure on prices. To repeat an important point, Keynesian economics is designed to deal with problems of unemployment and inflation through changes in demand.

In addition to their effects on aggregate demand in the economy, Arthur Laffer emphasizes that tax rates can have important effects on the supply of goods and services in the macroeconomy. This is because tax rates affect people's incentives to work and produce the goods and services that give rise to income. Up to a point, higher tax rates can lead to greater effort on the part of people as they attempt to offset, by way of more earnings, the effects of taxes on their purchasing power. However, Laffer reasons that there is some point beyond which higher tax rates can actually reduce the amount of time people spend at work and, thereby, reduce the national supply of goods and services.

Higher tax rates not only reduce people's purchasing power, but they also reduce the value of work and reduce the cost people have to incur when they forgo an hour of work and engage in leisure-time activities, like riding a bicycle, going fishing, or just talking with friends. Higher tax rates effectively reduce the price of leisure (since less is given up for an hour of leisure), inducing people to take more leisure—less work. (Remember the law of demand?)

These points are further developed in Figure 14–1. In that figure we have scaled income along the vertical axis and hours of leisure along the horizontal axis. The typical citizen-taxpayer has, let us suppose, some amount of time, like T_4 or 60 hours per week, that he or she can use for work or play. If he or she uses the time for work, a money income is earned and benefits are received indirectly through the goods that can be bought. How much money income is earned for the amount of leisure time forgone is dependent upon the individual's wage rate in the market. If a citizen-taxpayer uses the time for play, benefits are received directly from the activities. The individual can give up leisure for money income, giving up the direct benefits of leisure in the process for benefits received indirectly from the purchase of goods and services with money income. In other words, in terms of Figure 14–1, the individual has a transformation curve that extends from a point on the horizontal axis, like T_4, to a point on the vertical axis, like M_8 or $600 per week (assuming the wage rate is $10 per hour of work).

FIGURE 14–1

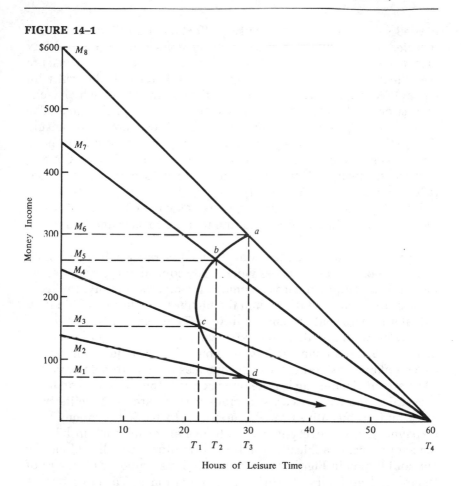

Hours of Leisure Time

Without any taxes being applied to money income, the individual can move from position T_4 to a position like a on the transformation curve. In moving to a, the individual gives up 30 hours of leisure for $300 per week in income. The individual could have more money but presumably the additional goods are not worth the additional hours of leisure that must be forgone.

Suppose the government imposes a 25 percent tax on money income. Such a tax means that the individual will take home $7.50 [$10 − .25 ($10)] for each hour worked. The tax also means that the price the individual pays for using an hour for some activity like talking with friends is reduced from $10 (which is the price without the tax) to $7.50 (which is the price after the tax is imposed). Embedded in the imposed tax are two effects: (1) an "income effect" revealed in the citizen's reduced purchasing power (or after-tax income) and (2) a "price effect" revealed in the lower price of leisure (and the higher price of goods and services than can be bought with money). With a tax rate of 25 percent, the income effect, which leads to greater work, may be more powerful than the price effect. The result: the taxpayer works longer and has fewer hours for leisure time activities. Graphically, the citizen-taxpayer moves from position a (which is on the transformation curve that reflects a tax rate of zero) to position b (which is on the transformation curve that reflects a tax rate of 25 percent).

If the tax rate is raised further, there is some point beyond which the power of the price effect (leading to more leisure and less work) outweighs the power of the income effect (leading to less leisure and more work). The consequence of higher tax rates will then be, on balance, more leisure and less work. The reduced hours spent on the job spell less output and less income in the macroeconomy. In Figure 14–1, more leisure is taken when the higher tax rates move the individual's transformation curve below M_4T_4 to, say, M_2T_4.

How do we know that higher tax rates will eventually lead to an increase in the amount of leisure, you ask. Your question can be answered by considering the consequences of an extreme tax rate of 100 percent. Under such a heavy tax rate, the government takes everything the worker earns in money; there are no benefits from work and no incentives for the taxpayer to work for money. The taxpayer then has every incentive to use all of his time in leisure-time activities. Graphically, the transformation curve lies along the horizontal axis in Figure 14–1. The individual chooses 60 hours of leisure and no hours of work, or combination e. To move from a point like c (when the tax rate is less than 100 percent) to point e (when the tax rate is 100 percent), the individual must move through combinations like d that represent fewer hours of work.

The same kind of analysis can be applied to the effects that higher and higher tax rates have on people's incentive to save and invest. Higher tax rates reduce the benefits received from not consuming (saving) and from taking the risks associated with investment. Up to a point, higher tax rates can spur saving and investment (since people can then try to offset the negative income effects of the higher tax rates by saving more and taking more risks). However, as in the case of taxes on income earned from work, higher tax rates can, beyond some point, reduce the benefits of saving and investing so severely that people save and invest less. The reduced investment means a lower capital stock for future generations and lower incomes than otherwise in the future (since less capital will mean lower productivity for workers).

The total tax collections (T) of the government are a function of two key variables: the tax rate (r) and income (Y). The mathematical relationship can be easily stated:

$$T = rY$$

For some increase in the tax rate (r), the income level (Y) can rise, giving rise to greater tax collections for the government. However, as we have pointed out, there is some increase in the tax rates that can have perverse effects on the income level: income can fall to such an extent that the product of r and Y, which is tax collections, actually falls.[1]

We noted in the preceding chapter that tax rates not only influence people's choices between work and leisure but also influence the form of income that is earned. Specifically, higher tax rates encourage people to take larger and larger shares of their incomes in nontaxable fringe benefits. High tax rates also induce people to move their work into the subterranean economy. In summary, tax collections of the government can, beyond some tax-rate level, be depressed due to (1) lower actual income and (2) lower reported taxable income.

With this knowledge of the incentive effects of tax rates, Laffer has devised a simple curve—the Laffer curve—that describes the relationship between tax rates and tax collections of the government. The general shape of the curve is illustrated in Figure 14–2. Initially, as tax rates in the figure rise from r_1 to r_2, tax collections of the government rise from T_1 to T_2. However, beyond r_2, taxable and reported incomes fall, resulting in an actual reduction in the tax collections of the government. At r_4 tax collections are zero.

THE LAFFER CURVE AND TAX POLICY

The Laffer curve has two important features. First, for every tax-collection level other than T_2 there are two tax rates—a high one and a low one—that yield the same revenue to the government. For instance, a tax rate of r_1 results in a tax collection of T_1, as indi-

---

[1] If the tax rate is raised from 30 to 40 percent and taxable income falls from $2.2 trillion to $1.6 trillion, tax collections fall from $660 billion to $640 billion.

FIGURE 14–2

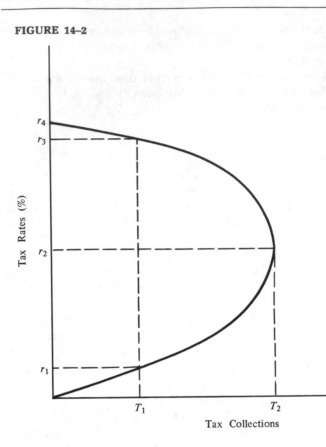

Tax Collections

cated above. However, a much higher tax rate, r_3, yields the exact same tax revenue. If given the choice between tax rates of r_1 and r_3, any government interested in maximizing its own welfare *and* the welfare of the public it is supposed to serve will choose r_1. The lower tax rate is certainly more desirable to taxpayers (aside from those with rather perverse preferences!), and it provides revenues for the same level of government programs as does the higher tax rate.

Second, as suggested in Figure 14–2, the impact of a tax rate increase depends critically upon the current *level* of taxation (as well as other factors). If tax rates are relatively low, then an increase in them will result in an expansion of tax revenues and of the ability of government to conduct its business. However, if the current level of tax rates is above r_2, an increase in rates can cause a reduction in government revenues and, accordingly, a contraction in government programs. Taxpayers are obviously hurt by such a rate increase, since they are then on lower utility levels. In addition, beneficiaries of government programs (like welfare recipients and military officers) are also harmed, since a cutback in programs can be a consequence of a reduction in tax revenues.

Observations regarding the effects of a tax-rate decrease are just as important. A tax-rate reduction can, at low levels of taxation, lead to lower tax collections and government expenditures. However, at very high levels of taxation, a tax-rate reduction can lead to an expansion of government. Under the latter condition, everyone presumably will benefit: lower tax rates will enhance taxpayer welfare. In addition, the lower tax rates will give the government the wherewithal to expand its programs and benefit people. The rate reduction will also give people greater incentive to work, save, and invest. The consequence is an expansion of national income and employment opportunities.

Professor Laffer and Congressman Jack Kemp and William Roth see in the Laffer curve a perspective for government fiscal policy that stands in sharp contrast with the Keynesian perspective. As we discussed, Keynesian economics leads to the conclusion that unemployment and sluggish national income growth can be alleviated by tax-rate cuts: tax-rate cuts lead to more consumer and business purchases—to greater aggregate demand. Laffer, Kemp, and Roth suggest that this Keynesian policy proposal not only has a questionable theoretical foundation but also is not very practical in times of high rates of inflation, such as the 1970s. Greater aggregate demand, without a change in the supplies of goods and services, can only contribute to inflationary pressures.

Laffer, Kemp, and Roth contend that tax rates should be reduced for the purposes of affecting the aggregate supply of goods. Tax-rate reductions will give people a greater incentive to work and produce, and the greater income earned from production will give people the means of buying the output. Further, they are convinced that, under the present tax system, tax rates in general are above r_2. Therefore, a tax-rate reduction will also have the effect of increasing tax collections of government. Therefore, a tax-rate reduction is good because it benefits both taxpayers and government.

The general shape of the Laffer curve is not a matter of dispute among policymakers and economists. On the other hand, there is considerable professional dispute over where we, as a nation, are on the Laffer curve. Stated differently, there is substantial disagreement over whether current tax rates in the United States are, on average, above or below r_2. The issue—which is really an empirical one—is important because of the consequences that a general tax-rate reduction will have on tax collections of government and on the ability of the government to develop its defense capability and to foster social-welfare programs. If we are above r_2, a tax-rate reduction will lead to higher tax collections. But if we are below r_2, a tax rate reduction will have the opposite effect.

Unfortunately, only a few, limited studies have been done on the supply-side effects of tax-rate reductions. The estimates that have been made are contradictory. In short, we just do not know whether tax collections will rise or fall with rate reductions. We suspect that the directional movement of tax collections will, in the final analysis, depend critically upon the type of taxes that are reduced (business and corporate income taxes and/or personal income taxes), the size of the general tax reduction, and the change in the structure of the tax-rate system.

SUPPLY-SIDE ECONOMICS AND INFLATION

Under Keynesian economics, inflation is viewed as a product of too much aggregate demand in the economy, or more goods being demanded than there are goods being produced. The difference between aggregate demand and aggregate supply places upward pressures on prices in general. Hence, Keynesians believe that inflation in the economy can be reduced by a decrease in aggregate demand. And the federal government can reduce the total demand of consumers, businesses, and governments in three principal ways: (1) a reduction in government expenditures, keeping taxes constant (and, when appropriate, running a budgetary surplus); (2) an increase in taxes by way of an increase in tax rates, holding government expenditures constant; and (3) a decrease in government expenditures along with an increase in taxes.

Supply-side economists tend to be monetarists; that is, they believe that the overwhelmingly important determinant of short-run demand in the economy is the money stock. They do not believe that government fiscal policy can do very much to affect short-run aggregate demand (at least in the way and to the extent Keynesians believe). If government reduces its expenditures and/or increases its tax collections, then monetarists argue the government will simply be less active in borrowing funds in the bond market. The lower demand for funds will lead to lower interests and greater investments and greater demand by businesses. The reduced demand brought about by government fiscal actions will be largely offset by greater demand in other sectors of the economy.

Supply-side economists, on the other hand, argue (as we have stressed above) that inflation can be fought by a reduction in tax rates—a policy recommendation that is diametrically opposite the Keynesian policy conclusion. The lower tax rates will lead to more production. And so long as the money stock is held constant, greater production will mean that the same number of dollars are chasing a larger quantity of goods and the overall price level should fall. If the money stock is growing at a constant rate that exceeds the rate of growth in output (at given tax rates), the economy will, of course, be experiencing inflation (since more dollars will then be chasing after relatively fewer goods). Under these circumstances, however, the greater production brought about by the lower tax rates should temper inflationary pressures—that is, should lower the inflation rate. In short, tax rate reductions "kill two birds with one stone," the production and unemployment problem and the inflation problem.

The reader should understand that the Keynesians have not yet, and for good reason, conceded the last word in the debate over appropriate anti-inflation tax policy to the supply-side economists. Keynesians may agree that lower tax rates will spur production, but they still point to the possibility that tax-rate cuts affect aggregate demand through increases in people's after-tax incomes. Whether or not inflation is quelled by a tax-rate cut depends upon the timing and relative magnitudes of the aggregate demand and aggregate supply effects. Given the tax-rate reduction, the demand effect may be larger than the supply effect, leading to greater inflationary pressures in the short and, possibly, long run. Further, Keynesians may point to the very real possibility that the supply effects of rate cuts may not occur until sometime in the future (when people are finally able to respond to the greater incentive of tax-rate cuts); but the demand effect may be almost immediate, meaning that rate cuts lead to greater inflationary pressures in the short run.

Supply-side economists are left unperturbed by the foregoing arguments. They might argue that even if the demand arguments of Keynesians turn out to be correct, the appropriate fiscal policy of the government may still be to lower (not raise) tax rates. Keynesians want to reduce aggregate demand by increasing government tax collections. If the average tax rate of people and businesses is above r_2 in Figure 14–2 and if tax rates are raised, then government will collect fewer, not more, taxes. Fewer goods will be produced (because of the negative incentive effects of the rate hike), and more income will go unreported to the IRS. The consequence: greater inflationary pressures, even following the Keynesian model of the macroeconomy. The Keynesians might retort by stressing that tax rates are, on average, below r_2 in Figure 14–2.

Where or when will the argument be settled? We wish we could answer that question. Much conceptual and empirical work remains to be done, as we have said. Our only advice is to stay tuned to subsequent editions of this book; perhaps we will be able to give you the answer if the issue is, in fact, ever settled.

SUPPLY-SIDE ECONOMICS: THE RICH VERSUS THE POOR

The discussion above has been developed in terms of an average tax rate for the entire population. We know, however, that tax rates vary across income groups. What constitutes appropriate tax policy for government (to accomplish whatever objective is set for government) depends critically upon the *structure* of taxes and the reaction of various groups to changes in their particular taxes. Again, consider the Laffer curve depicted this time in Figure 14–3. The United States operates under a progressive tax-rate system. This means that the higher the income, generally speaking, the higher the tax rate. Just for purposes of illustration, suppose the United States tax code is so constructed that the tax rates of high-income groups (the rich) are quite high and at position R on the Laffer curve. Suppose further that the tax rates of low income groups (the poor) are rather low and at position P on the Laffer curve.

Several points are apparent from the situation developed. An across-the-board, uniform cut in tax rates may indeed have all the incentive effects that supply-side economists contend will occur. However, it does not follow necessarily that the tax collections of the federal government will rise. The tax collections from the rich may rise, but the tax collections of the poor may fall and fall by more or less than the rise in the tax collections from the rich. However, this does not mean that the poor should necessarily be against tax-rate reductions for the rich. Such tax-rate reductions can conceivably lead to higher tax revenues that will enable the government to lower the tax rates of the poor. The government may or may not be able to lower the tax rates of the poor by as much as the rich, but both groups can still be better off. The economy can operate more efficiently and the government can maintain its current level of services.

Finally, we might note that analysis of government tax policy by way of the Laffer curve may suggest some rather odd and interest-

FIGURE 14-3

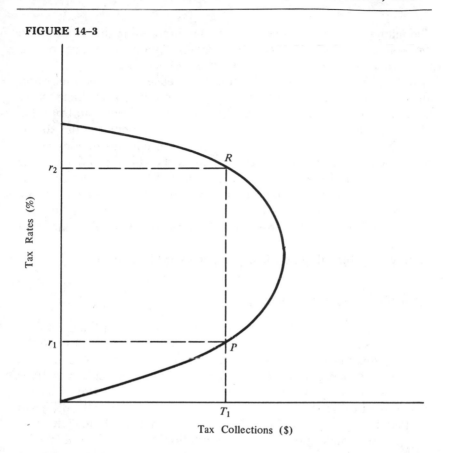

Tax Collections ($)

ing political proposals for Keynesian economists. Let us suppose that Keynesians believe the Laffer curve looks the way it does in Figure 14-3 (as we mentioned, no economist really questions the general shape of the curve), that inflation is prevalent in the economy, and that we want to formulate appropriate Keynesian policy recommendations to combat inflation. How do we do that? As we said before, we want to raise tax collections. However, a uniform increase in everyone's tax rates may not lead to higher tax collections. In terms of Figure 14-3, the tax collections of the poor will rise when their rates are raised above r_1. However, tax collections of the rich will fall if their tax rates are raised above r_2. The result of a uniform, across-the-board tax-rate increase may indeed be an increase in tax collections: the increase in the tax collections from the poor is greater than the decrease in tax collections from the rich.

The main problem with the uniform rate increase is that in order to increase government revenue by a given amount, the tax rates on the poor will have to be greater than they need to be.

Indeed, if the government wants to increase tax collections from all groups (or if the government wants to minimize the increase in the tax collections from the poor) then it should *raise* the tax rates of the *poor* and *lower* the tax rates of the *rich*. Of course, the conditions that underlie the analysis and lead to this conclusion may never really hold in the economy. Our point is that they *could* exist for some times and for some economies and that these are the types of policy conclusions that may be drawn from future research. If they are, we can only wonder how the electorate will receive the tax proposals and how well (or not so well) politicians who advocate such proposals will fair in elections. Supply-side economics may make for some very interesting political campaigns in the future.

CONCLUDING COMMENTS

Economics is fraught with controversy. Nowhere in the discipline is that truism more readily apparent than in macroeconomics and the growing debate between demand-side and supply-side economists. Both groups of economists have similar, if not identical, objectives —the reduction of unemployment and inflation. However as we have seen in this chapter, the two groups have distinctly different perspectives on how policy affects the economy. Hence, the two groups often make policy recommendations that are at odds with one another. For instance, to cure inflation demand-side Keynesian eonomists recommend tax-rate increases. Supply-side economists recommend just the opposite, tax-rate decreases. The debate on the issue vividly illustrates how important empirical studies are to the development of public policy. Because of the limitations of empirical studies, on the other hand, the debate may never be satisfactorily resolved.

QUESTIONS TO PONDER

1. Keynesian and supply-side economists both recommend tax-rate reductions as a way of increasing employment and income, but their recommendations are made for different reasons. What are those reasons? How do tax rate cuts at r_1 and r_2 in Figure 14–3 affect inflation in the Keynesian and supply-side models of the economy?

2. Using the supply-side model of the economy, how do lower tax rates affect business investment?

3. Suppose that national income is $2 trillion, that government takes 40 percent of national income in taxes, and that people are able to spend the remaining 60 percent. Suppose further the government is contemplating a 10-percent reduction in tax rates. Using the supply-side model of the economy, by how much must national income rise in response to a 10-percent tax-rate cut in order for government to collect the same taxes? Answer the same question assuming tax rates of 30, 50, 60, and 70 percent. From your calculations, what can be said about the relationship between the overall level of tax rates and the probability of government tax collections remaining the same when tax rates are reduced by a given percentage?

4. Suppose politicians and bureaucrats are out to maximize the size of government. What tax rate on the Laffer curve will be chosen by them? Under such a system and using the Keynesian model of the economy, how can the government, through the use of fiscal policy, fight inflation?

5. Consider the effects of a lump-sum tax cut of $10 to each and every taxpayer in both the Keynesian and supply-side models. Then consider the effects of a reduction in the marginal tax-rate structure that leads to an average tax cut of $10 in the Keynesian and supply-side models. Compare the effects. Does it matter in the two models how a tax reduction is brought about? Explain your answer.

CHAPTER 15

Rent seeking

In recent years, economists have been reconsidering a number of issues which most of them thought had been settled long ago. These issues fall mainly in the areas of the costs of transfers and restrictions on trade. The orthodox literature held that transfers were costless and underestimated the cost of restrictions. This reconsideration has tended to use analytical tools which go under the name *rent seeking*. Unfortunately, rent seeking is not a terribly good descriptive term, but once people begin using a word, it develops a life of its own, and it is probably true that rent seeking will continue to be the term used for this line of investigation.

THE BASIC MODEL

Let us begin by considering an old economic chestnut which is that transfers cost nothing to society. On figure 15–1, we have on the two axis Mr. X and Mr. Y. Let us assume that the total resource in our little two-man society is $1,000. This $1,000 can be divided between them in any way. Mr. X could have $1,000 and Mr. Y, nothing or Mr. Y, $1,000 and Mr. X nothing, or there could be some intermediate division. The line *PP* represents the locus of all possible divisions on it, and point *A* represents a division of these resources between the two so that X has $700 and Y, $300.

The standard economic discussion of this point would say that if we transfer some of Mr. X's wealth to Mr. Y, the result would be costless and we could end up on point *B* with X having $150 and Y, $850, but with society as a whole having as much as it had before. Mr. X's loss is exactly the same as Y's gain; hence, there has been no "social" loss. This proposition is no doubt true if we believe that the transfer of the resource from X to Y was imposed by God with no cost.[1] In the real world, however, transfers from one person

---

[1] Even in this case it is not certainly true since it is conceivable that the

FIGURE 15-1

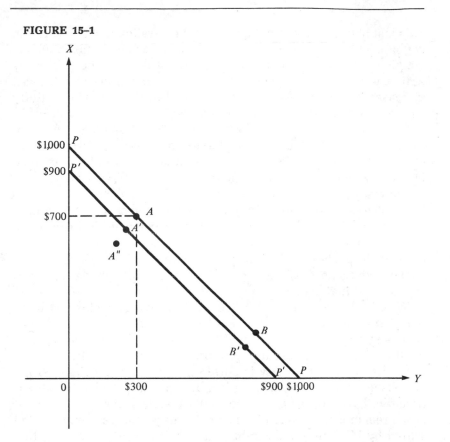

to another do not simply appear out of the blue. They are normally the result of hard work and investment of resources by the person who will receive the transfer. Sometimes they are the result of investment of resources by some third person (Z) who feels that redistributing funds from X to Y is desirable.

Note that the transfer cannot be the result of the investment of resources by X because if X wishes to give the money to Y, then we do not have a situation in which social wealth remains unchanged— it actually increases. If X wants to give a gift to Y, then X is benefited by the gift and so is Y. The same sum of money does double duty.

---

transfer of wealth away from X may lead X to work less hard; hence, total social wealth may be lower. This point will be ignored throughout the rest of this chapter, not because it is unimportant, but simply because the chapter is on another topic.

This last phenomenon might be called the paradox of charity. If you get satisfaction out of giving something to someone else and the recipient gets satisfaction out of receiving it, then the gift is, by ordinary measures, extremely productive. This is because the gift increases the utility of two people instead of the one whose utility would be increased if X, for example, spent the money on himself.

But if people have invested resources in obtaining the transfer of funds from X to Y (let us say they have gone to Washington lobbying at some cost), then the amount of resources that would be divided between X and Y after this expenditure is not PP, but some lesser amount, say $900, as shown by the line P'P'. Mr. Y will not get $850 but $765 as shown at the point B'. Of course, the cost of lobbying or engaging in some other kind of political maneuvering in order to cause a transfer may be much smaller than our example implies. Nevertheless, although any individual lobbying activity is not expensive, the sum over society as a whole is probably very great. But more of that below.

We must be cautious here, however, in drawing conclusions about the relative attractiveness of A and B'. It might be that point B' is in some sense a better location for this little two-person society than point A. Perhaps Mr. Y is in fact more deserving than Mr. X. If this is so, then in a way society is better off after transfer than before, but it is not better off in the rather simple meaning which the phrase *transfers have no social cost* normally conveys. Using the type of measurements the economist normally uses, the resources represented by P'P' are less desirable than PP, albeit it is possible that point B' is superior by some standard to point A. This gain, if there is such a gain, however, has been obtained at a cost and the move inward of the production frontier shows that cost.

Further, investment of resources by Y to obtain the transfer is not, in and of itself, enough to guarantee that the transfer will occur. Nor is it the total involvement of the resources here. It is likely that X will decide to lobby defensively also. The result will be, perhaps, that no transfer occurs, and the waste of the resources in the two lobbying activities that counterbalance each other will put society at A' or even if enough resources have been used, to point A''. In this case, by any standard, society has been injured by the attempts to redistribute, because it is clear that point A' is inferior to point A. *Everybody is worse off.*

Thus, transfers cost real resources even if they are successful, and if they are unsuccessful, their only effect may be a waste of resources, with the result that everyone is worse off. This conclusion was overlooked by economists for a long time essentially because economists paid little attention to the details of government behavior. Economists would say, perfectly correctly, that if the government transferred money from, let us say, the reader of this book to the two authors,[2] there would be no social cost, because your loss would be the same as our gain. The fact that we would have to engage in use of resources to make the transfer possible and that you would probably invest resources to defend yourself was overlooked. Thus, a good part of the real problem of transfers was overlooked, and the part that remains, i.e., the part that they did concentrate on, was a portion in which there was no resource cost. But before discussing further the problem of costly transfers, let us turn to another area in which somewhat the same kind of error has been made by traditional economics.

MONOPOLIES

In Figure 15–2, we show the diagram conventionally used to measure the cost of a monopoly. Temporarily we need not concern ourselves with the question of whether this monopoly is obtained privately by, let us say, merging steel mills or whether it is a result of some government regulation which prohibits import of foreign steel or prevents independent truckers from undercutting the prices being offered by chartered truckers.

In Figure 15–2, we have some price per unit of the monopolized product which is shown on the vertical axis and the quantity sold on the horizontal. It can be produced at a marginal (and average) cost of C, as shown by the horizontal line. Under competitive conditions, the quantity Q_C would be produced and price would be C. (Quantity Q_C is the point at which the marginal benefit of the last unit of the good equals the marginal cost.) Suppose, however, that a monopoly is organized; for simplicity, assume it is a private monopoly, although private monopolies are, of course, rarer than government-supported monopolies. The monopoly raises the price to M, and the total quantity produced falls to Q_M. The traditional measure of the welfare cost of this is the striped triangle. (Why?) The dotted rectangular area is the monopolist's profit. (Why?) Economists have traditionally argued that profits are transferred from the customers who continue buying the good. The gains of the monopolist, it is

---

[2] Obviously a meritorious transfer.

FIGURE 15–2

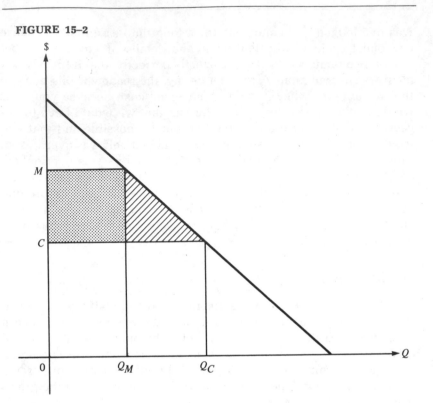

argued, exactly counterbalance the losses of the customers represented by this rectangle.

According to this conventional argument, the true loss was the striped area that represents the consumer surplus on quantity Q_C–Q_M that the monopolist refuses to produce. It is, of course, true that the striped area is part of the cost of the monopoly, but the belief that the dotted rectangle was not a cost was based on a failure to consider the process of organizing the monopoly. Clearly, if large profits can be made by getting a monopoly, whether this involves private maneuvering or talking the government into some kind of unwise legislation, we expect people to invest resources in obtaining that profit. Further, we expect them to invest resources up to the point where the return on the last dollar put into getting the monopoly or special restriction is equal to the return elsewhere. The result will then be that the resources invested in attempting to obtain the monopoly will be roughly equal to the present discounted value of the dotted rectangle.[3] Thus, the actual social cost is about the sum of the rectangle and the triangle. This is much higher than the conventional wisdom would have indicated. The error is the same as the error discussed above with respect to transfers: resources invested in obtaining the transfer or, in this case, the special privilege are ignored; hence, large social costs are overlooked.

The size of these social costs may perhaps be roughly approximated by two studies carried out by Anne Krueger.[4] She considered only one particular kind of special restriction which is the requirement that people importing merchandise to India and Turkey get foreign-exchange licenses. In this case, the beneficiaries of the restriction are not the importers or even the manufacturers who competed with imports, but the bureaucrats who handle the issuance of the licenses and take bribes. A monopoly is, in this case, created by the government for the benefit of its own employees rather than for the benefit of some outsider.

Professor Krueger found that in India, 7 percent of the national income and in Turkey, 15 percent was being wasted by these specific types of rent seeking. In both countries this was merely one example of many, and it seems likely that the total waste from all forms of rent seeking was much larger than these figures.

In order to fully understand this type of rent seeking, however, it is necessary to follow a rather complicated chain of reasoning. The central bank official who is bribed to give out foreign exchange licenses did not directly waste that bribe in rent seeking. He had already engaged in rent seeking in order to obtain his job as bank official. It was the resources wasted in competition to obtain a job in which he could get bribes that constitute the waste of rent seeking here. Many people had gone through Indian and Turkish colleges not with the intent of obtaining a training which would have value in later life, but simply because that was a requirement for having this kind of job. Having graduated from college, they devoted a great deal of time and energy to maneuvering in devious political channels for the job. In general, this meant that they could not hold

<hr/>

[3] Note the word *roughly.* Actually the problem of exactly measuring it is quite complicated. See Gordon Tullock, "Efficient Rent Seeking," *Towards a Theory of the Rent-Seeking Society* (College Station: Texas A & M Press, forthcoming). But the assumption that the rectangle represents the cost, although not precise, is a reasonably good one.

[4] Anne O. Krueger, "The Political Economy of the Rent Seeking Society," *American Economic Review* 64 (June 1974), pp. 291–303.

gainful employment at anything else for years on end. Of this large collection of people who invested so many years in political maneuvering, only a few lucky ones had received the bribe-rich jobs. They were, of course, making a sizeable profit out of their special privileges.

What happened in this case was that a great many people, in essence, bought lottery tickets at a very high cost, let us say, three years of their life devoted to political maneuvering. A few of them drew the lucky number. Those few, of course, did very well, but socially the total cost of the lottery was probably at least as great and very possibly larger than the benefit that these people gained. It was like any other lottery in that whoever got the winning ticket would do very well and those who do not get the winning tickets pay, or more than pay, for the prize of the winner. The conventional lottery, however, is a transfer which is entered into by its customers for what may be termed entertainment purposes. The cost of tickets partly goes to pay administrative cost including profits. The investments by the people engaging in devious political maneuvers in hopes of being appointed to the agency which distributes foreign exchange licenses are a pure waste in the sense that no one gets any direct benefit from them. Indeed, one of the reasons for the backwardness of India and Turkey is that so many bright, well-educated people devote their time to this type of activity instead of productive work.

RENT SEEKING THROUGH HISTORY

Looking back from the present, it seems quite astonishing that the economists missed the point we are making for so long. The two authors of this book can, however, testify that we, together with other economists, missed it for quite some time.[5]

It would appear, however, that in a way the astonishment in the economic profession indicates that we don't read our own history as carefully as we should. Adam Smith discussed the phenomenon, although not under the title rent seeking; and it was fairly well known by most of the economists in the early part of the 19th century. It gradually dropped out of the economic literature during the 19th century and has only recently been revived.

The history roughly parallels the importance of rent seeking in

---

[5] Gordon Tullock, "The Welfare Costs of Monopolies, Tariffs and Theft," *Western Economic Journal* 5, no. 3 (June 1967), pp. 224–32.

society. In Adam Smith's time, rent seeking was an important activity, and, hence, he brought it into his book. In the late 19th century, it declined to a very low level, and most economists ignored it. It is becoming important again in most western countries, and therefore, it is returning to the forefront of economic investigation.

EXAMPLES

The airlines

Before discussing the history in a little more detail, let us look briefly at a couple of examples of the way rent seeking in fact operates in our modern society. The first of these will be the Civil Aeronautics Board's (CAB's) regulation of the airlines, something which most economists profoundly hope will shortly be merely a historical category.

From 1937 when the CAB was created with the intent of reducing the competitiveness of the airline industry until the late 70s, the CAB ran a cartel for domestic American airlines and participated in the International Air Transport Association (IATA), which was an international cartel for international airlines.[6] The airlines had lobbied for and obtained the organization of the CAB as one of the New Deal reforms and obviously got a reasonable return on their lobbying efforts. But in the process of getting the bill through Congress, they found it necessary to make deals with various special interests. Further, in order to keep the whole cartel viable politically, it was necessary to continue catering to various special interests other than the airlines themselves.

To take a few examples from more recent times, Piedmont Airlines, a local line serving the area in which the authors of this book live, was compelled for many years to fly in and out of Pulaski, Virginia for the convenience of a very, very small number of people who wanted to fly from Pulaski to Washington or Atlanta. Because Pulaski is a very small town, Piedmont lost a good deal of money on this stop. Piedmont was also compelled to serve Chicago by way of Midway Airport instead of by way of O'Hare. From Piedmont's

---

[6] As a matter of fact, although the CAB and the American airlines did participate in this international cartel, not always but as a general rule, the American members of the cartel were interested in lowering prices. Apparently this was not because they believed in competition but because the American airlines were more efficient and, hence, had a lower cost structure, which meant that the optimal monopoly price for them was lower than the optimal monopoly price for an airline, such as British Airways or Airfrance.

standpoint, these were both significant costs, but their monopoly gains elsewhere made up for them.

On a more general level, the fee schedules were calculated in such a way that, in essence, people flying long distances were overcharged and people flying shorter distances undercharged. Further, the first class passengers paid somewhat less than the cost of their rather luxurious quarters, while the tourist passengers paid somewhat more. The income transfer from tourist-class passenger to first-class passenger and from people flying long distances to people flying short distances may perhaps serve some social goal, but it is certainly an obscure one.

Politically, these rules are not hard to explain. Small cities, the citizens of which normally take an airplane for a short distance rather than a long one,[7] are spread through far more congressional districts than our major cities in which the long flights originate. First-class passengers are almost certaintly on a per-capita basis more politically influential than tourists. Indeed, most senior government officials, including congressmen, travel first class. Under the circumstances, it is obvious why the airlines seeking support for their cartel would find it sensible to advocate these two special fare arrangements.

On a basic level, however, the cartel itself in the long run turned out to be not particularly profitable, which was perhaps the political reason it turned out to be possible to break it up. The CAB could set fares, and after a while it set standards of service.[8] The space between seats, for example, is regulated, and indeed now it is considerably smaller than it was in the late 50s. Individual airlines were attracting passengers by moving their seats farther and farther apart and making it possible for them to be inclined at flatter and flatter angles. Eventually the seat was, to all intents and purposes, a bed. Although the individual airline that did this attracted additional

---

[7] They then, of course, may get on another airplane for a long trip.

[8] Originally, tourist-class travelers were served only sandwiches. This led to a long and undignified squabble as to what a sandwich was. On the North-Atlantic run, a number of airlines like Swiss Air took the view that if there was a piece of bread somewhere on the plate, it was a sandwich. Of course, as anyone who has flown Swiss Air can imagine, the piece of bread was completely hidden under a pile of roast beef, liverwurst, salami, cheese, and so forth. The end of the squabble was the establishment of an agreed-upon standard for tourist meals, but these standards did not attempt to keep them at the sandwich level.

passengers and, hence, made money, it was obviously bad for the cartel as a whole, and the CAB came to the rescue of its members by forcing them to put the seats closer together.

But the CAB does not have the power to limit the number of flights which any airline may make between two points. The airline can increase the number of passengers by providing a denser schedule with the result that there are more passengers who find it convenient to fly American Airlines with a dense schedule than, let us say, United with a thin schedule. Since the prices that the CAB had set, together with the restrictions on the service, meant that the prices were considerably above what they would be without regulation, the airlines competed by putting more flights on with the result that the airplanes were flying half empty. This phenomenon is familiar to economists, and it almost always follows when prices are set above cost and competition is permitted on any single dimension. Resources are normally invested along that uncontrolled dimension until the full benefit of the cartel is exhausted. Instead of reducing the prices, service is increased. The result is that customers are worse off than they would be with lower prices, and the airline is not really benefited. This type of competition is very difficult for any cartel manager to avoid because there are so many ways to compete. In any event, this is what happened to the airlines. As a result, the reduction of the cartel restrictions actually permitted them to make better use of their aircraft and temporarily increased their profits.

Politically it is a little obscure why the CAB was not given the power to restrict the number of flights as well as controlling everything else about the airline business. Surely the cartel would have been more profitable if this had been so. It may be that in this case, the airline manufacturers were being "paid off" by an expanded demand for their product. If so, this would be a further case in which the cost of maintaining the monopoly has actually been dissipated in waste.

Postmen

Another example of rent being dissipated in waste can be seen in the postman who is overpaid. The evidence that postmen are overpaid is simply that they are willing to take examinations and then wait for a long period of time, usually several years, before getting their jobs. If the pay was just the opportunity costs of their work, they would not be willing to do this; hence, there would not be long queues of people waiting for the postal appointment. It is, however, these long queues that make up the social waste.[9]

Note that this system is brought into equilibrium by the length of the delay. Suppose that the postal salary is extremely high. Under those circumstances, enough people would study for the exam and pass it so that the delay before appointment to a postal job would be very long indeed. With a lower postal pay but with pay which is still higher than that of equivalent nonpostal jobs, the delay they would be willing to take would be shorter. If the post office simply paid the same amount that such organizations as United Parcel pay, no one would be willing to wait in queue for a postal job, and so people would be hired almost immediately after taking their exam. It would also be necessary to see to it that the exam did not require any special preparation. The waste here is in the delay which the successful candidates must undergo before taking up their main career. The rent has, in this case, very neatly been entirely consumed by waste.

Turn back to Figure 15–2. Assume that the actual cost of hiring a postman is C, but the price is M. We have, of course, the small shaded rectangle as the loss which occurs from not hiring as many postmen as would be hired at C. The large rectangle is entirely consumed by preparing for the exam and then waiting for appointment to the postal service.

Korea

Airlines and the Postal Service are merely two examples of rent seeking. Modern society and, for that matter, most societies in the world history before about 1800 provide many similar cases. If funds are transferred from X to Y, the transfer itself (and this is the element of truth in the conventional wisdom) does not have any social cost, but Y will put resources into attempting to get the transfer and X, to avoid it. The sum of these resources will normally be about the present discounted value of the transfer. The problem is a very general one and can have very great effects on the economy.

One of the authors of this book spent some time in the Orient. Specifically, he had one year under the Nationalist government of China, one year under the Communists, and about 18 months under

---

[9] He doesn't have to remain idle during this period, but he will be confined to a job for which the pay is relatively low because he is not planning on making it a career.

President Rhee's government in Korea. In all three of these regimes, the principal way of getting ahead was to obtain some special government privilege. These privileges varied a good deal from society to society. In Communist China, for example, it was mainly getting a high-ranking government job. In Nationalist China and Korea, government jobs certainly were desirable, but there were also ways of getting rents if you were not a government employee. The advantages of achieving these special positions of power and privilege were and are great, and individuals invested great resources in attempting to achieve them. For one example, the most important businessman in Korea took a trip to the United States. In order to understand what follows, it must be said that this was right after the war in Korea and things were in fairly bad condition. President Rhee traveled, when he left his palace, in an elderly Packard, which had been originally imported to Korea as the car of the American ambassador but had since been replaced by a more modern car.

The prominent businessman returned to Korea not by air but on a freighter which docked in Inchon very close to Seoul. The freighter contained a great many things belonging to the businessman, and on the deck were two Buick automobiles, one blue and one green. The businessman was told by customs that substantially everything on it was banned for import (which meant that he would have to bribe the customs inspectors). He went immediately to Seoul, leaving his baggage behind, and called on President Rhee. He said that he had been perturbed at the president's driving around in the streets of Korea in his elderly Packard and therefore had brought back a Buick for the president to drive in; in fact, he brought back two Buicks, and the president could take his choice. He would use the other himself. The president then asked where the Buicks were, and the businessman said they were being held at customs but no doubt President Rhee could get them released. President Rhee immediately told the customs officer in Inchon to release the businessman's personal effects including the large items. On the following day, the businessman turned up at the Korean White House with two cars, and President Rhee chose the blue one. The businessman not only improved his relations with President Rhee for various future transactions, but the cost of one Buick was no doubt much, much less than he would have had to pay the customs inspector to get the rest of his baggage through. It was an example of an intelligent man in a rent-seeking society taking action to minimize the rents he had to pay.

The point of this story is that activity like this is the thing that pays off most in societies in which rent seeking is common. Instead of seeking opportunities to cut costs and prices or produce commodities which people would like to have, the man who wants to get ahead in such a society will devote his attention primarily to trying to minimize the rents he has to pay other people and maximize the rents he receives. The private return is high in this area although there is no social return at all. Thus, immense resources in human capital are diverted from productive channels into areas where, although they benefit the individual, they have no social payoff.

Indeed, in most cases, they actually have negative social payoffs. Rents mainly are derived by putting restrictions on market activities. The net effect is that society is actually poorer after they are imposed than before. Thus, talking the government into giving you a monopoly on the sale of insurance on transpacific cargos[10] not only means that you have put great resources into an activity which will give you large rents, but also means that insurance itself will be produced monopolistically and, hence, relatively inefficiently.

Thus, if the steel industry succeeds in getting imports of steel reduced, this will not only mean a rent for the steel industry, it will mean that Americans will purchase their steel under less than competitive conditions with the result that there is a net loss there too. Not only does the society run the cost of the lobbying on the part of the steel industry together with a certain amount of counterlobbying on the part of steel consumers, but when the steel lobby wins, society is actually injured. Valuable resources are invested in causing injuries rather than in producing more wealth.

One of the authors of this book was mildly involved in a minor lobbying effort: specifically, he was hired to do some statistical work to support one side in a controversy about a particular government bill. In the course of his activities, he appeared before a senatorial committee[11] and read a paper before a conference organized by the Federal Trade Commission (FTC). In each case, there were large audiences. At first, he was puzzled by these large audiences but then quickly realized that they were representatives of various lobbying organizations interested in the legislation. Nor were these people attending these meetings mere clerks. One of the leading antitrust attorneys in the United States attended the whole of the very dull senatorial hearings and in fact testified himself. The total social cost of these hearings is probably very, very large indeed, not be-

---

[10] Which one clever businessman in Korea did indeed do.

[11] Actually two senators and several aides.

cause the government's investment is large but because the interested parties invested so much in the lobbying effort.

Consider the situation in England before about 1600. Suppose you want to make money selling soap. You could invent a new, improved kind of soap, invest in a cheaper way of making soap, or reduce your total cost as compared to your competitors by simply good organization and hard work. All of these would be ways of making money. There was, however, an alternative. You could get the king to give you a monopoly on selling soap in England.[12]

On the whole, the latter would be most profitable if one could obtain a monopoly; but not only did you have to talk the king into granting such a monopoly, you had to be certain he gave it to you and not to, let us say, the cousin of his mistress. Resources would be invested in these various ways of making soap out to the point where the marginal returns were equal. This would mean that there would be considerably less resources invested in improving soap or the technology for making it than there would be if the possibility of getting the king to give you a monopoly did not exist. Thus, we have the rent-seeking waste. Further, of course, if the king did give you a monopoly then the normal problems of monopoly, i.e., higher cost and the loss of the conventional welfare triangle shown on Figure 15–2, would also occur. Thus, the possibility of investing resources in rent seeking would tend to retard economic development.

It seems likely that one of the basic reasons for the relatively slow development of the world before what is called the Industrial Revolution and its fairly rapid development in the 19th century was the fact that rent seeking was major activity in most of the world during most of the history and became of relatively minor importance in England when the Industrial Revolution started in the 18th and 19th centuries. Certainly the situation observed in China and Korea was not conducive to growth. Investment in a factory or other capital installation for improving production was highly risky unless large resources had been invested in obtaining protection for that factory against rent seeking by officials. Thus, the actual cost of production was frequently half or more rent-avoidance activity of the sort described in connection with the Buick for President Rhee, and most of the higher management devoted their principal attention to this area. Production efficiency was a relatively minor interest.

---

[12] The actual soap monopoly turned out not to be terribly profitable because it was very difficult to enforce.

This was the situation of the world in general until really quite recent times. It is not clear exactly why rent seeking became relatively unimportant in England and England's American colonies in the early 18th century and then faded away to a very, very minor phenomenon in England and the new independent American colonies in the 19th century. Certainly the limited sphere of activity of the government was important. In 19th century England, the government did very little, and what it did do was not a potential source of very much in the way of rents. With the exception of tariffs, the same could be said with respect to the American government. Thus, rent seeking would have been confined to the creation of private monopolies, something that is always difficult. Further, during this period, England was a free-trade country with the result that private monopolies came very close to being impossible. It is well known among economists that tariffs are the mother of monopoly. Getting monopoly in one country is immensely easier that acquiring a worldwide monopoly, and indeed there have been very, very few such worldwide monopolies.[13]

Note, however, that laissez-faire type government is not absolutely essential to eliminate rent seeking. A government which controls the entire economy or large sectors of it but refrains from responding to rent-seeking activities, i.e., does not give special privileges to politically influential groups, would also have no rent-seeking waste. It might be inefficient for other reasons, but rent seeking would not be important. The pre-1700 governments were not enlightened in this way. They tended to give special privileges to all sorts of people including, of course, friends of the king, influential politicians, and bankers who were willing to advance money to the government. In a way, the rents were frequently sold and, hence, were a major source of government revenue. France actually went to the extreme of selling a large number of government jobs.

Still, the laissez-faire economy of England and the United States[14] without doubt made rent seeking difficult or impossible. The immense economic development of England and the United States in

---

[13] Most worldwide monopolies (and, to repeat, they have been fairly rare) have involved minerals which are found only in a few countries. The current OPEC organization is perhaps the most successful such worldwide monopoly in history.

[14] In the United States, laissez-faire was, of course, limited by the existence of an aggressive tariff policy. The internal market in the United States was so large, however, that although the tariffs were no doubt foolish, they never played a major economic role.

the 19th century was in part (but of course, only in part) the consequence of this elimination of rent seeking. Further, in the 19th century, many other countries copied the English and American institutions with the result that rent seeking declined all over the world. Here again this is one, although only one, of the reasons for the rapid spread of industry and economic development in the 19th century.

Rent seeking was never completely eliminated in the 19th century, and the fact that there was much less rent seeking in the government sphere does not, of course, mean that purely private rent seeking did not exist. The construction of private monopoly is an example, and any ingenious economist can think of numbers of others. Still, the total volume was very small compared to what it had been before.

CONCLUDING COMMENTS

Today, once again, one of the major ways of making money is to get the government to give you some kind of privilege. This special privilege may be hiring you as civil servant at more than what you can make elsewhere, restricting foreign imports of competing products, or prohibiting domestic competition, direct government grants, and so forth. The list is endless.

Measuring the exact amount of rent seeking is very difficult. The "influence" community, which is such an important part of Washington life and which combines with the highly paid federal civil service to make the Washington suburbs the highest income areas in the United States, is no doubt the source of considerable waste but a tiny portion of the total cost of rent seeking. The plethora of expensive French restaurants that have sprung up in Washington illustrate the expense of rent seeking.[15] But there are other and far more expensive ways of influencing the government. Lockheed once put a major defense plant in the constituency of the chairman of the House Armed Services Committee. This was, in all probability, not the best place to locate an aircraft plant, although as a matter of fact, it wasn't bad.

Similarly, General Dynamics beat out Boeing in a contest to build

---

[15] In part, of course, the customers of these restaurants are simply the very highly paid federal civil servants. To a very considerable extent, however, they are lobbyists seeing to it that the person whom they lobby listens carefully to what they have to say over a rack of lamb and a good wine.

a plane which eventually became the F-111 to a large extent because they had a factory in Texas and it was during Johnson's presidency. Since the F-111 turned out to be both very, very costly and poor, this was indeed an expensive bit of rent seeking. There was another expensive bit of rent seeking connected with this particular plane. The secretary of defense, McNamara, had decided that the Navy and Air Force should both have the same plane. Boeing, athough it made gestures towards producing the same plane for the different services, in fact was planning to produce two. Their engineers thought that it would be impossible to produce one plane to meet the demands of both the Air Force and the Navy. It seems likely that General Dynamics engineers agreed, but they devoted a great deal of energy and resources to a joint design. As a matter of fact, and we presume they knew this from the beginning, such a joint design was not feasible. This was, in a way, flattery directed at McNamara and turned out to be successful. McNamara chose them over the somewhat franker Boeing engineering staff. It, of course, turned out that the plane could not be used by both the navy and the air force, and in fact it wasn't very good for the air force.

Both General Dynamics and Boeing, of course, were well represented by lobbyists and sales representatives in Washington. Both indeed had members of the Senate and House who were deeply interested in getting the contract for their constituency. Nevertheless, it seems likely that the location of their plants and the engineering investment put in to make it appear that it would be possible to build one plane suitable for both the navy and the air force was immensely more expensive than this direct-lobbying effort. But this is merely one example. This kind of thing happens very commonly. Businessmen make business decisions not entirely in terms of price and benefit but also in terms of their probable political implications. The cost of these decisions can be very great.

It is clear that rent seeking leads to social waste, probably very large social waste. Unfortunately, so far economists have not worked out a way of measuring this waste; hence, we don't have positive measures in most cases. We referred, however, to two cases in which Ann Krueger approximated rent seeking—in one case 7 percent and in the other, 15 percent of the gross national product (GNP), and this was not for all rent seeking in Turkey and India but only for one particular type. So it is obvious that the total amount could be very large indeed. Frankly, we do not know how much rent seeking is reducing American GNP, although we think it probably is reducing it quite substantially. In any event, whether the waste imposed by rent seeking is large or small, it is a waste and we should do our best to eliminate it.

QUESTIONS TO PONDER

1. Can you suggest any reason why rent seeking first became relatively uncommon in the English speaking world in the 19th century and now is becoming much more common?

2. Many of the organizations which lead to extensive rent seeking, for example, the Interstate Commerce Commission (ICC), the Federal Communications Commission (FCC), and, until recently, the Civil Aeronautics Boards, were set up by people who at least ostensibly were simply trying to improve the functioning of some part of the economy. Do you think that they were sincere in attempting to bene- fit the economy and didn't know about the rent-seeking opportunities or that they were deliberately seeking rents? In this connection, it should be pointed out that the railroads were quite important in establishing the ICC; the radio industry, in setting up the FCC (and its predecessor); and the airlines, the CAB.

3. Can you think of any methods of reducing the amount of rent seeking?

Equal pay for equal work

By most conventional measures, women as a group do not have the same economic clout as do men. Many have known this simple fact for some time; it has only been, however, since the publications of such books as *The Feminine Mystique* by Betty Friedan and *Sexual Politics* by Kate Millet that the inequality of the sexes has been anything more than a passing concern to a substantial portion of the population. Currently, conversations on the subject are often emotional, and, frequently, the important questions of what exactly are the relative economic positions of women and what will be the effect of proposed remedies are lost in the heat of the argument. The purpose of this chapter is simply to clarify the status of women and the issues in the debate. We will pay particular attention to the probable effects of equal-pay-for-equal-work legislation. First, a look at the data.

THE ECONOMIC STATUS OF WOMEN

The labor-force participation of women

Historically, the proportion of women in the population has never been fully mirrored in the labor force. (The reader should recognize that the concept of the labor force, as defined by the Department of Labor, does not include housework.[1]) However, the labor-force

---

[1] The reason for the exclusion of housewives from the definition of the labor force is basically that since housewives do not enter any formal market in which a price for their work is set, it is difficult to determine the monetary value of work of women in the home and how much work is actually done. This is particularly true if differences in the quality of labor are recognized. As a sidenote, housework done by people for themselves is not included in the computation of gross national product, which means that such data understates the total value of productive activity (and the true level of employment) in the country. (However, the work done by a maid, as measured in the wages paid, is included in gross national product. A maid is also counted as a part of the labor force.)

participation rate of women *and* men has been changing as indicated in Figure 16–1. In 1900, women 20 years old and older constituted just over 18 percent of the labor force; by 1960 this figure had risen to just under 40 percent (see the graph below). By the beginning of 1980, slightly more than 51 percent of all women were participants in the work-a-day world outside the home.

On the other hand, while the total number of working men has increased markedly over the years, the labor-force participation rate of men (as a percentage figure) has been falling steadily since the early 1960s. In 1961, approximately 85 percent of all men were participants in the labor force; that figure fell to just under 80 percent by the first quarter of 1980. The lower labor-force participation rate of married men has very probably been stimulated by higher wages for all workers, which has enabled some men to drop out of the labor force for periods of time and to retire early. However, the greater willingness of women to leave the home to add to the family's income and to pursue careers has very likely given some men

FIGURE 16–1
Civilian labor-force participation rates by sex and age (seasonally adjusted)

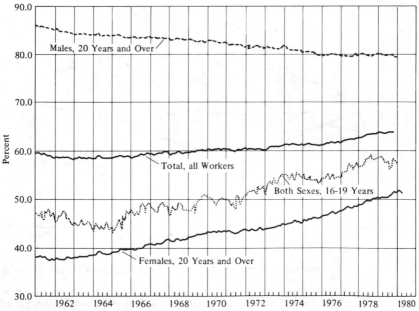

Source: U.S. Department of Labor, Bureau of Labor Statistics, *Employment and Earnings* (April 1980), chart 3, and table A–33.

the means and opportunity to leave the labor force from time to time and to take on some of the household responsibilities that were once assumed by women. Still, as evident in Figure 16–1, the labor-force participation rate of women 20 and older has traditionally been lower than the participation rate of both sexes in the age 16 to 19 category.

The change in the participation rates of young women is shown clearly in Figure 16–2. Women, for example, who may now be in college have had an initial participation rate approximately equal to the peak rate of women born much earlier, 1906–15, who could have been their mothers.

There are several reasons that can be given for the growth in the labor-force participation of women. First, real wages have been going up over time, and consequently, the cost of staying at home has become greater. Also, the costs of home-produced goods (since they

FIGURE 16–2
Labor-force participation over a working life of cohorts of women born in selected time intervals, 1886–1955

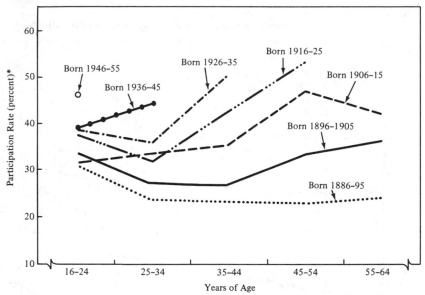

*Total labor force as percentage of total noninstitutional population in group specified.

For women born between 1886 and 1915, the first age plotted is 14–24 years. Cohorts reach age interval according to the midpoint of their birth years. Thus, the cohort born 1886–95 reached ages 25–34 in 1920 and ages 55–64 in 1950; the cohort born 1916–25 reached ages 25–34 in 1950 and ages 45–54 in 1970.

Source: *Economic Report of the President, 1973;* Department of Commerce.

are generally labor intensive) have become greater. Second, technological advances (in the form of such equipment as automatic washing machines) have occurred in housework. Women can now accomplish their work in less time. They can use a portion of their "greater real income" by going into the labor market, earning a money income, and buying clothes or other things they may want. They can thereby reap benefits from specialization.

Third, the divorce rate has been on the rise for some time. Since the divorce rate is currently somewhere in the neighborhood of two out of every five marriages, a married woman is assuming a considerable risk if she relies on her husband's income and stays at home. By staying at home, her education (or human capital stock) may depreciate for lack of use and can easily become obsolete with the changing times. If she is divorced after 15 years of marriage, she can find herself with very little earning power. She therefore may rationally go to work and self-insure herself against such consequences.

Fourth, there has been a disproportionate expansion of the service sector in the overall economy; and since women are disproportionately represented in that sector, one might expect a rise in the labor-force participation rate of women. In other words, more employment opportunities could have arisen for women, and perhaps more importantly, the real wage in the sector has risen, attracting women out of the home.

Fifth and finally, there have probably been some long-run changes in the values of women (as well as men). Women's attitudes toward work and careers have been changing, and their demand for children has been falling, causing a greater willingness to go out and stay in the working world. (We should note here that these changes in values should have kept women's wages from rising as much as they otherwise would have. Can you explain why?)

We have said nothing that would explain data that reflects very little change in the employment pattern of women among occupations within the working world;[2] we have only attempted to explain the change in the employment pattern between home and the working world. The fact that the distribution of women workers among occupations has changed very little may indicate that (1) the types of jobs women as a group want has not changed very much; (2) the

---

[2] See Barbara R. Bergman and Irma Adelman, "The 1973 Report of the President's Council of Economic Advisors: The Economic Role of Women," *American Economic Review* 63 (September 1973), pp. 509–14.

relative demand for women in "female occupations" has increased and the relative wages of women are greater by remaining in those occupations; or (3) the discriminatory barrier against women entering nontraditional fields is still as strong as ever. We suspect that all three forces are at work to some degree; which one is the most important is a question we feel cannot be answered with much conviction at this point in time. People in the forefront of the women's liberation movement, of course, are inclined to argue the case of the discriminatory barriers. It is also clear that the relative wage of people in the service sectors has been on the rise, and as noted above, women are disproportionately represented in the service sector.

Unemployment

Figure 16–3 illustrates the point that women have consistently experienced a higher rate of unemployment than men; 6.1 percent for women 20 and older as opposed to 4.7 percent for men in the first

FIGURE 16–3
Unemployment rates by sex and age

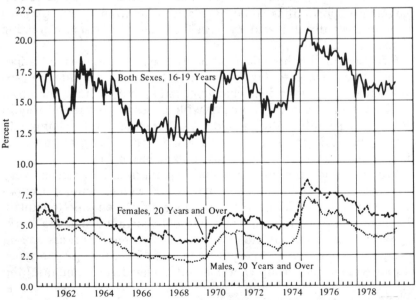

Source: U.S. Department of Labor, *Employment and Earnings* (April 1980), chart 10 and table A–36.

quarter of 1980. (As seen in the figure, the unemployment rate for teenagers is much higher than the unemployment rates for both men and women 20 years and older.) The reasons for the higher unemployment rates of women may include (1) layoffs, which tend to hit hardest among those who have the lowest seniority levels, and women tend to be on the bottom rung of the ladder in terms of seniority; (2) a man who is employed and is looking for work is not classified as unemployed whereas a woman working in the home who is looking for work is (because of the definition of the "unemployed") considered to be unemployed; (3) women are being discriminated against in employment opportunities; and (4) women are generally in the lower-skilled occupations (by choice or force), and the unemployment rates are typically higher in such categories. Many of these same reasons can be given for why the differential in the unemployment rates of the sexes has been increasing and why the unemployment rates of women tend to fluctuate more with changes in general economic activity and with such public-policy changes as increases in the minimum wage rate.

Earnings of men and women

There is perhaps no aspect of the economic status of women that can generate more emotional outrage than the wage differential between men as a group and women as a group. Tables 16–1 and 16–2 and Figure 16–4 give a reasonably clear picture of the earnings differential of men and women. Table 16–1 reveals that in 1977 women on average earned slightly less than 59 percent as much.

Furthermore, although there have been some up and down movements, the wage differential has been ever so gradually decreasing, not increasing as one might think from listening to all of the news reports about the improving economic opportunities of women. This does not mean that women are now worse off than they were, say, in 1955 (their absolute incomes from work have been increasing), but it does mean that the improvement in women's earning power has not, over the years, been as dramatic as men's.

Table 16–2 shows that in all categories of workers, from professional workers to common laborers, the wage differential between men and women is pronounced. Even among the self-employed people, women only earned about 34 percent as much as men. Figure 16–4 demonstrates that in the past women could expect to earn for most of their working lives less than men with high

266
CHAPTER SIXTEEN

TABLE 16-1
Comparison of median earnings of year-round full-time workers, by sex,
1955-1977 (persons 14 years of age and over)

Year	Median earnings (1) Women	(2) Men	(3) Earnings gap in dollars	(4) Women's earnings as a percentage of men's	(5) Earnings gap in constant 1976 dollars
1977	$8,618	$14,626	$6,008	58.9	$3,310
1976	8,099	13,455	5,356	60.2	3,141
1975	7,504	12,758	5,254	58.8	3,259
1974	6,772	11,835	5,063	57.2	3,433
1973	6,335	11,186	4,851	56.6	3,649
1972	5,903	10,202	4,299	57.9	3,435
1971	5,593	9,399	3,806	59.5	3,136
1970	5,323	8,966	3,643	59.4	3,133
1969	4,977	8,227	3,250	60.5	2,961
1968	4,457	7,664	3,207	58.2	3,079
1967	4,150	7,182	3,032	57.8	3,032
1966	3,973	6,848	2,875	58.0	2,958
1965	3,823	6,375	2,552	60.0	2,700
1964	3,690	6,195	2,505	59.6	2,696
1963	3,561	5,978	2,417	59.6	2,637
1962	3,446	5,974	2,528	59.5	2,790
1961	3,351	5,644	2,293	59.4	2,559
1960	3,293	5,417	2,124	60.8	2,394
1959	3,193	5,209	2,016	61.3	2,308
1958	3,102	4,927	1,825	63.0	2,108
1957	3,008	4,713	1,705	63.8	2,023
1956	2,827	4,466	1,639	63.3	2,014
1955	2,719	4,252	1,533	63.9	1,911

Notes: For 1967–77, data include wage and salary income and earnings from self-employment; for 1955–66, data include wage and salary income only.

Column 3 = column 2 minus column 1.
Column 4 = column 1 divided by column 2.
Column 5 = column 3 times the purchasing power of the consumer dollar (1967 = $1.00).

Source: U.S. Department of Commerce, Bureau of the Census: "Money Income of Families and Persons in the United States," *Current Population Reports*, 1957 to 1977. U.S. Department of Labor, Bureau of Labor Statistics: *Handbook of Labor Statistics*, 1977.

school diplomas. The relationship between the earnings of men and women with various amounts of education has not changed materially since that figure was first drawn and published.

What explains the differentials? First, it should be recognized that the computed annual earnings of women *could be* less because, for

EQUAL PAY FOR EQUAL WORK

TABLE 16–2
Median earnings of year-round full-time civilian workers, by occupation group and sex, 1977 (persons 14 years of age and over)

Occupation group	Women	Men	Dollar gap	Women's earnings as a percentage of men's
Total	$ 8,618	$14,626	$ 6,008	58.9
Professional and technical workers	11,995	18,224	6,229	65.8
Accountants	11,155	17,312	6,157	64.4
Computer specialists	15,135	18,849	3,714	80.3
Health workers (except physcians, dentists, and related practitioners)	12,093	13,360	1,267	90.5
Teachers	11,970	15,790	3,820	75.8
College and university	15,172	20,337	5,165	74.6
Elementary and secondary	11,732	15,029	3,297	78.1
Engineering and science technicians	11,566	15,147	3,581	76.4
Managers and administrators	9,799	18,086	8,287	54.2
Salaried	10,272	19,023	8,751	54.0
Manufacturing	11,277	22,523	11,246	50.1
Retail trade	8,437	15,076	6,639	56.0
Finance, insurance and real estate	10,684	19,696	9,012	54.2
Public administration	12,568	18,673	6,105	67.3
Other industries	10,839	20,220	9,381	53.6
Self-employed	4,258	12,428	8,170	34.3
Retail trade	4,732	10,554	5,822	44.8
Sales workers	6,825	16,067	9,242	42.5
Insurance, real estate, and stock agents and brokers	11,020	18,907	7,887	58.3
Retail trade	5,529	11,110	5,581	49.8
Sales clerks	5,413	10,114	4,701	53.5
Clerical workers	8,601	13,966	5,365	61.6
Bookkeepers	8,516	13,520	5,004	63.0
Cashiers and counter clerks (except food)	6,632	10,139	3,507	65.4
Office-machinery operators	9,019	13,076	4,057	69.0
Craft and kindred workers	8,902	14,517	5,615	61.3
Blue-collar worker supervisor, n.e.c.	9,138	16,202	7,064	56.4
Operatives, including transport	7,350	12,612	5,262	58.3
Manufacturing	7,479	12,644	5,165	59.2
Durable goods	8,305	12,648	4,343	65.7
Nondurable goods	6,736	12,631	5,895	53.3
Nonmanufacturing	6,401	12,536	6,135	51.1
Operatives (except transport)	7,342	12,384	5,042	59.3
Laborers (except farm)	7,441	10,824	3,383	68.7
Manufacturing	7,533	12,061	4,528	64.5

TABLE 16–2—(continued)

Occupation group	Women	Men	Dollar gap	Women's earnings as a percentage of men's
Service workers (except private household)	$6,108	$10,332	$4,224	59.1
Cleaning-service workers	6,353	9,201	2,848	69.0
Food-service workers	5,255	7,332	2,077	71.7
Health-service workers	7,050	8,643	1,593	81.6
Personal-service workers	6,097	9,553	3,456	63.8
Farm workers	1,635	6,412	4,777	25.5

Source: U.S. Department of Commerce, Bureau of the Census, *Current Population Reports,* P–60, no. 118.

FIGURE 16–4
Annual income by age, for male and female high school and college graduates

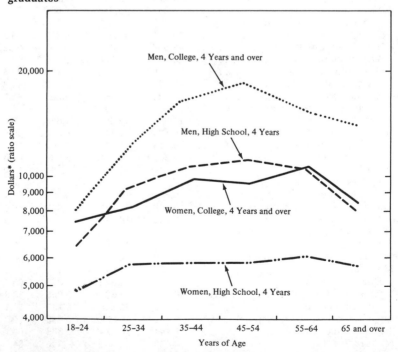

* Median income of full-time, year-round workers, 1971.
Source: *Economic Report of the President, 1973,* Department of Commerce.

example, they have less education or are in lower-skill jobs,[3] women have fewer years of seniority, and the working women are concentrated in regions that, as a general rule, have lower pay. These are possibilities, and the point that needs to be made is that before we can accept the argument that the gross differential in men's and women's wages reflects the amount or degree of discrimination, statistical manipulations must be performed on the data to account for the differences in the characteristics of the two groups. Because this is not a book on statistical inference and because of space limitations, we will not discuss how these adjustments can be made.[4] We will only discuss what adjustments have been made and how they affect the wage differential.

Several studies have tackled the problem of accounting for the differential in the annual earnings of the sexes. Table 16–3 summarizes the results. Because the different studies were undertaken in different years, used different samples, and adjusted for different variables, the gross and net differentials (that is, the differentials that remain after adjustments) are different. The gross differentials vary from 0.57 to 0.35 (the gross differentials in the studies conducted by the Council of Economic Advisors and Department of Labor could not be pinned down with precision in the sources that were used). The net differentials run from a low of approximately zero to a high of 0.57. In the case of the study by Sawhill, the differential went up substantially after adjustments.

How much of a differential is there between sexes? Barbara Bergman and Irma Adelman emphasize the importance of the findings in the second through seventh studies.[5] The Council of Economic Advisors concluded,

> Some studies have succeeded in narrowing the male-female differtial well below 20 percent. Indeed, Department of Labor surveys

---

[3] Many will argue that women are in lower-skilled jobs because of prejudice, as we have recognized, and because they are in lower-skilled jobs, their human capital does not rise as much as men, causing a greater differential in earnings as men and women become older.

[4] Actually, this is just a polite way of saying that the benefits of discussing methods used in statistically adjusting the data are not as great as the costs of doing so. This is also what other writers mean when they make similar statements. Would you expect the authors to use a few pages to add the necessary explanation if you or someone else would give them $10,000 to do so? Would you do it?

[5] Bergman and Adelman, *1973 Report*, p. 509.

TABLE 16-3
Summary of findings on sex wage differentials

Author	Gross earnings differential*	Net earnings differential*	Variables analyzed	Data base
Sanborn	0.42	0.12	Detailed occupations, hours, age, education, color, and urbanness within detailed occupations. Rough estimate of effects of turnover, absenteeism, and experience.	Experienced civilian labor force, 1950.
Morgan et al.	0.36	0.37	Broad occupation, education and age, population of city, urban-rural migration, movement out of Deep South, extent of unemployment in state, supervisory responsibility, attitude toward hard work and need achievement score, race, interviewers' assessment of ability to communicate, geographic mobility, physical condition, rank and progress in school.	Heads of household, 1959.
Fuchs	0.40	0.34	Color, schooling, age, city size, marital status, class of worker, length of trip.	Nonfarm employed persons, 1960.
Cohen	0.45	0.31†	Hours, fringe benefits, absenteeism, seniority, education, unionization.	Nonprofessional employees, aged 22–64, with a steady job, working 35 or more hours per week, 1969.
Oaxaca	0.35	0.29	Experience, health, migration, hours, marital status, city size, region.	Urban whites, 1967.
Suter and Miller ...	0.57	0.31	Education, occupation, work experience in 1966, lifetime career experience.	Male wage and salary workers, 1967, plus special longitudinal subsample of women, aged 30–44.
Sawhill	0.46	0.57	Age, education, race, region, hours and weeks worked, and time spent in the labor force.	Employed wage and salary workers in civilian labor force, 1967.

Council of .... Economic Advisers	NA	20	Training, continuity at work, lifelong work experience, and others.	Sample is unspecified.
Department of .... Labor	NA	close to 0	Detailed job classifications and being within the same establishment, and other factors.	Sample is unspecified.

* The earnings differential is equal to 1 = F/M where F and M represent female and male earnings in some form (varying from study to study). The Morgan et al. and Fuchs differentials are based on hourly earnings.

† Calculated by present author as 1 = F*/M where F* is female earnings adjusted for hours, fringe benefits and absenteeism, seniority, education, and unionization.

NA—data unavailable.

Sources: The summaries of the first seven studies were taken from Isabell V. Sawhill, "The Economics of Discrimination Against Women: Some New Findings," *Journal of Human Resources* (Summer 1973), pp. 382–96. The primary sources are:

Henry Sanborn, "Pay Differences Between Men and Women," *Industrial and Labor Relations Review* (July 1964).

James N. Morgan et al., *Income and Welfare in the United States* (New York: McGraw-Hill, 1962).

Victor Fuchs, "Differences in Hourly Earnings between Men and Women," *Monthly Labor Review* (May 1971).

Malcolm S. Cohen, "Sex Differences in Competition," *Journal of Human Resources* (Fall 1971).

Ronald Oaxaca, "Sex Differences in Wages" (Paper presented at a conference sponsored by the Woodrow Wilson School of Public and International Affairs, October 1971).

Larry E. Suter and Herman P. Miller, "Components of Income Differences between Men and Career Women" (Paper presented at the American Sociological Association meetings, September 1971).

Isabel V. Sawhill, "The Economics of Discrimination Against Women: Some New Findings," *Journal of Human Resources* 8 (Summer 1973), pp. 383–96.

The secondary source of last two studies is *Economic Report of the President, 1973* (Washington: U.S. Government Printing Office, 1973).

have found that the differential almost disappears when men's and women's earnings are compared within the same establishment. In the very narrow sense of equal pay for the same job in the same plant there may be little difference between women and men. However, in this way the focus of the problem is shifted but not eliminated, for then we must explain why women have such a different job structure and why they are employed in different types of establishments.[6]

WHY THE NET DIFFERENTIAL?

A net differential between men's and women's earnings can remain after adjustments because not all relevant variables are considered. It may also be that the quantitative data used may not accurately represent the qualitative differentials. For example, a group of men and women may have worked for the same number of years, but the quality of the work experience, or the human capital acquired, can be dramatically different. As pointed out by Bergman and Adelman, the male management trainee has surely acquired more human capital after ten years on the job than the female clerical worker. It may also be true that the number of years in college glosses over the quality differences in men and women's education.

There is also the pure and simple fact that women are often discriminated against. This may be because the employers have a definite preference for working with male employees; women employers can have the same preferences. Because of the lack of controls on their behavior, they are able to express their preferences in their hiring practices. Customers, who are the ultimate employers, may also have a preference for buying from men, which means that the marginal value of men is greater than the marginal value of women.[7] The demand for men is greater and their wage is correspondingly higher.

Many persons who discuss the topic point to the real-world fact that employers are inclined to presume that certain jobs are for women and certain jobs are for men. Women are, therefore, because of the decision rules that are formulated, crowded into typically

---

[6] *Economic Report of the President, 1973*, Department of Labor Statistics, p. 106.

[7] Is this a pure form of discrimination in the sense in which the term is normally used? What other aspects of customer behavior can we classify as discriminatory?

"female occupations." The crowding results in the wages of the workers (mostly female) in those occupations being depressed. (The crowding can also be partly the result of women choosing, because of inculturated attitudes or independent preferences, to go into those occupations.)

Decision rules can, from the standpoint of the employers, be rationally formulated. Hiring people is an expensive process at best, and obtaining more information about each individual person who applies is progressively more costly. By not obtaining the more detailed information on prospective employees, the employer can make mistakes. He can hire people who are not productive, and he may, after a short while, have to incur the cost of replacing them. Likewise, the employer may incur less cost by formulating a decision rule and making mistakes than he would incur if he obtained more information on each applicant[8] and made fewer mistakes.

As an illustration of the point being made, consider the continuum shown (Figure 16–5), which represents the "quality of work" (in any dimension that the reader would like) for a given job. Let us assume, just for purposes of illustration, that the distribution of women is

FIGURE 16–5
(Perceived) quality, distributions of women and men

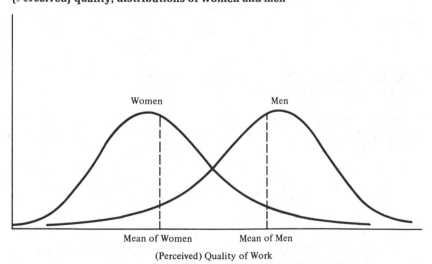

Women   Men

Mean of Women   Mean of Men

(Perceived) Quality of Work

[8] Remember that the probability of the information obtained being correct is likely to be less than one. (What will this do to the employer's willingness to obtain the information?)

to the left of the distribution of men. This can be either because the employer *knows* where the distributions lie or because he believes, and may be wrong, that they lie in the indicated positions. There are some women who are of higher quality than some men and vice versa. The mean for the women is still to the left of the mean for men. If the wages of men and women were the same and the cost of acquiring sufficient information to accurately place each applicant on the spectrum were quite high, the employer may find it profitable (in what sense?) to formulate the rule that men will be hired if a choice is to be made.[9] On *average*, the employer would receive (or would believe that he is receiving) a higher quality of work. This, of course, means that some women, particularly those who are of higher quality than the mean for men, would be discriminated against. This does not mean, however, that the employer is acting out of any sinister motive. He is merely attempting to maximize the accomplishment of his objectives, which may not include putting women down. When the wage differential results, it becomes rational for the employer to hire the women even though they are of less quality or are believed to be of less quality on average. (Why?) If the reason for decision rule is incorrect beliefs on the part of the employer or incorrect information, the solution is to educate the employer: he must be shown that his decision rule is not in his best interest. If the problem is a matter of taste, then preferences must be changed, which may be a long-term project.

SEX DISCRIMINATION: PROFIT VERSUS NONPROFIT INSTITUTIONS

Should we expect profit maximizing firms to discriminate more than nonprofit, say, governmental organizations? On the surface, one could argue that public, nonprofit organizations are set up for the purpose of operating in the public interest, which may mean in part that the people who work in such institutions are public spirited and are more tuned to social needs. One might expect them to be more fair when it comes to employment policies. As we discuss in more detail in a later chapter, this idealized picture of the public servant is probably inappropriate. As a group, it may be more appropriate to describe public servants as rational, utility-maximizing human beings who, as a group, are not distinctly different from everyone

---

[9] The reader should understand that the whole field of social science has been developed, at least in part, to derive beneficial decision rules.

else in the private sector. Indeed, it may be a little inconsistent to view public bureaucrats as private utility-maximizers when it comes to their nonworking lives and as social utility-maximizers when it comes to their work. Public servants do have their own preferences *and* prejudices. (The authors of this book are public bureaucrats— we teach in public universities—and we must confess that we do not believe we are materially different in our motives from the people that work for General Motors.)

In private institutions, profit is not the only incentive for behavior, but it is one of the incentives; and to the degree that the profit incentive is present, people can gain by making and increasing the profit. The objectives of the public institutions are not, in general, as clearly defined (take a look at the statement of objectives of your university, if you happen to be in school). Wages of employees, who can also be employers of other bureaucrats, are more closely associated with years of service or education as is the case in school systems (consider the civil-service pay scales) and are less closely associated with the profit of the organization. This seems to be a fairly reasonable expectation since profit is generally not an objective. Accordingly, one would expect that a public servant can, if he wishes, more easily express his own preferences with regard to employment practices or any other objective which he may consider to be in the public interest. If pay is fixed with years of work, for example, he can gain very little (or less, as a general rule, than he would if he were in a private institution) by setting his preferences aside. With a profit-incentive system, a person is in effect paid to do what may not be consistent with his personal preferences. We would, contrary to what may be the general view, expect more sex (and race) discrimination within nonprofit, governmental organizations than in profit-maximizing firms. This is not to say that profit-maximizing firms do not discriminate.

As far as we know, no one has done a study on the sex discrimination in profit and nonprofit organizations. There has been at least one study on *race* discrimination in the two types of organizations;[10] and as we would predict, the amount of discrimination within the nonprofit firms was significantly greater. This one study, of course, does not confirm our hypothesis regarding sex discrimination, but it is suggestive of what some future study may reveal.

---

[10] William J. Haley and John Paul Combs, "The Profit Motive and Labor Market Discrimination," Econometrics Workshop Papers (Ann Arbor: University of Michigan September 1973).

EQUAL-PAY LEGISLATION

Laws requiring equal pay for men and women doing the same jobs may appear on the surface to be an unambiguous solution to the achievement of greater social justice. However, as is often true in economics, appearances can be deceiving. The purpose of this section is to use supply and demand curves to demonstrate that, contrary to the good intentions of those who favor equal-pay legislation, effective enforcement of the law can reduce the employment opportunities of women and expand the opportunities of men. The analysis suggests that achievement of social justice for some will be at the expense of an injustice to others.

In demonstrating the above conclusion, we assume that men and women produce a homogeneous product, and for this women are paid less than men. We further assume that men and women are substitutes in employment, although not perfect substitutes,[11] and that the demand for both men and women has the normal negative slope. It is also assumed that the supply curves of men and women are upward sloping and, for simplicity, are equal and that the labor market is purely competitive.[12]

If the markets are competitive, the explanation for the higher wages of men must lie in the fact that the demand for men is greater (relative to the supply) than the demand for women. In Figure 16–6A, the demand and supply for men are respectively D_m and S_m; the demand and supply for women are similarly labeled in Figure 16–6B. The wage established in the market for women is W_w which is below the wage for men, W_m.

If the demand for men is greater relative to the supply, it must be due to one of two conditions: either the men are actually more productive (in some tangible or intangible sense), or the employers have been misguided and *believe*, although incorrectly, that men are more productive than women. (We will avoid engaging in the debate on which explanation is relatively more important.) In either case, the demand for men will still be greater and the predicted wage differential holds. Furthermore, any discriminatory "taste" factor for men employees can be fully accommodated in this analysis and does not alter the conclusions drawn. (If it is argued that women are crowded

---

[11] If men and women were perfect substitutes in the eyes of employers, it would be difficult indeed to explain why wage rates differ between the sexes.

[12] Given the relatively large number of employers in most labor markets, the assumption of competitive markets is reasonable.

FIGURE 16–6

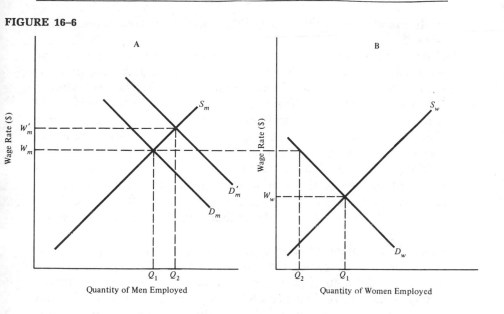

into female occupations, then the same model can be used since there will still be some wage differential.)

Assume now that the Justice Department requires (through effective enforcement) that the men and women in the two markets be paid the same and that the requirement is implemented by raising the wage of women to W_m.[13] The results are that, assuming the employers' attitudes toward the sexes are unaffected, the quantity of women employed falls from Q_1 to Q_2 in Figure 16–6B. As indicated in Figure 16–6B, there are women who will benefit from the legislation; these are the ones who retain their jobs and who receive the higher wage. However, this may be small solace to those women who lose their jobs and are forced onto the unemployment roles or to seek employment in jobs that do not come under the scrutiny and enforcement of the law. In fact, economic theory would predict that if the equal-pay-equal-work law is enforced, more women than at present would be forced to accept employment where their large numbers now determine the wage rate, such as cleaning, teaching, clerical and secretarial work, and cooking. Isabell Sawhill, in a

---

[13] It is highly unlikely that Congress would force the wages of men down to the level of women's.

study mentioned earlier, draws this conclusion from her empirical work.[14]

At the same time, just as an increase in the price of one good will increase the demand for its substitutes, *ceteris paribus*, the increase in the wage of women will increase the demand for their substitutes, for example, men; and if permitted, not only will the quantity of men employed rise (to Q_2 in Figure 16–6A), but their wage rate will also rise to W_m').[15] Pursuit of equality of pay scales for the sexes may only lead to an ever-shrinking market for women.

The policy implication is that if the economic status (that is, the wage) of women is to be improved, the basic market conditions (supply and demand) for women's labor must be changed, not just the price. If the supply is left unchanged, the way to narrow (or eliminate) the wage differential between the sexes is to increase the demand for women relative to men. Assuming that employers are in fact prejudiced against women or mistakenly believe women are less competent than men, employers must be reeducated, or proven wrong, and/or have their preferences changed. (Accomplishing this is a major thrust of the women's liberation movement.) In addition, the productivity of women can be upgraded by a change in women's skills and perhaps in their socially derived attitudes toward work, careers, and the family.[16] These changes mean, in essence, that in the eyes of the employers, women must become indistinguishable from men, which, in the final analysis, may be impossible. These changes will take time, and this may explain why so many have opted for the apparently simple solution of immediately raising the wage. In any event, the analysis suggests that if women are not to lose ground in employment opportunities, equal-pay laws may have to be accompanied by quantity controls.[17]

There are three major criticisms that may be leveled against the foregoing analysis. First, it may be argued that there are labor markets that are not competitive and that under monopsonistic con-

---

[14] Sawhill, "Economics of Discrimination against Women," pp. 383–96.

[15] If the wage rate of men is not allowed to rise, all of the traditional problems associated with price controls would develop, and the wage differential between men and women may be merely disguised.

[16] A frequently heard complaint from feminists is that women are culturally bound to low-paying jobs.

[17] One solution, which may not be politically practical, is to impose a legal minimum wage for men above their current wage level. This would increase the demand for women.

ditions, an increase in the wage for women will not reduce their level of employment. More sophisticated theories of market structures support this last inference, and it may be conceded that there are markets that are monopsonistic. However, the general conclusion—that an increase in the wage of women will result in a *marginal* reduction in their employment—will remain valid as long as there are labor markets that are competitive. To assume all labor markets are monopsonistic is indeed an extreme assumption. Besides, no one seems to be arguing that sex discrimination is the result of monopsonistic labor markets.

Second, the analysis does not consider the dynamic effects equal-pay-for-equal-work laws will have on employer attitudes: by paying women the same as men, employers will realize that women are every bit as valuable as men; and therefore, the demand for women will rise in the long run. It may be argued that the observed effects of other similar laws demonstrate the importance of the dynamic effects and that the analysis is probably wrong. These arguments are often voiced, but the mechanism through which the change in attitude occurs is left unclear. Statements such as the law will have a psychological effect are not very satisfying. Why would an increase in the wage paid to women change the employer's assessment of the laborers' value? An answer is needed because the issue raised goes to the heart of economic theory: does the employer look to the wage paid to determine what the value of a laborer is, or does he look to what the laborer produces to determine what the laborer's wage should be? Which provides the sounder basis for theorizing? Because of the experience economists have had with the latter approach, we as economists have a strong bias for it. Besides, if there is a short-run negative response to the increase in the wage of women, it would appear that since there will be fewer women employed, there will be less opportunity for the employers to "learn" that women are indeed as productive as men. There will be fewer opportunities for women to demonstrate their capabilities.[18]

The empirical evidence relating to the effects of legal wage floors tends to support our conclusions. Clearly, the equal-pay laws are a form of minimum wage legislation: women must be paid no less than

---

[18] Furthermore, not all dynamic effects are likely to be in favor of women. Because of the equal-pay laws, the employer may substitute capital, as well as men, for women and by doing so may discover that the capital equipment is more productive than he had originally thought. A greater effort may be made to develop new nonhuman substitutes for labor.

men. And the weight of the evidence supports the conclusion that minimum wage laws do have an adverse effect on the employment opportunities of those who are covered by the laws. Since John Peterson and Charles Stewart have made an extensive review of past studies of the effects of minimum wage laws, several of their conclusions may be noted:

> The impression created in most government studies that federal minimum wage policy has produced no adverse employment effects is erroneous.
>
> The general model of economic theory (that is, the competitive model) most clearly corresponds to the observed results of statutory minimums, whereas the alternative models used to be non-predictive in theory and in fact.
>
> Minimum wage rates produce gains for some groups of workers at the expense of others. . . .[19]

A recent study of Kosters and Welch[20] found that in addition to reducing the level of employment, minimum-wage rates increased the instability of those who have been covered by the laws, particularly nonwhites and the young. Is there any reason to believe that equal pay laws for women will have any different consequence than the more conventional minimum wage laws? In support of minimum-wage rates, many advocates have argued forcefully that those who are covered would otherwise be the victims of discrimination and would, once covered, demonstrate that they deserve the higher wage.

Third, it may be contended that the adverse effects of the law may be inconsequential and that the benefits to the many far exceed the harm done to the few. Such a position would not, as noted above, be very comforting to those women who are made worse off because of the law. The fact that there will probably be many more women whose wages are raised than there will be women who are adversely affected by the legislation probably goes a long way toward explaining why congressmen are prone to support such laws. It increases the numbers of votes they receive.

----

[19] John M. Peterson and Charles T. Stewart, *Employment Effects of Minimum Wage Rates* (Washington: American Enterprise Institute for Public Policy Research, 1969).

[20] Marvin Kosters and Finis Welch, "The Effects of Minimum Wages on the Distribution of Changes in Aggregate Employment," *American Economic Review* 62 (June 1972), pp. 323–31.

CONCLUDING COMMENTS

The whole argument does suggest a strategy for women leaders: equal pay laws should be coupled with quantitative controls to insure against adverse employment effects. In addition, by requiring employers to hire more women than they otherwise would (for example, through affirmative action programs), the result can be an increase in the demand for women *and* an increase in their wage rates. This, of course, brings into focus the problems associated with controls and the prospects of reverse discrimination.

QUESTIONS TO PONDER

1. Suppose the government requires that women be paid the same but that the wages of men must, on average, be reduced to the level of women's. What will be the consequences of such a law? Explain with the use of supply and demand curves.

2. Suppose the government does not mandate equal pay for equal work but requires that employers hire more women and fines employers who do not comply. What will be the market effects of such a law? Use supply- and demand-curve analysis in your answer.

3. We noted in the text that even self-employed women earn substantially less than self-employed men (See Table 16–2). Explain that differential.

4. What will equal-pay-for-equal-work laws do to the willingness of women to stay in the home, to the birth rate, to the national income level, and to the number of meals bought at restaurants?

PART **6**

COLLEGE AND
UNIVERSITY
EDUCATION

CHAPTER 17

The university setting

Typically, universities catch hell from their students. Students frequently complain about the quality of food; they deplore "meaningless" general education requirements and criticize professors who are more concerned with their research and professional standing outside the classroom than they are with the quality of their instruction. They do not like being bored to tears while in their classrooms, and some tire easily of humbling themselves before the "lords" of the university, the administrators. Students beef about poor or remote parking facilities or about regulations that prohibit cars on campus altogether. In years gone by, they have grumbled about and demonstrated against "petty" rules—such as dress codes, curfew hours, and sign-outs—that restricted their social conduct. More recently, the hot issue on some campuses has been whether or not coed suites within dormitories should be allowed.

On the other side of the desk, professors are not without their complaints. They bemoan what they sense has been a deterioration of academic standards. They are very concerned with what has come to be known as "grade inflation," or the gradual increase in grades given to students. Now, more than ever, there is concern over pay raises not keeping up with the cost of living. As one professor recently complained at a faculty meeting, "I wish the administration would stop talking about 'annual raises'; I haven't had a *real raise* in years."

In this chapter we are not concerned with the legitimacy of student and faculty complaints. Nor will we spend time evaluating the tactics employed by students or faculty to get what they want. We prefer to consider the more interesting question of why the university *can* operate the way it does. At the start, we readily admit that part of the basis for much student and faculty discontent may simply be an unbridled attempt on their part to get more and more for little or nothing. However, we think a fuller understanding of modern university operations requires some reflection on the institutional setting of the education process.

UNIVERSITY PRICING

The modern public university has one notable feature, and that is, it typically receives part of its funding from state appropriations and/or grants, endowments, and charitable contributions. The rest, generally less than 50 percent, comes from students (or their parents) in the form of tuition and fee payments. Until very recently, there has been a shortage of openings in higher education; more students have wanted to get in than could be admitted. The reason for past shortages, as we will show, can be traced to the way in which education has been financed. Many of the problems students have confronted in their college careers can also be laid at the feet of the subsidies given to education. That may be a mouthful, but we intend to explain in detail. First, we need to lay out the framework for the analysis, which means the market for education.

In Figure 17–1, we have scaled the number of university openings (that is, the number of students that can be admitted) along the horizontal axis and the price (which amounts to the marginal value of education) along the vertical axis. The *student* demand for education, labeled D_1 is viewed as the horizontal summation of all stu-

FIGURE 17–1

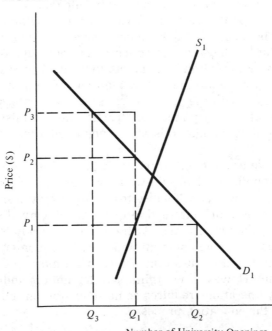

Number of University Openings

dents' individual demand curves. It is the market demand for education, and it is a function of anything that gives value to being an educated person, such as the inherent satisfaction from learning, the additional lifetime income the educated person can receive, and any change in social status that may be experienced by students and attributable to education. In the discussion, the demand is assumed to have its normal negative slope. (Why?) This means that more people will want to enter college if the price falls.

The supply of education (how many openings will be offered at each price) is a function primarily of the number of faculty members and/or classroom seats available and of the teaching technology being employed; that is, the greater the number of faculty members employed and/or the greater the number of classrooms and seats, the greater the supply of university openings students can fill. Also, if television or large lecture rooms are used, then more students may be accommodated.

To give some realism to the model, the supply of education, S_1 in Figure 17–1, is assumed to be upward sloping but highly inelastic with respect to tuition and fee payments from students. We make this assumption recognizing that the number of students universities can admit is determined in large measure by decisions of state legislatures or, in the case of private institutions, charitable organizations. They are the ones who make appropriations for dormitories and classroom buildings. However, it seems reasonable to assume that schools can and do respond to a limited degree to changes in the price they can charge their students. Hence, the upward sloping curve.

If education were provided on a free-market basis, the market clearing price would be the price at which the supply and demand for education intersect in the graph. On the other hand, assuming that the legislature both subsidizes the students' education and limits the physical size of the university, the price charged students in the form of tuition and fees will be below the market clearing price —for example P_1. (For simplicity, we assume all universities charge the same price.) Note that at P_1, the number of student openings in universities will be Q_1; however, the number of students wanting to enter will be much greater, Q_2. In other words, given the supply and demand and price of education in this illustration, there is a shortage of openings for college students (Q_2–Q_1), and this, we believe, fairly accurately describes the situation of universities and colleges until the late 1960s and early 1970s. (If this were not true, one must wonder how else we could have experienced a shortage.)

The existence of the shortage goes a long way toward explaining the behavior of universities. Because of the shortage, the available openings must be distributed among those who want to be admitted in some extra-market manner. Since there are more students knocking at the doors than can be admitted and since the students are not paying the full cost of their education, there is certainly little incentive for the university (when a shortage exists) to pay much attention to the wishes of the students. It is also clear why the criteria for admission has traditionally been on the basis of who the most intelligent students are and who are the best or most efficient learners. Not only do such standards permit the faculty to fashion students after their own idea of what an educated person should be, it may make life in general a little easier for the instructors. It is often much easier to teach an intelligent person than one who may not be so well-endowed mentally.

Those students who want to go to college but who cannot get in represent a threat to those students who are admitted. If the admitted students do not conform to the requirements (standards) of the university or faculty, they can be replaced by those who would otherwise be a part of the shortage. Therefore, as opposed to accepting a total payment of P_1 from each student, the demands of the optimizing university can be raised. The *effective price,* meaning the money price plus the nonmonetary "payments" the university will charge, can in fact be raised to P_2 in our illustration. P_1 is paid by the students in the form of tuition and fees and the rest, P_2-P_1, can be extracted from the students in any number of forms. The university can impose general education requirements the student may not appreciate and can impose social regulations that are not liked. The university can also neglect the quality of the accommodations, such as food and dormitory facilities, and it can require students who want to drive cars on campus to park in a remote area. The professor can require more work than students will freely choose and can require that they learn material that is of little interest to the student but of considerable interest to the professor. If students do not like the way they are treated in or outside the classroom, they can be replaced or less severely penalized with low grades.

Notice that P_2 is the highest price that can be charged. If the university attempted to extract a higher money and nonmonetary price than P_2, for example, P_3, the number of students wanting to go to college would fall to Q_3. Given that Q_1 openings will be available, a surplus of openings (Q_1-Q_3) will exist; universities can anticipate a cutback in funds from students and state appropriation; and professors will be threatened with a possible loss of jobs and income. In such a situation, what can we expect to happen? Being economists and university professors and recognizing that competition *does* exist among faculty members and universities, we would anticipate that the demands placed on students would fall back to P_2. This means that something would have to give, such as the extensiveness of general education requirements, the toughness of courses, the attitude of university personnel, the quality of food, and so on.[1]

From this analysis, we may conclude that what professors and universities view as their standards may be primarily an expression of their market position and their ability to extract a nonmonetary price from students. It also follows that their ability to lay claim to standards and induce compliance from students is dependent in part upon public subsidies; this is revealed in the gap between P_2 and P_1, and their ability must rise and fall with the difference. For example, suppose that the university raised the tuition and fee payment to something above P_1 and there is no offsetting increase in demand. The result would be, barring a change in supply and demand conditions, a reduction in the shortage and, more importantly for our present purposes, a reduction in the gap between P_2 and the price charged for tuition and fees. Here again, if something did not give, the number of students wanting to enter college would drop, and we would have the surplus problems discussed above. The anticipated results would be, as above, that the optimizing university would have to concede some of its demands in other areas of university life. Having to make such concessions is one possible constraint on universities' abilities to raise their tuition and fees.

If the university does not concede in areas such as rules governing social conduct and parking, then a reduction in demands may have to be realized in the area of expected academic performance. The reader may think professors have their standards and will maintain them at all costs, and we agree that there are professors who are like that. However, visualize for the moment a professor who may have a family to support and very few employment opportunities outside the university. Consider also that this professor may not have tenure. If there exists a surplus of university openings, such as Q_1-Q_3, then there will be unfilled seats in someone's class-

---

[1] An aloof attitude on the part of professors and administrators is one means of reducing the utility of education to students, and, to that extent, it is one means of extracting a nonmonetary price from students.

room, portending a possible cutback in the number of faculty members needed. If the university cuts back on faculty, who would you guess would go first? Given the attention administrators pay to student credit hours generated by faculty and departments, it is quite likely that if a cut is made, it will be where the number of students in class is low. Recognizing this prospect and remembering that faculty members are not all irrational when it comes to their own welfare, the individual faculty member can attract more students to his or her classes in two basic ways. He or she can attempt to change the nature of the course, improve its inherent value to the students, and increase the demand for the courses. This option has the disadvantage of requiring more work on the part of the professor. The other basic way he or she can attract more students is by cutting back on demands on students. In other words, the price to students of taking these courses can be reduced by lowering requirements and/or raising the grades students can expect to receive for any given level of achievement.

If one professor, by such methods, attracts more students, then other professors, who may not have originally been caught with an enrollment problem, may now be saddled with unfilled seats and the threat of losing their jobs. The result *can be* a competitive devaluation of academic standards and inflation of grades. This is not necessarily bad for the *students* because remember that we originally said that professors may have been imposing what they thought was important on the students and they may now be catering more to student desires. At the same time, we must recognize the possibility that the public (and parents) may have been subsidizing college education in order that the professors' will (which is thought to be more in the long-run interest of students and society) could be imposed. Because tuition and fee payments can influence the ability of professors to extract work from students, it is understandable why they may side with students in opposing higher tuition payments and in promoting government subsidization of education.

We can complicate the analysis a little by considering the impact of changes in demand and supply conditions. If the demand for college education increases while the supply remains constant, as described in Figure 17–2, the expected result is an increase in the shortage of openings from Q_2-Q_1 to Q_3-Q_1. Note also that the effective price unversities can charge can go up from P_2 to P_3, meaning the universities can increase their tuition and fee payments and/or increase their demands in other areas of academic life. (Similar conclusions could be drawn if the supply increases but the demand in-

FIGURE 17-2

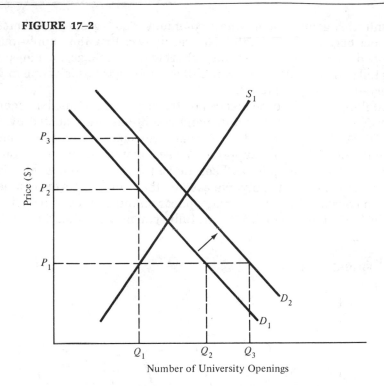

Number of University Openings

creases by more than supply. Try showing this on a graph of your own.) This situation may be reasonably descriptive of universities in the late 1950s and early 1960s. The value of a college education was definitely on the rise during that period of time. In addition, incomes and the population of potential college students were increasing. The college diploma was generally considered to be a surefire ticket to the pie in the sky all young people and parents dream about. All of these factors were increasing the demand for college education faster than openings could be made available.

In the late 1960s, the supply and demand conditions in the university education market began to change dramatically. The growth in the number of potential college students began to taper off, the college diploma became much more common and its prestige value began to drop, and surpluses of college graduates, especially in teaching fields and engineering, began to emerge—all of which led to a significant drop in the growth of demand for college education and, in some states or areas, to an absolute drop in the demand. On the supply side, state appropriations for classroom buildings and dormitories gained momentum; community colleges and technical schools began to proliferate. The result was that the supply outstripped the growth in demand; shortages of college openings at first fell and then later evaporated all together; surpluses of openings emerged on many campuses.

To illustrate the consequences of these changes, consider Figure 17–3. The initial supply and demand conditions are depicted by S_1 and D_1. We have increased the demand and supply curves to D_2 and S_2, but notice that the supply has been increased by more than demand (that is, supply has been moved further to the right). For purposes of simplicity only, we assume that tuition and fee charges remain constant.[2] The graph may appear on the surface to be a little confusing; but if you look at it carefully, you may see that the results of the changes are a reduction in the shortage from Q_2–Q_1 to Q_1–Q_3

FIGURE 17–3

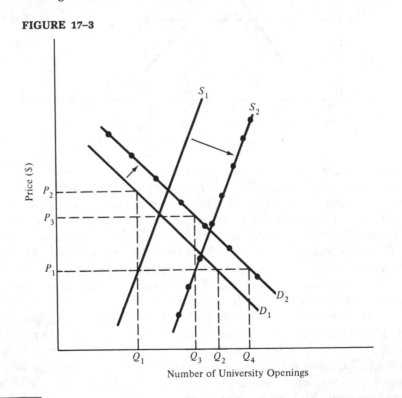

Number of University Openings

<hr/>

[2] We realize that tuition charges have gone up dramatically during the period with which we are concerned; however, such changes do not harm our conclusions. In fact, such changes, if introduced, would serve to reinforce our conclusions. Can you show why?

and a reduction in the *effective price* universities can charge, from P_2 to P_3. Given this latter reduction and the constant tuition price, the university and/or faculty must reduce their demands on students. We would predict that the changes that occurred in the educational market during the late 1960s would be reflected in one or more of the following areas: reduced social regulations, a relaxation of general education requirements and other restrictions on students' college programs, a change in the attitudes of administrators and professors toward students, and perhaps lower academic standards, however defined.

Interestingly enough, those of us who have been a part of university systems during the past decade have seen almost all of these changes come about. Colleges and universities have reduced their general education requirements, and some have eliminated them altogether. Universities are turning more and more toward student evaluations of faculty and courses as a means of evaluating faculty performance and ensuring that faculty members pay more attention to the desires and feelings of students. Social rules, which used to be very stringent on the activity of women in particular, have been abolished.[3] Students are being allowed much more freedom in taking independent study courses and in designing their college programs to meet their own needs.

Grades were going up in the 1970s so much that on many campuses more than two thirds of all grades given were As and Bs. On many campuses, the dean's list became a joke to those who knew what had been happening. *Newsweek* magazine reported the following on grade inflation:

> In 1961, about half of the seniors at Harvard College graduated with honors; this month, when the class of '74 received their di-

---

[3] As a sidenote, one of the authors has been associated with two schools that, when he was there, had very strict dress codes and sign-out requirements for women. For example, at one school women had to be in their dorms by 10:30 p.m. during the week and could not be gone from campus for more than four hours without signing out again. They also could not wear bermuda shorts on "front" campus. At another campus, women could not date men of another race without written permission from their parents. When students demonstrated against such rules in the early 1960s, the administration would respond by arguing that they were doing what they thought was right and in the best interest of the women students. At both schools, when enrollment problems began to appear, the rules were scrapped almost *in toto*. The justification given was that women in the middle and late 1960s were more mature and responsible than were their counterparts in earlier years. Such statements made good press releases, but few in the college communities took them very seriously.

plomas, degrees *cum laude* or better went to an astonishing 82 percent. The average University of Colorado student in 1964 maintained a grade-point average of 2.4 (out of a possible 4 points), but
his counterpart today has a GPA of 2.82. Between 1962 and 1972,
the University of North Carolina doubled the percentage of As it
handed out. The average grade at the University of Wisconsin has
soared from C-plus to B-plus in just nine years. And the dean's list
at the University of Virginia included 53 percent of the student body
last year—compared with 21 percent in 1965.[4]

In a survey of over 400 colleges and universities, Roy Burwen found
grade inflation to be prevalent during the 1960s, which was a time
of considerable expansion in universities and colleges.[5]

In addition, one should realize that grades went up in the face of a
downward drift in Student Achievement Test scores of entering
freshmen. Employers, graduate schools, and organizations such as
Phi Beta Kappa no longer looked upon high grades as clear evidence
of superior ability. At one time, employers looked to colleges and
universities that screened the bad students out and graduated the
people who were markedly better than those who failed to make it
through. In the 1970s, with rising grades and a growing uncertainty
over what they meant, more and more employers were turning away
from seeking college graduates and were turning toward training
their own people. To the extent that this has occurred, the value of
the college degree has deteriorated, reducing the demand for education.

Before closing this section, three points need to be stressed. First,
we have discussed the problem of education in the context of an
environment in which the shortage of openings has been reduced.
In the late 1970s, many colleges and universities found that their
demand was once again expanding more rapidly than their available
openings for students. The result was a tightening of academic
standards some places, especially in colleges of business. However,
with the slow down in the growth in the number of college-age students in the 1980s, this recent trend should be shortly reversed and
the shortage of openings should again decrease.

Second, we recognize that many of the changes that have occurred in education are in part the results of fundamental social
changes in attitudes and preferences of people toward what educa-

---

[4] "Grade Inflation," *Newsweek*, July 1, 1974, p. 49.

[5] Roy Burwen, "Institutional Research Notes" (San Francisco: Office of Institutional Research, San Francisco State College, March 1971), unpublished.

tion is and should be. We merely submit that the market has played a significant role in the development of educational policies and attitudes.

Third, the faculty of any given university could get together and could put restrictions on the grades any given faculty member could distribute to his students. However, such a move is likely to run headlong into the opposition of those who believe that such policy would be a violation of academic freedom. In addition, if one university restricts its grades and other do not, the result can be a movement of students to other universities, jeopardizing jobs in the university that restricts faculty grades.

FACULTY SALARIES

Because of the tremendous growth in universities during the 1950s and 1960s, there was a corresponding increase in demand for faculty members. Salaries rose substantially and graduate schools geared up to satisfy the increasing demand for persons with doctorates. Because education appeared at the time to be a sound investment, many persons eagerly sought advanced degrees. The usefulness of the graduate programs that sprung up, however, was predicated on a strong growth in university systems; and when this growth began to level off, graduates continued to be pumped out. The eventual consequence of a system in which salaries could not be readily adjusted downward was a surplus of prospective faculty members. Many Ph.D.s in the humanities went begging for jobs and ended up selling hotdogs and driving trucks.

Although money wages of existing faculty members could not be easily reduced, salaries of beginning faculty members began to stabilize and, in some areas, to fall. In a situation in which more faculty members abound than can be hired, one might anticipate state legislatures and university administrations taking every opportunity to reduce the *real income* (that is, the purchasing power of money income) of the faculty members. As a result, pay raises have in most states not kept pace with inflation. (If legislatures did not permit this to happen, they would have had a difficult time, perhaps, explaining the rather high salaries of faculty members to their constituencies.) One might also expect universities to reduce the income of faculty members by putting greater demands on them; and so we have had a growing trend toward eight-to-five days for faculty, whereas in the past they have been relatively free to come and go as they pleased. Administrations have imposed standardized student evaluation on faculty and have been able to raise their demands in the areas of research, publications, and community and regional service. In the past, tenure has been offered to prospective faculty as a fringe benefit; now the probationary period before one can receive tenure is being lengthened, and many schools are moving to abolish tenure altogether. All of these changes and cutbacks in graduate programs are working to reduce the surplus of Ph.D.s on the market.

In the foregoing paragraphs, we have been generalizing about the broad market for faculty. When the market is segmented by discipline, these generalizations do not always hold. They do appear to hold very well for professors in the humanities and education but not so well for professors of accounting and finance. Herein lie potential pitfalls for university administrators who may attempt to make sweeping rules for all faculty. If the administration dictates that all faculty raises are to be the same, the university may hold on to those faculty whose employment market is glutted, but they may lose, for example, their accountants whose market wage rate may have risen by more than the standardized salary increase. If the university does not pay the market wage to those accountants it has, it will then have to enter that same market they tried to ignore and hire other accountants at the going market wage. If they refuse, their accounting program can suffer.

This is one aspect of market forces many administrators fail to appreciate. As an illustration and as discussed above, universities are putting more reliance on student evaluations in determining salary increments. This may mean that the mean scores received by the different faculty members in different disciplines are ranked and raises are dispensed accordingly. To reveal the inherent problems of such schemes, suppose that all of the accountants are basically "crummy" teachers in the eyes of their students but they are typical of others in the profession. (Believe it or not, some of our best friends are accountants!) In the college of business, let's suppose that they score relatively low among other faculty in the college; economists (being inherently superior in all aspects of university life!) score relatively high. The evaluation scheme of allocating raises on the basis of student evaluations would mean that the economists receive more than the accountants. However, suppose that the market for accountants is much tighter than the market for economists; the market wage of accountants would rise comparatively more. The market would dictate that the accountants receive a higher raise. If the university or college employs student evaluations as a criterion for raises, what do you think would happen? You can rest assured that unless the accountants were bound to the school for nonmonetary reasons, the college of business would lose their accountants. The school would then have to enter the market to hire the accountants at the higher wage. The university could avoid all of the expense associated with faculty turnover by simply looking to market as a guide for adjusting salaries.

CONCLUDING COMMENTS

The reader should understand that the foregoing analysis does not necessarily reflect the way we think university students, administrators, and faculty *should* behave. As has been our goal throughout the book, we have only tried to explain why they have behaved the way they have and how they might be expected to behave, given changes in market conditions.

QUESTIONS TO PONDER

1. If the university increases its tuition and fees while the demand for and supply of educational openings remains constant, what will happen to educational standards, social regulations, and attitude of faculty and university officials?
2. Suppose the demand for education switches from the humanities to business, everything else held constant. What will be the effects of the change on the academic standards in humanities and business?
3. Suppose that the salaries of college business graduates goes up relative to the salaries of other graduates, what will happen to academic standards in the colleges of business? Does your answer have anything to do with the supply response of universities?
4. Explain the following statement: "An increase in the state subsidy to higher education will directly and indirectly increase the welfare of faculty members."

CHAPTER 18

Learning behavior

Psychologists and educators have been concerned with learning behavior for some time. We now know a good deal about the learning process, particularly among the lower-order animals; however, it is abundantly clear from experience that educators have a long way to go before much can be said about how learning among students within a classroom setting can be improved. The federal government and foundations such as Ford and Rockefeller have spent literally billions of dollars over the past decade researching the learning and educational processes. Unfortunately, researchers have frequently concluded that there is no difference between their experimental and control groups—that nothing appears to work in the classroom. For example, Robert Dubin and Thomas Taveggia found this to be the case in their examination of 91 major studies of experiments that had evaluated different techniques, methods, and classroom conditions.[1] H. Kiesling concluded that "It is striking to note that such pay-parameter variables (as teacher experience and training) were seldom found to be related to pupil performance."[2] After a decade of actively funding projects to change education in the public schools, the Ford Foundation in the early 1970s concluded that very little that was done made much difference.

Where there has been a favorable difference between experimental and control groups, researchers have been very reluctant to suggest that their conclusions be generalized to other similar (but not identical) situations. Policymakers have readily questioned whether or not the marginal benefits achieved were worth the cost incurred.

---

[1] Robert Dubin and Thomas Taveggia, *The Teaching-Learning Paradox* (Eugene: University of Oregon, 1968).

[2] H. Kiesling, "Multivariate Analysis of Schools and Educational Policy" (Santa Monica, Calif.: The Rand Corporation, 1971). Darrell Lewis and Charles Orvis drew basically the same conclusions from their review of the literature in economic education, *Research in Economic Education: A Review, Bibliography, and Abstracts* (New York: Joint Council on Economic Education, 1971).

The inability of educators and psychologists to demonstrate how learning in the classroom can be upgraded stems in part from the terribly complex nature of the classroom environment. In that environment, students are being constantly bombarded with thousands of bits of information (stimuli); and if one assumes that a change in the flow of any one type of information will actually have a material impact on student learning, he may rightfully be guilty of presumption. In addition, we feel that the failure of the educational establishment to explain the educational process may be more fundamental in origin—that is, it may be at least the result of the way in which the learning process is perceived by those who are doing the research. This can mean that the wrong questions have been asked and the evidence has been misinterpreted.

THE TRADITIONAL VIEW

The dominant view of learning among psychologists appears to be a very mechanistic one—and perhaps overly so. The subjects or students receive stimuli and respond accordingly. The task of the teacher is one of providing the right stimuli in order that the right response can be imprinted in the behavior of the students. In this way, the students learn by connecting stimulus and response. From the perspective of traditional learning theories, it appears to us that the students do not have *real choice* in the sense that the theories allow them to choose in some rational manner among viable options. This may be because students are not credited (from a theoretical point of view) with having a preference that is independent of the stimulus-response mechanism and that can operate on or alter that mechanism. They merely respond. Once the imprint—that is, the connection between stimulus and response—is made, students can be likened to a computer. The data cards can be fed in and a printout is received without any intervening creative thought process. The main reason for this approach may be that the admission of choice can muddy the "theoretical waters." One purpose of any social science, such as psychology, is to make predictions regarding human behavior and, more specifically for our purposes, the learning processes. If the choice is admitted to the discussion, then one may suppose that it is impossible to say anything about learning; that is, if choice is to be real choice, then it must be unpredictable. If choice is predictable, then one must wonder how it can be *real choice.* Seeing this roadblock, psychologists tend to avoid the subject.

In these few pages, we hope to introduce choice into the discussion of learning.[3] The individual student or instructor is not viewed as an academic robot, responding mechanistically to stimuli from the environment, past and present. We accord the individual a preference that is, to a degree, independent of environmental factors. The student or faculty member can therefore choose from a range of options or combinations of goods and services, which may include learning or education.

Our approach to learning is different from conventional views in one important respect. Educators, in an attempt to explain the learning process, are inclined to point to genetic and environmental conditions (such as sex, age, race, class size, and method of instruction) as causes of student learning behavior; whereas we, in applying the economic approach to learning, look to the choice calculus of the individuals as a primary explanatory factor and one that tends to be overlooked in more conventional studies. This is not to say that environmental and genetic conditions do not constrain the choice process.

THE RATIONAL STUDENT

We begin by assuming that students are rational in the conventional economic sense of the term. As discussed in Chapter 1, this means that students know what they want and attempt to maximize their satisfaction by consuming from a range of commodities that are available. Perhaps, the reader feels that an assumption of rationality is inappropriate in any discussion of education. A person can only make *rational* decisions among those alternatives which are *known*. By definition, what is to be learned is not known; and therefore, a person cannot make rational decisions regarding learning he or she knows little about. The fact is that people make decisions that involve unknowns and uncertainties all the time. The decision to research involves what is yet to be found. People regularly buy cars and appliances (often used ones, at that) they know

---

[3] In this chapter we are at best able to outline certain broad themes in the economics of learning and conventional psychological theories. Robert Staaf deserves considerable credit here for originating and developing the economic approach to learning. For a more detailed and rigorous treatment of the economist's approach, the reader may want to see Richard M. McKenzie and Robert J. Staaf, *An Economic Theory of Learning: Student Sovereignty and Academic Freedom* (Blacksburg, Va.: Center for the Study of Public Choice, 1974). There are actually a number of psychological theories of learning; for a good review of these, see Winfred F. Hill, *Learning: A Survey of Psychological Interpretations*, rev. ed. (Scranton, Pa.: Chandler Publishing, 1971).

virtually nothing about. It is certainly questionable whether or not the public knows more about the costs and benefits of the cars they buy than they know about, say, a course in economics before they enter the class. Remember, students are not completely in the dark about the classes they sign up for; they do spend a significant amount of time attempting to acquire information about courses and professors they take. People make decisions on the basis of the information they have at hand and can rationally justify acquiring, and this goes for the decision to learn.[4]

At any rate, if you can accept our assumption, you may further recognize that students will *fully* allocate their resources—that is, time and material and monetary wealth—and will equate the ratios of the marginal utility of the goods they buy to their respective prices. Including knowledge *(k)*, which is the end product of the learning process as a good that can be "consumed" by the students, the marginal condition is: $MU_a/P_a = MU_k/P_k = \ldots = MU_n/P_n$, where *MU* denotes marginal utility, the subscript *a* can represent any good such as an apple, and subscript *n* can stand for any other good. P denotes price, which in the case of knowledge may mean the money and time expenditure required to obtain a unit of knowledge. If the equality has not been attained and, for example, $MU_k/P_k > MU_a/P_a$, then the students have gotten more utility for the last \$1 (or resource) spent on knowledge than on apples. (For a more detailed explanation, see Chapter 1.) They can consequently increase their utility by shifting resources from apples to the acquisition of knowledge. In other words, if they are rational, we can expect them to choose to learn more and to continue to expand their knowledge until equality is attained among the ratios.

Here, knowledge has been treated as a composite good, whereas we know that it comes in many diverse forms. This means that the actual utility-maximizing condition is a little more complicated. Letting subscripts *e*, *f*, and *h* denote knowledge in the fields of economics, French, and history, the marginal condition becomes: $MU_a/P_a = MU_e/P_e = MU_f/P_f = MU_h/P_h = \ldots MU_n/P_n$. If, instead,

---

[4] A fruitful departure (but one that cannot be taken) would be the consideration of a question economists have pondered for years: When does a person stop acquiring information and make a decision? Remember that the acquisition of information itself can be a rational act. Aside from this issue, one economist, Gary Becker, showed that even if people are irrational in at least one sense of the term, many of the deductions made from an assumption of rationality still hold ("Irrational Behavior and Economic Theory," *Journal of Political Economy* 70 [February 1962], pp. 1–13).

302
CHAPTER EIGHTEEN

$MU_e/P_e > MU_fP_f$, students can increase their utility by learning more economics and less French.

Another way of saying the same thing is that Paul Smith, a student, will "purchase" knowledge or any particular kind of knowledge up to the point that the marginal benefits equal the marginal costs. *He will purchase only so much,* and he will vary his "consumption" of any kind of knowledge, such as economics, not only with the price he himself pays (that is, the demand curve for economic literacy is downward sloping) but also with changes in the marginal utility and price of other goods. For illustrative purposes, suppose that the marginal utility of apples (which, by the way, is totally outside of formal classroom setting) increases; this means that MU_a/P_a will become greater than MU_e/P_e. It would then be rational for Paul to consume more apples and less economic knowledge. If on the other hand, P_e were to rise, it would be rational for Paul to spend less on economics and more on other goods, such as apples, or even more on other subjects. If he does not do this, assuming equality among the ratios before the price increase, MU_e/P_e will be less than the other ratios. (To test your understanding of what has been said, what would the student choose to do given the following changes: an increase in MU_e; a reduction in P_f; and an increase in P_a.)

A simple conclusion that deserves special note is that the amount of knowledge Paul acquires may not be the same the professor believes he should acquire, or in other terms, any disagreement between what Paul does in fact accomplish in class and what the professor expects him to accomplish may simply be due to a difference between what the professor perceives the benefits for him to be and what Paul perceives them to be.[5] Also, recognize that in our view of student behavior, Paul does not automatically respond to stimuli; rather, he is viewed as receiving information about relative costs and benefits about matters to be learned, weighing it in terms of his own preference, and then choosing an appropriate response. The extent of his response depends on what happens to the marginal utilities of the goods as more or less is consumed. For example, going back to the situation in which $MU_e/P_e > MU_f/P_f$, we concluded that Paul would choose to learn more economics, but how much depends on the rate at which MU_e falls as more is consumed. If MU_e dimin-

---

[5] We also wish to point out that any disagreement could just as easily be due to the fact that the instructor and student do not evaluate the MUs of other goods as being the same. Can you explain why?

ishes rapidly, he will learn less additional economics than if the MU diminished slowly. Keep in mind that he will increase his knowledge in economics until the ratios are equal.[6] This leads to the point that new classroom device or technique can, from a technical point of view, increase the ability of the student to learn economics. However, because of the cost involved and perceived benefits to the student, the student may choose to increase his understanding by less than what is technically possible.

To illustrate this last point with more precision, assume for simplicity that there are two subjects, French and economics, open to Paul; that both subjects yield positive benefits; and that he has allocated a given amount of time to the study of these subjects.[7] In Figure 18–1, we have scaled his achievement in economics along the horizontal axis and achievement in French along the vertical axis.

We do not know a great deal about Paul, but we do know that if he allocates *all* of his time to the study of economics, he can achieve only so much in that field. We have arbitrarily selected E_1 in Figure 18–1 as that limit. We also know that if he chooses to achieve E_1 in economics, he will learn nothing in French. This, of course, assumes that learning French requires some time and that learning economics has nothing to do with learning French. The same can be said about his ability to learn French. If he devotes all of this time to the study of French, he can learn only so much; we have indicated this limit by F_1.

Alternately, Paul can choose to divide his time between the study of French and economics in any number of ways, changing the relative achievement in the two subjects. By taking time away from the study of French and applying it to the study of economics, he can increase his achievement in economics while giving up achievement in French (that is, the cost of achieving in economics). It is from this line of reasoning that we have drawn a line between F_1 and E_1. This line (or more properly, transformation curve) depicts the numerous combinations of French and economics achievement

---

[6] We have sidestepped the possibility that MU_f will increase as fewer units of French are learned.

[7] Admittedly, as we have discussed, the amount of time available for educational purposes is note likely to be fixed. However, the assumption does simplify the discussion and does not detract from the limited argument we have in mind. Also see Robert J. Staaf, "Student Performance and Changes in Learning Technology in Required Courses," *Journal of Economic Education* 3 (Spring 1972), pp. 124–29.

FIGURE 18–1

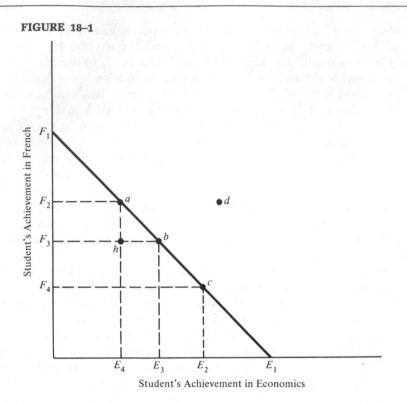

Student's Achievement in Economics

that can be "produced" by Paul. He can therefore choose to consume any combination along F_1E_1. Although it does happen, it is doubtful that the typical student will choose either combination F_1 or E_1. Assuming that Paul must pass both courses, he cannot afford to have zero achievement in either field.[8] Consequently, we would expect him to choose some interior combination, such as a, b, or c. Combination d is out of the range of possibilities; it requires the use of more resources than Paul has available for education. (For some other student, who may be more efficient at learning economics and French, d migh be possible. Why?) If Paul chooses combination h, he will not be fully using his resources; he can have more achievement in French and/or economics. Therefore, any combination inside and not on F_1E_1 will not be chosen by the rational student.

---

[8] We recognize that some students come to a class with such a backlog of knowledge in a given subject area that they do not have to do anything to pass the course. Here again, we are attempting to concentrate on the typical student in the typical class.

Hence, Paul's task is to sort through all combinations along F_1E_1 for that one combination that will maximize his own satisfaction. If he chooses b, it must be because it is preferred over a and c.

The task of the professor can be viewed as twofold. First, the professor of economics can attempt, by various persuasive techniques, to change the student's preferences toward economics. The result may be that the student prefers combination c over b. The student learns more economics, but notice that the greater achievement in economics in this case is at the expense of achievement in French. (The efforts, on the other hand, can induce the student to allocate more time to education, in which case the transformation curve will move out to the right.)

Second, the economics professor can attempt to increase the efficiency with which the student learns economics. If he accomplishes what he sets out to do, the student can achieve more in economics; the limit of the student's achievement can move, for example, from E_1 to E_2 in Figure 18–2. Assuming that the French professor does nothing to improve learning in his discipline, the

FIGURE 18–2

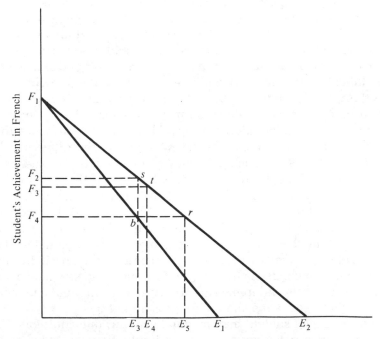

Student's Achievement in Economics

---

student's transformation curve will, pivoting on F_1, move to F_1E_2. The student can then choose any combination along this new curve. He can choose combination r; his achievement in economics increases while his achievement in French remains constant. On the other hand, the student can choose combination s, in which case his achievement in French would rise and his achievement in economics would remain constant. It we had put some leisure activity, such as golf, on the vertical axis instead of achievement in French, the result of the efficiency change in economics could have meant more rounds of golf for the student. The common sense explanation for s is simply that since the student can now learn more economics in the same amount of time, he can reduce the amount of time spent studying economics, learn the same amount, and spend the time on some other activity such as golf or studying French.

The student can also choose combination t in which case he increases his achievement in both subjects. However, in our example, the increase in economics is much smaller than the increase in French. This might be the expected result of the student who is a French major and is taking economics as a means of satisfying his general education requirement.

This analysis suggests a possible explanation for the outcomes of experiments conducted by educators and which appear to have no impact. The researcher can have two classes of students. In one class, he teaches the conventional way, and the mean student achievement may be measured at level E_3. In the other class, he does something that is innovative and in effect moves the transformation curve out to F_1E_2. However, he really does not know if or how much the curve has moved. Besides, he may not even think in terms of the students' transformation curves. All he does is measure their mean achievement, which may be E_4. Because the difference between E_3 and E_4 is quite small, he may conclude that the experiment was a failure. While it is possible that what is done did not have any effect on learning efficiency (that is, the curve actually does not move), the failure of the researcher could have been the oversight of the increase in the student's achievement in French or the greater amount of time the student spends goofing-off or out on dates. If he had broadened his research and had considered the possibility that students may have been choosing to do something else, his conclusion may have been different. This is only a possibility but one which researchers in education should not pass by lightly.

Before leaving student maximizing behavior, one additional, important point can be made. We have implicitly assumed that the marginal utility of knowledge, MU_k, is positive, which is in accord with the paradigm that there are benefits to education. Therefore, the student is *willing* to pay some price to acquire some finite amount of knowledge. However, some types of knowledge may have no perceivable benefits *to the student*. This may be descriptive of many of the courses included under general education requirements. In such a case, the student must be *paid* before he can be expected to bear freely the cost of learning the subject. Of course, one way of paying the student is to impose a cost on him if he does not voluntarily learn the material. This can be done by making the coursework a requirement for graduation or entry into a profession. The student can also be penalized with low grades, damaging his future income-earning ability. If he takes the coursework, he is permitted to obtain his degree. The degree then becomes the payment. As discussed in the previous chapter, such tie-in sales can be made to the student as long as the price charged in the form of tuition and fee payments is below the market-clearing price.[9]

THE RATIONAL PROFESSOR

The professor can be viewed as a rational human being and as facing a transformation curve. Consider Figure 18–3. In that graph, we have put the leisure time of the professor on the vertical axis. Assuming the professor's field is economics, we have scaled the mean achievement of the professor's classes along the horizontal axis. If the professor does nothing with his classes except walk into class, he will have only so much leisure time available for doing other things, such as playing golf or undertaking research. We have arbitrarily indicated this limit as L_1. On the other hand, he can use all of the time raising his students' understanding in economics. In this event, the students' mean achievement can rise to E_1. Like the student, the professor can divide his time between leisure activities and increasing his students' achievement, in which case he will have open a number of leisure-achievement combinations, which may be described by L_1E_1. Also like the student, the professor is faced with the problem of choosing the combination along L_1E_1 that will maximize his utility. Remember, the professor does have academic freedom, which gives him considerable leeway in deciding how he will use his time.

If he chooses combination *b*, the student's mean achievement

<hr>

[9] We force students to go to public schools. The element of compulsion suggests that the perceived benefits of education for those who actually have to be forced is not sufficient to cover the students' private cost of the education.

FIGURE 18–3

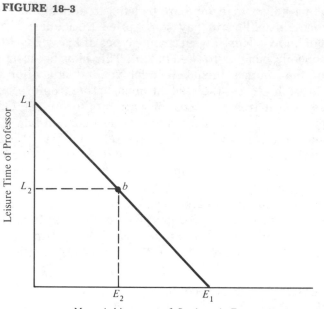

Mean Achievement of Students in Economics

level will be E_2. This implies that the students will, given their abilities and effort, learn only so much, and this is, in part, the result of the utility-maximizing behavior of the professor. If the professor had chosen to work harder, the students would have learned more, possibly as much as E_1. However, the professor would have had less leisure time available or less time for research, and he apparently, in this example, did not believe the additional achievement was worth the cost in terms of leisure time.

If we now introduce some innovative technique into the classroom that can improve the efficiency of the learning process, the professor's transformation curve will, pivoting on L_1, shift to L_1E_3 in Figure 18–4. The professor can now choose any combination along this curve. He can choose combination c, in which case the full benefits of the change in classroom efficiency is revealed in student achievement, which rises from E_2 to E_4. On the other hand, the professor can trade some of the gains in learning efficiency for additional leisure time. He can choose combination d, or any other between c and L_1; in this example, the net increase in student achievement from the innovation is very slight. If this were a part of an experiment, the researcher might conclude that the innovation was ineffective. Recognizing the possible choice behavior of the

FIGURE 18–4

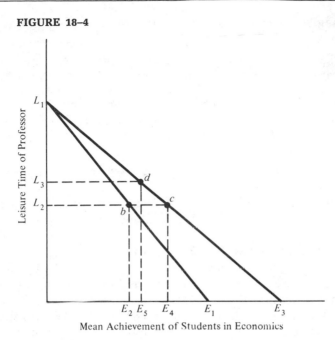

Mean Achievement of Students in Economics

student and faculty and recognizing that most educational experiments are undertaken in public schools and general education courses at the college level, it may be understandable why researchers so often may have found that their experiments have had little effect.

STUDENT EVALUATIONS

Increasingly, universities are turning to student evaluations as a means of evaluating faculty performance. However, the issue of whether or not student evaluations can be influenced by the grades the professor gives his students is unsettled. Allen Kelley, in a study in economic education, found a positive relationship between grades and student evaluations but concluded, "Providing students with high course grades does not appear to exert an important impact on evaluations."[10] Furthermore, he suggests that if the instructor had raised his quality point average from 2.27 to 3.50, the mean ratings for the course would have increased by only two to three percentage points. Conversely, Dennis Capozza, in another study

---

[10] Allen C. Kelley, "Uses and Abuses of Course Evaluations as Measures of Educational Output," *Journal of Economic Education* 4 (Fall 1972), pp. 13–18.

in principles of economics, came to a dramatically different conclusion.

> The results indicate that every 10-percent increase in the amount learned reduces a professor's rating by half a point. On the other hand, if a professor's grades average 3.5 instead of 2.5, he improves his rating by one and a half points. Another way of expressing the relationship would be that if a professor wishes to receive a perfect rating of 1.0, then he should teach nothing and give at least two thirds of the class As.[11]

In this section, we will demonstrate what economic (choice) theory can say on the subject.

On student evaluation forms, students are typically asked to respond to such questions as "What is your overall appraisal of the way in which your professor conducted the course?" The students are asked to rate the professor on a scale that may range from "far below average" to "far above average." At best, student evaluations reflect the degree to which the course and instructor agree with the student's preference for such factors as grades, leisure, course content, and, we might add, classroom entertainment. We can therefore reasonably assume that the higher the *relative* utility (or the lower the relative disutility)[12] the student acquires from attending class under one professor, the higher the relative evaluation of the instructor and course.[13]

GRADE INFLATION

Setting aside the multidimensional nature of student preference, assume for the time being that all professors, other than the one with which we are concerned, hold their grades constant and that the student is rational and views grades (or quality point average) and

---

[11] Dennis R. Capozza, "Student Evaluations, Grades and Learning in Economics," *Western Economics Journal* 11 (March 1973), p. 127. For other studies on the same subject, see V. M. Voeks and G. M. French, "Are Student Ratings of Teachers Affected by Grades?" *Journal of Higher Education* 31 (June 1960), pp. 330–34; Miriam Rodin and Burton Rodin, "Student Evaluation of Teachers," *Science* 177 (September 29, 1972), pp. 1164–66; Alan Nichols and John C. Soper, "Economic Man in the Classroom," *Journal of Political Economy* 80 (September/October 1972), pp. 1169–73; and John C. Soper, "Soft Research on a Hard Subject; Student Evaluations Reconsidered," *Journal of Economic Education* 5 (Fall 1973), pp. 22–26.

[12] The student can possibly dislike all of his instructors; but if asked to rate the instructors, he will give the one whom he dislikes least the highest rating.

[13] These statements seem reasonable to us because if the student is asked to give comparative ratings to different professors in different fields or differ-

leisure time as goods from which he receives some utility. Assume also that higher grades (As and Bs) are preferred to lower grades and that leisure time (which can be used for anything inside or outside academic life) available to the student is limited to L_1 in Figure 18–5. These assumptions appear to us to be reasonably descriptive of the typical student. Grades (or quality point average) in an economics course are scaled along the horizontal axis.

Given the professor's standards and assuming the student has to work for his grades, we know that the student will have to forgo leisure time to raise his grades. Because other things may be important to him, we would not expect him to spend all of his time studying and attempting to raise his grade to the highest point possible, which in this case is B.[14] The student may *choose* combination *a*, at

FIGURE 18–5

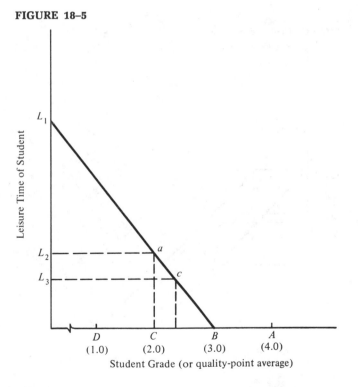

ent courses, he must be able to reduce the comparative problem to one common basis. We use the economist's concept of utility as that common denominator.

[14] For illustrative purposes, we have arbitrarily assumed that this particular student is incapable of making an A under the instructor's initial standards.

which he makes a grade of C and has L_2 leisure time available for studying other subjects or going out on dates. (He used the difference between L_1 and L_2 for studying economics.) The student may choose combination c—that is, he could have made a higher grade—however, since he did not, we must assume that the additional time spent studying $(L_2–L_3)$ was worth more to him than the marginal increase in his grade.[15]

The professor can change his grading structure in any number of ways, but to keep the discussion short and simple, we will focus attention on one way and assume that the professor will give the student the opportunity to make a higher grade for the same amount of effort. Furthermore, we assume that he eases up in such a way that the student's tranformation curve between grades and leisure time shifts out in a parallel manner, from L_1B to L_1A in Figure 18–6. Given

FIGURE 18–6

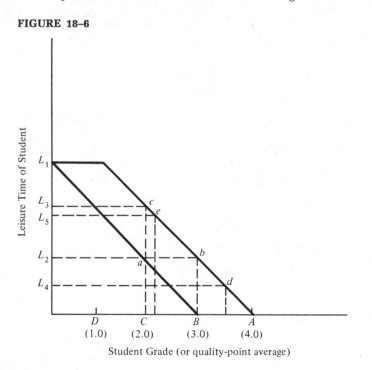

Student Grade (or quality-point average)

---

[15] A point worth mentioning at this juncture is that if a researcher observes several students making higher grades than others in the class, he cannot on *a priori* grounds expect their ratings of the instructor to be higher for the simple reason that they may have worked harder to obtain their grades and are therefore no better off.

the shift, the student has the opportunity to move from combination a (on L_1B) to any point on L_1A. He can move to b, in which case he will have a higher grade and the same amount of leisure time. This means that his effort (L_1–L_2) and achievement in the course should remain constant. On the other hand, the student could *choose* combination c; there he would end up with the same grade but with more leisure time. If he chooses c, he will spend less time studying economics and presumably will achieve less.

Alternately, the student can choose any combination between c and b and end the course with a higher grade and more leisure time. Since he can have more of both if he wishes, we must assume that from the student's point of view, he is better off and conclude that the professor's rating will rise because of reduced standards. How much, however, we cannot say. Even if the student chooses a combination like d, in which even he would have a higher grade but less leisure time, we would still expect the professor's rating to rise. The student can choose, say, combination e—that is, more of both—and in the event he chooses d, we must deduce that d is preferred to e. Since e is obviously preferred to a (because there is more of both at e), d must also be preferred to a. Therefore, the instructor's rating should be up at d. (This is a little tricky and you may want to reread this paragraph to insure that you follow it.)

There are two points that fall out of the graph that need to be especially stressed. First, if the students as a group choose a combination like e, it means that the grade they receive under the new grading structure may rise by an insignificant amount; but the instructor's ratings will still be up. If a researcher correlates the grades that professors give with their student evaluations and never looks at what the student achieves in the course or what he does with his leisure time, he may find very little or no correlation. He may actually conclude that higher student ratings cannot be bought with changes in the grading structure. However, there are professors who in fact may be "buying" higher student ratings with an easing of their standards. The problem is that the researcher has failed to see that students are taking the benefits of the professors' lower standards in terms of more leisure.

Second, as noted above, it is possible for the student to choose a combination like d (less leisure and a higher grade). If he does, he will be studying and achieving more in the course; however, it is interesting to note that Capozza, in the study quoted in the first part of this section, found an inverse relationship between achievement and student evaluations, meaning that the students may be choosing combinations like *e* (more leisure). The suggested inverse relationship between achievement and student evaluations was also borne out in studies by Attiyeh and Lumsden[16] and by Rodin and Rodin.[17] Interestingly enough, most studies on the relationship between student ratings and grades have been, for the most part, undertaken in courses like principles of economics, which are required for one reason or another. In such courses most students may not want to be there in the first place; and under such conditions, if given the chance, they may move from *a* to, say, *e*—that is, they may take the benefits of the higher grading structure in terms of more leisure time. If the course is one students want to take because they like the subject or because they believe the knowledge acquired can be used to bolster their income, then one may more likely find a strong positive relationship between achievement and student ratings of the professors.

REAL GRADE INFLATION

In the foregoing discussion, we explicitly assumed that other professors held their grades constant. However, if all professors inflate their grading structure, which has tended to be the case over the past decade,[18] the value to the student of any absolute grade falls. This is because the student's own ranking among his classmates falls if he continues to receive the same grades while their grades go up. The student's utility from taking a course under a professor who does not inflate should fall and so should the student's rating of the professor. Therefore, if student evaluations are used in determining salary increases, the professor who does not inflate can experience a drop in relative income. Also, if grade inflation is the general rule among professors, a professor may, to raise his (relative) ratings, have to inflate grades relative to the general trend.

AN ADDITIONAL EMPIRICAL TEST

Testing any hypothesis regarding the impact of grade inflation on student ratings and performance is fraught with difficulties. *Ideally,*

---

[16] Richard Attiyeh and Keith G. Lumsden, "Some Modern Myths in Teaching Economics: The U.K. Experience," *American Economic Review* 62 (May 1972), pp. 429–33.

[17] Rodin and Rodin, "Student Evaluations of Teachers."

[18] See Roy Burwen, "Institutional Research Notes" (San Francisco: Office of Institutional Research, San Francisco State College, March 1971).

a given set of students should be taught a course under a given grading policy, and their ratings of the course and professor should be taken. They then should be given the same course with the only change being in the grading policy. The results of such an experiment would have meaning only if we could assume that in the process the students' preferences and opportunity sets are not changed, which is, of course, a totally unrealistic assumption.

In order to obtain some idea of the impact of grade inflation, Paul Combs and one of the authors (McKenzie) took a second-best approach, which was to conduct a control-experimental group-type study.[19] Combs taught two sections of the same introductory course in statistics, and McKenzie taught two sections of the same course in introductory economics. In each case, Combs and McKenzie gave their classes pre- and post-tests, taught their sections as closely similar as possible and gave the same tests during the course. The only difference in their instructional methods was their grading policy. Each designated one class as being the "easy" class and one as the "hard" class. In the case of Combs, the easy class was given partial credit for incomplete answers, which was not the case in his hard class; the difference in the numerical grade on the last day of class was approximately one half of a letter grade. McKenzie, on the other hand, gave the same numerical scores on the tests of the two classes; the difference was that his grading scale was much lower for his easy class. That is, a B began at a lower numerical score for his easy class than for his hard class. The difference in the mean grade given in his two classes was a little over a full letter grade on the last day of class.

As we have hypothesized, Combs' mean student ratings were approximately 10 percent higher in the *easy* class than in his hard class. However, the students in his *hard* class had a greater improvement in their understanding of statistics; their improvement was approximately 10 percent greater. Since McKenzie had a much larger differential in his grading distribution in the two classes, one might expect a much larger differential in student ratings and performance, and this is exactly what was found. The students in McKenzie's easy class gave him a 25-percent higher mean rating than did the students in his hard class. On the other hand, the improvement in economic understanding of his students in his hard class was 85

---

[19] J. Paul Combs and Richard B. McKenzie, "The Empirical Effects of Grade Inflation on Student Evaluations and Performance" (Boone, N.C.: Economics Department, Appalachian State University, 1975).

percent greater than the students in his easy class. In our preceding analysis, all we could possibly say is that we should have found an inverse relationship between student ratings and performance, given a difference in the grading structure; but we frankly did not anticipate the difference to be so dramatic.

Upon more sophisticated regression analysis (for those who understand statistics), we standardized for a number of characteristics of the students, such as sex, age, race, marital status, quality-point average, and so forth. We found in the McKenzie test, the dummy variable introduced to distinguish between the students in his hard and easy classes was statistically significant at 0.001 in the equation in which the professor ratings were used as the dependent variable and in which the differences in the student's performance on the pre- and post-test were used as the independent variable. This dummy variable was not significant in the analysis of Combs' results, but the sign of the variable was in the predicted direction. This suggests, but does not prove, that if Combs had increased the difference in his grading structures, the differences in ratings and performance would have been significant. The study also suggests that if student ratings had been used in ranking the faculty within the department for purposes of raises, Combs and McKenzie could have, assuming other faculty members held to their grading policy, raised their rankings and raises by inflating their grades.[20]

CONCLUDING COMMENTS

At this point, the reader may believe that we look upon student evaluations of professors as a totally perverted device for evaluating teaching. On the contrary, we recognize that students can see good qualities in teachers. We believe that students can fairly accurately tell when a professor is prepared for class and if he is sufficiently competent to teach the course. They can also make judgments about his treatment of themselves and other students. All of these judgments can be reflected in their rating of the professors they have. The main point we have been trying to make in this section is that given the quality of the professor, economic theory suggests that

---

[20] For those that may be concerned with this study from a moralistic point of view, the authors of the study maintained a difference in their grading policy until the last lecture session at which the student ratings were taken. In the final analysis, the classes were graded on the same basis. In fact, because we realized that we had "framed" the students, the student grades were higher than they normally are in classes of the professors.

student evaluations can be distorted by the professor's grading structure. If two professors are *equal in every other respect,* we would predict that the professor with the higher grading structure (in the sense that we have used the term in this section) will tend to receive the higher student ratings. In a similar manner, if two professors are distinctly different in the eyes of the students, one being better than the other, our analysis suggests that the professor who would otherwise have the lower rating can (partially) offset the differential by easing up on his grades.

QUESTIONS TO PONDER

1. Suppose that two professors increase the efficiency of the learning process in their classes at the same time but they increase the efficiency by different amounts (or percentages). What effect will such changes have on the choice behavior of the student with regard to the two courses and some other leisure time activity?
2. Do professors have an incentive to increase the efficiency of the learning processes in their classes? If they do, what is it? What other institutional changes can be made to increase this incentive?
3. Suppose a professor can inflate grades by changing the grading curves (see accompanying graphs).

FIGURE 18–A

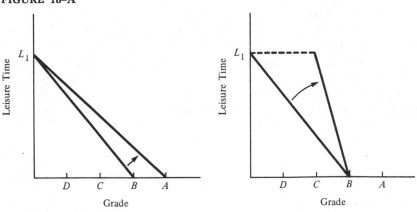

What effect do the changes have on the "price" or "cost" of a higher grade? In which case is the student most likely to "choose" to learn the most after the grading structure is inflated? Explain in terms of basic economic principles.

Committees and comment pollution

Committees are an integral part of the internal governance of colleges and universities. They are typically delegated major responsibilities such as determining admissions standards, developing curricula, handing out awards, and making policy recommendations on such important matters as internal resources allocation, grading systems, tenure, and other faculty and student welfare measures. Although one may like to think of the committee process as one in which learned men and women, through an in-depth evaluation of a problem area, make sound judgments, faculty members and administrators commonly characterize their committee meetings as dull, boring, and a monumental waste of time. They are also prone to suggest that what may appear to be informed judgments are often (though not always) nothing more than the personal expressions of members who throughout the committee sessions made little or no attempt to come to grips with the issues at hand (and it should be noted that, generally speaking, the larger the committee, the more common the complaints). If these criticisms are correct, not only may the university be employing its resources inefficiently through direct support of the committees themselves, but it may be operating on the basis of very poor judgments.

The purpose of the analysis in this chapter is not to suggest that *all* university committees operate, in some sense, badly but rather to develop an economic explanation as to why there is likely to be an excessive "production" of comments (or "comment pollution") within *many* committee meetings (or why meetings may be long and dull), and why the judgments of the individual members may often (though not always) be uninformed, or why little effort may be made in studying the assigned task of the committee. Once the sources of the problems of the committee are recognized, remedies do emerge as is indicated below. In developing the argument, we

take the usual position that committee members—faculty, administrators, and students—are similar to their counterparts in other
walks of life in that they weigh the costs and benefits of taking
action, will take an action if the benefits exceed the costs, and will
extend "production" of the activity up until the point at which the
marginal private benefits of the action equal the marginal private
costs. In a word, the committee member is rational.[1]

COMMENTS AS PUBLIC GOODS

A comment made by a committeeperson in a meeting is a public
good (or perhaps as frequently as not, a public "bad") in much the
same sense as is police protection or industrial pollution. (What is a
public good? A public bad?) Take, for example, the situation of the
industrial polluter. When it fouls the air, it imposes a cost on persons
who may live or work in the surrounding area: the people on the
street may experience eye irritation, and the pollution may soil the
clothes on the line. If the property rights to the air are left unassigned
(as has been the case in the past), the polluter need not consider
these external costs in its production decisions. Consequently, its
private costs are less than the social costs of the industrial activity,
and we can expect that production (and the emission of pollutants)
will be extended beyond the social optimum.[2] It is only through the
internalization of the external costs through user charges or taxes
that an economically efficient output can be achieved.

---

[1] The chapter is in part the application to a specific problem area of the
general line of analysis that was developed in Chapters 11 and 12.

[2] The social optimum is the output level at which the marginal *social* costs
equals the marginal *social* benefits. The social costs include all costs incurred
by those directly involved in a transaction and those who are not a party to
the transaction but who are affected indirectly. It is the emission of particles
beyond the point of social optimum that economists would call pollution. One
Indian can urinate in the Hudson River (as many did for a long time) without
affecting (in the sense that anyone is disturbed) the aesthetic beauty of the
area or the quality of the water. The problem of pollution exists when all
people start throwing their waste in the river at basically the same place and
same time; that is, they go beyond the social optimum amount of waste
disposal.

Problem: several years ago people who were very concerned about the
destruction of the environment gathered on what was then called "Earth Day"
at the Washington Monument. After all the speeches on what human beings
were doing to the world were over, they left, leaving the grounds covered with
litter. Realizing that the mess was created by "concerned citizens," how could
it happen? Would you as an economist have expected them to create the
mess? Why?

In the case of the committeeperson's comment, once the comment is made, all members of the committee must hear it. There are external costs (as in the case of the industrial production) involved since people other than the one making the comment must, if they are present, spend the time to hear what is said. The private cost to the individual making the comment is mainly equal to the time he or she spends listening to himself or herself.[3] (There may be those who fear making a fool of themselves with their comments; however, we find that there are many in the universities who get a great deal of positive utility in making comments to any group. They enjoy sounding off before the committee in the same way that a musician likes to perform before an audience.) The social costs, on the other hand, are equal to the summation of the opportunity cost incurred (or value of time spent) by all members of the committee listening to the comment, and it needs to be emphasized that the discrepancy between the private and social costs for a comment expands with the size of the committee. The rational committeeperson will extend the production of comments until the marginal *private* benefits equal the marginal *private* costs; and since the private costs are likely to be less than the social costs, we should expect there to be a natural tendency for committees to overproduce comments for the same reason that the industrial producer (when external costs are not internalized) can be expected to pollute.

A solution for efficient operation of a committee is for the chairperson to impose costs on members making comments to the extent necessary to achieve equality between the private costs actually considered by each committeeperson and the costs to the committee as a whole. This may be easier said than done; however, recognition of the problem of inequality between private and social costs may suggest to the chairperson attitudes and devices that have the effect

---

[3] The individual who is concerned about the feelings of others may also include in his own calculations the additional factor that his comments may inconvenience others or may lower his stature in their eyes. This still does not mean that the assessed private costs of the individual making the comments are necessarily equal to the social costs as calculated by the other members of the committee and that the committee will necessarily work "properly." There are committees that do in some sense work properly; however, our purpose here is to develop a model of committee behavior that will enable us to understand why so many committees do not. In addition, full inclusion of all "charitable feelings" in the choice calculus of the individual committeeperson makes the model so general that all predictive content is lost. Our assumption regarding the costs that are considered is similar to the assumption of profit maximization in more conventional economic discussions of the firm.

of raising the effective private cost of a comment to the individual.[4] Firmness would indeed be a desirable characteristic of any good chairperson, and such a tack may be easier for the chairperson to embrace if he or she understands that controlling the comments of individual members can be desired by all members. It may appear to be paradoxical, but it is still the case that even though each individual member may freely choose to "pollute" the committee with comments, he or she could still desire some form of collective (chairperson) control over the comments made by all committee members. The simple reason is that although his or her own freedom may be restricted, he or she does not have to endure the comment pollution generated by others.[5]

THE JUDGMENT OF COMMITTEEPERSONS

If Mr. Sims, a doctoral candidate, were to select as his thesis topic the effectiveness of the Interest Equalization Tax Act from July 1963 through December of the following year, he would no doubt undertake an exhaustive review of the relevant literature, make a point by point evaluation of the provisions of the act, collect mountains of data and evaluate them in different ways, and end up spending no less than nine months in *concentrated* study. If Mr. Sims was hired by a university and appointed to a committee whose function was to make recommendations on the internal allocation of university resources, most of his colleagues (given the typical committee organization) might indeed consider him to be a little unusual (if not queer) if he addressed the task of the committee with the same thoroughness with which he developed his doctoral thesis. He would probably get the same reaction even though the problems confronting the committee were considered by all to be more important than the subject of a doctoral thesis.

---

[4] We must hedge the issue at stake here since an economist has no particular expertise in suggesting what may actually constitute an increase in cost, barring the use of such things as taxing income or, what can amount to the same thing, charging for each comment made. The authors seriously doubt that such techniques would be an acceptable or necessarily efficient means of controlling a committeeperson's behavior.

[5] Of course, the most desirable situations for any *individual* committeeperson would be for the chairperson to permit *him* completely free range in making comments while at the same time restricting the comments of the other members. We are suggesting in the text that the committeeperson would be willing to compromise this position to move away from a completely free and open committee session.

One obvious explanation for the disparity in the amount of effort expended on a thesis and a committee task is that Mr. Sims must, once employed, divide his allegiance and work effort among the demands of his students, department chairperson, and professional activities: he simply may not have the time for committee work.[6] In addition, he may not have any particular personal interest in the problem facing the committee, whereas his doctoral research may have been personally gratifying, and many committee tasks, admittedly, require only that the committee members express their own preferences. Our concern, however, is with those committees that do require study and preparation on the part of the members, but yet the effort expended may never come close to being that which may be required; and we seek explanations for the behavior of committee members that have largely gone unrecognized by university officials but which are no less important than those reasons frequently cited.

Committee work can be exceedingly costly to committee members. Mr. Sims, studying the issue of internal resource allocation, for example, can be expected to spend, if he does a good job, five to ten hours a week for a period of a year or more trying to assess the scope of the problem at hand and evaluating current programs on campus. If he has no particular expertise in such areas—for example, he is in English or music—the magnitude of his task is considerably multiplied. This means he must forgo other activities that may have value to him. If he is inclined to operate within the publish-or-perish world or consults a great deal, serious effort on the business of the committee can reduce his future income stream. Otherwise, time spent on committee work can deny him rounds of golf or conversation with students or his family. In short, in absence of compulsion, the decision to undertake committee work at any level is an economic (choice) problem for him.[7] Therefore, to understand his behavior, one must compare the costs with the benefits of committee work as perceived by Mr. Sims.

The cost of Mr. Sims' work potentially includes the value of the time spent on research, as indicated above, plus the time spent in

---

[6] It is interesting to note, however, that many faculty members are employed before they finish their doctoral thesis; they (generally speaking) will still make a concentrated effort to complete their thesis.

[7] Although he may have no choice with regard to whether he is appointed to a particular committee, the committee member typically has a great deal of latitude in determining how many meetings he will attend, how well prepared he is for the meetings, and how attentive he is during the sessions.

committee meetings listening to others, relating what he has learned, attempting to synthesize the information he receives from others with that which he has collected, and attempting to convince others of the relative correctness of his own position. There are in essence two basic types of potential costs: research costs and costs associated with dealing with the committee. Note that almost all costs are under the control of the committeemember—the exception being the minimum number of times he must attend meetings—and that many of the costs of dealing with the committee escalate exponentially with the size of the committee.[8] As suggested earlier, comment pollution—or the length of the meetings—is likely to rise with the number of members since there are more perspectives and, therefore, potentially more comments to be made. And when there are more members, there are more people to convince that any given position, should be taken.[9] Again, there are more perspectives in the larger committees, which must be won over to a given position, if one is to be taken; and therefore, the variety of tactics required to convince (develop) a winning coalition is likely to be greater.

On the benefit side of Mr. Sims' "choice ledger," one can distinguish between indirect and direct benefits of committee work. Indirect benefits may include such factors as the effect Mr. Sims' work will have on his own income, security, and prestige through the actions taken by the committee. In the case of the committee on internal resourse allocation, Mr. Sims, through his effort, can possibly affect university policy and, therefore, the demands for his own services as a teacher. The direct benefits may include the entertainment value (for want of better words) associated with being in on what is happening on campus, giving the impression that he is doing something, and having interesting conversations with people with whom he does not normally associate.

The amount of work he is willing to undertake depends on the perceived benefits from his action and how they compare with the cost of achieving those benefits. As we assumed in the beginning,

---

[8] Research costs are more directly related to the assigned task of the committee than to anything else.

[9] Because of the public-goods nature of comments made within committee meetings, the cost of persuasion is not likely to rise proportionately with the number of committee members. This does not mean, however, that the cost will not rise.

One of the reasons for forming committees in the first place is to make comments public goods and therefore reduce the costs of forming a consensus among a number of people who may represent various aspects of campus life.

Mr. Sims will undertake no work unless the benefits exceed the costs, or the payoff is positive. In many instances, the indirect benefits from committee work can be small for the individual member; the decisions made may have nothing to do with the member's own welfare (but may have a great deal to do with welfare of, say, students). In the event that the effects of the committee decisions are generalized over the entire faculty, the effect can be small for any one individual, and if so, he will make his decision on how much research to undertake on the basis of the *individual* benefits he receives and not on the basis of the total effects. Since the decisions of the committee are public goods themselves, the effort expended by each member can easily be sub-optimal.[10] It is indeed apparent that one tends to observe greater effort expended by those committee persons who are directly or indirectly affected substantially by the decisions of the committee.

As for the direct benefits, committee work, and particularly the quality factor, is given very little attention in the evaluation of faculty members. Student credit hours generated and research are by far the dominant considerations. Clearly, the typical department chairperson who is primarily responsible for evaluation may never do anything more than count the number of committees his or her faculty are on. In fact, inquiry into the quality of the individual's committee work can be considered in many circles of academia as a violation of commonly accepted professional ethics.[11] We do not mean to suggest that there is never any feedback but only that it may be so scant that it does not reflect the true effort of the committeemember and may be too unreliable to use as a basis for evaluation.[12] The other direct benefits (entertainment) may explain his attendance at meetings but tend to detract from his research effort.

Mr. Sims' work can also be related to committee size but in an inverse manner. The larger the committee, the smaller the perceived benefits from expended effort. In a large meeting of faculty—take, for example, a faculty meeting as an extreme case—the vote of an

---

[10] Gordon Tullock, "Public Decisions as Public Goods," *Journal of Political Economy* 79 (July/August 1971), pp. 913–18.

[11] It would be in the interest of the faculty member to employ some personal resources attempting to give the impression that he is working harder on his committees that he actually is. It *may* be rational for him to work harder at giving a false impression than on committee business.

[12] Our model of rational behavior would clearly suggest that the committeeperson who knew that his work was being scrutinized by those who have power over his income would exhibit more effort.

individual faculty member is one among many. The probability of his individual vote determining the outcome of the meeting is rather small, and, one may add also, that the probability of what he does or says in the faculty meeting affecting the outcome of the meeting is also rather small (or smaller than for smaller committees). For smaller committee meetings, the probability goes up. However, Mr. Sims will be rational and will still discount the benefits resulting from the committee actions by (1) the probability that his own vote will be affected by research (A; see below); (2) the probability that his position, determined by his own research, is the correct one (D); (3) the probability that his research will affect the outcome of the committee vote (E); and (4) the probability that the committee decision or vote will actually affect the individual committeemembers (F).[13] Even for the smaller committees, it might be deduced that these probabilities and corresponding discounts can be so low that the expected personal benefits, resulting from the research efforts, will have to be far greater than the expected costs, which can in themselves be quite large.

For example, assume that the following values are associated with the probabilities noted above: $A - 0.5$, $D = 0.75$, $E = 0.2$, and $F = 0.5$. (These values seem to us to be reasonably generous for purposes of illustration.) Mr. Sims will undertake the cost of research (C) if the discounted benefits (B) are greater than the costs or if $(ADEF) (B) - C > 0$. *For this example, this means that the expected benefits would have to be greater than $26.67 for each dollar value of research cost incurred.* Even if it were conceded that the probabilities are too low and should be adjusted upward, we should still find that the expected benefits will have to be several times the expected costs. In light of the analysis, it is quite understandable why many committee members, even in relatively small committees, do very little to become informed on the subject matter facing them.[14]

The foregoing analysis also suggest several general guidelines for committee organization:

---

[13] This last factor must be added since many committees are set up for the purpose of making recommendations and not for taking action directly. In such instances, it is not certain what the committee recommends will actually be adopted as university policy.

[14] In a large faculty meeting, E would be much smaller than in the example above. If $E = 1/500$, the benefits would have to be greater than $2,666 for each $1.00 of cost. This would mean that to expect the committeepersons to incur $1,000 worth of cost on committee work, one would have to expect $2,666,000 worth of benefits. The obvious paradox is that a few people actually work as hard as they do.

1. University committees that are organized to study a problem for which there is no obvious answer should be kept small. From personal experience, the authors doubt that a committee with more than six members will actually study any problem before it. Larger committees should be reserved for those areas of university life for which study is not required or the mere expression of individual preferences toward an issue is the underlying function of the committee. As is now virtually axiomatic within the study of groups, large groups should be used for reaction and not for action.

2. In the interest of reducing the cost of research to the individual committeeperson, the task of the committee should be segmented and responsibility for research in the different areas should be delegated to the members. This means that if large committees are thought to be necessary for some political purpose, for example, subcommittees should be organized, and clear lines of responsibility should be drawn and made known.[15] Since all members will not be studying the entire problem facing the committee, there is a cost embedded in this suggestion. However, if the entire problem is laid on the committee as a whole, the cost of a complete study of the whole problem *can be* too great for any one to undertake *any* research. In addition, each committee member may attempt to become a "free rider," meaning that no one does anything.

3. Before a committee is organized, there should be a high probability that the recommendations of the committee will be put into action. If an administrator frequently organizes committees and almost as frequently ignores their recommendations, this behavior will reduce the diligence with which the committees will tackle any problem that is assigned. In other words, it will reduce the probability that he or she *can* accept the recommendations of the committees that are appointed.

CONCLUDING COMMENTS

There have been two overriding conclusions that come out of the foregoing discussion. First, committee meetings are likely to be dull and boring because, given their typical organization, there is likely to be an overproduction of comments and these comments are likely to be based on uninformed judgments; this goes for students as well

---

[15] An alternative would be for the committee to be given the authority to hire someone to undertake the research and draw up proposals the committee can approve or disapprove.

as faculty committee meetings, and it is just as applicable to committee meetings that are wrestling with the question of what to do about industrial pollution as well as how to reallocate faculty resources. If the reader has difficulty accepting this as a generality, then it is clear that he has not been on many committees. Second, many of the problems universities have experienced in the past may be the result of the extensive use of committees and the general lack of concern over (or understanding of) the operations of the committee. A university may well be advised to be more selective in the use of committees, particularly the larger ones.

PART 7

ECONOMICS
AND ITS
SCIENTIFIC
NEIGHBORS

CHAPTER 20

Basic needs and human behavior: a digression into psychology

A. H. Maslow, a psychologist, argued that basic human needs can be specified with reasonable clarity and can be ranked according to their importance in providing motivation and influencing behavior.[1] Embedded in Maslow's hierarchy of needs is a theory of human behavior that is to some degree foreign to the economist's way of thinking. In this section. Maslow's system will be outlined so that we may be able to use it for comparative purposes. This, admittedly, is a digression of sorts, but we think it is an important one because we have a suspicion that Maslow's system (at least in terms of its basic structure) is not terribly dissimilar from the views of many laymen in economics.

Maslow's need hierarchy is pictured in Figure 20–1. The importance of the needs, in terms of how powerful or demanding they are in affecting human behavior, ascends as one moves downward

FIGURE 20–1

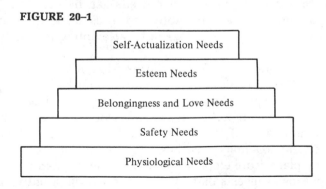

Self-Actualization Needs

Esteem Needs

Belongingness and Love Needs

Safety Needs

Physiological Needs

---

[1] A. H. Maslow, *Motivation and Personality* (New York: Harper and Row, 1954). See primarily chap. 5.

through the pyramid; that is, the most fundamental or prepotent needs, which are physiological in nature, are on the bottom. This category of needs includes on one level all attempts of the body to maintain certain chemical balances (such as water, oxygen, hydrogen-ion levels) within the body. On a higher level, the physiological needs include the individual's desires for food, sex, sleep, sensory pleasures, and sheer activity (meaning the need to be busy).

The need for safety, which is next in prepotence, may include the desires of the individual for security, order, protection, and family stability. The next category, belongingness and love needs, may include, among other things, the desire for companionship, acceptance, and affection. Maslow lists under the heading of esteem needs the individual's desire for achievement, adequacy, reputation, dominance, recognition, attention, appreciation, and importance. He argues that the need for self-actualization "refers to man's desire for self-fulfillment, namely, to the tendency for him to become actualized in what he is potentially. This tendency might be phrased as the desire to become more and more what one is, to become everything that one is capable of becoming."[2]

Maslow stresses that such an individual may indicate he is striving after one need when in fact he is pursuing something else. For example, the individual may say that he is hungry because by doing so and going out to dinner, he can acquire companionship, affection, and attention. This may be the case because the individual may find it useful to deceive another person or because he does not *consciously* know what his true motivation is. In addition, Maslow argues that certain preconditions, such as the freedom to express oneself, are necessary before basic needs can be satisfied. Consequently, the individual can be motivated to establish the necessary preconditions; he may not appear to be attempting to satisfy basic needs.

Maslow does not hold rigidly to the ordering of needs as indicated in Figure 10–1. He specifies this particular ranking because it appears to him to be descriptive of the people with whom he has associated and because it appears to be a reasonably good generality concerning human motivation. Because of cultural or environmental factors or because, for example, love has been denied in the past, some people may place more emphasis on esteem needs than on the need for love. He also suggests that "There are other apparently innately creative people in whom the drive to creativeness seems to be more important than any other counterdeterminant. Their creativeness

---

[2] Ibid., pp. 90–92.

might appear not as selfactualization released by basic satisfaction, but in spite of the lack of basic satisfaction."[3]

Although he qualifies his argument, the core proposition in Maslow's theory of human behavior is the argument that a person will first satisfy his most basic needs (physiological needs) before he attempts to satisfy needs of higher order. He writes:

> If all the needs are unsatisfied, the organism is then dominated by the physiological needs, all other needs may become simply non-existent or be pushed into the background. It is then fair to characterize the whole organism by saying simply it is hungry, for consciousness is almost completely preempted by hunger. All capacities are put into the service of hunger-satisfaction, and the organization of these capacities is almost entirely determined by the one purpose of satisfying hunger. . . . Capacities that are not useful for this purpose lie dormant, or are pushed into the background.[4]

If the most basic needs are satisfied, "At once other (and higher) needs emerge and these, rather than physiological hungers, dominate the organism. And when these in turn are satisfied, again new (and still higher) needs emerge, and so on."[5] One gets the impression from reading Maslow that the individual will not attempt to satisfy his second most prepotent needs until the most prepotent needs are (almost) fully satisfied; he will not move to the third tier in the hierarchy until the needs at the second tier are (almost) fully satisfied.[6] Apparently, the individual will not attempt to effect any self-actualization until he has moved through all former tiers. If any tier in the hierarchy is skipped entirely, it is because of insurmountable environmental or physiological barriers.[7]

Maslow's approach to human motivation and behavior resembles the approach of economists in several respects. First, they are similar because the essence of both theories is an assumption that the individual is able to rank all of his wants (or needs) according to their importance to him. In the Maslow system, anything that is not directly a basic need is ranked according to how close it is to a basic

---

[3] Ibid., p. 98.

[4] Ibid., p. 92.

[5] Ibid., p. 83.

[6] We use the term *are (almost) fully satisfied* because of such statements as "If both the physiological and safety needs are fairly well gratified, there will emerge the love and affection and belongingness needs" (Ibid., p. 89). Maslow never explains what will keep the individual from fully satisfying any given need level before moving on to a higher tier.

[7] Admittedly, this is an interpretation of Maslow and may be an unfair statement of what his true position is; however, he does tend to write in black and white terms—either the barriers are there or they are not.

need. Other needs beyond the five categories mentioned, such as the need to know and/or understand and the need for aesthetic quality, can be handled by adding additional tiers.[8] As pointed out in Chapter 1, the economist simply starts with an assumption that the individual knows what he wants and is able to rank all possible goods and services that are able to satisfy his wants.

The two systems are dissimilar, however, when it comes to the specification of the ranking, Maslow is willing to argue that in general the basic needs and their ranking can also be identified; that is, he can say what the individual's needs are and is willing to venture a statement about their relative importance. On the other hand, an economist would generally take the position that the relative importance of the needs varies so much from person to person that a hierarchy of needs, although insightful for some limited purposes, does not move us very far in our understanding of human behavior. The economist may specify whether a good or service may add to or subtract from the individual's utility and will argue that more of something that gives positive utility is preferred to less; but he would be unwilling to try to say exactly where the good (or need) may lie on some relative scale. We must presume that the specificity Maslow seeks is to him a useful, if not necessary, basis for predicting human behavior. Economists believe that they can say a great deal about human behavior without actually specifying the relative importance of the things people want. We certainly admit that the economist's inability to specify the relative importance of needs is a limitation to economic theory. (Given some of the areas into which economists are now delving, more and more economists are beginning to wish that they could somehow specify the ordering of people's preferences.)

Both systems are similar to the extent that they view the individual as consuming those things that give him the greatest satisfaction, Even in the Maslow system, which lacks a direct statement to the effect, there is the implicit assumption that the individual is a utility maximizer. Maslow also assumes diminishing marginal utility as more of the need is consumed; if this is not the case, it is difficult to understand how the individual can become fully or almost fully satisfied at any need level.

The systems are different because of their views of the constraints that operate on the ability of the individual to maximize his utility.

---

[8] Maslow, in his 1954 book, is less certain about the relative positions of the need to know and the need for aesthetic quality because of the limited research that had been done on the subject at the time he wrote the book.

The constraints in the Maslow hierarchy include environmental and cultural factors and the individual's character, or his beliefs about what is right and wrong. There is no mention of the individual's productive ability or income (unless these are implied in the environmental or cultural constraints) or of the costs of the means by which his basic needs can be fulfilled. These considerations are basic constraints in the economist's view of human behavior. By not considering cost, Maslow appears to assume that either there is no cost to need gratification and/or (in spite of an implicit assumption concerning diminishing marginal utility) the demand curve for any need is vertical (or perfectly inelastic). This means that the quantity of the need fulfilled is unaffected by the cost. An implied assumption of the vertical demand curve is that the basic needs are independent of one another. They are not substitutes; for example, a unit of an esteem need fulfilled does not appear in the Maslow system to be able to take the place of even a small fraction of a unit of physiological need.

Maslow recognizes that most people only partially fulfill their needs at each level. He writes:

> So far, our theoretical discussion may have given the impression that these five sets of needs are somehow in such terms as the following: if one need is satisfied, then another emerges. This statement might give the false impression that a need must be satisfied 100 percent before the next need emerges. In actual fact, most members of our society who are normal are partially satisfied in all their basic needs and partially unsatisfied in all their basic needs at the same time. A more realistic description of the hierarchy would be in terms of decreasing percentages of satisfaction as we go up the hierarchy of prepotency. For instance. . . . it is as if the average citizen is satisfied 85 percent in his physiological needs, 70 percent in his safety needs, 50 percent in his love needs, 40 percent in his self-esteem needs, and 10 percent in his self-actualization needs.[9]

Maslow does not, however, explain why this will be the case, nor does he provide an explanation as to why a person will not fully satisfy the higher needs before he moves to the next tier.

The economist might concede for purposes of argument, as we do, that the demand for a physiological need is greater (and more inelastic) than the demand for a safety need, which in turn is greater than the demand for a love need. However, it does not follow that, as Maslow suggests, the love need will be less fulfilled in percentage

---

[9] Maslow, *Motivation*, pp. 100–101.

terms than the safety or physiological needs. To what extent the different needs are gratified depends upon the cost or price of each unit of the means for satisfying a need and the elasticity of demand of each need. To illustrate, consider Figure 20–2. The demand for a means of gratifying a physiological need is depicted as being greater (meaning it is further out to the right) than the other demands. (For the sake of simplicity we consider only three needs.) We assume that any given need is fully satisfied if the quantity of the need "purchased" is equal to the quantity at the point where the respective demand curves intersect the horizontal axis.[10]

If as in this example, the cost of satisfying each need is the same, P_1, the individual will consume Q_{P1} of the means of satisfying his

FIGURE 20–2

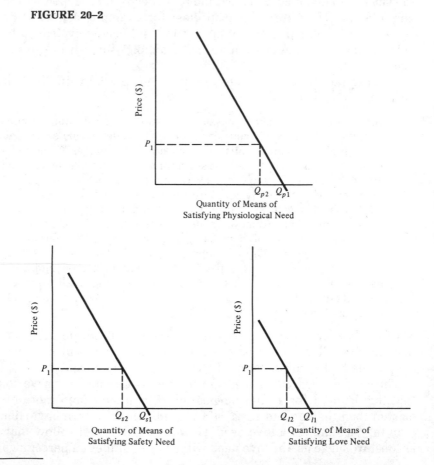

Quantity of Means of
Satisfying Physiological Need

Quantity of Means of
Satisfying Safety Need

Quantity of Means of
Satisfying Love Need

[10] At that quantity, the marginal utility is zero, implying that the person's utility level from the consumption of that need is at its maximum.

physiological need. As far as units are concerned, this is greater than the quantity of units consumed of the other needs; however, the percentage of the need gratified does not have to be greater. If demand for the physiological need were sufficiently inelastic, the percentage of the need gratified could be greater.

It is doubtful, however, that the costs of satisfying the different needs are the same. The availability of the resources needed for satisfying the different needs can easily be different; consequently, the costs of need gratification can be different. If the cost of fulfilling the physiological need were substantially greater, even though the demand for the need were greater, the percentage of the physiological need fulfilled could be less than the percentage of the other needs fulfilled. In Figure 20-3, the prices (or cost per unit) of the means by which a physiological need can be satisfied (P_p) are greater than the prices of the means for satisfying the other needs. The price of satisfying the safety need (P_s) is also assumed to be greater than the price of satisfying the love need (P_l). The result in this case is what we suggested could be: the individual will fulfill a lower percentage of his physiological need than he will fulfill of his other needs. In fact the order of need fulfillment is reversed from the order suggested by Maslow: the individual fulfills a higher percentage of his love need than the other needs.

Maslow apparently has observed that people fulfill a higher percentage of their physiological needs than other needs. Our line of argument suggests that this may have been the case because the price of physiological need fulfillment is lower than the prices of fulfilling the other needs.[11] The point we wish to make is that a change in the price (or cost) structure can bring about a change in the extent of need gratification at each level. In such an event, our (and psychologists') definition of what may be considered normal as far as need gratification is concerned should be reconsidered. People's behavior need not have changed in any fundamental sense: they may merely be responding to different prices, while their basic preferences and attitudes remain the same.

QUESTIONS TO PONDER

1. Do people you observe fully satisfy their physiological needs before they attempt to satisfy other needs? Can you offer any evidence?

---

[11] It may also be that the demand for physiological satisfaction is more inelastic than the other demands. This could be considered normal as far as need gratification is concerned.

FIGURE 20-3

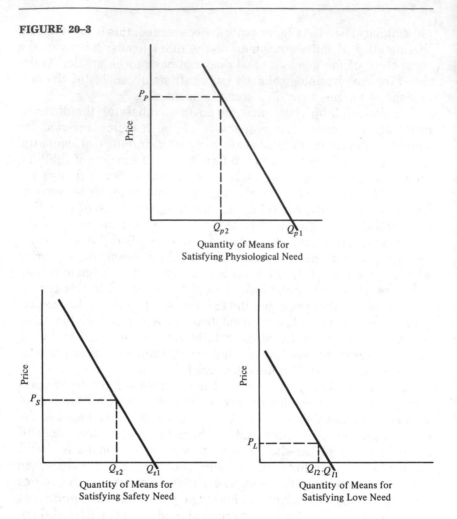

Quantity of Means for
Satisfying Physiological Need

Quantity of Means for
Satisfying Safety Need

Quantity of Means for
Satisfying Love Need

2. Attempt to make rough estimates of the cost of obtaining an "additional unit" of some physiological need and some self-actualization need. (What is the relationship between their cost?) What difficulties do you encounter in making those estimates?

3. In the chapter, we assumed for simplicity that the demands for three methods of satisfying needs were the same. Is this a reasonable assumption? Why or why not?

4. Are people willing to make tradeoffs in satisfying their needs? If they are, does this mean that the Maslow or the economic approach to consumer behavior is the more descriptive of people's behavior?

Rationality in human and nonhuman societies

RATIONALITY IN ECONOMICS: THE EXPERIMENTAL EVIDENCE

In Chapter 1, we outlined the economic approach to human behavior. One of the foundations of this approach is the assumption that human beings are rational. As we pointed out in that chapter, the standard of rationality is not a very high one, but nevertheless economists do believe in the essential intelligence of human beings in the very limited sense that their demand curves slant downward and that they will select the preferred choice over the less preferred.

Among scholarly critics of economics, this rationality assumption is perhaps the most frequently criticized aspect of economics. Economists have answered this criticism in a number of ways, first by pointing out that the requirement of rationality in economics is actually a very low requirement. Second, Gary Becker has argued that the demand and supply relationship can be generated by random behavior; hence, people do not have to be rational to fulfill the basic postulates of economics.[1] This argument by Becker was criticized in part by Israel Kirzner,[2] but the basic point is generally accepted. It is not true that all of the participants in a market process have to be rational.

In this chapter, we will turn to the experimental evidence of the rationality assumption. We will begin with discussion of the experimental economics in which special experiments are set up for

---

[1] Gary S. Becker, "Irrational Behavior and Economic Theory," *Journal of Political Economy* 70 (February 1962), pp. 1–13.

[2] Israel M. Kirzner, "Rational Action and Economic Theory," *Journal of Political Economy* 70 (August 1962), pp. 380–85. See also, Gary S. Becker, "A Reply to Kirzner," *Journal of Political Economy* 71 (February 1963), pp. 82–83.

normal human beings. The outcome of these experiments is consistent with the rationality hypothesis. Indeed, Vernon Smith, one of the pioneers in the area, regards these experiments as the first real proof of both rationality and what we normally refer to as consumption theory. It should be said, however, that these experiments were originally designed for other purposes and their proof of rationality is a secondary consequence. Nevertheless, they do prove that at least a great many people behave rationally. Incidentally, these experiments can, if desired, be repeated in almost any classroom. They are an interesting game for the first one or two times they are tried but tend to be boring if run a large number of times.

After we have discussed these examples of experimental economics, we will turn to another set of experiments which deal with rationality in quite a different way. These experiments demonstrate that *rationality* in the sense that it is used in economics characterizes not only human beings but human beings who are formally judged insane (and therefore are hospitalized), birds, rats, and a group of microscopic animals called rotifers. We do not know if these animals are rational, but they certainly behave as if they were. In other words, their demand curves slope downward. They try to buy in the cheapest market, adjust consumption in terms of prices, and so on.

AN EXAMPLE

Let us then turn to some very simple experiments that support the idea that markets tend to equilibrium and that this equilibrium is an efficient one. These experiments were originally carried out by Vernon Smith, and they can be duplicated in any class with no great difficulty.[3] They are less enlightening than some of the later experiments we will discuss for a number of reasons, the most important of which is that the students were simply asked to play the game of buying and selling without having any real money riding on their action. Later experiments, many of them also devised by Smith, have provided the students with cash they can earn by efficient performance in this experimental market.

In the original experiment, students are divided into sellers and buyers. Then they are given a card which tells them their minimum sale price if they are the sellers or their maximum purchase price if

---

[3] See Vernon Smith, "An Experimental Study of Competitive Market Behavior," *Journal of Political Economy* 70 (April 1962), pp. 111–37.

they are the buyers. One student, for example, might receive a sale card with $2.50 as the lowest price at which he or she can sell, and another might receive a purchase card with $3.50 as the highest purchase price at which he or she can buy. They are also told how many units they can buy or sell. For simplicity, this is usually one unit.

The students are then instructed to buy and sell to each other in a simulated market. Each one is to attempt to maximize his or her profit. The profit is defined as the amount that the price which the seller receives exceeds his or her minimum price. The converse rule applies to the buyer.

The technique is very informal. The students simply announce an offer to buy or sell whenever they feel like it, and some other student may then accept the offer, or perhaps no student will accept it. In professional markets—for example, the grain exchange—that operate on roughly these rules, the procedure is very disorderly, with a great deal of shouting and a set of hand signals. But for classroom purposes, it is sensible to provide some rule that guarantees that everyone understands what everyone else is saying. For example, the students could hold up their hands if they want to make or accept an offer, and the professor may indicate which one of the several raised hands will be recognized. This is some departure from the real world, but it is a little easier to follow.

The cards that have been distributed to the students are normally arranged in these experiments so that there is an equilibrium price. For example, see Figure 21–1.[4] Each of the dashes on the line marked *DD* represents a student holding a demand card for the price shown. Similarly, each dash on the line *SS* represents a student holding a seller's card for the price shown. The equilibrium price is a trifle less than $3.50, and the number of units that will be sold is 15. A few students will be left with transactions incompleted, but this is true of the market also.

The game is played until there are no longer any acceptable offers. Normally the price and quantity at which this occurs can be predicted quite accurately by anyone who knows the shape of the demand and supply curves represented by the cards distributed to the students. The student experimental subjects do not know this; hence, their information is incomplete. Under the circumstances, it takes a little while to establish equilibrium. On the right half of Figure 21–1, we show the process through time of the price of trans-

---

[4] This is a mildly revised version of Smith's Figure 2, Ibid., p. 118.

FIGURE 21-1

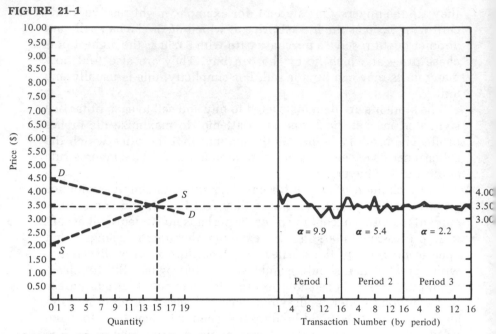

Source: Smith, "Experimental Study," p. 118.

actions. You will note that the prices start at the left with considerable variance, but toward the right end of the chart (after some
experience has been accumulated), they are quite stable.

The method in which these time charts are produced is fairly
simple. The individuals play the game until there are no more offers
that are acceptable. This is called a period, and, for example, the
first such play is shown as period 1.

Once there are no more acceptable offers forthcoming, the beginning round of the game is declared finished, and each student is
then told the game will start again. He will still use in the second
round of the game the same prices and designation of seller and
buyer that he used in the first round. In the second round of the
game, however, each of the students has more information about the
structure of the market than in the first round, and therefore, we
would expect that the variance of prices would be lower in period 2
than in period 1. Examination of Figure 21–1 indicates that this is
what happens. In this particular experiment, only three rounds of
the game were played, and the reason is obvious from observation
of the transaction chart in period 3. By period 3 with this rather

simple structure, almost everyone was well enough informed so that the price was extremely stable. Smith felt that little was to be gained from further repetitions at this point, and he stopped the game.

All that we have learned so far from these experiments is that the price does indeed approach the equilibrium but that it does not do so instantaneously, because people do not have adequate information. This will surprise very few students of economics, but some noneconomists have expressed doubt on this point. However, there is a little more information to be obtained from our very simple experiment. We could make measures of the speed with which equilibrium is approached, and this is a topic upon which formal economics has very little to contribute. Economists have normally simply said that equilibrium would be achieved but not very fast.

As a matter of fact, in the article from which this experiment was drawn, Smith proceeded to test a number of hypotheses having to do with the stability of the market price and the speed at which equilibrium was approached, depending on such matters as the steepness of the demand and supply curves, whether they have roughly the same slant or one is fairly flat and the other is steep, and so forth. Not surprisingly, in general, the flatter the demand and supply curves, the faster equilibrium was approached. Although there had been speculation on this matter beforehand, the information obtained was first real evidence.[5]

FURTHER EXPERIMENTS

Of course, a game in which nothing really rides on success in trading is realy not very close to the real world. In fact, it is surprising how good the results are. After Smith had done the initial work, has was able to interest the National Science Foundation in funding more elaborate experiments in which the participants actually had

---

[5] Some of this work had been foreshadowed in S. Siegel and L. Fouraker, *Bargaining and Group Decision Making* (New York: McGraw-Hill, 1960). One nice feature of this set of experiments, however, is that they do not require any complicated setup or sizable resources; hence, any economics class that wishes can duplicate them and indeed develop more complicated hypotheses to be tested by the same method. A word of caution, however, is necessary. From personal observation of Vernon Smith, the students playing these games tend to become bored. This is not surprising, since the games are not designed for entertainment; but a rapid boredom rate means that it is undesirable to do very much of this experimentation, even though one or two rounds of the game would probably be a good way to break up the classroom routine.

something to gain from efficient behavior. Students really made a cash profit. Cards were distributed in much the same way as the earlier experiment, but the individuals received a money payment equal to the difference between their minimum sale price or maximum purchase price and the actual transaction price (if they were sellers), or below their maximum purchase price and the actual transaction price, assuming that the price was above their minimum sale price (if they were sellers), or below their maximum purchase price (if they were buyers).

Smith mainly used these funds for more complicated experiments than the one described above. But Charles Plott, building on Smith's work, duplicated the above experiment using cash payments in this manner.[6] The principal difference between Plott's experiments and Smith's is, we suppose, readily predictable. When there was something actually riding on the results, the people engaged in the game were more careful and paid closer attention, with the result that they approached equilibrium more rapidly.

Barry Keating, as a byproduct of teaching managerial economics, produced some further experimental data along these same lines. In his class, the students are divided into 15 "companies," each with a small board of directors (three to five students). These companies routinely make decisions on various management policy matters including price and production schedules. The experiment is intended to be realistic in the sense that market conditions change, so that the students can never be perfectly informed about the demand situation, just as real-world companies are never perfectly informed. The students are rewarded in grades if their company is "profitable."

Keating's result would surprise no economist. The companies responded to changes in the basic underlying market conditions by experimental activity with new prices and production schedules. Since different companies tried different prices and production rates, this would lead to an increase in the spread of their policies. Rather quickly, however, the spread between different companies' prices and policies narrows. Note that it never actually gets down to zero, since some of the companies are always searching to determine whether market conditions have changed. All of this, of course, is very similar to the real market.

---

[6] All of the Plott experiments discussed in this chapter are very recent and, hence, unpublished. Since he continues to do work, anyone interested in this field can simply write to him at California Institute of Technology, Division of Humanities and Social Sciences, Pasadena, California 91109, and he will be glad to send you a large pile of papers reporting his experimental results.

Pollution

Plott continued his experiments into more difficult areas. One of these areas, voting procedures, was the subject of a set of experiments that rather neatly confirmed the basic proposition of Chapter 16. In that chapter, we argue that in a two-party system, even with more than one issue, the two parties tend to be very close together and at approximately the middle of the distribution. He also dealt with the problem of regulating pollution. By an ingenious technique,[7] he generated a pollutant in his experiment; that is, each individual completing a transaction imposed a cost on all other individuals, but the cost was, for him or her, lower than his or her gain. As any economist would predict, the equilibrium reached by the experiment was socially inferior, although it was privately optimal. The individuals, like real-world polluters, maximized their own profit and ignored the injury they inflicted on others, with the result that all of them were worse off than they would have been had they each taken the well-being of others into account.

In such a situation, economists usually argue that a properly calculated tax is the optimal policy, but in the real world, governments very commonly rely on regulations, a quota for example. Plott tried both of these techniques and found, as no economist would be surprised to hear, that the tax achieved the socially optimal number of sales in an efficient manner, and the quota achieved the same number but with a good deal of waste.

CRAZY BUT NOT IRRATIONAL

The experiments discussed above were intended to demonstrate various economic propositions and test rationality as a sort of byproduct. Further, normal human beings were used. Let us now turn to the evidence which indicates that abnormal human beings and at least some animals are also rational. Let us begin with people who are insane. Most patients in mental hospitals do not require any kind of physical restraint, although their behavior may be peculiar at times. Further, most are in reasonable physical health. As a consequence, the management of most mental hospitals usually tries to get a certain amount of maintenance work from from their patients.

---

[7] Limitations of space, together with our lack of knowledge as to the background of our readers, make it necessary for us to condense sharply some descriptions of experimenters, such as this one. Full descriptions can be obtained, however, by writing to the author or if you are willing to wait a little while, by reading them in the published literature.

For example, the patients may be asked to make up their beds, keep the area around their beds (or their room, if they have one) clean and orderly, perhaps assist in other tasks, such as mopping the hall floor. Since most of the patients are free to associate with each other, a certain amount of disciplinary control is also desirable. In particular, patients are restricted from doing things likely to irritate the other patients in their wards.

Until recently, it was always rather difficult to get the patients to cooperate. Lately, however, the introduction of "token economies" has led to significant improvements in patient behavior, with very little effort on the part of the hospital management.

The system is fairly simple. A special money (token) is issued by the hospital management. Since theft is frequently a major problem, the tokens are usually similar to traveler's checks in the sense that each token is issued to one particular patient and only that patient can use it.[8] Thus, if one of the patients steals the tokens of another, it does him no good.

These tokens may be used to purchase small comforts within the hospital community. For example, there may be a ward shop selling candy, cigarettes, and so forth. Further, it may be possible for the token holders to "buy" better-than-standard meals, the use of recreational facilities, visits to town, and so forth.

It should be said that this new technique was not originally introduced to make the life of hospital managers easier. It began as a rather controversial method of treating patients. Although there is still some controversy about the procedure, it does seem in many cases to cure (or at least suppress the symptoms of) some mental diseases. Unfortunately, although it works in many cases, it does not work in all.

The individuals under treatment would be paid in tokens for an activity the doctors thought would benefit them. For example, an individual suffering from agoraphobia (fear of open spaces) might be given a token for walking ten yards out into an open field and then back. After several days in which tokens were earned this way, the distance he had to go would be increased. This rather simple technique, believe it or not, does cure a fair number (unfortunately not all) of the cases of agoraphobia.

But our purpose here is not to discuss the use of token economies as a technique for curing mental illnesses but as a way of obtaining

---

[8] Presumably the management would have no objection to bargained exchanges, but the economy is a fairly simple one, and this happens rather rarely.

economically rational behavior from the patients in mental hospitals. After using tokens as a curative measure for a time, the caretakers of mental hospitals soon realized that the token economy could also be used for improving inmate behavior in other ways. The patient might be given a token, for example, for bedmaking, be paid in tokens for mopping the floor or assisting in other routine tasks. Indeed, in some cases the patients can actually be "employed" in simple, factory-type assembly jobs. It should be said that in general these jobs were assigned not because the institution wanted to make money but because it was thought desirable both to keep the patients busy and to give them continuing work experience, in order that they can support themselves when and if they are released. Nevertheless, in a number of cases, institutions have in fact made modest profits on the operation, although in most cases there are losses if the curative aspects of the matter are disregarded.

Disciplinary problems became relatively unimportant with the token economies. Further, when difficulties did arise, in general they could be dealt with very simply and easily by changing the price. For example, in one hospital, the patients objected to mopping the floor. The caretakers simply raised the wage for floor mopping and found themselves deluged with volunteers.

Psychologists tend to be interested in improving their art; hence, they perform experiments. Changing the price of goods in the patients' shop turns out to lead to exactly the kind of behavior that economists would anticipate. For example, in one rather elaborate experiment, prices of various commodities were changed at unannounced intervals.[9] The patients in general adjusted just the way that economic theory would predict for rational beings; that is, they increased their purchases of things whose prices had gone down and reduced their purchases of those that had gone up. In some cases, the change was slow rather than immediate (which would indicate that a learning process was involved), and in some cases, errors in observation threw a good deal of sand into the procedure. Still, in general these people who had been certified as insane behaved quite rationally.[10]

In another case, the management of an institution had the pa-

---

[9] R. C. Battalio, "A Test of Consumer Demand Theory Using Observation of Individual Consumer Purchases," *Western Economic Journal* 11 (December 1973), pp. 411–28.

[10] Presumably the doctors, like other people, are not perfect, and there were some errors in diagnosis among the patients; but it would be very surprising if the average patients were not in fact mentally ill.

tients employed in various activities for which they were paid. As an experiment, the management gave the patients a "paid vacation." The patients were given opportunities and encouragement to continue their work during their vacation, but they would be given no additional payments. Needless to say, this was an experiment, and the results are not surprising. The patients all chose not to work, thus indicating that their previous work had been a rational effort to obtain the tokens and not the result of "conditioning" or some other irrational characteristics.[11] The same management also arranged a set of experiments in which individuals were first trained for a number of different jobs and then given their choice of the jobs with token payment. After they had become accustomed to the job, they were then suddenly informed that the payment would be discontinued for their preferred job but that they could earn the same wage in a less-preferred job. As would be expected, all but one of the patients instantly changed to the less-preferred job, and the one exception changed after a day or so of experience of getting by without a "wage."[12]

R. C. Winkler, working with chronically psychotic female patients, tested more complex behavior patterns.[13] He distinguished luxury items from necessities and measured the responsiveness of the patients to price changes of several items, reaching the standard conclusion that the demand for necessities was "price inelastic," meaning that the patients were relatively unresponsive to price changes and that the patients had greater *total expenditures* when the price of the necessities went up. They also found that the demand for luxuries was "price elastic." This means that the patients made lower total expenditures on the luxuries when their prices were raised.

In the above experiments, nothing in the way of age, IQ, educational level, type of mental disorder, or length of time in institutions seemed to affect the results. In other words, even seriously disturbed and/or very stupid people with no education who had been institutionalized for long periods of time behaved as if they were

---

[11] T. Allyon and N. H. Azrin, "The Measurement and Reinforcement of Behavior of Psychotics," *Journal of Experimental Analysis of Behavior* 8 (November 1965).

[12] Ibid.

[13] R. C. Winkler, "An Experimental Analysis of Economic Balance: Savings and Wages in a Token Economy," *Behavior Therapy* 4 (January 1973), pp. 22–40.

rational. It is only those people who were so seriously disturbed or so mentally impaired that they had only a few available behavior patterns—and were therefore not capable of earning and spending tokens—who did not respond to the types of experiments described above in a rational way.

In general, what these experiments indicate is that standards of rationality required for economic behavior are so low that certified patients in mental hospitals meet them. The argument that economics assumes rationality and that people are not rational is not, strictly speaking, refuted by these observations; but they certainly cast doubt on it.[14]

RATS

Let us proceed to consider some other entities normally thought to be even less rational—specifically, laboratory rats. Recently, a few economists, particularly John H. Kagel and Raymond C. Battalio of Texas A & M University, have been borrowing experimental techniques from the psychologists and using them to test whether behavior of nonhuman species is similar in restricted ways to that of human beings.[15] Since the research has only begun, they have so far tested only some of the simplest propositions of economics. It should be said at the start, however, that in these special, simple areas, rats seem to behave rationally.

Let us consider briefly the existing experimental technique in which the rats are confined individually in separate cages. We will in fact talk about only one rat, although Kagel and Battalio have, of course, tested their hypothesis on more than one. The box used to test the rats in these experiments is a bit of standard psychological apparatus. It consists of a box which has an internal environment wholesome enough so that the rats can be kept there indefinitely provided that food and water are supplied and the box is regularly cleaned. Attached to the box is a small computer that can be used to both meter the behavior of the experimental animal and carry out whatever provision of food or other stimuli to the animal the experi-

---

[14] For a general survey of token economies, see David G. Tarr, "Experiments in Token Economies: A Review of the Evidence Relating to Assumptions and Implications of Economic Theory," *Southern Economic Journal* 43 (October 1976), pp. 1136–43.

[15] John H. Kagel et al., "Demand Curves for Animal Consumers" (Paper presented at Southern Economic Association meeting, Atlanta, Georgia, November 1976).

menter has planned; that is, the computer keeps track of all things going in and can be instructed to deliver various items under various conditions.

Since the rat would have great difficulty in handling token currency, the experiments charge the rat prices not by giving it a small collection of tokens and having it insert them in a slot but by having the rat push a bar at the back of the cage. The pushes on the bar are the "payments" made by the rat, and this leads the computer to meter out to it, let us say, a small quantity of root beer, cherry cola, or whatever else the experimenters choose. They change the price of the various commodities by changing the amount delivered each time the bar is pushed. Thus, the price of .1cc of cherry cola might be one bar-push, or two, or four.

Suppose then we consider one of their experiments in which a rat is given an adequate supply of food and water automatically by the machine and, in addition, is confronted with two bars—pushing one leads to root beer being provided and pushing the other provides cherry cola.

The computer can now be instructed to change the "price" of root beer and cherry cola by changing the amount received each time the bar is pressed.[16] In one experiment, for example, the amount of root beer delivered per bar-push was held constant,[17] but the amount of cherry cola per bar-push was changed. It was found that when the payoff to a bar push was 0.025cc of cherry cola, the rat consumed only a little over 0.1cc per day. When the price was lowered so that the rat could get 0.5cc per push, he consumed 65, and at one bar-push per 0.1cc, he consumed 200. Of course, the rat changed its consumption of root beer at the same time; that is, since the price of root beer was being held constant in real terms, the exchange ratio between the root beer and cherry cola for the rat was improving; hence, the rat reduced its consumption of root beer and increased its consumption of cherry cola. The rat's consumption of both cherry cola

------

[16] Note for the instructor: these experiments studied two different types of demand curves, one holding apparent real income constant and the other holding money income constant. For the purpose of this chapter, the matter is unimportant; but details of the experiment would provide a particularly easy way of explaining problems of demand curves under changes of wealth, the Slutsky-Hicks theory, and so on, if the instructor feels this material is suitable for an elementary course.

[17] One of the results of this experimentation has been the discovery that rats seem to like root beer more than almost anything else. It must be genuine root beer, however. The rats apparently regard diet root beer as little better than water.

and root beer at varying prices of the cherry cola can be seen in Figure 21–2.[18] It can be seen that for the rat, root beer and cherry cola were substitute goods; that is, the more it consumed of one, the less it consumed of the other. There was, however, an element of complementarity (that is, the two goods are not perfect substitutes) in that the rat did not reduce its consumption of root beer at exactly the same rate as it increased its consumption of cherry cola.

FIGURE 21–2

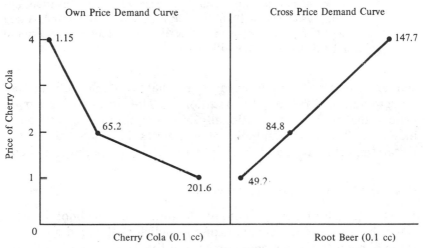

Apparently the rat was behaving rationally. Its consumption of a given product increased as the price went down, and it lowered its consumption of a competing product at the same time, just as we assume rational human consumers do. The rat was equally rational in dealing with necessities. At one point, the rat, instead of being given as much water as it wished to drink and then the choice of two luxury drinks, was required to push the bar to get water. It turned out that the rat drank almost as much water per day at a low price as at a high price. Water was clearly a necessity to the rat, not something it drank for pleasure. Hence, it pushed the bar enough to get its daily demand for water and no more. We can say that the rat had an elastic demand for cherry cola and root beer but an extremely (almost perfectly) inelastic demand for water.

Thus, it seems that the minimum rationality assumption normally

---

[18] Kagel et al., "Demand Curves for Animal Consumers," Fig. 5.

used by economists is met by quite simple animals. Those who say that human beings are not able to behave in an economically rational manner may be saying we are as dumb or dumber than rats! Note, however, that we are discussing behavior and not the actual preferences of the rat. But we do, for subjective reasons, believe that a downward sloping demand curve reflects a desire to obtain some goal, and action is taken to that end. The other view is possible. The prominent behavior psychologist, B. F. Skinner, said:

> A rat could be said to know when to press a lever to get food, but it does not press because it knows that food will be delivered. A taxi driver could be said to know a city well, but he does not get around because he possesses a cognitive map.[19]

Skinner, of course, believes that rats and human beings are very similar in that neither one engages in what we might call *rational thought* and both respond to conditioning. The authors of this book believe that both behave rationally in attempting to achieve goals they value. From the standpoint of economics, however, the issue is not an important one, and either point of view can perhaps be held.

BIRDS, SNAILS, AND ROTIFERS

Let us go a little further. One of the authors of this book investigated theoretically the behavior of an English bird called a coal tit. He explained the bird's behavior on the theory that the bird is rationally allocating its time between two different kinds of searches for food in order to get the most food with the least effort.[20] Kagel and Battalio repeated on pigeons the experiments similar to those performed on rats. The results were similar also.[21] Even such simple animals as snails seem to have at least some ability to make rational choices.[22]

David Rapport has investigated a microscopic animal, *Stentor coeruleus,* and he finds that its behavior is simple-minded but still rational.[23] Since this very small animal has practically nothing that

---

[19] B. F. Skinner, *About Behaviorism* (New York: Alfred A. Knopf, 1974), p. 139.

[20] Gordon Tullock, "The Coal Tit as a Careful Shopper," *The American Naturalist* 105 (January–February 1971), pp. 77–80.

[21] Personal communication.

[22] Gordon Tullock, "Switching in General Predators: Comment," *Bulletin of the Econological Society of America* 51 (September 1970), pp. 21–24.

[23] D. J. Rapport and J. E. Turner, "Determination of Predator Food Pref-

we would recognize as a brain or even a nervous system, it obviously has only very limited abilities to make rational choices. Nevertheless, when it was confronted with different types of food under circumstances in which the effort it had to undertake to consume each varied, it responded as would human beings or rats. When its preferred food was hard to get, the *Stentor* made do with second-rate food. However, when the cost of the "better" food was lowered, the *Stentor* would spit out the less-preferred food and concentrate on the more preferred.

Although the experiments summarized above are, as far as we know, the only formal studies of animals in which the question of whether they behave as rational consumers has been investigated, it seems to be a rather general feeling among biologists that all animals behave this way. It should be said, however, that biologists normally do not use the same language as do economists. Rapport, who performed the experiment on *Stentor* mentioned above, wrote two articles in which he attempts to introduce his fellow biologists to the vocabulary and methods of economics.[24] In these articles, he presents standard economic models, with appropriate introduction for the biologist. Towards the end of one of these articles, he says:

> The use of optimization principles has been implicit in much of theoretical biology. As Rosen points out, "that idea that nature pursues economy in all her workings is one of the oldest principles of theoretical science" (Rosen, 1967). The assumption of optimizing food selection behavior appears valid provided natural selection is efficient in "weeding out" species or individuals which failed to make optimum food choices.[25]

Rapport goes on to discuss the deductions that can be drawn from this rational model for biology and methods of testing them. He

---

erences," *Journal of Theoretical Biology* 26 (1970), pp. 365–72; and David J. Rapport, Jacques Berger, and D. B. W. Reid, "Determination of Food Preference of *Stentor Coeruleus,*" *Biological Bulletin* 142 (February 1972), pp. 103–9. Since the authors assume that the readers are not much interested in either the exact nature of *Stentor coeruleus* or the details of its feeding habits, we have not described them. Any reader who finds our discussion too general can turn to the original sources.

[24] David J. Rapport, "An Optimization Model of Food Selection," *The American Naturalist* 105 (November–December 1971), pp. 757–87; and Rapport and Turner, "Economic Models in Ecology."

[25] Rapport, "Optimization Model of Food Selection," pp. 583–84; inner quote by Rosen refers to R. R. Rosen, *Optimality Principles in Biology* (London: Butterworths, 1967).

then performed some of the tests in the articles listed above and confirmed the theory.

CONCLUDING COMMENTS

Thus, human beings in experimental situations, microscopic animals, bird, rats, and inhabitants of mental hospitals choose to buy in the cheapest market. Obviously, it does not follow directly from all of this that everyone is rational in his daily life. What we have attempted to demonstrate in this chapter is not that human beings are necesarily rational (although we do believe that they are quite rational) but that the requirement of rationality used in economics is a very modest one. We are not saying anything very complimentary about human beings when we say that they are economically rational. On the other hand, people who say that human beings are not rational are saying something extremely insulting. They are saying that microscopic animals are brighter and better able to make intelligent consumption decisions than is the average human being.

QUESTIONS TO PONDER

1. Design a simple experiment to test some additional economic propositions.
2. Are most people you know smarter than pigeons?
3. Can you think of any reasons why the evolutionary process would tend to develop animal behavior patterns which demonstrate what we call *rationality*?
4. How would you account for the fact that many critics of economics attack the rationality assumptions? Is it because they perceive people as not being up to the level of intelligence of a pigeon or for some other reason?

CHAPTER 22

Sociobiology

That some animals have fairly complex social orders has been known for a very long time. The ant was held up as an example in the Old Testament, and beekeeping seems to be an immensely ancient human profession. The study of animal societies has, of course, always been part of biology. In recent years, however, a new subdiscipine within biology, called sociobiology, has been developed. It studies the social interactions of nonhuman species.

The popular press has given sociobiology a good deal of attention with prominent sociobiologists such as E. O. Wilson and Robert L. Trivers appearing on the cover of *Time* or being interviewed on talk shows. It is of great interest to economists and indeed, economists have made contributions to the sociobiological literature.[1]

HUMAN AND NONHUMAN SOCIETIES

In part, the popular interest in sociobiology is the result of a mistake. Suppose some particular type of behavior is observed among a number of social species. It is sometimes erroneously deduced that this must also be characteristic of man. The error is, of

---

[1] For example, see Gordon Tullock, "Biological Externalities," *Journal of Theoretical Biology* 33 (December 1971), pp. 565–76; "Altruism, Malice and Public Goods," *Journal of Social and Biological Structures* 1 (January 1978), pp. 3–9; "Altruism, Malice and Public Goods: Reply to Frech," *Journal of Social and Biological Structures* 1 (January 1978), pp. 187–89; "Switching in General Predators: A Comment," *Bulletin of the Ecological Society of America* 51 (September 1970), pp. 21–24; "The Coal Tit as a Careful Shopper," *American Naturalist* 105 (January–February 1971), pp. 77–80; "On the Adaptive Significance of Territoriality: Comment," *The American Naturalist* 113, no. 5, pp. 772–75; "Comment on 'The Physiological (and Sociological) Causes of the Evolution of Man from Apes'," *Speculations in Science and Technology* 1, no. 5 (December 1978), p. 528. See also, Paul A. Samuelson, "Complete Genetic Models for Altruism, Kin Selection, and Like-Gene Selection," (forthcoming), and Jack Hirschleifer, "Natural Economy Versus Political Economy," *Journal of Social and Biological Structures* 1, no. 4 (October 1978), pp. 319–37.

course, particularly attractive if the social species which have the particular traits are primates and, hence, close to men. Still, perhaps the most amusing example of this dealt with ants. In the 1890s there was a prominent student of ants and their behavior, who was also a Baptist clergyman. In his articles and books on ants (which were actually very good in terms of the knowledge of the times) he occasionally inserted little sermons on how much better off humans would be if we all behaved as the ants do.

In more recent times there is less of a religious drive and more of what we might call the naturalistic fallacy. To take one example which has trapped several sociobiologists, the Hamadryas baboon is, of course, a primate and, hence, reasonably closely related to human beings. It is also a social animal, and its habits make it particularly easy to study. In consequence, we probably know more about the society of the Hamadryas baboon than that of any other social animal. It happens that the Hamadryas baboon males are about twice as big as the females. Under the circumstances, it is not surprising that the Hamadryas baboon society is completely male dominated. Several sociobiologists have come to the conclusion that male dominance is "natural" because the baboons (and other primates) have it. A very prominent sociobiologist, E. O. Wilson, who happens also to be politically in favor of women's lib, has written at length about the natural male dominance and how it can be overcome if we only work hard enough. Of course, the fact that baboon society is male dominated tells us substantially nothing about male/female relationships among human beings. Nor should we regard ants as our mentors. Jan Marais was a pioneer in the study of baboons, and there is now a Jan Marais Chair of Ecology at the University of Pretoria. Its occupant remarked that careful study of the baboon tribes would permit us to live like baboons if that is what we wanted, but that personally he preferred to live like a man.

There is, however, some small element of truth in the statement that we may learn something about human society by studying animal society. First, studying animal societies may raise new questions in our minds. The answers to these questions may be of importance to the students of human society. It is in raising questions, however, rather than giving answers that the study of nonhuman societies is of direct relevance.

More importantly, but a problem for the future, it may be that we will eventually develop a general theory of society in which human society, baboon society, ant society, the society of the sponges, the society of the slime molds, and so forth will all be seen as special cases. On the other hand, it may well be that the things that we refer to as societies in, let us say, humans and bees are in fact radically different institutions; hence, no general theory covering both will ever be developed. But at the moment we know too little about animal societies and, for that matter, about human societies to have much hope of developing such a general theory of society in the immediate future. Still, if we do study both our own society and the various animal societies,[2] we may someday find this general theory of society. On the other hand we may not.

ECONOMICS AND BIOLOGY

What, however, are economists doing in biology? In the first place, economics and biology have a fairly old relationship. The two co-inventors of the theory of evolution, Darwin and Wallace, both specifically said they got the idea from reading Malthus's essay on population. Malthus was, of course, the world's first professor of economics.[3] From this early interaction between the two disciplines until just recently, however, biology and economics developed their separate ways with little interaction.

In the last 15 to 20 years, biology and economics have begun to come together again. The basic reasons for this encouraging development were discoveries in biology and not in economics. Traditionally, biology, with the exception of genetics, had been essentially an observational and experimental subject with little in the way of formal theory. Recently, biologists realized that the general theory of evolution could be particularized into a detailed theory which could then be tested by statistical or experimental means.

As the reader may recall, Darwin argued that the development of all existing species was a result of an evolutionary process. Modernizing his thought a little bit, the genes which control the heredity of any plant or animal change very slowly, but randomly. Each change either increases the likelihood that the particular plant or animal will leave descendants or, much more commonly, lowers it. Since those genes which increase the likelihood of leaving descendants (fitness) will be more common in future generations and those which lower fitness will be rarer, over time the world pop-

---

[2] There are also plant societies, but they tend to be ignored by the sociobiologists.

[3] As a matter of fact, his book was good biology but poor economics, as the history of human population since he wrote it has demonstrated.

ulation of plants and animals will evolve. The present vast collection of different plant and animal species on the surface of the earth is simply the result of this process.

Recently economists realized the evolutionary hypothesis tells us not only something about history, but something about the present day world too. Animals and plants should be reasonably efficiently designed for their place in the web of life. It is possible to make calculations about efficient characteristics. Birds, for example, should have certain size beaks if they feed on particular types of insects, the teeth of animals should be adjusted to their diet, and so forth. It turns out that these very general propositions can be reduced to detailed and highly specific statements and then one can go and look at the data and see whether they fit. The result in general has been that evolution as a hypothesis has been overwhelmingly confirmed but also that biology is becoming a theoretical rather than observational science. Biologists might not like to hear this, but as a matter of fact, *The American Naturalist* and *The American Economic Review* these days look very much alike. The average article in both begins with a theoretical discussion of some point, usually developed mathematically, and then proceeds to a statistical examination of the real world to test the theory.

The resemblance between economics and biology today is not, however, a merely superficial similarity in appearance. In both cases, theory is based on the premise that subjects will maximize subject to constraints. Human beings are assumed by economics to attempt to maximize their utility subject to various restrictions put on them by the environment. The biologists assume that plants and animals are maximizing their biological fitness subject once again to restraints put upon them by the environment. Although there are, of course, many differences, there are also very strong similarities in the two approaches. It has been possible for economists to publish articles in biology and at least one biologist, Garrett Hardin, has done excellent work in economics.[4]

THE FINDINGS OF SOCIOBIOLOGY

But so much for generalities. What have the sociobiologists found out about nohuman societies? The first and, in some ways, most astonishing discovery is that many animals, birds, insects, and for that matter, plants, are real-estate owners. They control specific

---

[4] Garret Hardin and John Baden, eds., *Managing the Commons* (San Francisco: W. H. Freeman and Company).

pieces of ground, sea bottom, or airspace. Sociobiologists have largely ignored the plants, but it should be said that plants can be real-estate owners too. A number of trees, bushes, and, for that matter, even some grasses, exude chemicals into the soil around their base which makes it impossible for direct competitors to grow there. This means that the particular plant does not need to be concerned about other plants growing close enough to it to seriously damage its prospects.

From the economic standpoint, there is immediately here a cost-benefit calculation. Does the plant gain enough from removing all competitors a distance which, for a small plant, may be one inch or so away to pay for the cost of producing and exuding into the soil chemicals which make the growth of other plants unlikely? Since some plants do this and others don't, one can deduce that sometimes this is an efficient technique which is likely to contribute to survival and sometimes it is not.

Note here a characteristic of animal "property" which they do not share with humans. The plant or animal itself must defend its living space. There is no possibility of calling in the sheriff to evict a trespasser. Clearly this is less efficient than the concept of private property in human society. We don't depend completely on our own strength to maintain our property ownership, and indeed, in any community there are some elderly people who would be unable to defend themselves against even a most modest attack who nevertheless peacefully hold large pieces of property. This would be impossible in the biological realm.

There seems to be reason to believe that the human approach to property is more efficient than the animal approach, but let us nevertheless continue talking about animal property. First, the existence of property in this sense means that the property owner, whoever he or she is, must be prepared to defend the property one way or another. Usually among the animals and birds this means fighting, and of course, there is some cost to the fighting. There are two species of ground squirrels which live in the Rocky Mountains. One, which we shall call A, is the dominant specie in the higher altitudes where the trees and brush are rather open. As you move down the mountain to areas where the brush is much thicker and visibility is poor, the other, which we shall call B, becomes dominant.

The explanation for this division of property seems to be simple. A is a territorial ground squirrel which protects a given territory by patrolling and fighting intruders. B is nonterritorial, simply picks up its food where it can find it and if attacked by a member of the A specie, runs away. In the high area where trees and brush are rather sparse and, hence, visibility is good, the A specie drives the B specie away from all suitable sources of food because each member of the A species established territorial control over an area large enough to feed itself and there are no areas left for the B squirrel.

In the lower parts of the mountain where the trees and brush are thick and visibility is poor, the A ground squirrel attempts to set up a territory, but it isn't able to see the boundaries easily. The result is that the B squirrels can live in an area even if there are A squirrels there, and since the B squirrels do not put any energy into patrolling territory or attempting to fight off intruders, they are, in the long run, able to survive better than the A squirrels. The A squirrels run the cost of protecting their property and don't get the protection because of the technological problem of poor visibility in this area; hence, they are less fit than the B squirrels.

An economist would immediately recognize this as a simple cost-benefit problem. It takes a certain amount of energy to patrol and guard the property. In the upper areas where there is little brush and you can see an intruding squirrel quite a ways off, the return on this exertion of energy is positive; that is, the benefit is greater than the cost. Farther down the mountain, where the brush and other undergrowth makes it hard to tell whether there is another ground squirrel intruding on your property, the benefit is much less, but the cost is as great or even greater with the result that the A squirrel is not viable there. Although we have said that an economist would immediately recognize this as a case of cost-benefit analysis, the biologist, of course, recognized it even before the economist and used exactly the same kind of analysis except that some of the details of the mathematics are different.

Territoriality is not confined to higher mammals and birds, and nests frequently have a home territory which they defend. Almost certainly some members of any college class will have seen a war between two ant colonies, probably fought over a boundary question. These wars, which involve immense numbers of ants and may last for days, are normally not very conspicuous, since they are fought in the grass and brush. Occasionally, however, they occur on sidewalks or other paved areas, and then they are very conspicuous indeed.

DEFENSE OF PROPERTY

So far, we have simply talked about the owner of the property defending it, and we have not said much about how he or she does it or, indeed, how the intruder tries to take advantage of the property. In some cases, as in the example of the ground squirrel B, the intruder simply sneaks in and runs if he is detected. In most cases, however, there is a more direct confrontation between the existing owner and the trespasser who very commonly is interested in ejecting the owner and taking over the property himself. The easiest and most obvious explanation as to who wins in such an encounter is simply that the biggest and toughest member of ground squirrel. A species, or biggest and toughest bird, or biggest and toughest fish, either retains his property and ejects the intruder or seizes property from a smaller and weaker member of his or her own species. This conclusion is not unanimously held by biologists.

Biologists point out quite properly that fighting is costly and individual members of species who engage in a great deal of it lower their fitness by the energy consumed in the fighting. Of course, a fight which is quite costly but which leads to the winner obtaining possession of very attractive pieces of real estate may nevertheless pay. But over time, if he has to defend that real estate in a number of other costly fights, the end product may be that he is worse off than he would have been had he not engaged in the fights at all. The B squirrels have apparently decided that fighting doesn't pay in their environment.

If we observe conflict among animals, the first thing we note is that there is a great deal of the animal equivalent of threatening and name calling before any actual fighting occurs, and very commonly, all that happens is a good deal of threat behavior by the two birds, shall we say, at the end of which one of them flies off, admitting defeat. Some biologists have argued that the elaborate threat behavior is a ceremony, but it seems more likely that the threats are real. During the period in which the birds maneuver, threaten, and call each other names, they (like two humans working up towards a fight) are obtaining information as to who is likely to win and the severity of the fight. Obviously they don't scientifically analyze the problem, but their genes could transmit built-in reaction pattern which would have much the same effect as if they had indeed carefully weighed the probability of success, the probability of injury, and the net benefit of engaging in a real fight.

The problem is here quite complicated. There are cases in which one can imagine a specie continuing to exist with part of the members of the specie being programmed to fight very easily, and part being programmed to fight not at all, and both (hawks and doves) remaining viable at a particular ratio. It is not clear whether this mathematical possibility is actually presented in nature or not.

In most cases, however, it seems that the posturing and threats of the two animals are genuine, and if one or the other doesn't decide to give up, there will be a fight; mostly the fight doesn't occur because one or the other does decide that it is not worth the risk of injury. Professor E. O. Wilson once said that any animal species which had been observed for less than 1,000 hours had a reputation for being peaceful and nonbelligerent. As soon as the observation time rose well above 1,000 hours, however, examples of severe fights and deaths occurred.

The famous sociobiologist, Jane van Lawick-Goodall, was a victim of this problem, although in her case the number of hours she had put in before she discovered that the chimpanzees whom she was studying could be quite belligerent, was a good deal more than 1,000. She was studying chimpanzees in Africa, and it is now clear, although it was not when she began her studies, that the particular area where the studied was completely enclosed within the boundary of a chimpanzee band (animal bands are discussed below). She found that although there was a certain amount of threat behavior and mild fighting, nothing very serious in the way of fighting occurred, and she wrote books and gave lectures about how peaceful the chimpanzees were.

Then the chimpanzee group with which she was dealing split into two, and war immediately broke out between the two groups. The larger group apparently killed every single male in the smaller group. About the same time, she discovered that two females in the tribe were systematically killing and eating the children of other females. So much for the peaceful chimpanzee. Van Lawick-Goodall is not alone in having made this kind of mistake. For a while it was thought that wolf fights were always determinated rather quickly by the surrender of one or the other party without any great injury. It turned out that that does indeed happen frequently, but by no means always, and wolves can be killed in fights with other wolves. With lions it would appear that murder by another lion is actually the commonest single cause of death. It is particularly true for the juveniles. Both wolves and lions are property owners although in their case, the property is held by a larger group than an individual or a mating pair.

But let us now go on to discuss these larger groups. The bulk of the property-owning species is not particularly social. An individual, or a pair, or, in some cases, a male with a harem own a piece of real estate which they defend, but they have relatively little contact with their neighbors except occasional fighting. There are other animals which operate in larger groups which we shall call bands, although biologists would use a different name for different species (a pride of lions, for example). These larger groups sometimes are real-estate owners, but they have a national or band territory rather than simple ownership of the property. In most cases no individual member of the group owns any particular subsection of the larger plot that is owned by the tribe itself. Sometimes these bands do not seem to have any particular real estate area and wander across the country-side with different bands, operating in much the same territory at different times (gorillas, for example).

In those cases in which the band does have a specific piece of real estate, however, they normally defend it, sometimes marking the boundaries much the same way as the domestic dog would mark the boundaries of his master's land, and they are willing to fight over the borders. In Hans Kruuk's study of the hyenas of the Ngorongoro crater,[5] there is an account of a quite spirited border battle at which the losing hyena band was forced to move its boundary back by a considerable distance. The real-estate quarrels of these bands, how-ever, are really very similar to those of individual property owners among animals except for their larger scale.

DOMINANCE

The internal social organization of the mammals and birds is in general some modification of a dominance order. In the chickens in which the dominance order was first carefully studied, it was noticed that there would be one chicken in the flock who could peck on any of the others and to whom the others deferred when it came to going for food; another who could peck on anyone except the first; and so on down to the bottom where there would be a chicken which could be pecked by anyone and whose life expectancy would not really be very long in the wild (although in a farm yard, presumably it would be kept alive).

The dominance order is not stable because there are occasional confrontations between members of the group in which a lower-ranking one beats a higher-ranking one, with the result that it moves up on the scale and the higher ranking one moves down. Neverthe-less, the higher the rank of the individual in this scheme, the more access he or she has to food, mates, and so forth. In some cases (among the wolves, for example), the top dominant also plays a very

---

[5] Hans Kruuk, The Spotted Hyena (Chicago: University of Chicago Press, 1972).

modest policing role within the tribe by breaking up fights among his juniors.

The advantage of this system for the dominants (the ones at the top of the order) is obvious, but why do these more lower-ranking animals stay in the tribe rather than striking out on their own? The answer seems to be simply that the lower-ranking ones do better than they would on their own. The tribe offers them some protection against predation since such a group is less likely to be attacked than an individual animal, and in addition, there are a number of eyes and ears watching for predators. In some cases, the hunting technique used will only work if there are a considerable number of animals. It is impossible for a single wolf to pull down a moose, but a wolf pack can do so with no great difficulty.

The final reason an animal who is far down the dominance order may stick with the band is simply that the death rate of almost all species in the world is high, and the prospect that he will rise to top rank through the death of his superiors is never zero.

LESSONS FOR HUMAN SOCIETY

It is perhaps sensible here to discuss one aspect of fighting between animals which we have so far sidestepped. In general, if a quarrel between two animals proceeds far enough so they actually fight, one of them realizes he is losing and gives up. The other will usually not continue the attack. (Note, we said in general.) There are cases in which the attacker will continue until the beaten animal is dead. There are other cases in which the beaten animal doesn't realize it is beaten until it is too late and, hence, dies of its wounds even though it did try to give up.

Some people who attempt to draw lessons for human behavior from animal behavior have pointed out the pattern of behavior in which the losing animal gives up and the winning animal stops attacking as a pattern for humans. Once it is clear who is going to win, the one that is going to lose obviously has nothing to gain from continuing the fight. His or her decision to give up at that point is therefore understandable. If, however, the winner continues the attack, presumably the potential loser would attempt to defend itself. It might well inflict serious injury on the winner during the last stage of the fight. Thus, it is, on the whole, sensible for the winner to let the loser off, having "taught him a lesson" rather than to continue with the fight. Human beings in fact behave this way, but, of course, we have institutions under which the loser can be permanently penalized for losing, let us say, a war.

Naturally, the animals may not make these complex computations. Nevertheless, those who behave according to an efficient pattern will survive and produce offspring and those who don't, will not, with the result that over time heredity leads to behavior which, in many cases, is rather similar to that which would be recommended to the animal by a game theorist with a Ph.D. from Massachusetts Institute of Technology. If, however, the most efficient behavior is extremely complex, it may be beyond the rather limited capacity of an animal brain; hence, the animal will not behave with optimal efficiency simply because the energy cost of carrying around the large and complicated brain necessary to provide optimal efficient behavior in unusual circumstances is greater than the benefit from the fitness standpoint.

VARIABLE BEHAVIOR

We quite frequently find that animals are able to change their pattern of behavior from a social one to an individualistic one and from property owning to nonproperty-owning. Sometimes they will be social or property owning in some aspect of their lives and not in others. The wolves of Isle Royale, for example, hunt moose in the winter but a large number of smaller animals in the summer. In consequences of this pattern, they organize themselves in a pack for the winter, because an individual wolf cannot bring down a moose. In the summer, on the other hand, they break up and operate individually or perhaps in sets of mated pairs. The fact that biologists aren't quite certain which pattern they use in the summer is indicative of the fact that it is harder to observe wolves in the summer when there are leaves on the trees and bushes than it is in the winter when the branches are bare. Initial studies of the Isle Royale wolf pack were in fact carried on from a small plane circling over the island. This technique was only suitable for winter observation.

Similarly, most sea gulls get their food from the sea, and fish move around a good deal so that ownership of a particular piece of the sea (even if it could be marked out) would be of little value. Under the circumstances, they do not own fishing grounds.

Many gulls, however, put their nests in highly restricted areas which are apparently selected because they are protected from predators. These gulls normally have very, very strict ownership arrangements with respect to the nest area.

We tend to think of insects as having fixed behavior patterns and being unable to adjust to changes in their environment, but at least in some cases, this is not so. Most tropical wasps have several queens in the nest while all those in the temperate zone maintain single-queen nests. It seems likely that this is an adjustment to the cold winter which will kill any but the healthiest and best-fed queen. This, however, would not apply in the tropics. There is at least one example of temperate-zone wasps which were accidentally reestablished in Tasmania (which does not have cold winters) and which promptly developed multiple-queen nests.

As a final example, Kruuk's study of the hyenas of the Ngorongoro crater shows that the hyena bands have real-estate holdings. His further studies of the hyenas in the vast Serengeti Plain is not absolutely clear on the point, but it certainly seems likely that the hyenas there do not really have specific hunting ranges. They travel over very large areas, and the animals they hunt also travel over large areas so that specific hunting grounds would not be very valuable. In the more confined areas of the Ngorongoro crater, real-estate ownership for the pack is worthwhile but apparently not in the Serengeti.

A sort of compromise is found among the lions of the open areas of Africa. The grass-eating animals upon which they prey move according to the seasons to areas where grazing is good. The lions must follow, but they are basically a territorial animal with each pride maintaining, insofar as it is possible, a monopoly over its own territory. The way this has worked out in the case of the lions is that the territories hunted and guarded by each pride move with the prey animals. You have what amounts to migrating property ownership.

TERMITE AND ANT SOCIETIES

Although we are apt to feel somewhat more at home in dealing with the societies of other warm-blooded animals, particularly the primates, and also to feel at least some fellow feeling for other vertebrates, the most interesting social organizations are probably those found among the insects. There are wasps, bees, and ants which are all related to each other, the social spiders (a little known group), and the termites. Of these, the oldest and in some ways best-developed are the termites. Termites are a rather primitive family of insects related to the cockroach. Although they are something of a nuisance in the United States, their highest development can be found in the tropics. Indeed, the traveller in some parts of Africa can actually take his direction from the tall, blade-like termite nests which are always rigidly oriented north and south.

Such a nest may have up to 2 million termites in it. The nest itself is, of course, only the center from which a large number of tunnels go off in all directions to permit the termites to find and consume dead wood. The nest and the tunnels are full of busy worker termites who are engaged in collecting wood, in some cases bringing water into the nest (although that is not always necessary), and maintaining the nest itself. They will be guarded by a special caste of soldier termites who are equipped with quite a wide variety of different kinds of defensive armament. Perhaps the most interesting ones are those who are provided with a sort of nozzle on the top of their heads from which they can spray a sticky substance. Others have large jaws, and in some cases, the head of the soldier is specially designed for blocking the entrance into the tunnels of the nest.

The workers have much to do in addition to bringing in wood. The nest itself requires maintenance and repair, and the ventilation of the nest is important. The termite inside the nest of one of the large African colonies lives in an environment which is remarkably stable. First, the atmosphere in the nest is a great deal more moist than the outside air and contains much more carbon dioxide. It is also quite stable in temperature. The nest is built in such a way that there is a regular circulation of air through it driven by the heat generated in the nest, and there are arrangements so that the speed of circulation can be changed by termite workers so that the amount of heat radiated through the upper portion of the blade-like structure can be adjusted; hence, the temperature of the nest is kept quite stable. The inside of a termite nest is not quite as stable in temperature as the interior of a heat-regulating mammal like the human being, but it is a good deal more stable than the interior of a lizard or a fish. Last, but by no means least, the termite reproductives are, of course, the heart of the nest. Normally, there is a king or queen, but in some cases, a number of pairs of so-called secondary reproductives may be found.

The termites have another peculiarity which is that most of them, indeed all except the highest termites, don't actually digest the wood themselves. They have in their intestine colonies of small single-celled animals which do the actual digestion. Thus in a way, there is a colony inside the colony. Further, some of the termites engage in gardening. They build fairly large caverns in their nest in which they raise a special type of fungus.

It can be seen that the termite nest is a complex social organization with a great deal of division of labor. Further, except for the reproductives and the specialized soldier classes,[6] the division of labor among the termites does not depend on their physical constitution. Most of the termite workers are capable of carrying on any of the tasks in the nest. How then are the termites allocated to their jobs?

Theoretically, it could be, of course, that they simply come out of the egg with instruction for some to repair walls, others to attend to the royal pair, and so forth. We know that this is not true, however, because the number of termites engaged in any activity changes depending on the needs of the nest. If you damage the nest, for example, the number of termites engaged in repair and reconstruction immediately rises sharply. In times of drought, more termites are involved in obtaining water.

Again, it might, of course, be that the termites are simply randomly distributed among their various activities, but if this were so, the termite nest would be highly inefficient. We do not have any positive proof that termites, ants, and so forth are highly efficient, but there is fairly good evidence that they are from the role they play in the world. Next to man, the social insects are probably the most successful single group of species on the planet. Further, the fact that both the ants and the termites, two totally unrelated species using different food sources, have found much the same social organization is evidence of their efficiency.

There is further evidence of the efficiency of these social insects, in this case taken from the ants. E. O. Wilson examined the division of ants among the various casts, specifically workers and soldiers, in his nest. In order to understand this test it should be pointed out that workers and soldiers are produced by the nest by the feeding and care of otherwise identical larva. Thus, the ratio between them is something determined by the nest just as the ratio between those ants engaging in repairing the walls of the nest and those seeking food are determined by the nest.

Wilson, using linear programming techniques, investigated the efficient proportion of worker and soldier ants in a number of species. In all cases, he found the actual allocation was close to the allocation that his calculation showed to be efficient. It was not perfect, but this is as likely to be because his calculations did not perfectly fit the real world as because the ants were themselves inefficient.

Similar tests have not been carried on with respect to most other aspects of the efficiency of ant and termite nests, but nevertheless,

---

[6] There may be other specialized classes in some termite nests.

we think we can accept that they are indeed efficient and that the allocation of labor within the nest between the various tasks is well carried out.

How is this allocation controlled? It certainly is not controlled by a central planning board, nor is there a system of formal orders transmitted from some center of the nest which says in essence: "the temperature in the nest has risen by one half a degree, open ventilation channels 13a, 26b, and 45c." Before answering this question we should keep in mind that a somewhat similar puzzle exists inside the human body. Within us are white corpuscles which are ameoba-like entities within our bloodstream. These cells attack and ingest foreign matter in the bloodstream, particularly bacteria. If a human being suffers an injury, let us say, a cut to a finger, the white blood corpuscles will immediately congregate at that spot where they provide what amounts to a guard force against infection. How are they guided to the right locations?

It is certainly not true that they are ordered to the right location by the brain, because the white corpuscles have no connection with the nervous system. They will go to areas the injury has affected even if, due to the injury itself, the nerves have been severed in that area. The simple explanation seems to be that these corpuscles are self-motivated in the sense that they "decide" where they will go and are provided with some kind of drive or motivation[7] to ingest things in the blood that should not be there. We can regard this as a "taste." Further, they are motivated to seek out places where such things are particularly common. Probably the clues which they follow are chemical. It seems likely that a cut releases into the bloodstream various bits of cell debris and chemicals from the cells which are normally not found there, and it is these chemicals and bits of debris that attract the white corpuscles. It is easier to assume that the white corpuscles are programmed to respond to these stimuli and do so than that they receive special orders.

Probably the same is true with the termites. In part, they are no doubt responding to chemicals, particularly chemicals exuded by the queen, which get transmitted around the nest from termite to termite whenever they are in close contact. But this message system can hardly control the temperature of the nest.

If, on the other hand, we assume that termites respond to temperature, then temperature changes could affect their behavior. Assume

---

[7] It is hard to talk about these things with a single-cell animal which does not even have nerves, but it is clear than an amoeba in the outside world has a drive to attack and ingest bacteria.

a termite in the upper part of the nest who feels that it is too hot. There is immediately available an opportunity to lower the temperature both for itself and for the nest by opening a few more ventilation channels. Similarly, if he feels too cold, the reverse behavior is called for. The same termite if deep down in the nest, even if he was too warm, would not be stimulated to do anything about the temperature because there would be no ventilation channels in the immediate vicinity to deal with. By complicating this set of drives and assuming that each termite has quite a number of them, we can produce something that is roughly analogous to a human-utility function for each termite. The termite (again using the human analogy) attempts to maximize this utility function with the particular action he undertakes being determined by his or her immediate environment. This pattern of behavior could be elaborated into a complete structure for controlling any of the social insects' behavior.[8]

But although this explains why the individual termite behaves in a manner which is efficient from the standpoint of the nest, it does not explain why evolution has given the termites this set of drives. After all, many social insects (termite soldiers, for example) will sacrifice themselves for the good of the nest without, as far as one can see, the slightest hesitation or doubt. This would superficially appear to be a counter-evolutionary pattern of behavior.

Once again, if we consider the human body, the explanation is fairly simple. The human body has a very small set of cells which are involved in reproducing other human beings, but the bulk of the body cells simply exist to keep the body as a whole alive. Your skin cells sacrifice themselves by the millions for your well being every day. Evolution has selected the human being as a complicated mechanism in which most of the cells have the duty of protecting those few who can reproduce. The nonreproducing cells have no effect on evolution at all in the future because they simply won't be around.

The same is true with the termite. Only the reproductives are involved in transmitting the genes to future generations. Therefore, there is no reason why the genes should be programmed so that there is any self-protection drive for the workers or the soldiers, and as far as we can see, they are not.[9]

---

[8] Gordon Tullock, *Coordination Without Command* (Blacksburg, Va.: Center for the Study of Public Choice), unpublished.

[9] In the case of the bees, wasps, and ants there is another and more complicated explanation based on the peculiar hereditary mechanism used by these animals. We are dubious about this alternative mechanism, but, in any event, it is irrelevant for the termites.

The analogy between the termite's nest and the human body is strong enough so that a great many biologists tend to think that in the case of the termite the actual nest should be regarded as the individual rather than the termite itself. They refer to a "super-organism." Certainly, the termite nest with its controlled internal environment does have a great deal of resemblance to the warm-blooded animal, but there seems no point here in quarreling about words. We can easily tell a termite from a termite nest and we can talk about them separately. But there are many gaps to fill in our knowledge of termites and, indeed, of all other social animals. In many of them, the gaps are much more prominent than the few places where we have knowledge. The social spiders would be a good example. Earlier we mentioned the theory that a general science of society can be developed, with human society and the various animal societies merely being specific instances of the theory. We cannot say for certain that this is untrue, but what we can say is that if we are going to have such a general theory, we have to know a great deal more about nonhuman societies than we do now.

CONCLUDING COMMENTS

Altogether then, what we learn from studying animal societies is that on the whole we are better off not following their example. On the other hand, the societies are interesting themselves, and they permit us to think about society in a new and different way, which may lead to additional insights about human society.

Here we have talked only about the societies of higher animals and of the social insects. But there are many other societies in nature. We mentioned the societies of plants which have been totally overlooked by the sociobiologists, probably because all of the socio-biologists are zoologists rather than botanists. Even in the animal kingdom, however, there are sizeable areas about which we know very little. Jelly fish, for example, are representatives of a type of animal society which is theoretically relatively comprehensible but the details of whose organization is relatively unknown. The sponges, an immensely ancient group, are societies of great complexity, and again we know almost nothing about how this society functions.

There are two other social animals which are totally unknown to the layman but reasonably well known to the professional biologist —the slime molds and the ectoprocts. Our knowledge of the actual social behavior of these two types of societies is almost nil. Indeed, we are primarily confined in this case to observations of the behavior of the entire society rather than of the individuals which constitute it.

Sociobiology is then a fascinating field which offers great opportunities for further research. However, it is unfortunately still a large field for further research. We have only made the smallest of starts in our study in this area. A student of human society may by examining other societies have new questions raised in his mind. He may get new ideas for human society from them. In the present state of our knowledge, however, it is very unlikely that he will be able to offer any real insight into human functioning from the study of slime molds, baboons, and termites.

QUESTIONS TO PONDER

1. Human property relations are different from those found among territorial animals. It is possible that humans inherited property relations from their primate ancestors and then changed them. It is also possible, of course, that this is an independent invention. Which do you think is more likely?

2. Why do you suppose dominance relationships are weaker in the human society than among animals?

3. Suppose it were true that some particular behavioral trait was characteristic of all mammals. Would this be evidence that human beings also share the trait?

PART 8

A PARTING
WORD

CHAPTER 23

Where do we stand?

The total social system consists of all the
people in the world, all the roles which they
occupy, all their patterns of behavior, all their
inputs and outputs which are relevant to
human beings, and all the organizations and
groups that they belong to. This is, of course,
a very large, complicated system. Nevertheless,
it is convenient to separate it from other systems of the world even though all the world's
systems interact and form a total system of
the planet. Just as the geologists and oceanog-
raphers study the lithosphere and the hydro-
sphere, meteorologists study the atmosphere,
and biologists study the biosphere, so we say
that social scientists study the sociosphere,
which operates as a system at a somewhat
different level of organization than the others.

Kenneth Boulding[1]

The vast expansion of economics as a discipline is one of the
more interesting intellectual developments of this generation. The
number of economists involved in this expansion and the variety of
topics analyzed is on the increase; there is every reason to believe
that this trend will continue, blurring the traditional boundaries
which have separated economics from the other social sciences. In
fact, we encourage the breaking down of these boundaries in order
that more cooperation can take place among the different social
sciences.

In this book, we have outlined the economic approach to the study
of human behavior and the social order and have used this approach

---

[1] Kenneth E. Boulding, *Economics as a Science* (New York: McGraw-Hill,
1970), p. 1.

to discuss a wide range of topics, many of which are not normally thought of as being within the scope of economics as a discipline. We hope that in the process, we have been able to demonstrate how fruitful this approach can be in terms of improving our understanding of the world around us. More importantly, we hope we have stimulated the reader to employ this approach in his own attempts to come to grips with issues and problems outside the scope of this book.

In considering a wide range of topics with a single approach—that of economics—we are fully aware that at times our efforts may be misunderstood or misinterpreted. A major point of controversy concerns the concept of rationality, which has been at the base of many of our discussions. To be sure, many noneconomists will make the point again and again and again that human beings are not rational; hence, the economists' assumption of rationality is false. In discussions with people of this persuasion, we have always found that they define *rational* in a way not characteristic of the economists. They define a rational person as one who is perfectly informed and cold-blooded, who takes very long views, gives considerable attention to all decisions, and invariably aims at direct, selfish ends. With this interpretation of the word rational, it is easy to demonstrate that people are not rational. Even though we point out that the disagreement amounts to a difference in definitions—and that the economists' definition is relatively immune to such criticism—we expect economic analysis to continue to be attacked at this level.

Economic beings, normally perceived as money-grubbing materialists, are a caricature. Human behavior encompasses the aesthetic, religious, and ethical dimensions, as well as the economic, and a complete understanding of man's existence must account for them all. In this book, we have attempted to alert the reader to be mindful of all of these aspects of human experience, and where possible, we have introduced aesthetic and ethical considerations into our discussions. We have concentrated on what may be called the *economic dimension*, broadly defined, because that is our area of expertise and because there is much to be gained by the clear recognition of the economic motive in all areas of human experience.

By the same token, much work needs to be done in the way of exploring the full dimensions of human behavior and integrating them to a greater degree than social scientists are presently capable of doing. The problems of doing this are indeed formidable. In general, we need to know much more about value formation. More specifically, ethics is an area of human behavior which has been barely touched by economists; we know very little about how ethics emerge, become altered, and consequently, how they affect social order. If we are in an "ethical crisis," as many suggest, we need to know why. Much has been done over the past decade on the economics of politics, but much remains to be understood regarding the limitations of political order. We need to know more about how the market, politics, and ethics are interrelated as social organizers. It has been only recently that such economists as Kenneth Boulding have begun to address the roles that love, fear, benevolence, and malevolence play in the social order.

Perhaps many more economists, as well as other social scientists, will search these problems, and by the time this book is rewritten again, we will be able to add more insight into what we already understand about social order. Although many new tools and techniques of analysis may be necessary, we suspect that the economic approach to problems, which has been at the heart of all that we have written, will play a significant role in our attempts to address ever more complex problems, and it is this prospect that makes economics an exciting field to be in.

Index

This book has been set lintoype, in 10 and 9
point Melior, leaded 2 points. Part numbers
are 12 point Melior, and part titles are 18
point Melior. Chapter numbers are 9 point
Melior and chapter titles are 18 point Melior.
The size of the type page is 26 by 45 picas.